LEGAL PRACTICE COURSE

# ENFORCEMENT AND
# DEBT RECOVERY

D1615092

WITHDRAWN

LEGAL PRACTICE COURSE

Other titles available from Law Society Publishing:

**Civil Costs Assessment Handbook** (2nd edn)
Peter Burdge

**Civil Litigation Handbook** (2nd edn)
General Editor: District Judge Suzanne Burn, Consultant Editor: Professor John Peysner

**Consumer Credit Act 2006**
Julia Smith and Sandra McCalla

**Insolvency Law Handbook** (2nd edn)
Vernon Dennis

**Renewal of Business Tenancies**
Michael Haley

All books from Law Society Publishing can be ordered through good bookshops or direct from our distributors, Prolog, by telephone 0870 850 1422 or email **lawsociety@prolog.uk.com**. Please confirm the price before ordering.

For further information or a catalogue, please contact our editorial and marketing office by email **publishing@lawsociety.co.uk**.

# ENFORCEMENT AND DEBT RECOVERY

A Guide to the New Law

*Peter Levaggi, David Marsden and Peter Mooney*

The Law Society

All rights reserved. No part of this publication may be reproduced in any material form, whether by photocopying, scanning, downloading onto computer or otherwise without the written permission of the Law Society and the authors except in accordance with the provisions of the Copyright, Designs and Patents Act 1988. Applications should be addressed in the first instance, in writing, to Law Society Publishing. Any unauthorised or restricted act in relation to this publication may result in civil proceedings and/or criminal prosecution.

Whilst all reasonable care has been taken in the preparation of this publication, neither the publisher nor the authors can accept any responsibility for any loss occasioned to any person acting or refraining from action as a result of relying upon its contents.

The views expressed in this publication should be taken as those of the authors only unless it is specifically indicated that the Law Society has given its endorsement.

The authors have asserted the moral right under the Copyright, Designs and Patents Act 1988 to be identified as authors of this work.

# CONTENTS

# ABOUT THE AUTHORS

## Peter Levaggi

Peter is joint Head of the Property Litigation Group at Charles Russell LLP. He heads the Property Insolvency team and has particular expertise in insolvency related property issues. Peter also has particular expertise in dealing with forfeiture and distress claims. He is a member of the r3 Group of Insolvency Professionals Association and has sat as legal counsel to the membership committee of the Insolvency Practitioners Association. Peter is well known as an advocate and holds right of higher audience. He was the lead advocate in the House of Parliament hearings before the select committee on Crossrail in relation to four petitions opposing various aspects of the bill and amendments.

## David Marsden

David heads the Mortgage Disputes team at Charles Russell LLP. He is a member of the Property Litigation Association and specialises in commercial property disputes with an emphasis on the retail market. David is well known in the enforcement industry and is a regular contributor to the legal press.

## Peter Mooney

The word 'bailiff' dates back to medieval times. According to the dictionary, it means 'an officer executing writs and processes and performing distraints' and also 'an agent or steward of a landlord'. Whilst Peter cannot claim quite such lengthy antecedents he has built up the experience and expertise over more than three decades fulfilling these dual roles in an extremely complex area of the law. Peter is the senior partner of County Bailiff Company.

# TABLE OF CASES

# TABLE OF STATUTES

# TABLE OF STATUTORY INSTRUMENTS

# TABLE OF EUROPEAN LEGISLATION

# LIST OF ABBREVIATIONS

| | |
|---|---|
| AE | Attachment of Earnings |
| AEA 1971 | Attachment of Earnings Act 1971 |
| AEO | Attachment of Earnings Order |
| AO | Administration Order |
| CAB | Citizens Advice Bureau |
| CAEO | Consolidated Attachment of Earnings Order |
| CAPS | Centralised Attachment of Earnings Payment System |
| CCR | County Court Rules |
| CCJ | county court judgment |
| CPR | Civil Procedure Rules 1998 |
| CRAR | Commercial Rent Arrears Recovery |
| CSA | Child Support Agency |
| DEO | Deductions from Earnings Order |
| DMS | debt management scheme |
| DRO | Debt Relief Order |
| DVLA | Driver and Vehicle Licensing Agency |
| ECHR | European Convention On Human Rights |
| ERO | Enforcement Restriction Order |
| HCEO | High Court Enforcement Officer |
| HMRC | Her Majesty's Revenue and Customs |
| IVA | Individual voluntary arrangement |
| JCHR | Joint Committee on Human Rights |
| NACAB | National Association of Citizens Advice Bureaux |
| PEA 1977 | Protection from Eviction Act 1977 |
| RSC | Rules of Supreme Court |
| SIA | Security Industry Authority |

# PART I    **GENERAL TYPES OF ENFORCEMENT**

# 1 INTRODUCTION

## 1.1 INTRODUCTION

**1.1.1** The Tribunals, Courts and Enforcement Bill was published on 25 July 2006 and the Act received Royal Assent on 19 July 2007 ('the new Act').

**1.1.2** The reforms have been a long time coming and we are still waiting for the regulations to the new Act to be published ('the regulations').

### Debt

**1.1.3** The new Act comes at a time when record numbers of people are being caught in the debt trap and the signs are that the situation is becoming progressively worse. In 2006 the Citizens Advice Bureaux (CAB) dealt with 6,500 new cases of debt every day, a rise of more than 20 per cent on the figures in 2005. The National Association of Citizens Advice Bureaux reported that 1.7 million people needed help with money problems and the number wanting advice about bankruptcy rose 53 per cent up to 99,000. CABs are now dealing with twice as many debt inquiries than they did 10 years ago. This has been attributed to an unprecedented consumer credit boom. David Harker (Chief Executive of CAB) has said:

> These figures are worrying evidence that, where many have enjoyed benefits of the credit boom, a large and growing number continue to pay the price.
>
> They are becoming overwhelmed by serious debt which can have a devastating impact on their lives. Even more worryingly are the signs that people are struggling not only to repay credit but also to afford the day-to-day essentials.

**1.1.4** In 2006 the number of county court judgments increased for the second year running. Commercial judgments increased by 6 per cent to £178,313 in 2006.

**1.1.5** The figures in Table 1.1 are obtained from the annual statistics of the Registry Trust Limited.

**1.1.6** Over the last five years the number of county court judgments has been steadily rising. In 2005 the number of judgments against consumers rose dramatically.

**Table 1.1**    County court judgments

| County court judgments (excluding DVLA judgments) | 2002 | 2003 | 2004 | 2005 | 2006 |
|---|---|---|---|---|---|
| Consumer | 632,568 | 631,368 | 538,383 | 635,222 | 843,853 |
| Commercial total CCJ | 182,256 | 170,689 | 161,882 | 167,664 | 178,313 |
| Total | 814,824 | 802,057 | 700,265 | 802,886 | 1,022,166 |
| Y/Y change | −8.1% | −1.6% | −12.7% | 14.7% | 27.3% |

**Table 1.2**    Amounts paid on judgments

| CCJ satisfactions | 2002 | 2003 | 2004 | 2005 | 2006 |
|---|---|---|---|---|---|
| Consumer | 131,429 | 96,581 | 98,967 | 93,443 | 108,079 |
| Commercial total CCJ | 14,869 | 14,554 | 14,287 | 15,476 | 20,586 |
| Total | 146,298 | 111,135 | 113,254 | 108,919 | 128,665 |
| Y/Y change | 10.1% | −24% | 1.9% | −3.8% | |

**1.1.7**    The rise in consumer debt has risen sharply in recent years. This has resulted in a substantial increase in the number of bankruptcies and individual voluntary arrangements (IVAs). The growth in personal insolvency has undermined the enforcement process. Increasingly creditors find that they are unable to use enforcement action because a bankruptcy intervenes to prevent enforcement, or the debt is compromised by an individual voluntary arrangement.

**1.1.8**    The number of IVAs has increased by more than 900 per cent between 1998 and 2006.

**1.1.9**    The number of bankruptcies has increased by 320 per cent between 1998 and 2006.

> There has been an explosion of personal insolvency work in the last 10 years. This seems to be mainly driven by Consumer Credit. A number of insolvency businesses have been set up just to deal with the large volumes of IVAs. This remedy is aggressively advertised on television and through the media as a rapid way for individuals to write off debt. It is often used to stop enforcement action and is sometimes misused.
>
> Brian Johnson (Insolvency Practitioner: HW Fisher)

**1.1.10**    Partly as a consequence of the rising number of personal insolvencies, the majority of judgments are not paid.

## New Act

**1.1.11**    Obtaining a court order does not ensure that the debt is paid or possession is given of the land. As important as actually obtaining the order is the ability to enforce it. What these figures show is that all too often a party with judgment in his favour may still end up not getting paid.

**1.1.12**    There are, of course, various methods of enforcement available to a creditor with the benefit of a judgment. The new Act has amended both the methods of enforcement and also the method of obtaining information about the debtor, with the purpose of affording to creditors a higher chance of obtaining payment under a judgment.

**1.1.13**    The new Act seeks to strike a balance between the enforceability of judgments and the need to protect vulnerable debtors who are genuinely unable to pay their debts. This balancing act gives a series of new advantages to creditors countered by a series of new remedies and requirements to protect debtors.

| New Act creditor advantages | New Act debtor advantages |
| --- | --- |
| The creation of commercial rent arrears recovery (CRAR) | The abolition of the law of distress for landlords |
| The creation of a unified easily accessible new enforcement system in 'taking control of goods' | The unified system benefits both sides |
| Allowing enforcement agents reasonable force to gain entry to a premises | The requirement that force cannot be used without a court order |
| An upgraded system allowing information to be obtained about debtors from third parties (such as banks and government departments) | |
| | A new range of remedies allowing debtors who are unable to pay to postpone repayment and reduce the level of debt, i.e. Management Schemes, Administration Orders and Enforcement Restriction Orders |
| The rebuilding of creditor confidence in enforcement remedies that are modern and are in compliance with the European Convention on Human Rights (of particular importance to institutions that place a value on social responsibility) | Measures to bring enforcement remedies into compliance with the European Convention on Human Rights |
| | An upgraded certification process for enforcement agents and a step towards the creation of a governing body for the enforcement industry |

**1.1.14**    This book will chart the improvements made by the new Act, illustrated by a comparison with the pre-Act position (where the comparison is relevant to understand and interpret the new provisions). This book will also be a comprehensive review of the law of enforcement.

**1.1.15**    Throughout the book the procedures will be illustrated by reference to quotes and stories obtained from bailiffs, commercial landlords and insolvency practitioners.

**1.1.16**    The objective of the new Act is to:

- represent the government's commitment to improving the efficiency of civil justice;
- aim to enhance the ability of creditors, with legitimate claims, to pursue enforcement through a simplified and accessible system;
- seek to protect those debtors who genuinely do not have the means to pay.

Whether the new Act will succeed in these objectives remains to be seen.

## 1.2    SUMMARY OF CHANGES UNDER THE NEW ACT

1. *Obtaining information about the debtor* – The new Act introduces the information order and the departmental information request (**Chapter 5**).
2. *Enforcement agents* – The new Act creates a foundation for the regulation of bailiffs, now called enforcement agents (**Chapter 6**).
3. *Taking control of goods* – Distress for landlords is abolished and replaced with a new system on commercial rent arrears recovery for landlords (**Chapters 7–9**). Execution and all forms of seizing a debtors goods are unified under a system of taking control of goods.
4. *Attachment of Earnings Orders* – The new Act allows a creditor with the benefit of a debt to be paid in instalments to obtain a charging order even where there is no default in payment of those instalments. The new Act also imposes a financial limit on charging orders and orders for sale (**Chapter 15**).

# 2 GENERAL RULES ABOUT JUDGMENTS AND ORDERS

## 2.1 INTRODUCTION

**2.1.1** An understanding of enforcement requires knowledge of the thing being enforced: the judgment or order.

**2.1.2** This book will review enforcement of court based judgments and orders. In addition we will review the ancient right of a landlord to levy distress for rent (enforcement without a court order/judgment).

## 2.2 DEFINITIONS OF JUDGMENT/ORDER

**2.2.1** The general rules about judgments or orders are set out in Part 40 of the Civil Procedure Rules 1998 (CPR). Throughout this book, the terms 'judgment' and 'order' are used. They generally mean the same thing in the context of enforcement. It used to be that there was a distinction between them which was important for enforcement, but that is no longer the case.

**2.2.2** Under CPR rule 70.1(2)(c), a judgment or order:

includes an award which the court has –

(i)     registered for enforcement;
(ii)    ordered to be enforced; or
(iii)   given permission to enforce

as if it were a judgment or order of the court . . .

**2.2.3** A frequent error in relation to judgments is their spelling. A court judgment is spelt 'judgment' not 'judgement'.

## 2.3 REQUIREMENTS OF JUDGMENT OR ORDER

**2.3.1** Every judgment or order must:

- state the name and title of the person who ordered it (except for default judgments, judgments following admissions, consent orders, orders to enforce awards and Orders to Obtain Information (for which see **Chapter 5**));
- show the date on which it was made;
- be sealed by the court.

## 2.4    DATE OF EFFECT OF JUDGMENT

**2.4.1**    A judgment takes effect 'from the day when it is given or made, or such later date as the court may specify' (CPR rule 40.7(1)).

**2.4.2**    The judgment can often be enforced on the day it takes effect. However, this is subject to the debtor's right to apply for a stay of execution (see **9.1.20**) and the debtor's right to seek the new Act remedy of a debt management scheme or relief (see **Chapters 19–23**).

## 2.5    DATE FOR INTEREST

**2.5.1**    Under CPR rule 40.8 and Judgment Act 1838, s.17 or County Courts Act 1984, s.74, interest on a judgment or order runs from the date of the judgment or order unless provided otherwise in the CPR or the court orders that it is to run from a different date. The court can in fact order that interest is to run from a date before the date of the judgment.

## 2.6    INTEREST

**2.6.1**    A creditor is entitled to claim interest:

- *On High Court judgments* – Under Judgments Act 1838, s.17, which states that 'every judgment debt shall carry interest at a rate of 8% per annum'.
- *On county court judgments* – When specified by the County Courts (Interest on Judgments) Order 1991 and County Courts Act 1984, s.74. This provides that interest is generally payable on most (but not all) county court judgments. Interest is not payable on:
  - Consumer Credit Act proceedings;
  - suspended possession orders.

**2.6.2**    The rate of interest is the same rate as for High Court judgments (County Courts (Interest on Judgments) Order 1991, art.5(1)).

**2.6.3**    A creditor who wishes to claim interest when making an application to enforce a judgment debt must include in the application:

- the sum on which interest in claimed;
- the amount of interest claimed;

- the dates from and to which interest has occurred; and
- the rate of interest applied (CPR PD70 para.6).

## 2.7   TIME FOR COMPLIANCE WITH JUDGMENT OR ORDER

**2.7.1**   Payment of a money judgment must take place within 14 days of the judgment or order unless:

- the order specifies a different date;
- the CPR specify a different date; or
- the court has stayed proceedings or the judgment (CPR rule 40.11).

After this date, the creditor can adopt any method (or methods) of enforcement of his choice.

## 2.8   CORRECTING JUDGMENTS OR ORDERS

**2.8.1**   Historically, this is known as the 'slip rule'. It can happen that either in court, or when the Order is being typed up by the Court Officer, minor (but sometimes important) typographical errors can occur in the Order. This rule allows typographical errors only to be amended.

**2.8.2**   The procedure is set out in Practice Direction B to CPR Part 40, para.4:

- a simple application without a hearing is usually sufficient;
- the court has an inherent power to vary its own orders to make the meaning clear.

## 2.9   GENERAL RULES OF ENFORCEMENT

**2.9.1**   Enforcement is generally governed by CPR Part 70.

**2.9.2**   CPR rule 70.1(2) defines 'judgment creditor' as:

a person who has obtained or is entitled to enforce a judgment or Order

and 'judgment debtor' as:

a person against whom a judgment or Order was given or made.

**2.9.3**   The new Act has refined these definitions, using just 'creditor' and 'debtor'. They have the same meaning as under rule 70.1(2). The new Act terminology will be used in this book.

## 2.10    ENFORCEABILITY OF COSTS ORDERS

**2.10.1**    An order to pay costs (once assessed or agreed) can be enforced in the same way as if it were a judgment or order (CPR rule 70.1(2)(d)).

## 2.11    ENFORCEMENT AGAINST A NON-PARTY

**2.11.1**    Where a court makes an Order either in favour of or against a party not named in the proceedings, the Order can be enforced by or against that party in the same way as if he were actually named in the proceedings (CPR rule 70.4). The classic example of such an Order is a wasted costs order (where a non-party that has meddled in the proceedings can be ordered to pay a party's costs). Sometimes such an order is made against a solicitor acting for one of the parties where there has been an abuse of process.

## 2.12    HOW MANY METHODS OF ENFORCEMENT CAN BE USED?

**2.12.1**    Under CPR rule 70.2(2) unless provided otherwise, a creditor can use any method of enforcement that he wishes. The choice is entirely his and the debtor's convenience does not hinder him in his choice of method to use.

**2.12.2**    A creditor can also use more than one method, either at the same time or consecutively, until the judgment debt is paid.

**2.12.3**    When using more than one method of enforcement, if one method obtains part payment from the debtor the creditor should notify the court and any enforcement agent of the payment received.

**2.12.4**    If a creditor is unsure of the most appropriate method of enforcement, he can apply for information about the debtor's assets by means of an Order to Obtain Information under CPR Part 71 or he can ask the court 'what kind of action it would be appropriate to take . . . to recover that particular debt' under s.95 of the new Act.

**2.12.5**    One of the amendments to the law under the new Act assists a party in deciding which enforcement method to use. A party can now ask the court to apply to, for example, a government department, requesting information from that department to provide information about the debtor. This new procedure can be used to obtain the name, address, date of birth and national insurance number of the debtor from a government department. The new Act is designed to prevent parties who owe a judgment debt from 'going to ground' to avoid payment.

**2.12.6**    These new 'departmental information requests' and 'information orders', introduced by ss.97 and 98 of the new Act, are dealt with in **Chapter 5**.

## 2.13   METHODS OF ENFORCEMENT

**2.13.1**   The following methods of enforcement are available to a creditor:

- *Distress* – Levied on behalf of landlords (replaced by 'commercial rent arrears recovery' by the new Act).
- *Writ of* fieri facias *or Warrant of Execution (RSC Orders 46 and 47 and CCR Order 26)* – The procedure involves the debtor's goods being seized and sold to pay off the judgment debt. These have been renamed as Writs/Warrants of Control under the new Act. They are the only method of enforcement that does not require a judicial decision (other than distress/CRAR).
- *Third Party Debt Order (CPR Part 72)* – This is where the creditor asks that a third party who owes money to the debtor pays that money direct to the creditor rather than to the debtor. The classic example is where the debtor's bank is ordered to pay money in his account to the creditor.
- *Charging Order, Stop Order, Stop Notice (CPR Part 73)* – This acts like a mortgage over the debtor's property to secure the judgment debt. In the case of property, the debt can then be enforced by an Order for Sale.
- *Attachment of Earnings Order (CCR Order 27)* – This is governed by the Attachment of Earnings Act 1971 and CCR Order 27. An 'attachment of earnings order' provides that an employed debtor's employer (where he is employed) must pay part of the debtor's earnings to the creditor.
- *Appointment of a Receiver (CPR Part 69).*
- *Committal or Sequestration* – This is only available where the debtor fails to do something ordered to be done by a certain date and time.

# 3 REGISTRATION OF JUDGMENTS

## 3.1   INTRODUCTION

**3.1.1**   The Register of Judgments, Orders and Fines has replaced the Register of County Court Judgments, which had been in existence for over 150 years. The reason for the replacement is that from 6 April 2006 the new Register was extended to include High Court judgments and fines registered by local justice areas.

**3.1.2**   The Register now contains details of county court judgments, county court Administration Orders, High Court judgments, magistrates' court fines and Child Support Agency (CSA) Liability Orders.

**3.1.3**   The Register can be searched. Further details are held at **www.registry-trust.org.uk**.

**3.1.4**   Centralising the Register in this way now makes it easier to search for all forms of judgments against a party. Anyone can search the Register, which is in three sections:

- *Section one* – county court judgments, Administration Orders and Child Support Agencies;
- *Section two* – High Court judgments registered after 6 April 2006; and
- *Section three* – fines registered by Local Justice Areas.

**3.1.5**   Details in sections one and two remain on the Register for six years from the date of the judgment. Details in section three remain on the register for five years from the date of conviction.

**3.1.6**   For each judgment on the Register a person applying for details will be given the name and address of the debtor, the original amount of the judgment, the name of the court and the date of the judgment. Details of the claimant (where he is not the judgment debtor) are not provided.

## 3.2    CREDIT RATING

**3.2.1**    The major concern for individuals about being on the Register is that it will have an effect on their credit rating and (as a result) their ability to obtain future credit, for example, when applying for a mortgage.

**3.2.2**    If a debtor pays the judgment within one month, the debtor's details are not put on the Register. This allows a debtor the possibility to pay promptly and not appear on the Register.

**3.2.3**    If the debtor does not pay (or takes longer than one month to pay) then the debt will be placed on the Register. When a court is provided with evidence that a judgment debt has been paid in full that court should notify the Register so that it can be amended to show that the judgment debt has been satisfied.

**3.2.4**    This happens when the debt has been repaid outside one calendar month of the judgment date – it remains on the Register but shown as satisfied.

**3.2.5**    A judgment can only be removed from the Register:

■    if it was entered in error;
■    if it was paid before the court date; or
■    if it was cancelled because full payment was made within one calendar month of the judgment date.

In these cases only, a party on the Register can apply to court to be removed from the Register.

**3.2.6**    For this reason, the Register can, immediately following a judgment, be used as an enforcement tool. Informing the debtor that if they pay the judgment debt within one month, they will not appear on the Register (and so their credit rating will not be affected), may encourage prompt payment by the debtor.

**3.2.7**    Similarly, notifying the debtor that (even after one month) their credit rating may be improved by the Register showing that the judgment is 'satisfied' could also encourage payment.

# 4 TRANSFER OF PROCEEDINGS

## 4.1 TRANSFER OF COUNTY COURT PROCEEDINGS TO ANOTHER COUNTY FOR ENFORCEMENT

**4.1.1**   Where a creditor is required to enforce a judgment of one county court in a different county court (for example where he is obliged to carry out enforcement proceedings in the county court local to where the debtor resides) the creditor must make a request in writing to the county court where the case originated (and judgment handed down). The debtor requests in writing that the proceedings be transferred to the other county court.

**4.1.2**   Once the court officer receives the request for a transfer, he will transfer the proceedings to that other court unless a judge orders otherwise. The court will then give notice of the transfer to all parties in the proceedings.

**4.1.3**   All further steps in the proceedings (including enforcement proceedings) should then be taken in the court to which the proceedings have been transferred unless provided otherwise.

## 4.2 TRANSFER OF COUNTY COURT PROCEEDINGS TO THE HIGH COURT

**4.2.1**   Transfer of county court proceedings to the High Court are governed by the County Court Rules (CCR) Order 25, rule 13.

**4.2.2**   The transfer of a county court judgment to the High Court for enforcement is usually to enable a creditor to be able to use the services of a High Court enforcement officer. (Now an enforcement agent, see **Chapter 6** in relation to enforcement agents under the new Act. See also **9.1.5** on the financial limits for enforcement in each court.)

**4.2.3**   In transferring a matter to the High Court for enforcement, the first step for a creditor is to make a request for a certificate of judgment under CCR Order 22, rule 8(1). The application for a Certificate of Judgment is made in writing to the court. If the applicant is a party to the claim, he must state whether the certificate is:

- required in order to take proceedings in another court on the judgment;
- required to enforce the judgment in the High Court; or
- as evidence only.

**4.2.4**    If the application is being made to enforce a judgment in the High Court, the application must also include:

- A statement that:

    - the applicant intends to enforce the order by execution against goods; or
    - the order is a possession order against trespassers.

- Confirmation that an application has been made for an order to transfer the claim to the High Court.

**4.2.5**    If the application is not party to the proceedings, he must state in the application:

- the purpose for which the certificate is required;
- his capacity for requesting the certificate; and
- any other facts showing that the certificate may be properly granted.

**4.2.6**    Where the Order is being enforced by execution against goods or where the Order is an Order for possession of land made in a possession claim against trespassers, the county court will grant a certificate of judgment and the certificate will act as an Order to transfer the proceedings to the High Court and takes effect as soon as the certificate is granted.

**4.2.7**    The court will not issue a Certificate of Judgment (and so will not transfer proceedings to the High Court until the application has been dealt with) where one of the following is pending:

- an application to vary the date or rate of payment of money due under the Order;
- an application under Civil Procedure Rules (CPR) rule 39.3(3) (application to set aside judgment where a party failed to attend trial);
- an application under CPR rule 13.4 (application to set aside judgment and the matter is being transferred to another court);
- a request for an administration order – this will now be extended to a request for one of the other debt management procedures created by the new Act, including Enforcement Restriction Orders, and Debt Management Schemes and Debt Relief Orders; or
- an application for a stay of execution.

**4.2.8**    Once proceedings have been transferred, the court will notify the debtor or the person against whom the Order was made.

## 4.3   TRANSFER OF PROCEEDINGS FROM HIGH COURT TO COUNTY COURT

**4.3.1**   This is usually done where a creditor wants to use a county court method of enforcement (i.e. an Attachment of Earnings Order). It is governed by CPR rule 70.3(1).

**4.3.2**   Under CPR rule 70.3, where a creditor wants to transfer High Court proceedings to a county court, he must make an application to the High Court, asking that the proceedings to be transferred.

**4.3.3**   The application notice requesting transfer should be in form N244 and should include:

- a copy of the judgment or order;
- a certificate verifying the amount due;
- a copy of the enforcement officer's return to the writ if a writ of execution has previously been issued in the High Court to enforce the judgment; and
- a copy of the order transferring proceedings to the county court.

# 5 OBTAINING INFORMATION ABOUT THE DEBTOR

## 5.1 INTRODUCTION

**5.1.1**  Once a party has obtained judgment, a major decision which must be taken is how to enforce it.

**5.1.2**  The most appropriate method (or methods) of enforcement depends on the assets held by the debtor. For example, if a debtor is cash rich, a Third Party Debt Order (see **Chapter 14**) against his bank accounts may be more appropriate than a Charging Order over property (**Chapter 15**). A Charging Order is only available if the debtor actually owns some property.

**5.1.3**  To assist with making an informed decision as to the most appropriate method of enforcement, especially where the debtor's assets are not obvious, a creditor can apply to the court for an Order to Obtain Information.

**5.1.4**  An Order to Obtain Information is not a form of enforcement. It is a means by which the creditor obtains information from the debtor about the debtor's assets to decide whether it is worthwhile to take an enforcement step and which method is most likely to obtain payment of the judgment.

## 5.2 EFFECT OF THE NEW ACT

**5.2.1**  In the first consultation paper of the Department for Constitutional Affairs' Civil Enforcement Review, the procedure for obtaining information about a debtor was the most heavily criticised of all the procedures under review. The criticism of the procedure was that it was too slow, too easily prolonged by the debtor and the information provided was often either incomplete or not to be believed. It was felt that the main problem with the procedure was that it relied too heavily on co-operation by the debtor.

**5.2.2**  Despite this, the mechanism of an Order to Obtain Information is unaffected by the new Act.

**5.2.3**  The new Act has, however, introduced two new mechanisms which will assist a creditor in making his decision about the most appropriate method of enforcement and supplement existing rights. The two new mechanisms are:

- the Information Order (which is served on third parties); and
- the Departmental Information Request (which is served on government departments).

5.2.4    These mechanisms allow a creditor to verify via third parties any information provided by a debtor, or even go to those third parties direct. The inability to do so previously was the major failing of the pre-Act system.

5.2.5    The new mechanisms are dealt with later in this chapter.

## 5.3    ORDERS TO OBTAIN INFORMATION

5.3.1    Orders to Obtain Information from debtors are governed by Civil Procedure Rules (CPR) Part 71 and are unaffected by the new Act.

5.3.2    The effect of an Order to Obtain Information is that a debtor is ordered to attend court and give details of his assets.

5.3.3    Although the application involves judicial input, once a compliant application is made, the court will issue an order for the debtor to attend court (CPR rule 71.2(6)). A debtor can be asked to attend court to provide information about:

- the debtor's means; and
- any other matter about which information is needed to enforce a judgment or order.

### Popularity of Orders to Obtain Information

5.3.4    The popularity of Orders to Obtain Information has steadily declined over the last five years.

**Table 5.1**  Orders to Obtain Information

| Year | Orders made |
| --- | --- |
| 1995 | 66,397 |
| 1996 | 57,339 |
| 1997 | 51,375 |
| 1998 | 65,630 |
| 1999 | 67,976 |
| 2000 | 61,092 |
| 2001 | 68,040 |
| 2002 | 57,987 |
| 2003 | 43,159 |
| 2004 | 34,673 |
| 2005 | 31,444 |
| 2006 | 28,354 |

**5.3.5**    The figures in Table 5.1 from 1995 to 1999 have been obtained from the Business Management System and from 2000 onwards from the main Civil Law Case Management System. They are provided by the Economics and Statistics Division of the Ministry of Justice.

**5.3.6**    There could be a number of reasons for the decline in the popularity of Orders to Obtain Information. Personal insolvencies have risen dramatically in the last five years (bankruptcies and individual voluntary arrangements (IVAs)). IVAs have increased by approximately 900 per cent from 1998 to 2006 and bankruptcies have increased by 400 per cent during the same period. Obviously, where a debtor enters into a formal insolvent arrangement there is no merit or prospect of recovery, and the limited ability to obtain information in this way becomes meaningless. On bankruptcies all the debtor's assets become automatically vested in the Trustee in Bankruptcy pursuant to Insolvency Act 1986, s.306. The difficulty of recovering the full cost of the application could also discourage applicants from using this method.

## Timing of application

**5.3.7**    An Order to Obtain Information can be made at any time after judgment has been obtained. The debtor does not have to be behind with payments.

**5.3.8**    An application cannot be made where:

- the judgment debt has been paid in full; or
- there is a moratorium due to insolvency proceedings (see **Chapter 8** in relation to insolvency moratoria).

**5.3.9**    An application for an Order to Obtain Information may be made without notice (CPR rule 71.2(2)(a)).

## Applicant

**5.3.10**    Only a creditor (i.e. the person with the benefit of an unpaid judgment) can apply for an Order to Obtain Information (CPR rule 71.2(1)).

## Procedure

**5.3.11**    The procedure involves the debtor being ordered to attend court. In this case, a debtor need not be a money debtor, he could also be, for example, subject to an Order to return goods.

**5.3.12**    At court the debtor or company officer of the debtor is questioned, on oath, by a court officer who will ask him questions designed to find out what his assets are.

## Fee

**5.3.13**    There is a fee for making the application. The fee can be checked at paragraph 7.3 of the Guide to Civil Proceedings Fees at: **www.hmcourts-service. gov.uk/publications/guidance/fees/index.htm**.

**5.3.14**    The fee can be added to the amount recoverable from the debtor.

**5.3.15**    Under CPR rule 45.6 fixed costs can also be recovered and a fixed fee of £15 can be recovered to cover the cost of personal service. It will cost a lot more to have a document personally served, but £15 is all that can be recovered.

## Forms

**5.3.16**    Where the debtor is an individual, the creditor must complete form N316 (application for an Order that the debtor attends court for questioning).

**5.3.17**    Where the debtor is a company, the creditor can ask that one of the officers of the company be questioned about the company's assets. In that case, the creditor should fill out form N316A when making his application.

**5.3.18**    To take either step, the creditor will need to know the name and address of the debtor (which should be stated on the claim form).

## Contents of Application

**5.3.19**    Under CPR rule 71.2(3) the application in form N316 or form N316A must:

■    contain the name and address of the debtor;
■    identify the judgment or order which the creditor is seeking to enforce;
■    state the amount currently owed by the debtor under the judgment or order (for Orders to pay money);
■    if the debtor is a company state:

   –    the name and address of the officer of that body whom the creditor wishes to be ordered to attend court; and
   –    his position in the company;

■    if the creditor wishes the questioning to be conducted before a judge, give reasons;
■    identify any documents that the creditor wishes the debtor (or other person to be questioned) to be ordered to produce at court;
■    if the application is to enforce a judgment or order which is not for the payment of money, identify the matters about which the creditor wishes the debtor (or officer of the debtor) to be questioned;
■    any further questions that the creditor wishes the court officer to ask.

**5.3.20**    Where the application requests that the debtor be questioned before a judge on receipt of the application, the court officer will refer the application to a judge to consider the request.

**5.3.21**    If the judge decides that there are compelling reasons for questioning to take place before a judge then he will order that it does. Otherwise, he will pass the application back to the court officer who will issue form N39 and the questioning will take place before the court officer.

## Appropriate court

**5.3.22**    An application for an Order to Obtain Information must be made either in the court that made the judgment being enforced or, if the proceedings have since been transferred to another court, in that court (CPR rule 71.2(2)(b)).

**5.3.23**    If the debtor lives in an area covered by a court other than the court in which the claim was brought and the application has been issued, the questioning will take place at the court local to where the debtor lives unless the judge decides otherwise.

## Hearing of the application

**5.3.24**    There is no preliminary hearing. The application for an Order to Obtain Information, requiring the debtor to attend court, can be made without a hearing. An order for the debtor to attend court will be issued provided the application complies with the requirements of CPR rule 71.2(3) (set out above).

## Order

**5.3.25**    Once the court officer receives a compliant application, and subject to any need to refer the matter firstly to a judge (at the applicant's request in the application), the court officer will draw up an Order to Obtain Information, form N39. This is an Order that the debtor must attend court for questioning. The order contains:

- a time, date and place for the debtor to attend to be questioned;
- an explanation that he must answer on oath the questions asked by the court officer;
- information for the debtor in relation to his right to provide money to cover travel expenses (CPR rule 71.4);
- information for the debtor that if he wants to pay the money now, he can do so. Given the debtor may have defaulted in paying money due under a court order, it is harsh on the creditor to have to pay the debtor's travelling expenses, but it is a requirement of making an application;
- a warning to the debtor that if he does not comply with the Order to attend court, he may be imprisoned.

## Service of the Order

**5.3.26**   A copy of the Order to Obtain Information (requiring the debtor to attend court) must be served personally on the debtor. The court will only arrange service if the creditor is a litigant in person. Any other creditor must arrange service himself or through an enforcement agent or other third party.

**5.3.27**   The Order to Obtain Information (to be served) cannot be left with someone at the debtor's address or posted through the letter box, it must be personally served. The rules for personal service are set out in CPR rule 6.4.

**5.3.28**   The Order must be served not less than 14 days before the questioning is due to take place (CPR rule 71.3(1)). The 14 days includes weekends and bank holidays, it is not 14 working days. The rules about calculating dates are set out in CPR rule 2.8.

**5.3.29**   If service cannot take place at least 14 days before the questioning is due to take place, the court must be notified and a new date will be listed. This must be done no later than seven days before the date set down for the questioning (CPR rule 71.3(2)).

**5.3.30**   If personal service cannot be arranged, the applicant can apply to the court under CPR rule 71.3(1) for the court to allow another method of service.

## Affidavit of service

**5.3.31**   As service is a prerequisite for the hearing, service of the Order to Obtain Information is confirmed by providing a sworn affidavit saying how and when the debtor was served (CPR rule 71.5). This affidavit of service can be provided in form EX550 but it is not obligatory to use that form.

**5.3.32**   If a process server is used to serve the Order to Obtain Information then the process server must swear the affidavit. A copy of the Order to Obtain Information served must be exhibited to the affidavit.

**5.3.33**   The affidavit of service must be filed not less than two days before the date of questioning or produced at the hearing (CPR rule 71.5(2)).

**5.3.34**   The affidavit of service must cover:

- details of how the order to attend court was served;
- whether the debtor has asked for his travelling expenses to be paid and, if so, confirmation that they have been paid; and
- how much of the judgment debt remains unpaid.

**5.3.35**   Where service is carried out by a process server, this may require two affidavits (one to deal with service and the other to cover the balance of the points set out above).

## Effect of the Order to Attend Court

**5.3.36**   Under CPR rule 71.2(6) the Order will require the debtor (or other person) to attend the county court local to where he resides (or carries on business) unless the judge decides otherwise.

**5.3.37**   Questioning will take place before a judge only if there is a request in the application for it to do so and the judge considers that the request in the application provides compelling reasons for questioning to take place before a judge.

**5.3.38**   Creditors often find that the standard questioning by the court officer is impotent and prefer the more vigorous cross-examination by the creditor's barrister before a judge. Unfortunately, this in itself is not a 'compelling reason' for questioning to take place. A compelling reason may be evidence of misrepresentation or serious omission of the debtor or if, during proceedings, the debtor's witness evidence under oath was not believed.

**5.3.39**   Where a person is served with an Order to Obtain Information he must attend court at the time and place specified in the Order and produce at court documents in his control which are specified in the Order. He must also answer on oath any questions put by the court.

**5.3.40**   The Order will specifically state:

> You must obey this Order. If you do not you may be sent to prison for contempt of Court.

The effect of a party refusing to attend court following service of an Order to Obtain Information is dealt with below.

## Hearing

**5.3.41**   The normal procedure for the hearing is that it will take place before a court officer who will ask a standard set of questions. It is only if the judge decides that, following a request in the application, the hearing should take place before a judge that it will take place before a judge.

**5.3.42**   Creditors tend to prefer the ability to cross examine before a judge and comprehensively interrogate the debtor with questions that the debtor may not be expecting. The creditor needs, however, to provide compelling reasons as to why this should happen.

**5.3.43**   The prescribed questions that the court officer will ask are set out in Form EX140 and Appendix A to the Practice Direction to Part 71 of the Civil Procedure Rules (where the person being questioned is an individual debtor) and in Form EX141 (Appendix B) where the person is an officer of the debtor company.

**5.3.44**    The questions asked by the court officer set out in form EX140 for an individual and EX141 for an officer of a company include:

- *Personal information* – Name, address, marital status, intention to move, dependant children.
- *Employment status* – Occupation, place of work, gross pay, dates of payments, account numbers, how long unemployed for, steps being taken to obtain employment, state benefits, date of retirement, details in relation to pension, other people who are employed in the household, other state benefits.
- *Property* – Whether the debtor owns his own property, how much is paid on the mortgage, whether any part is let, whether he rents, how much he is paid by way of rent.
- *Savings* – Other property owned, bank and building society details, whether he owns a car.
- *Other debts* – Council tax, water charges, mortgage etc.

The form ends with an offer for payment. At this point, the debtor can offer to pay in full by a certain date or by instalments by a certain amount at regular intervals.

**5.3.45**    It may well be that the regulations to the new Act will require the provision of information about debt management and relief to be made available to the debtor at this stage.

## Further questions at the hearing

**5.3.46**    Where the hearing takes place before a court officer (which is the normal procedure) the creditor or his representative can attend court and ask questions themselves or can request that the court officer ask additional questions by attaching a list of proposed additional questions to the application notice.

**5.3.47**    The court officer records the evidence. The person being questioned will be asked to sign it at the end of the hearing. The hearing is relatively informal compared to a hearing before a judge.

**5.3.48**    Where the hearing is to take place before a judge, it is the creditor or his representative who ask the questions. In that case, the standard questions do not have to be used. The proceedings will be tape recorded and the court will not make a written record of the evidence.

## Attendance at hearing

**5.3.49**    Although the debtor is obliged to attend the hearing, there is no need for the creditor to attend questioning of the debtor by a court officer. The creditor has the right to attend if he wishes. If the hearing takes place before a judge then the creditor (or his representative) should attend as, in that case, it is he or his representative who puts the questions to the debtor. If the debtor does not attend the hearing or attends but refuses to give an oath or refuses to answer questions, the matter will be passed to a circuit judge.

## Debtor non-compliance

**5.3.50**   If the circuit judge believes the debtor has not complied with the Order to Obtain Information, the judge will issue a Suspended Committal Order (form N79A). This could arise because of:

■   failure to attend; or
■   misrepresentation; or
■   a material omission.

**5.3.51**   The Suspended Committal Order is an Order for the debtor to be committed to prison. The Committal Order is however suspended and does not take effect immediately and will not take effect if the debtor attends a new date to be questioned and fulfils his obligations at that new date.

**5.3.52**   The Suspended Committal Order needs to be served personally (CPR rule 6.4 deals with personal service).

**5.3.53**   If the debtor fails to attend the hearing on the date in the Suspended Committal Order a warrant of arrest will be issued, giving a county court bailiff ('enforcement agent' under the new Act) the power to arrest the debtor. If, upon arrest, the debtor agrees to be questioned by the court then the judge will usually discharge the Suspended Committal Order. If the debtor refuses to be questioned or fails to comply with the Order to Obtain Information, a Warrant of Committal will usually be issued. That warrant authorises the enforcement agent to take the debtor to prison for the time specified in the Suspended Committal Order.

## Further applications

**5.3.54**   Further applications to obtain information can be made, following the first application. For example, if following standard questions by a court officer, the creditor is not satisfied that the debtor has replied correctly, the creditor can make a further application and ask that the application take place before a judge.

**5.3.55**   If the debtor believes that the creditor is abusing the process by repeat applications, the judge could use the court's general case management powers or penalise the creditor in costs.

## 5.4   NEW ACT POSITION – INFORMATION ORDERS AND DEPARTMENTAL INFORMATION REQUESTS

**5.4.1**   As set out above the pre-Act procedure for orders to obtain information remains unchanged. However, it has been supplemented by the new procedures set out below.

**5.4.2**   One of the purposes of the new Act is to enable creditors to enforce their judgments more effectively. An essential component of this is to facilitate a creditor's access to information about the debtor and his assets.

**5.4.3**   In the Department for Constitutional Affairs' Civil Enforcement Review (www.dcs.gov.uk/enforcement/indexfr.htm) it was suggested that a creditor may enforce a judgment more effectively if he were allowed to seek information about the debtor from parties other than the debtor (who may be unwilling to co-operate despite the sanction of imprisonment or who may not co-operate fully). Orders to Obtain Information, where the person giving the information has a very real interest in not disclosing information about himself may not be as useful as they could be. Provision of information about the debtor by third parties in both the public sector (Department for Work and Pensions etc.) and in the private sector (banks, building societies etc.) can only help in providing the creditor with sufficient information about the debtor to make an informed decision as to the most appropriate method (if any) of enforcement.

**5.4.4**   Following the comments in the Civil Enforcement Review, the new Act has introduced two new mechanisms:

■ *Information Orders* – Information Orders apply to the private sector, who are ordered to provide information.
■ *Departmental Information Requests* – The court is more polite to the government and public sector who are simply issued with a 'request' for information. Departmental Information Requests and Information Orders are not designed to take the place of an Order to Obtain Information. They are designed to complement Orders to Obtain Information.

## Does the creditor apply for a request or an Order?

**5.4.5**   These new mechanisms only apply for enforcement, i.e. where there is a judgment debt.

**5.4.6**   The creditor does not make an application for a Departmental Information Request or an Information Order, it is made by the court (s.96(2)):

> *The relevant court* may make one or more of the following in relation to the debtor –
>
> (a)   a departmental information request;
> (b)   an information order. [Emphasis added.]

**5.4.7**   Once the creditor has applied to court (under s.95 of the new Act), it is for the court to decide (under s.96(3) of the new Act) whether it would be assisted by a Departmental Information Request or an Information Order.

## Overview

### *What action can the court take?*

**5.4.8**   Under s.96(3) of the new Act, the court has a discretion whether or not to make a Departmental Information Request or grant an Information Order.

**5.4.9**   The court will exercise that discretion to make a Request or an Order 'only if it is satisfied that to do so will help it to deal with the creditor's application'.

### *Multiple applicants*

**5.4.10**   If the court makes a Departmental Information Request or an Information Order, the court can use the information it receives under a Departmental Information Request or an Information Order to make further Departmental Information Requests or Information Orders (s.101(2) of the new Act).

### *What does the court do with the information it receives?*

**5.4.11**   The court may use the information it receives under a Departmental Information Request or an Information Order to provide the creditor with information about the most appropriate action to take to enforce the judgment debt (s.101(3)) but only once regulations are in force to govern the way in which this is to happen (s.101(6)).

**5.4.12**   The court may use the information in assisting the creditor in enforcing the judgment debt (s.101(4) of the new Act) or may pass it to another court if enforcement is taking place in that court (s.101(5)).

### *Procedure*

**5.4.13**   Information Order and Departmental Information Requests cannot be made unless the creditor has first made an application to the court under s.95(1) of the new Act, which provides:

> A person who is the creditor in relation to a judgment debt may apply to the High Court or a county court for information about what kind of action it would be appropriate to take in court to recover that particular debt.

**5.4.14**   Section 95(2) of the new Act leaves it open for the procedure to be set down by regulations:

> An application under subsection (1) must comply with any provision made in regulations about the making of such applications.

**5.4.15**   Under s.96(1) of the new Act, a creditor cannot benefit from either of the two new mechanisms unless he has first applied under s.95(1) for 'information about what kind of action it would be appropriate to take in court to recover that particular debt'.

**5.4.16** So, s.96 of the new Act gives authority to the court to make a Departmental Information Request or an Information Order but s.96(1) is also specific in that it only 'applies if the creditor in relation to a judgment debt makes an application for information under section 95'.

**5.4.17** If the court decides to make an Information Order or a Departmental Information Request, the court will firstly notify the debtor that it intends to make a Departmental Information Request or an Information Order (s.96(4)) but the debtor does not have the right to object.

**5.4.18** In making a Departmental Information Request or an Information Order, the court can disclose as much information as it feels necessary to aid the third party (being asked the questions) in responding to the Departmental Information Request or Information Order (s.96(6) of the new Act). This specifically includes disclosing the identity of the debtor.

## Departmental Information Requests

**5.4.19** These are governed by s.97 of the new Act. They are:

> a request for the disclosure of information held by, or on behalf of, a government department.

### To whom is the request made?

**5.4.20** The request is made by the court to 'the Minister of the Crown, or other person, who is in charge of the department' under s.97(2).

**5.4.21** A request cannot be made, however, to the Scottish Administration, a Northern Ireland department or the Welsh Assembly government (s.97(6)).

### Use

**5.4.22** The most obvious use for a Departmental Information Request is for the court (and creditor) to obtain from the Secretary of State the name, address, date of birth and national insurance number of the debtor. Using that information, a request can be made to Her Majesty's Revenue and Customs (HMRC) to find out whether the debtor is employed and the name and address of the employer. That would then be useful in making, for example, an Attachment of Earnings Order.

### Responding to a Departmental Information Request

**5.4.23** The recipient of the request (i.e. the government department) 'may' disclose to the court any information it considers necessary to comply with the request.

**5.4.24**    The use of the word 'may' in s.99(2) of the new Act implies a discretion which, although in line with the idea of a 'request', limits the efficacy of the new Act when it comes to governmental departments. Technically, there is nothing to stop the government department from simply ignoring the Departmental Information Request.

**5.4.25**    The reaction of government departments to the receipt of a Departmental Information Request, and whether they respond within a short enough timescale to be of use in any enforcement proceedings, remains to be seen. How government departments are to respond to a Departmental Information Request is to be set out in non-legislative agreements between the Department for Constitutional Affairs and the respective departments. These are likely to be finalised after the Regulations have been drafted.

**5.4.26**    Had the new Act introduced a timescale for responding, it would have avoided the court waiting unnecessarily to see if a government department decided to respond. During this time the creditor still may not have enough information to decide how best to enforce his judgment. Any delay could be costly to the creditor.

**5.4.27**    In that respect, the new Act does not address a common criticism of methods of obtaining information about debtors – that the methods are too slow.

## Information Orders

**5.4.28**    Departmental Information Requests are likely to be used for an Attachment of Earnings Order. An Information Order is likely to be used before applying for a Third Party Debt Order. They are extremely important because, without specific information about the debtor's accounts, the creditor cannot apply for a Third Party Debt Order.

**5.4.29**    Information Orders are governed by s.98 of the new Act and are designed to obtain information from third parties (i.e. anyone other than the debtor himself or a government department). The most likely use will be in obtaining information from banks or building societies.

**5.4.30**    Like Departmental Information Requests, Information Orders are made by the court.

**5.4.31**    Unlike Departmental Information Requests, a response to an Information Order is obligatory. Section 98(1) of the new Act uses markedly different terms to those used in relation to Departmental Information Requests in s.99(2). Section 98(1)(c) of the new Act actually *orders the information discloser to disclose the required information to the relevant court.*

**5.4.32**    Information Orders can be used to order only particular information from particular people. The definition of the information discloser is very broad and will be more particularly defined in the Regulations. However, it is likely to include not only a particular person (corporate or individual) but also a particular description of person. It is not clear at this stage whether a general order against 'all high street clearing banks' could be made.

**5.4.33**   In practice, Information Orders are only likely to be ordered by the court where either the debtor refuses to give bank (or other financial) details or where there is a reason to doubt the truth of the information he has provided.

**5.4.34**   Once again the new Act does not impose a time limit on, or even a suggested deadline for, a response. It is hoped the regulations will introduce time limits. If not, it reduces the usefulness of the new measures in a situation where, for example, banks do not respond for months. In that situation, a creditor is left not knowing his position while a debtor could be dissipating his assets.

## Procedure

**5.4.35**   Under s.97(3) and (4) (for Departmental Information Requests) and s.98(1) of the new Act (for Information Orders), if the court makes:

- a Departmental Information Request then the 'Minister of the Crown' may provide the 'prescribed information';
- an Information Order then the 'prescribed person' must provide the 'prescribed information'.

What is meant by 'prescribed' will be set out in regulations that are yet to be drafted.

**5.4.36**   For an Information Order, the 'prescribed person' (i.e. the 'information discloser') is likely to be banks and buildings societies. The 'prescribed information' is likely to be information about bank account numbers and funds held.

**5.4.37**   In making a Departmental Information Request, the information discloser is likely to be the Commissioners for HMRC and the 'prescribed information' is likely to include matters such as how long a party has been employed, how much they earn each year, how much tax they pay and other such matters.

## Extent of duty of disclosure

**5.4.38**   Under s.99(2) the information discloser under a Departmental Information Request may disclose any information the discloser considers necessary to comply with the request.

**5.4.39**   The extent of disclosure is therefore governed by:

- the wording of the request; and
- the information discloser's opinion on what is 'necessary'.

If a government department considers that it does not have to provide the information because it is not necessary, there may well be no remedy against this decision save for making an application under an authority such as the Local Government Commission.

**5.4.40**    Information Orders, however, will most likely define exactly what is required and so the information discloser's opinion of what is necessary will not affect the Order.

**5.4.41**    If the party receiving an Information Order (who then becomes an information discloser) does not hold the information required from that Information Order, he is protected from breach under s.100 of the new Act.

**5.4.42**    However, a failure to disclose some or all of the required information is only allowed by one of the 'permitted reasons' set out in s.100(2) of the new Act. These are that:

■    the information discloser does not hold the information; or
■    the information discloser is unable to ascertain whether the information is held because of the way in which the Information Order identifies the debtor; or
■    the disclosure of information would involve the information discloser in unreasonable effort or expense.

The last of these is of course open to abuse by an unscrupulous, busy (or just plain lazy) information discloser.

**5.4.43**    There are methods to combat this although it must be questioned just how effective these measures are. If an information discloser wishes to rely on a 'permitted reason' in s.100(2) for non-disclosure, he must file a certificate at court (s.100(3)). The certificate must state what of the required information is not being disclosed and must give the permitted reason(s) for the failure to disclose that information.

## Use of disclosed information

**5.4.44**    A court cannot make a Departmental Information Request to the Commissioners for HMRC until regulations are in place relating to the use and disclosure of information disclosed by them (s.96(5) of the new Act). These regulations are to follow.

**5.4.45**    Information disclosed under an Information Order does not breach any confidentiality obligations (s.101(9) of the new Act):

> The use or disclosure of information in accordance with this section is not to be taken to breach any restriction on the use or disclosure of information (however imposed).

Similarly, in providing information under a Departmental Information Request, this will not breach the Data Protection Act (s.101(3) of the new Act).

**5.4.46**    This, quite rightly, affords the protection to the information provider and the court to be able to disclose the requested information without fear of reprisal.

**5.4.47**   Under s.103 further regulations will be passed showing the way in which debtor information may be used or disclosed to provide the creditor with information about what kind of action it will be appropriate to take in court to recover the judgment debt. The regulations may prescribe the relationship between the duties of information disclosers under the Data Protection Act 1988 and the obligation to comply with an Information Order or Departmental Information Request.

**5.4.48**   In obtaining information under a Departmental Information Request, a creditor must obtain the consent of the Commissioners before using that information to recover a judgment debt.

## Offences

**5.4.49**   The information disclosed under an Information Order or Departmental Information Request must be used with care.

**5.4.50**   Under s.102 of the new Act, it is an offence to use disclosed information under a Departmental Information Request or an Information Order unless it is used in one of the following ways:

- in accordance with s.101 (i.e. to provide the creditor with information about what kind of action (if any) it would be appropriate to take in court to recover the judgment debt);
- in accordance with an enactment or order of court and it is in accordance with regulations;
- for the purposes of any proceedings before a court and it is in accordance with regulations;
- if the information has previously been lawfully disclosed to the public;
- if it is in accordance with rules of court that comply with regulations yet to be passed.

**5.4.51**   It is a defence (under s.102 of the new Act) for a person charged with unlawful use or disclosure of this information to prove that he reasonably believed that the use or disclosure was lawful.

**5.4.52**   A person guilty of an offence under s.102 risks (on indictment) imprisonment of up to two years and/or a fine or (on summary conviction) imprisonment of up to 12 months and/or a fine not exceeding the statutory maximum.

## Transitional provisions

**5.4.53**   The sections of the new Act relating to Departmental Information Requests and Information Orders (ss.95 to 104) are retrospective. They apply to any judgment debt once the new Act is in force, whether that judgment debt became payable or recoverable before or after the commencement of the new Act (s.105(1) of the new Act).

## 5.5    OVERVIEW FLOWCHART

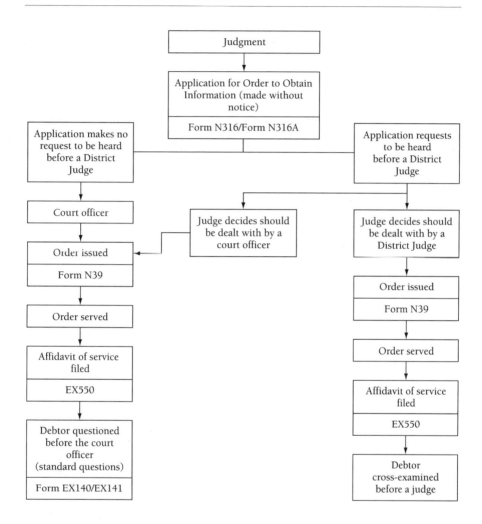

## 5.6    FORMS

| | |
|---|---|
| N316 | Application for order for debtor to attend court for examination |
| N316A | Application for order that the officer of a debtor company attend court for examination |
| N39 | Order to attend court for questioning |
| N40 | Warrant for arrest and committal for disobedience |
| N40(HC) | Warrant of arrest and committal for disobedience |

| N40B | Warrant of committal for disobedience |
| N40B(HC) | Warrant of committal for disobedience |
| N79 | Suspended committal order for disobedience |
| EX140 | Examination Record (Individual) |
| EX14 | Examination Record (Company) |

# PART II  **TAKING CONTROL OF GOODS**

# 6 ENFORCEMENT AGENTS AND WARRANTS OF CONTROL

## 6.1 INTRODUCTION

6.1.1 The new Act reforms the law which regulates bailiffs and the process of seizing the goods of a debtor to enforce payment of a debt ('distress'). The reforms are comprehensive and far-reaching and include:

- the abolition of the 'law of distress' for landlords;
- the replacement of distress for landlords with commercial rent arrears recovery (CRAR);
- the unification of the process regulating all forms of distress into one system of 'taking control of goods';
- the creation of a foundation for the regulation of bailiffs ('enforcement agents').

### Pre-Act position

6.1.2 Under the current system bailiffs and enforcement officers (together renamed 'enforcement agents' by the new Act) can seize goods for a wide range of debts. Accordingly enforcement agents are able to levy distress in relation to unpaid taxes, property rents, non-domestic business rates, court fines, judgment debts, and the list goes on.

6.1.3 A different system applies to each type of forum. There are separate systems for each type of civil court which gives judgments. Landlords and local authorities have their own systems.

- High Court Enforcement Officers (HCEOs) enforce High Court judgments by executing a writ and are governed by the provisions set out in the Courts Act 2003;
- county court bailiffs enforce county court judgments by executing a warrant and are governed by the County Courts Act 1984;
- private bailiffs certificated by a county court District Judge pursuant to the Distress for Rent Rules 1988 levy distress for rent without a court order and execute a warrant of distress;

- private bailiffs certificated by a county court District Judge enforce Liability Orders made in the magistrates' court and levy distress to collect unpaid council tax and non-domestic business rates.

6.1.4   These differences are highlighted by the different approach taken by enforcement agents under the various regimes. The diversity of types of enforcement agent and systems of enforcement gave rise to a call to unify the processes.

6.1.5   Landlord's distress was perhaps the biggest impetus for change, having been singled out for attention by the Law Commission since 1966 (Interim Report on Distress for Rent (1966), Law Comm. No.5) and recommended for abolition (Landlords and Tenant Distress for Rent (1991) Law Comm. No.4 194). This is dealt with in **Chapter 7**.

## 6.2    EFFECTIVENESS OF ENFORCEMENT – REFORM AND THE FOUNDATIONS FOR THE NEW ACT

6.2.1   Pre-Act enforcement through the appointment of county court bailiffs accounts for the majority of actions which can be taken by a creditor to seize goods. The county court system is often considered to be ineffective because:

- the system is slow and sometimes suffers from long waiting periods between the issue of a warrant and execution;
- a significant proportion of warrants are deemed unenforceable.

6.2.2   Questions have long been raised about the Courts Services Performance Measure, which only takes account of enforceable warrants. Creditors are often dismayed by how many warrants are classified as unenforceable by the court service. This is often blamed on a lack of proper detail to locate the debtor. Between 1998 and 2002 approximately 52 per cent of all warrants issued were classified as unenforceable. There is a perception within the enforcement industry that private bailiffs paid by result are 'more tenacious'. This view was identified within the consultation process for the new Act. There was a general feeling that the county court system was slow, understaffed and sometimes produced poor results.

Table 6.1   Warrants of execution: amounts issued and recovered in England and Wales, 1999–2006

| Year | Amount received in all warrants (£) | Amount issued in all warrants (£) | Pence-per-pound recovered on all warrants |
| --- | --- | --- | --- |
| 1999 | 46,015,501 | 196,287,059 | 23.44 |
| 2000 | 49,579,112 | 181,682,532 | 27.27 |
| 2001 | 47,832,846 | 168,291,967 | 28.42 |
| 2002 | 48,491,378 | 170,676,955 | 28.41 |
| 2003 | 49,819,049 | 186,294,217 | 26.74 |
| 2004 | 48,550,116 | 195,831,506 | 24.79 |
| 2005 | 47,417,447 | 200,347,628 | 23.67 |
| 2006 | 46,173,497 | 211,262,049 | 21.86 |

*Source*: Ministry of Justice.

## Can't pay/won't pay

**6.2.3**   It was considered important to preserve creditor confidence. Enforcement should not fail merely because a particularly hardened and recalcitrant debtor refuses to pay ('won't pay'). The Lord Chancellor's Department published a research paper in March 2003 which identified two groups of debtors, i.e. those who can't pay and those who have set out not to pay (*Can't Pay or Won't Pay* by Nicola Dominy and Elaine Kempson, March 2003). The research paper highlighted the difficulty of distinguishing between those who fall into the following categories:

- *'can't pay'* – those people who did not have the money when they fell into arrears and have insufficient funds to pay when a creditor takes action;
- *intermediate group* – those who had the means to repay when they incurred the debt but as result of changed circumstances are not able to pay when recovery action is taken. This may include, people who have lost their jobs, faced a marriage breakdown or who have suffered an illness etc;
- *'won't pay'* – the people who had the money to pay when they fell into arrears and were still in a position to pay when their creditors are taking recovery action – this group wait until the last possible moment before paying.

**6.2.4**   There is a balance to be struck between the action which should be permitted against those without the ability to pay, and the steps which should be allowed against those without the commitment to pay. Accordingly there is a distinction between debtors who 'can't pay' and debtors who 'won't pay' a debt. The research paper estimated that the 'won't pay' group might be as high as 12 per cent. Within the 'can't pay' group there is also those who have incurred debt recklessly. However even though the hardened debtor is a significant proportion of the total it does not justify a one size fits all process. Enforcement law needs to be flexible enough to provide a proportionate response to each category of debtor (also see **6.4** below in relation to human rights).

**6.2.5**   Creditors do not want to waste time and money taking action against debtors who do not have the means to pay a debt. Conversely, debtors who genuinely cannot pay must be protected from overzealous creditors. Finally, debtors who are able to pay should not be able to exploit the rules intended to protect the vulnerable members of society where they are not vulnerable themselves.

## Benefits of bailiff enforcement

**6.2.6**   The four principal objectives of bailiff enforcement are:

(a) *realisation* – so that creditors can attach and realise valuable goods owned by a defaulting debtor;

(b) *identification of assets* – bailiff enforcement helps a creditor understand what assets (and sometimes what other liabilities) the debtor has. However, it might be more proportionate for a creditor to establish what assets can be identified prior to enforcement taking place;

(c) *deterrent* – the possibility that a creditor may use bailiff enforcement helps to prevent debtor default;

(d) *spur to payment* – the use or threatened use of bailiff enforcement operates to induce payment often without an actual seizure and sale.

6.2.7    The key concern is whether these objectives can be achieved within the confines of proportionality and in compliance with the European Convention on Human Rights. When the law confers a right it should also supply an effective mechanism to give the right practical effect. The Scottish Law Commission recognised this principle but thought that it should be moderated on the basis that the system should permit the least coercion that can be used whilst still being effective to achieve the four objectives.

6.2.8    The effectiveness of any enforcement process has to be tempered by proportionality. This will always be a delicate balancing act.

## Growth in debtor default

6.2.9    In recent years creditors have become frustrated with the process. There has been an increase in default. The success of the process has also been eroded by the explosion in the number of personal insolvencies.

■    bankruptcies have increased from 19,647 in 1998 to 62,956 in 2006;
■    individual voluntary arrangements have increased from 4,902 in 1998 to 44,332 in 2006.

6.2.10    There has been a consumer credit expansion in the last 10 years. Each adult in the UK, on average, accounts for in excess of £18,000 worth of unsecured consumer credit. This has not only affected the large credit suppliers, it has also had a knock-on effect in relation to recoverability of debt for all creditors. The Enterprise Act 2002 liberalised the system for bankrupts (reducing the period of bankruptcy from three years to a maximum of one year for most bankruptcies). Some commentators referred to this as a 'rogue's charter'. The Enterprise Act has to some extent removed the stigma for debtors who cannot pay their debts.

6.2.11    With rising levels of default there is an increased need to preserve creditor confidence with a better method of enforcement. With the introduction of a simpler, unified system for bailiff enforcement under the new Act, it is hoped that the process will become more effective.

## General principles and objectives of the new Act

6.2.12    These reforms came after an extensive consultation process which took place over a period of six years. The aspiration of the new Act is to create a system of enforcing debt based on two principles:

- the system should operate effectively and give creditors confidence enabling them to obtain payment of their debts with reasonable success;
- the system should be designed to have proper regard to protecting debtors from undue economic hardship.

Accordingly a system of bailiff enforcement needs to be effective and proportionate. The new Act seeks to reconcile the conflict between these two opposing principles.

**6.2.13**   In the white paper entitled *Effective Enforcement* published by the Lord Chancellor's Department in March 2003, Lord Irving in a foreword stated:

> Society wants those who owe money judgments to pay their dues but also wants to protect the vulnerable. We all want to prevent unacceptable behaviour from those with the difficult task of making debtors pay but we also want to ensure that creditors, many of whom may be in financial difficulties themselves, receive the money to which they are properly entitled. It is important that individuals have the right to manage their own financial affairs, but we are all concerned to address issues of over indebtedness. We must protect individual's rights to privacy while recognising that controlled access to information about debtors circumstances is essential since there will always be those who deliberately seek to avoid payment.

> The courts and those who bear the responsibility of enforcing the courts' judgments have to find a way to balance these competing demands and achieve the fair balance between rights and responsibilities, for both debtors and creditors which we all expect in a modern and democratic society.

## 6.3   THE NEW ACT POSITION

**6.3.1**   The new Act is designed to improve the effectiveness of bailiff enforcement. Given the antiquity, diversity and complexity of bailiff law, it was a prime candidate for rationalisation. Therefore one of the main objectives was to simplify and clarify the law making it more transparent and certain.

**6.3.2**   The new Act sweeps away all the current systems, including landlord's distress. In replacement there will be a unitary system which applies to all enforcement that involves seizing goods. Landlords, also, have access to this new process (although with limitations). The new Act creates:

- one kind of bailiff/enforcement officer – to be called an 'enforcement agent';
- one system for seizing the goods of a debtor to be known as 'taking control of goods'.

**6.3.3**   For the new provisions applying to enforcement agents see **6.5**. For the new provisions applying to taking control of goods see **Chapters 9–10**.

## 6.4    PROPORTIONALITY: COMPLIANCE WITH THE EUROPEAN CONVENTION ON HUMAN RIGHTS

### Pre-Act position

**6.4.1**    The Human Rights Act 1998 gave direct effect in the UK to the European Convention on Human Rights 1950 (ECHR). The current systems of bailiff enforcement have been seen to be out of kilter with the ECHR and perhaps open to challenge.

**6.4.2**    The relevant convention articles are:

- *Article 6* – the right to a fair trial before an independent tribunal;
- *Article 8* – the right to respect for private and family life and the home;
- *Article 14* – the right to enjoy the Convention rights without discrimination;
- *Article 1 of the First Protocol* – the right to peaceful enjoyment of possessions.

**6.4.3**    Each one of these ECHR Articles potentially influences the law of enforcement. Bailiff enforcement does not, necessarily, breach the ECHR. It was considered that without adequate safeguards, particular instances of enforcement against vulnerable debtors could be the subject of an ECHR challenge. A challenge could be made on the basis of lack of proportionality and unlawfulness. Possible challenges would include:

- for small debts, the cost of enforcement might be disproportionate to the value of the debt;
- the right to use reasonable force to gain entry to premises might be appropriate in limited circumstances but an abuse in other circumstances;
- the process must be undertaken with adequate safeguards for third party rights.

**6.4.4**    The ECHR can affect particular aspects of enforcement. A clear example of this is the decision in *McGonnell* v. *UK* (Application number 28488/95 handed down on 8 February 2000) (2000) 8 BHRC 56. In this Guernsey case the European Court decided that a bailiff should not also be the judge who determines a challenge to an enforcement action. In the county court this is what happens. Under County Courts Act 1984, s.123 District Judges are personally responsible for the actions of their bailiffs. The *McGonnell* case criticises this position where a judge has a dual administrative and judicial role. If there were a challenge to the county court process (such as an interpleader application) then this could be determined by the same District Judge that is responsible for the potentially unlawful distress in the first place. For example, the same District Judge could rule in an interpleader dispute in circumstances where under the pre-Act system the District Judge is technically one of the parties.

**6.4.5**    It must also not be forgotten that creditors have rights under the ECHR. For example, landlords, as well as tenants, have a right to peacefully enjoy their property.

## The new Act position

**6.4.6**   The new Act took account of and accepted the recommendations put forward by the consultation process. The new Act sets out to remove the uncertainties of bailiff enforcement and to clarify the grounds upon which enforcement can be exercised. One of the aims was to minimise the risk of a successful ECHR challenge and to set out the regime of bailiff law clearly in one place. The modifications created by the new Act have been driven by the requirement to ensure compliance with the ECHR. Particular steps have been taken to ensure compliance:

- County Courts Act 1984, s.123 has been repealed and the third party interpleader process reformed (see **12.2**);
- one system of enforcement will replace the diversity of regimes and minimise the risk of debtors being confused (see **Chapters 10–12**);
- the law of distress has been abolished and replaced with CRAR (see **Chapter 7**);
- a debtor's claim of set off will have to be taken into account in accordance with the guidance of Lightman J in *Fuller v. Happy Shopper Markets Ltd* [2001] 1 WLR 1681 (see **6.4**);
- a regulatory body for enforcement agents will in time be set up to deal with complaints;
- a clear regulatory framework will be set up for all enforcement agents.

**6.4.7**   The new Act will not remove all possibility of an ECHR challenge. It will be open to particular debtors in particular circumstances to argue that there has been a breach of the Convention. However, in most cases, the new Act will reduce the prospect of any such challenge being successful.

## 6.5   ENFORCEMENT AGENTS

### Pre-Act position

**6.5.1**   The enforcement profession is fragmented with some firms and individuals operating outside of any structure. Enforcement agents (with certain exceptions) hold a certificate issued by a county court. The current system of bailiff enforcement is not subject to any uniform regulatory system.

**6.5.2**   The Department of Constitutional Affairs has estimated that there are currently 5,200 enforcement agents operating in England and Wales, made up of approximately:

- 600 county court bailiffs;
- 1,600 other state employed agents (such as tax collectors, customs officials etc.);
- 200 local authority employee enforcement agents;
- 1,600 certificated bailiffs; and
- 1,200 non-certificated private bailiffs.

It has also indicated that there are approximately 150 firms operating within the industry, many of these operating without any formal or statutory regulation.

6.5.3   The regulations under the new Act will introduce a new unified certification process. However, this process is likely to adopt the important parts of the existing regime in force for certificated bailiffs.

## Certification process

6.5.4   The current statutory regime for providing certificates to landlords' bailiffs is contained in two nineteenth century statutes (Law of Distress Amendment Act 1888 and Law of Distress Amendment Act 1895) and the Distress for Rent Rules 1988. Accordingly the certification process has evolved in a perfunctory and pragmatic way over a period of time.

6.5.5   There is only one certification process for bailiffs administered by a select number of county courts (as set out in Part 4 of the Distress for Rent Rules 1988). Certificates last for two years from the date issued. An application for a certificate is made on a prescribed form (form 3 under the 1988 Rules).

6.5.6   The application requires:

■   two references, which must evidence the applicant's knowledge of the law of distress;
■   a certified copy of a search of the register of county court judgments against the applicant's address(es) over the last six years;
■   two passport size photos;
■   copies of three advertisements placed in newspapers local to the issuing county court, all to have been placed at least 60 days prior to the hearing of the application and filed at the court at least three days prior to the hearing;
■   bailiffs to provide a security bond of £10,000.

6.5.7   The hearing is dealt with by a Circuit Judge. The judge must be satisfied that the applicant:

■   is a fit and proper person to hold a certificate;
■   possesses a sufficient knowledge of the law of distress;
■   is not engaged in the business of buying debts.

6.5.8   In relation to the 'knowledge' requirement the applicant can demonstrate this by successfully sitting the examination set by the Certified Bailiffs Association. However, this is not an absolute requirement. In reality there is a high degree of inconsistency from District Judge to District Judge as to the certification process. The applicant attends the hearing in person. If he makes any misrepresentation to the court then this would be contempt.

## Complaints

**6.5.9**   Complaints are remarkably rare, given the huge potential for disgruntled debtors who might want to take action. Debtors and third parties are able to make a complaint. The complaint is made on form 4 or 5 of the Distress for Rent Rules 1988 and is first dealt with by a Court Officer who sends details of the complaint to the bailiff. The bailiff has 14 days to reply in writing and a judge then decides whether to summons the bailiff to a hearing to show cause why the certificate should not be cancelled.

**6.5.10**   The complaint is made against the bailiff personally and not the firm. This can put individual junior bailiffs in a difficult position if their employer is in effect making the decisions and controlling the process.

## The new Act position

**6.5.11**   The new Act introduces a single legal framework for all enforcement agents. All bailiffs are to be known as enforcement agents. The objective stated in the White Paper was that:

> All enforcement agents must be required to balance their duties to the court, the creditor and the debtor. They all do a difficult job, they all have broadly the same powers and must all behave in an appropriate way. All service users – whether creditors or debtor – are entitled to expect high professional standards. [*Effective Enforcement* – White Paper 2003 – CM 5744.]

**6.5.12**   Part 3 of the new Act unifies the law governing the activities of enforcement agents when taking control of and selling goods. It also modernises and unifies most of the pre-Act terminology used in various pieces of legislation. The new unified procedure will apply to almost all systems allowing enforcement agents to seize goods.

## Will a regulatory body be set up?

**6.5.13**   The new Act provides a foundation for regulation, but falls short of creating a regulatory body. The White Paper proposed a system to guard against malpractice and to protect debtors. It suggested that a licensing regime would be put in place and implemented through a new regulatory body. It is clear that this remains the government's long term aim. The Lord Chancellor's Department has considered the merits of creating an Enforcement Services Commission to act as a regulatory body. There was some discussion as to whether this body would be the Security Industry Authority (SIA). The SIA was set up to regulate between 300,000 and 800,000 personnel in the private security industry and has operated as an executive NDPB since 1 April 2003. The SIA currently has powers in relation to wheel clampers, door bouncers (bouncers), manned guards and key holders, private investigators and security consultants.

**6.5.14**    The regulatory body, when it materialises, is likely to provide for:

- inclusion of all enforcement services;
- licensing of all enforcement agents;
- approving of authorised enforcement service providers;
- accreditation of professional associations;
- authorising training providers;
- setting up a complaints board; and
- allowing the SIA (or other regulatory body) to make recommendations to the Lord Chancellor.

**6.5.15**    On this basis there is also likely to be secondary legislation dealing with:

- criteria for licences;
- issuing of a code of practice;
- requirements for applications;
- requirements for obtaining licences;
- the complaints process.

**6.5.16**    While it remains the government's long term objective to set up a new regulatory body, as an interim measure the new Act replaces, by extending and modifying, the landlord's certification process that currently exists for bailiffs under the Distress for Rent Rules 1998. The extended and modified certification process will apply to persons taking control of goods who are not Crown employees or constables (the justification for such an exclusion being that the Crown employees and constables by virtue of their status are already subject to adequate systems of control).

## Certification process – regulation and control under the new Act

**6.5.17**    The new Act extends the certification process giving county court District Judges the power to issue certificates subject to regulations to be made by the Lord Chancellor. The regulations will include provision (s.64 of the new Act):

- for fees to be charged on applications;
- for certificates to be issued subject to conditions including the giving of security;
- for certificates to be limited to purposes specified by or under the regulations;
- about complaints against certificate holders;
- about the suspension and cancellation of certificates;
- to modify or supplement the provisions of the Act relating to executing warrants of control (Sched.12 to the Act) for cases where a certificate is suspended or cancelled or has expired; and
- requiring courts to make information available relating to certificates.

**6.5.18**    Eventually the certification process will be administered by the regulatory body set up by the government to oversee bailiff enforcement.

**6.5.19**  Section 63 specifies the criteria to be met for an individual to act as an enforcement agent. This includes acting under a certificate under s.64. This clause also creates an offence where an individual acts as an enforcement agent and does not meet the specified criteria. Under the new Act an individual may act as an enforcement agent only if he has a certificate under s.64 or if he is exempt. Enforcement agents are the only individuals who are able to execute an enforcement power conferred by a writ or warrant under the terms of the new Act.

### EXEMPTIONS

**6.5.20**  All enforcement agents will require a certificate to execute an enforcement power unless they are exempt under the new Act.

**6.5.21**  An individual does not require a certificate to act as an enforcement agent if the individual:

- is a constable;
- is an officer of Her Majesty's Revenue and Customs, under s.63(4) of the new Act;
- is a civilian enforcement officer. For the purposes of an enforcement power being exercised in the magistrates' court, civilian enforcement officers (as defined by Magistrates' Court Act 1980, s.125A) are also exempt;
- already has a certificate in force granted under the Distress for Rent Rules 1988 (s.64);
- is a person who works as a court officer (or is employed by the Court Service) (Courts Act 2003, s.21 and s.63(3) of the new Act);
- is a third party directed by an enforcement officer to help and assist with his activities (s.63(2)(c)). Any such third party is not required to obtain a certificate (the Department of Constitutional Affairs Regulation of Enforcement Agents, 30 June 2007, CP2/07).

## What extra requirements will the regulations impose when they come in?

**6.5.22**  The regulations have not yet been through the complete consultation process. However, there are some clues as to what they may contain. The regulations are likely to be influenced by ECHR concerns. In February 2007 the Joint Committee on Human Rights (JCHR) canvassed heavily for the introduction of a clear regulatory framework for enforcement agents. The JCHR had serious concern that the lack of a clear unified regulatory framework provides insufficient safeguard for rights of debtors and third parties.

**6.5.23**  The JCHR published a report entitled *Legislative Scrutiny: Third Progress Report* in February 2007. As a consequence of this report and other consultation it is currently intended that the regulations will require enforcement agents to meet certain conditions before being granted a certificate including:

- professional qualifications;
- the level of approved training that has to be undertaken on an ongoing basis;
- compulsory criminal record checks;
- references;
- confirmation that the applicant is not an undischarged bankrupt or involved in certain trades (such as the buying and selling of debt); and
- the provision of a security bond of up to £10,000 to have been lodged.

**6.5.24**   This is similar to the current requirements under the Distress for Rent Rules 1988. However we will have to see the detail. Currently bailiffs can take the Certified Bailiffs Association's exam but are not compelled to do so. The regulations are likely to introduce compulsory tests. They are also likely to introduce a level of supervision to ensure that the powers of the Act are exercised in a proportionate manner and in compliance with the ECHR. It remains to be seen whether the Security Industry Authority is to become the appointed regulatory body for all enforcement agents. It is highly likely that in due course an enforcement commission in some form will be constituted to take on the role.

## Complaints

**6.5.25**   Until a regulatory body is set up to supervise and administer the certification process, complaints will continue to be administered by the county court system.

**6.5.26**   When a regulatory body is constituted (whether the SIA or other 'enforcement commission') this will have as a primary function the obligation to oversee a complaints scheme for enforcement services. The commission may, in time, be granted power to revoke certificates for failing to act with the conditions set by the court. However, the Lord Chancellor's Department also envisages that a complaints board will be established to oversee the complaints procedures of enforcement agents, service providers and accredited professional associations. The complaints board will monitor the conduct of enforcement agents in relation to taking control of goods under Sched.12 to the new Act. The complaints board will also deal with abuse of fee scales and charges (*Effective Enforcement* 2003 White Paper).

**6.5.27**   The county court system will continue to monitor the complaints process until these bodies are created or empowered to deal with complaints. For landlords the current complaint process is governed by the Distress for Rent Rules 1988.

# 7 COMMERCIAL RENT ARREARS RECOVERY

## 7.1 PRE-ACT POSITION: DISTRESS FOR RENT

### Background

**7.1.1** The new Act abolishes distress and replaces it with a new mechanism (see new Act position below). Landlords have long enjoyed the common law right to levy distress for rent. Distress for rent under the pre-Act regime is one of the main weapons by which a landlord can recover rent arrears. It is an ancient common law remedy which generally gives the landlord a right as soon as rent is overdue to enter the demised property and to seize and hold goods found there. The initial right to levy distress can be exercised irrespective of who owns the goods, until the rent is paid. Where goods belonging to someone other than the tenant have been seized, some third party owners have limited rights of 'after-the-event' protection granted by the Law of Distress Amendment Act 1908.

**7.1.2** In relation to commercial premises distress was a very popular remedy available to the landlord when rent was in arrears. It is an automatic right arising from the obligation to pay rent. A landlord using the remedy has to comply with a complex and sometimes anachronistic set of rules developed over the centuries in a haphazard fashion. These then have to be applied to the modern world of landlord and tenant.

**7.1.3** For commercial premises, the use of distress was not subject to prior judicial control. In other words no prior court order was necessary in order to authorise a bailiff to enter commercial premises and attempt to levy distress. In some respects this gave landlords a significant advantage over other creditors (almost all other creditors first need a court order to instruct an enforcement agent to seize goods).

**7.1.4** In principle distress is a simple operation. A landlord who is owed rent is able to take goods from the demised premises and sell them. From the proceeds he is able to satisfy the arrears of rent together with the costs of using the remedy. However, over the centuries a complex body of rules developed through case law and supplemented by statutory control. Both govern the conditions for the exercise of each and every step of the procedure; such as who may exercise the remedy, the subject matter of the distress (i.e. the goods distrained upon), the amount recoverable (i.e. rent, monies reserved as rent) and when and how the distraint may be put in place.

7.1.5   As soon as the tenant falls into rent arrears the power to levy distress becomes exercisable and the landlord could proceed without any advance notice to the tenant and without observing any other preliminary formality. There are some limited instances where distress is prohibited by statute without first obtaining the court's permission. However in relation to the majority of distress actions the landlord does not need the court's permission. The court's permission is required in limited circumstances including:

■   under Rent Act 1977, s.147, no distress can be levied on a dwelling house let on a protected tenancy or subject to a statutory tenancy without the permission of the county court;
■   under Housing Act 1988, s.19, no distress can be levied on a dwelling house let on an assured tenancy without the permission of the county court;
■   under certain types of insolvency no distress can be levied without the permission of the companies court or the county court (see **Chapter 8** in relation to insolvency).

7.1.6   In practice, therefore, landlords rarely levy distress in relation to residential premises (unless part of the demise is being used for business purposes or for ground rents). Therefore in the majority of cases being in relation to commercial premises the landlord could proceed without giving the tenant any notice. Under the pre-Act regime, the landlord is able to ambush the tenant with no notice being given.

## The impetus for reform – and the ECHR

7.1.7   The potential to ambush a tenant was one of the most severe criticisms that has been levelled at distress. The absence of (in most cases) any advance warning to the tenant, let alone any preliminary check on the validity of the claim was potentially in conflict with the European Convention on Human Rights (ECHR).

7.1.8   The Law Commission report entitled *Landlord and Tenant Distress for Rent* published in 1991, concluded that:

> Distress for rent should be abolished when improvements to the court system make the other remedies effective. At that time the reforms to the court procedure will offer a good prospect to the court system being able to cope efficiently with the extra work.

7.1.9   In recent years, concern has been expressed that distress for rent is contrary to the ECHR in that it potentially breaches:

■   Article 6, right to a fair trial – the remedy was used in a way which gave the tenant little chance of making representations;

- Article 8, right to respect for the home, privacy and family life; and
- Article 1 of the First Protocol, the right to quiet enjoyment of possessions.

**7.1.10**   The ECHR position for enforcement generally is dealt with in **6.4**. However the law of landlord's distress has been a focus of ECHR concern. It is therefore surprising that, since the Human Rights Act 1998 came into force in 2002, there had been little direct challenge to the right to levy distress for rent. The possibility of a challenge was entertained by Lightman J in the case of *John Lesley Fuller* v. *(1) Happy Shopper Markets Limited (2) Nurdin & Peacock plc* [2001] 1 WLR 1681:

> The ancient (and perhaps an anachronistic) self help remedy of distress involves a serious interference with the right of the tenant under Article 8 of the European Convention on Human Rights to respect for his privacy and home under Article 1 of the First Protocol to the peaceful enjoyment of his possessions. The Human Rights implications of levying distress must be in the forefront of the mind of the landlord before he takes the step and he must fully satisfy himself that taking this action is in accordance with the law.

**7.1.11**   However, Lightman J did not consider the use of distress would always place the landlord in conflict with ECHR. He was concerned that this form of rapid, direct approach, should only be used after proper consideration was taken of the tenant's position. Account should be to whether the tenant had any right of set-off or counterclaim in relation to the rent claim.

**7.1.12**   Naturally the rights of the landlord under the ECHR must also be taken into account, particularly in relation to commercial premises. Here the balance sometimes changes. The landlord could be a private individual with an investment property and the tenant could be a large incorporated business attempting to extend its payment terms. An individual landlord also has the right to the peaceful enjoyment of his property under the ECHR.

**7.1.13**   Landlords are in the business of supplying accommodation, both commercial and residential. This places landlords in a potentially more difficult position than other types of suppliers. Suppliers of other commodities usually have the ability to stop future supplies until payment of arrears is made. Although landlords often have the common law right to terminate the tenancy/lease (by forfeiture), repossessing a property can sometimes be difficult. There are a number of statutory obstacles which often prevent an immediate termination of the lease by peaceable re-entry. Accordingly a small private landlord relying on the income from the property may find himself in an invidious position, i.e. he has a corporate tenant that is in default. He may also find that he is unable to forfeit or levy distress. This could be a breach of the landlord's rights under the ECHR.

**7.1.14**   Accordingly, the human rights implications for distress were unclear. What was clear to the advisors to the Lord Chancellor's Department was that the new Act had to at least reform the law of distress.

## 7.2    THE EXTENT OF THE DEBT PROBLEM IN THE COMMERCIAL PROPERTY MARKET

**7.2.1**    For all of its faults, the law of distress represents an important remedy for landlords. There are an estimated total of 684,000 commercial tenancies in England and Wales. Of these, an estimated 121,000 tenancies (17.7 per cent) are in rent arrears at any one time (based on a Lord Chancellor's Department Survey of Landlords).

**Table 7.1**    Responses to landlord's questionnaire

| | |
|---|---|
| Number of tenancies with rent arrears | 121,000 |
| Percentage of tenancies with rent arrears | 17.7% |
| Total amount of rent arrears by value of total rental income | £365 million |
| Total percentage of value of total rental income | 8% |
| Percentages and amount of the arrears successfully recovered | 45% amounting to approximately £163 million |
| – with recourse to agents, the use of distress or court action | 43% successfully recovered £71 million |
| – where agents successfully recovered the arrears without the need to take goods | 12.5% – £20.4 million |
| – through taking legal control of and sale of goods | 0.87% successfully recovered £1.4 million |
| – through debt recovery procedures and the court | 1% of arrears successfully recovered £1.8 million |

**7.2.2**    Distress has been a major tool for the commercial property industry, reducing the amount of rent arrears significantly. Distress has been used by both large and small landlords/property companies. The major advantage of the current system is that it was on many occasions quick and effective for landlords and did not require any court procedure. The new Act represents a compromise whereby the law of distress will be abolished. However, landlords will be able to continue to use a non-court process which is to be unified with the process available under the Act for the enforcement of county court judgments (and all other enforcement mechanisms allowing a bailiff/enforcement agent to take control of goods, whether through the magistrates' court, High Court etc.).

## 7.3    THE NEW ACT: ABOLITION OF DISTRESS

**7.3.1**    Section 71 of the new Act abolishes the common law right to distrain for arrears of rent in its entirety. However, in replacement landlords are able to use the procedure in Sched.12 to the new Act to recover unpaid rents. The new procedure for landlords is called 'commercial rent arrears recovery' (CRAR) (s.72 of the new Act).

**7.3.2**    The enforcement industry has been prepared for these reforms and has evolved with the changing times. One of the bailiffs interviewed for this book summed up the way the industry has adjusted to the new environment:

> Over the last 20 years the industry has undergone a major change in its attitudes and approaches. We have become more aware of human rights issues and act in a much more sensitive way.
>
> 20 years ago a bailiff would be more inclined to remove assets for sale to recover the debt as quickly as possible. Bailiffs today sometimes help put in place repayment plans. We can quickly appraise if a particular debtor genuinely has the inability to pay. We only remove goods where there is no other option. For real hardship cases there is often no real point in uplifting goods which might be of insufficient value to cover the costs position.
>
> We have seen a rise of new issues such as the language barriers and new communities who are not familiar with the legal system in Britain. On occasion we are faced with foreign nationals who are very scared of the process. This sometimes arises because the bailiffs or police in their country of origin use violence and coercion.
>
> *Our job is more about negotiation and discussion with debtors. It is a minority of cases where we actually uplift.*

## 7.4    CRAR – COMMERCIAL RENT ARREARS RECOVERY (SS.71 AND 72 OF THE ACT)

**7.4.1**    CRAR retains the essential ingredients of distress in that generally the process can be used without obtaining a court order. The new Act sets out strict preconditions for the exercise of CRAR which are more restricted than the current distress for rent process. In order to exercise CRAR the following conditions must be met:

1.  The lease must be of commercial premises (where not a single part of the premises can be let as a dwelling) (ss.71 and 72 of the new Act).
2.  CRAR is limited to the recovery of outstanding rent (together with interest and VAT). The rent must be in excess of the 'minimum amount' (to be set by regulators). It does not include any sum in respect of rates, council tax, services, repairs, maintenance (even where these sums have been reserved as rent) (s.76).
3.  The lease must be evidenced in writing and still in existence.

These preconditions are dealt with more fully below.

### Landlord – who can use CRAR?

> The law of distress may be an archaic remedy. However it has been used by many commercial landlords as a valuable counter balance to the growing number of insolvencies. In our experience we, like most landlords, are generally very sensitive to the prospect that some tenants are in a vulnerable position. We only use the remedy in the most appropriate of situations and often as an exercise to start reasonable negotiations.

I believe that the proposed changes to the law of distress will force landlords to fall back on insisting on larger rent deposits, more stringent reference requirements and tighter lease terms.

Anthony Farrant – Dawnay, Day Property Investments Ltd

**7.4.2**    The new Act empowers commercial landlords to use CRAR providing that the landlord is entitled to the immediate reversion in the property comprising the lease. CRAR is not available, directly, to superior landlords (s.73(1)).

**7.4.3**    Under s.73 a 'landlord' is defined as the person 'being entitled to the immediate reversion in the property comprised in the lease'. However, the definition is open to broad interpretation as to what constitutes a landlord.

## Does the landlord have to own an interest in the property?

**7.4.4**    In short, no. There are circumstances where the landlord might not have any legal interest in the property at all. A person may be deemed to be the landlord if he is entitled to assert that role as between landlord and tenant. This right can arise where the tenant in equity is stopped from denying that a person is his landlord (estoppel). This is expressly provided for under s.73(3):

in the case of a tenancy by estoppel, a person is entitled to the immediate reversion if he is entitled to it as between himself and the tenant.

**7.4.5**    The circumstances might be where:

- the person claiming the right to be landlord granted the lease of the property to the tenant;
- the true owner did not and does not object; and
- the tenant has peacefully enjoyed the use of the property under the terms of the lease.

**7.4.6**    On this basis a lease may be created by estoppel and may exist between the parties on that basis. Estoppel in this context is a principle which prevents the landlord from invalidating a lease he has granted (even though he may not have enjoyed the right to grant the lease in the first place). The estoppel arises out of the relationship of landlord and tenant. The question is whether the parties have willingly entered the relationship. If so then each is estopped from denying the consequences which flow from that relationship. Accordingly, the effect of a lease where a landlord had no title to create this tenancy is to create a tenancy by estoppel between himself and the tenant.

**7.4.7**    The principle of 'tenancy by estoppel' is described succinctly by Hoffmann J in *Bruton v. London & Quadrant Housing Association* [1999] 3 WLR 150 at 157:

It is not the estoppel which creates the tenancy but the tenancy which creates the estoppel. The estoppel arises when one or other of the parties wants to deny the ordinary incidence or obligations of the tenancy on the ground that the landlord has no legal estate. The basis of the estoppel is that, having entered into an agreement which constitutes a lease or tenancy he cannot repudiate that incident or obligation.

7.4.8   This principle can have important implications. A tenant will not be able to defeat the use of CRAR only on the basis of some defect in the landlord's title. Where the circumstances show that the tenant has peacefully enjoyed the premises pursuant to an agreed lease, granted by a person holding himself out to be the person 'entitled to the immediate reversion', as landlord, then the parties will be estopped from denying the validity of the lease (s.72(3)).

## What happens if more than one person owns the property?

7.4.9   Landlords who jointly own the property are known as joint tenants. Where there is more than one owner (i.e. joint tenants of the immediate reversion) then any one of them can exercise the right as landlord. In fact any one or more landlord (of joint landlords) is able to exercise CRAR and recover rent due to each and all of them (s.72(4)).

## Can a mortgage lender use CRAR?

7.4.10   Where the landlord's interest is mortgaged, then the mortgage lender (mortgagee) has no right to exercise CRAR unless he has given notice to the mortgagor (landlord) of an intention to:

- take possession; or
- appoint a receiver; or
- directly enter into receipt of rents and profits (s.73(5)).

7.4.11   However, a mortgagee cannot exercise CRAR if the lease granted does not constitute a lease which binds the mortgagee. For example, if the lease was granted without the mortgagee's knowledge and contrary to the provisions of the mortgage, then it would not be binding (s.73(6)).

## Can the landlord appoint someone to exercise CRAR on his/her behalf?

7.4.12   Any authorisation to exercise CRAR on behalf of the landlord must be in writing and the new Act envisages that prescribed requirements will be set for such indirect authorisation (s.73(8)).

## What happens if the court appoints a receiver?

7.4.13   Where a receiver is appointed by the court in relation to the landlord's interest, CRAR is exercisable by the receiver in the name of the landlord (s.73(7)).

## The lease

**7.4.14**    Section 74 of the new Act defines the lease to mean:

> a tenancy in law or in equity, including a tenancy at will, but not including a tenancy at sufferance.

## 7.5    LEASE

### Pre-Act position

**7.5.1**    The position is broadly the same under the current regime, i.e. as to what constitutes a lease. However the new Act gives statutory definition to the requirement that there must be a lease.

### The new Act position

**7.5.2**    In order to exercise CRAR there must be a lease. This section will investigate the necessary factors which make up a lease.

### *Definition of lease*

**7.5.3**    The new Act (at s.74) defines a 'lease' as:

> a tenancy in law or equity, including a tenancy at will, but not including a tenancy at sufferance.

The words 'lease' and 'tenancy' are to some extent interchangeable. A lease is the grant of a right to the exclusive possession of a property for a term less than the landlord enjoys himself. Accordingly the landlord might be the freehold owner or in possession of a superior lease. A lease may be for a term of years absolute or it may run on a period by period basis, determinable on notice (periodic) (Law of Property Act 1925, s.1(1)).

### *There must be a lease – a licence will not do*

**7.5.4**    The important distinction lies between a lease as opposed to the right to occupy premises pursuant to a more contractual arrangement (i.e. a 'licence').

**7.5.5**    The pre-Act common law right to levy distress for rent arose out of the relationship of landlord and tenant. Distress was not available in respect of a payment provided for by an agreement which created a licence (which did not establish the relationship of landlord and tenant). Accordingly CRAR is only exercisable where the relationship of landlord and tenant exists, whether in law or in equity (s.74(1) of the new Act).

**7.5.6**   CRAR is not available if the occupier/tenant has only a licence to occupy (i.e. no interest in land). A lease or tenancy confers an interest in the land demised. A licence does not confer this interest. There has been a great deal written about the differences between a lease and a licence. The mere fact that a document is entitled licence (rather than lease) is not the only factor. The question as to whether a written agreement creates a licence or a tenancy can only be determined by a full review of the terms of the agreement (*Addiscombe Gardens Estate v. Crabbe* [1958] 1 QB 513 CA):

> The relationship is determined by the law, and not by the label which the parties chose to put upon it.

This does not mean that the written terms have no effect, but a landlord cannot alter the legal nature of the rights he has granted just by calling it something else (*Street v. Mountford* [1985] AC 805).

## Exclusive possession: the difference between a lease and licence

**7.5.7**   Perhaps the most important factor in determining whether an agreement has created a licence or a lease is the degree of exclusive possession that is enjoyed. That is, the ability of the tenant to exclude any third party (including the landlord) from the property.

**7.5.8**   A tenant with exclusive possession can keep out the landlord unless the landlord is exercising limited rights reserved under the terms of the lease (e.g. to inspect or carry out landlord's repairs). Whereas all tenants have exclusive possession, confusingly, some licences have exclusive possession and some do not. One example of the difficulty faced by landlords is the grant of a right to erect and operate a stall at a trade exhibition. Such an agreement, in one sense, provides the stall holder with exclusive possession, but the full facts of the position may be construed to equate to a licence. It will be difficult in these circumstances to know whether CRAR can be used.

## Lease must be evidenced in writing

**7.5.9**   CRAR may be exercised in relation to a lease which is granted on express written terms or one where it may be inferred (e.g. where the owner of a property accepts weekly or other periodical payments from the occupier (*Swindon BC v. Aston* [2003] HLR 610)). However, the lease must be evidenced in writing (s.74(2)).

**7.5.10**   There is no provision that the lease must be made in writing, merely evidenced (unlike, for example, the requirement in Law of Property Miscellaneous Provisions Act 1989, s.2 in relation to a contract for entering into a lease which must be made in writing).

**7.5.11**    Therefore the lease could be an oral tenancy with no express written terms. The evidence could come in the form of rent demands and payments made against these rent demands and also any correspondence between landlord and tenant in relation to the tenancy.

### Equitable lease: where a lease arises without the creation of a legal demise

**7.5.12**    CRAR can be exercised where there is an equitable lease. It is not strictly necessary to satisfy all the legal requirements to create a lease. An agreement for lease (or contract to create a lease) may have the effect of establishing a relationship of landlord and tenant. So if there is an agreement for lease and the proposed tenant enters the property, the relationship arises and a tenancy in equity is created. In this way a tenant in possession of a property (under a contract for a lease), has the right, in equity, to enjoy the property, as if the lease had been granted. Accordingly, a relationship of landlord and tenant is created in equity (see 7.4.4).

**7.5.13**    To establish this equitable right, the person claiming to be able to exercise the right to be landlord, must be able to show that he could compel the tenant to complete an agreed form of lease through an action for specific performance. Where this can be shown CRAR can be exercised.

**7.5.14**    However the landlord must act quickly. As it is only an equitable right it might be defeated by delay (laches). The equitable right could be eroded as a consequence of taking too long to implement the CRAR process.

Example: *Walsh v. Lonsdale*

The well known case of *Walsh v. Lonsdale* illustrates the point. In this case the tenant had entered into a contract for a seven year lease and entered into possession. However, the landlord had not compelled the tenant to execute a formal lease. The landlord claimed rent in accordance with the contract and the tenant refused to pay. The landlord threatened to use distress. The tenant made an application for an injunction to restrain the landlord from levying distress. The tenant claimed that in the absence of a formal tenancy there could be no right to use distress. The court decided that as the landlord would have (in any event) been entitled to specific performance then a tenant holding under an agreement for lease holds under the same terms in equity as if a lease had been granted. The landlord was permitted to exercise the right to levy distress for rent despite the equitable nature of the lease.

### Tenancy at will and sufferance

**7.5.15**    CRAR can be used where there is a tenancy at will but not where there is a tenancy at sufferance (s.74):

## Tenancy at will

**7.5.16**    A tenancy at will is commonly created where the landlord and tenant are negotiating the terms of a new lease and the landlord allows the tenant to occupy the property before terms are finally agreed. A tenancy at will can be brought to an end by either party without notice (*Javad* v. *Aqil* [1991] 1 All ER 243).

**7.5.17**    To exercise CRAR the tenancy at will must be evidenced in writing (see above). Where negotiations are taking place between landlord and tenant in relation to proposals for a new tenancy and the landlord has allowed the tenant early access, it is not sufficient that such negotiations should be evidenced only orally (*Cardiothoracic Institute* v. *Shrewdcrest Limited* [1986] 3 All ER 633).

## Tenancy at sufferance

**7.5.18**    Section 74 excludes a tenancy at sufferance from CRAR. This is consistent with the current law of distress (pre-Act) where it is not possible to distrain in relation to a tenancy at sufferance.

**7.5.19**    *What is a tenancy at sufferance?* A tenancy at sufferance arises where the tenant wrongfully continues in possession after the lease has ended. A tenancy at sufferance requires neither the assent nor dissent of the landlord and therefore it can never be created by express agreement. In practice, a tenancy at sufferance can only be created by operation of law. A tenancy at sufferance is typically created where the tenant holds over (without any statutory justification or landlord's consent).

**7.5.20**    If a tenancy at will is terminated by the landlord then the tenant becomes a tenant at sufferance only.

Example:

A lease of commercial premises comes to an end. The lease had been contracted out of the provisions of Part II of the Landlord and Tenant Act 1954 and was not protected. The tenancy comes to an end on the date that the fixed term expires. There is no automatic continuation as the 1954 Act does not apply. The landlord allows the tenant to remain in the premises hoping to agree new terms. The tenant does not give up vacant possession.

In this example if the tenant has been given the landlord's consent (whilst negotiations for a proper new tenancy continue) then it will constitute a tenancy at will. Conversely if no consent is provided then it will be a tenancy at sufferance.

## 7.6   COMMERCIAL PREMISES

### Pre-Act position

**7.6.1**   The new Act removes the landlord's rights to use distress (CRAR) in relation to residential premises.

**7.6.2**   Currently, distress can be levied against commercial premises or residential premises. However, the permission of the court is required to levy distress in relation to a dwelling house let on a protected tenancy or subject to a statutory tenancy under the Rent Act 1977. Permission is also required in relation to an assured tenancy under the Housing Act 1988. This leaves a limited number of residential tenancies where distress can be used without obtaining permission (for example those tenancies that fall outside the provisions of statutory protection – or long leases for ground rents). Landlords rarely apply for permission and these applications are very rare.

**7.6.3**   However, distress can be levied against mixed use premises, where part is used as a dwelling. This is an important factor because distress is most commonly used in relation to tertiary rated business premises (i.e. premises where the tenant is likely to be a small business). In this sector it is very common for the property to be a retail let with an upstairs flat. Sometimes the retailer does not use the flat as a dwelling but uses it for storage purposes. Sometimes the flat is sub-let. Sometimes still the tenant occupies the flat as his residence and trades from the shop below. These tenancies fall within the protection of the Landlord and Tenant Act 1954 and are classified as business tenancies, provided any part of the holding is used for business purposes.

**7.6.4**   The National Association of Citizens Advice Bureaux report *Undue Distress: CAB Clients' Experience of Bailiffs* (Alison Green, May 2000) concluded that the use of distress as a method of enforcement for domestic debt should be abolished. The *Independent Review of Bailiff Law* produced by Professor Beatson in June 2000 for the Lord Chancellor's Department also concluded that, with regard to residential property, there is a risk that the current practice would not comply with the ECHR in relation to residential premises.

**7.6.5**   Given that the court's permission is required to levy distress for most residential premises it was, perhaps, unfair to focus on landlord's distress in this way (Rent Act 1977, s.147 and Housing Act 1988, s.19). In reality the use of distress in residential premises (with or without court permission) has, for a long period of time, been virtually non-existent.

**7.6.6**   At one time bailiffs were instructed to collect ground rents on long leases (where no court permission is required), but even this limited use has declined sharply. The majority of bailiffs would not contemplate levying distress in relation to residential premises and if a premises was mixed use (e.g. shop with integral flat) then distress would in practice be taken only in relation to the commercial part of the premises.

## The new Act position

**7.6.7** CRAR can only be exercised in relation to commercial premises. However, it is important to note that the premises must be purely commercial (s.75).

**7.6.8** Under s.75 of the new Act the definition of commercial premises includes only premises where no part of the demised premises is:

- let as a dwelling;
- let under an inferior lease as a dwelling; or
- occupied as a dwelling.

**7.6.9** In such respects s.75 really amounts to codifying what had already become industry practice. The only significant effect on the industry will arise in relation to mixed use premises. Section 75 restricts distress in relation to commercial premises if any part has been let as a dwelling or any part has been occupied as a dwelling. This would prevent CRAR being used in circumstances where a shop (with a flat) has been let even where the tenant elects not to actually use the flat as a dwelling.

**7.6.10** This embraces a range of leases where the integral flat might not have been used as a dwelling for an extended period of time. Even if not actually used as a flat, if the permitted user clause in the lease allows a residential element, then CRAR cannot be used. As the premises in part had been let as a dwelling this would preclude the use of CRAR for the entire premises.

**7.6.11** 'Let as a dwelling' is defined in s.75(3) as 'let on terms permitting only occupation as a dwelling or other use combined with occupation as a dwelling'.

**7.6.12** Even where the lease grants no express permission to use premises as a dwelling, providing there is no express prohibition for such use, mere occupation as a dwelling deprives the landlord of the ability to use CRAR. Accordingly, unless there is an express prohibition in the lease (or a superior lease) whereby the tenant (or a superior tenant) has covenanted not to use any part of the premises as a dwelling, any form of residential occupation of any part of the premises will remove the ability to instruct an enforcement agent to exercise CRAR (s.75(5)).

**7.6.13** This creates potential for an unscrupulous tenant to claim that he is in occupation of the premises as a dwelling (e.g. a small room at the back of the shop) and thereby rendering impossible the use of CRAR. There is no statutory definition of the expression 'occupied as a dwelling'. This could possibly include occasional occupation as a dwelling. The tenant may sleep in a back room from time to time and subsequently argue this deprives the landlord of the CRAR remedy. There could be a very large commercial warehouse where such a back room represents a tiny part of the demised premises and the principle would still apply, CRAR would be rendered ineffective.

## 7.7    RENT

### Pre-Act position

**7.7.1**    Distress has always been a remedy which can only be used for the recovery of 'rent'. It was not available in the case of non-payment of other monies due under the terms of the lease. However, landlords often seek to expand the definition of rent under the terms of a lease. If payments such as insurance premiums and service charges have been expressly reserved as rent and the amount properly ascertained in accordance with the lease then distraint could be used.

### *Pre-Act set off*

**7.7.2**    If a lease required a tenant to pay rent without deduction or set off, then the landlord could levy distress for the whole amount, even where the tenant might have a valid counter claim. This position was questioned by Lightman J in *Fuller* v. *Happy Shopper Markets Ltd* [2001] 1 WLR 1681 on the basis that depriving a tenant of the right to set off was a breach of ECHR (see **6.4**).

### The new Act position

### *Pure rent only*

**7.7.3**    The potential to recover sums other than pure rent have been taken away by the new Act. Section 72 provides the right to use the CRAR procedure in relation to rent payable under a lease. Rent is then defined by s.76:

> 'Rent' means the amount payable under a lease (in advance or in arrear) for possession and use of the demised premises, together with –
>
> (a)    any interest payable on that amount under the lease, and
> (b)    any value added tax chargeable on that amount or interest.

**7.7.4**    However, rent is defined not to include any other sum such as:

- rates;
- council tax;
- service charges;
- other maintenance charges;
- insurance; or
- any other ancillary payments.

This is the case whether or not these sums are reserved as (or in any way called) rent under the terms of the lease (s.76(2)).

**7.7.5**    The provisions go on explicitly to confine the use of CRAR to the amount payable for possession and use of the demised premises (s.76(3) of the new Act). Why this distinction should be made (e.g. between rent and service charge) is a mystery. Presumably if a payment is contractually due and owing and properly claimed by the landlord under the terms of a lease there can be no real distinction in terms of enforcement methods from an ECHR compliance perspective. There is no good reason why such a distinction should have been made. Whereas there is obviously merit in excluding issues such as damages or unascertained amounts from CRAR, commercial leases have, as a matter of routine, provision for the payment of standard ascertainable running costs for the property.

## Other conditions for rent

7.7.6    CRAR can only be exercised to recover rent that:

(a)  has become due and payable before notice of enforcement is given; and
(b)  is certain or capable of being calculated with certainty (s.77(1)).

7.7.7    This is subject to two further provisions which affect rent:

(1)  Minimum amount
     CRAR can only be exercised if the net unpaid rent is at least the minimum amount at the time:

     –    immediately before a notice of enforcement (under Sched.12 to the new Act) is given; and
     –    immediately before the first time goods are taken control of after that notice (s.77).

The regulations will set the minimum amount. To qualify, the unpaid rent must be more than the minimum amount (not counting interest, VAT or permitted deductions) at both of these times. Therefore if the tenant pays after receiving a notice of enforcement and prior to the visit of the enforcement agent to take control of goods, the ability to use CRAR will be lost. In fact the tenant would only have to pay enough to reduce the rent due to below the minimum amount.

(2)  Double rent
     The new Act repeals most of the Distress for Rent Act 1737 but leaves in place s.18, which entitles the landlord to recover double rent if a tenant gives notice to quit but does not give up possession at the time of the expiry of the notice. The section provides:

     In case any tenant or tenants shall give notice of his, her or their intention to quit the premises by him, her or them holding, at a time mentioned in such notice, and shall not accordingly deliver up possession thereof at the time in such notice contained, then the said tenant or tenants, his, her or their executors or administrators shall from thence forward pay to the landlord or the landlords, lessor or lessors, double the rent or sum which he, she or they should otherwise have paid, to be levied, sued for and recovered at the same time and in the same manner as a single rent or sum before the giving, such notice could be levied, sued for, or recovered; all such double rent or sums shall continue to be paid during all the times such tenant shall continue in possession as aforesaid.

The 1737 Act only applies where the tenant has served a notice to quit and actually given a valid notice terminating his lease.

Under the terms of s.18, double rent can be recovered at the same time and in the same manner, as single rent. It seems that CRAR can be used. However this possibility contradicts s.79 of the Act which restricts the use of CRAR after the end of the lease (see below). This principle also potentially conflicts with s.74 in that CRAR applies only to a lease which is not a tenancy at sufferance.

As set out above, a tenancy at sufferance is typically created where tenants hold over or continue in possession without agreement. Nonetheless, s.18 of the 1737 Act gives the landlord the right to recover double rent in the same manner as he may have recovered the single rent prior to the tenant's notice to quit having been served. This only applies where a tenant has served a notice to quit. It does not apply to any termination notice served by a landlord.

## 7.8   PERMITTED DEDUCTIONS

**7.8.1**   Section 77(7) of the Act is exercisable in relation to an amount of rent to be reduced by any permitted deduction. The permitted deductions against the rent are any:

> deduction, recoupment or set-off that the tenant would be entitled to claim (in law or equity) in an action by the landlord for that rent.

**7.8.2**   Many leases exclude the right of set-off. A covenant to pay the rent without any set off or deduction was originally thought to allow a landlord to bring an action either by distress or through the courts for the full amount of rent, even where the tenants may have a valid complaint. The tenant was then left in a situation where this complaint had to be dealt with separately. If the landlord brought court proceedings then any such complaint could be the subject of a counterclaim (even though it couldn't be validly set off as a consequence of the express covenant).

**7.8.3**   The draftsmen of the new Act were anxious to avoid an invitation to the real estate lawyers out there to draw up express lease provisions to sidestep this restriction, so permitted deductions include all forms of set-offs and deductions. In addition any form of 'recoupment' forms part of the permitted deductions.

**7.8.4**   Whereas a landlord can sometimes block a right of deduction or set-off in a court action, it is very difficult to remove the tenant's right to bring a claim (or counterclaim). So if the tenant would be able to recoup the amount due in rent, through a claim or counterclaim then the landlord must remove these sums from CRAR (s.77(7)). This could also include a claim for an unascertained sum in damages. This creates difficulty for landlords as it might on occasion be impossible to accurately assess the magnitude of the permitted deduction.

7.8.5   With the use of recoupment it is clear that an express covenant to exclude a right of set-off (either in law or equity) would not be enough to allow a landlord to use CRAR in relation to that part of the rent which could be recouped by the tenant through a valid claim or counterclaim.

## Deductions that can be made

7.8.6   There are many types of deductions which are authorised by statute and common law.

7.8.7   Tenants are authorised by various statutory provisions to make deductions which include the following items:

- unpaid tax payable by superior landlords recouped from a tenant by HMRC pursuant to the Income and Corporation Taxes Act 1988 (s.23(2));
- compensation due to the tenant of an agricultural holding under the Agricultural Holdings Act 1986 where the compensation has been ascertained;
- compensation due to the tenant who has made improvements and has complied with the provisions or under the Landlord and Tenant Act 1927;
- payments of instalments made to local authorities by a tenant on behalf of his landlord under the Public Health Act 1936;
- certain payments made in relation to highway expenses under the Highways Act 1980;
- payments to superior landlords made to avoid CRAR in respect of arrears of rent or the superior lease (s.82 of the new Act).

7.8.8   At common law a tenant can make deductions from the rent in a number of situations including:

- Repairs – where the landlord is in breach of its repairing obligation and the tenant has carried out the repairs on the landlord's behalf, then the costs of those repairs are recoverable and can be deducted providing the sum is clear and ascertainable. This is a very long-standing common law right (*Taylor* v. *Beal* (1591). However, under the new Act a tenant is permitted to deduct any sum which might be 'recouped'. Accordingly this is likely to extend to unliquidated (i.e. non-ascertained) amounts.
- Where the landlord is in breach of its other covenants which has resulted in losses or expenses being incurred by the tenant, the same principle applies.

7.8.9   In equity a tenant can set-off in certain situations including:

- It is possible for a tenant to exercise a right to set-off where a counter-claim arises out of the same contract (which in this case is the lease). A set-off could be ascertained or unascertained provided it relates to a counter claim arising out of the lease. This can extend to any breach of the landlord's obligations. However, the tenant has to have 'clean hands' (consider *Bluestorm* v. *Portvale* [2004] EGLR 38).
- Over-payments made by the tenant by way of mistake.

■    Where a landlord has promised a tenant to accept a lower payment and the tenant has acted upon this to its detriment by way of promissory estoppel.

## 7.9    USE OF CRAR AFTER THE END OF LEASE

### Pre-Act position

7.9.1    Distress for rent could only be levied when there was a continuing landlord and tenant relationship. Accordingly where the landlord had elected to forfeit the lease for breach of a covenant, the right to distress was lost (*Serjeant* v. *Nash Field & Co* [1903] 2 KB 304). Once the tenancy came to an end the right to distress was generally lost (see 7.5.15).

### The new Act position

7.9.2    Section 79 of the new Act codifies this principle, so that CRAR ceases to be exercisable once the lease has come to an end. However, there are exceptions to this principle and CRAR can be exercised:

1.    Where a lease expires by effluxion of time but continues by virtue of Part II of the Landlord and Tenant Act 1954 (s.79(7)).
2.    If the tenancy which comes to an end had been contracted out of the provisions of Landlord and Tenant Act 1954, s.2 and the tenant remains in the premises negotiating terms for a new lease (providing the tenancy becomes a tenancy at will) (*Javad* v. *Aqil* [1991] 1 All ER 243). Where a person remains in possession under these circumstances then any such tenancy at will need not be evidenced in writing (s.79(5) of the new Act).
3.    In relation to goods where the CRAR process is commenced prior to the lease coming to an end (s.79(2)(a) of the new Act).

7.9.3    CRAR can also be exercised after the lease comes to an end providing six conditions are met, as follows:

(a)    the lease did not end by forfeiture;
(b)    not more than six months have passed since the day the lease ended;
(c)    the rent was due from the person who was a tenant at the end of the lease (i.e. not a previous assignor);
(d)    the tenant remains in possession of at least part of the demised premises;
(e)    if there was a new lease then it must be a lease of commercial premises;
(f)    the person who was the landlord at the end of the lease remains landlord and entitled to immediate reversion in relation to the new period of possession.

7.9.4    Any new period of possession (whether by way of tenancy at will, new periodic tenancy or fixed term lease) does not have to comply with the provision that it needs to be evidenced in writing (as provided by s.74(2) of the Act). In the case of a tenancy by estoppel the person who is the landlord remains entitled to the immediate reversion providing the circumstances which gave rise to the estoppel continue (see 7.4.4).

7.9.5    Accordingly, CRAR can be used in relation to rent arrears falling due under the terms of an old lease which has come to an end where the tenant remains in possession and the conditions of s.79(4) are met. This does not stop the landlord from exercising CRAR in relation to arrears of rent which have arisen in relation to the new period of occupation. So where a landlord faces a defaulting tenant that hasn't paid its rent for a lease which has now come to an end and continues not to pay rent for any new arrangement, the landlord can exercise CRAR in relation to both periods (subject to the s.79(4) conditions).

Example under the Landlord and Tenant Act 1954:

Any tenancy continued by virtue of Landlord and Tenant Act 1954, s.2 will not have ended for the purposes of s.79. The landlord retains the ability to exercise CRAR as the 1954 Act process continues. CRAR can be used whilst the tenant progresses his application for a new tenancy. The landlord is free to exercise CRAR during any statutory continuation. If during the 1954 Act process, rent arrears arise prior to the granting of a new lease then the landlord is able to exercise CRAR for a period of six months following the grant of a new lease in relation to rents which fell due under the terms of the old lease. If the court makes an order for a new tenancy then the lease commences three months later (Landlord and Tenant Act 1954, s.64). The landlord could then, for a period of six months, use CRAR for arrears under the old lease. He could also use CRAR for arrears under the new lease.

## 7.10    AGRICULTURAL HOLDINGS

7.10.1    CRAR can only be used in relation to agricultural holdings for rent arrears which are less than a year old (taking the year from the date that the rents fell due) prior to a notice of enforcement being given (s.80).

7.10.2    Where rent has been deferred as a consequence of the ordinary course of dealing between landlord and tenant to the end of a quarter or half a year after it legally became due, then the one year period commences at the time of the deferred due date (s.80(4)).

7.10.3    Tenants of agricultural holdings are allowed to insist that the landlord deduct from the amounts which are subject to CRAR any compensation which is due to the tenant in respect of the holding under the Agricultural Holding Act 1986 or under custom or agreement (providing the level of compensation has been ascertained) (s.80(5)).

## 7.11    ANTI-AVOIDANCE PROVISIONS – LANDLORDS CANNOT EXTEND THEIR RIGHTS

**7.11.1**    The new Act prevents a landlord from creating a contract which would extend his rights to seize or otherwise take control of goods or modify the effects of CRAR in any way (s.85).

**7.11.2**    This is a measure designed to protect tenants from their landlords' insisting upon a contractual right to extend the use of CRAR to such things as service charges, varying the requirement to serve an enforcement notice, or generally to affect the workings of the CRAR system.

## 7.12    RIGHT TO RECOVER RENT FROM SUB-TENANT

### Pre-Act position

**7.12.1**    Under Law of Distress Amendment Act 1908, s.6 a superior landlord is able to serve a notice requiring sub-tenants to pay their sub-rents directly to him where rent is in arrears under the head lease.

**7.12.2**    This is a powerful rule, as it provided the superior landlord with the right to recover sub-rents from the sub-tenant (which are due to be paid to the tenant as the immediate landlord of the sub-tenant) in priority to the rights of:

- an administrative receiver of the tenant; or
- a fixed charge receiver appointed by the tenant's mortgage company;
- an administrator of the tenant;
- a liquidator of the tenant;
- a trustee in bankruptcy of the tenant.

The Court of Appeal decided in *Rhodes* v. *Allied Dunbar Pension Services Ltd* [1989] 1 All ER 1161, CA that where a s.6 notice has been served the sub-rents were payable to the superior landlord even where a bank had previously appointed receivers under the terms of a debenture. There is no restriction in the service of a s.6 notice where there is a creditor's voluntary liquidation. Service of a s.6 notice arguably is not restricted by a compulsory liquidation or an administration. In an administration the court's permission is required to take action against a company or commence any legal process but this does not prevent a s.6 notice being served (Insolvency Act 1986, s.43, Sched.B1).

**7.12.3**    Taking action such as serving a s.6 notice is not something which would be restricted by the moratorium against commencing a legal process. Millet J decided in the case of *Re Olympia* v. *York Canary Wharf Limited* [1993] BCLC 453 that the service of a contractual notice to complete was not restricted by an administration moratorium (formerly covered by Insolvency Act 1986, s.11 and now by Insolvency Act 1986, s.43 or Sched.B1 under the pre-Act regime following the amendments made by the Enterprise Act 2002). So a s.6 notice would also be a right that is unlikely to be affected by the moratorium.

**7.12.4**  Accordingly the service of a s.6 notice was an important remedy to landlords. The effect of a notice was to transfer to the superior landlord by way of assignment the right to recover, receive and give a discharge for rent. Following the service of a notice, the superior landlord could then secure payment from the sub-tenants by an action through the courts or through the levy of distress. It did not prevent the superior landlord taking steps to pursue his immediate tenant for default. Both the tenant and the sub-tenant could be pursued at the same time.

**7.12.5**  Section 6 could be used in relation to residential premises, mixed use premises and in circumstances where the tenant had vacated. It had become a powerful tool. In the majority of circumstances, sub-tenants were happy to pay their rent to the superior landlord. The degree of priority afforded by s.6 was perceived by the industry as being fair in circumstances where the head landlord was in fact continuing to supply the right to occupy the premises to the sub-tenant.

**7.12.6**  Law and Distress Amendment Act 1908, s.3 creates a direct landlord and tenant relationship between the superior landlord and the sub-tenant, whilst the effect of a s.6 notice continues.

**7.12.7**  It was rare to have a situation where both the tenant and the sub-tenant would be defaulting parties and therefore the service of a s.6 notice was a relatively successful remedy for landlords.

## The new Act position

**7.12.8**  The new Act reforms the remedy created by s.6. The new Act abolishes all forms of distress and the Law of Distress Amendment Act 1908 in its entirety. Accordingly s.6 will no longer survive. In its place, s.81 of the new Act creates a new right to recover rents from a sub-tenant in line with CRAR and the provisions within the new Act for taking control of goods.

**7.12.9**  If a tenant is in default (in circumstances where CRAR would be exercisable) then the landlord may serve a notice under s.81 on any sub-tenant. As this right only arises where CRAR is exercisable it only applies to commercial premises and pursuant to all the other provisions of Chapter 2 Part 3 of the new Act (Rent Arrears Recovery).

**7.12.10**  This will mean that s.81 will have significantly more limited effect than the provisions of s.6.

### New procedure

**7.12.11**  The s.81 notice will have to be in a prescribed form. Regulations will state the form of the notice including:

- what it must contain;
- how it must be served; and
- what must be done to withdraw it (s.81(6) of the new Act).

**7.12.12**    The regulations are likely to provide that the notice must be served in the same way as the service of a s.6 notice, which could be served by registered post or personally on the premises (*Jervis v. Hennings* [1912] 1 Ch 462).

## The notified amount

**7.12.13**    The notice must state the amount of rent and that the landlord has a right to recover these rents from the immediate tenant by CRAR. This becomes the notified amount (s.81(5)).

**7.12.14**    Although the notice can only be served where CRAR is exercisable the landlord does not have to first serve an enforcement notice. The minimum amount under s.77 for the purposes of s.81 can be calculated at the time when the s.81 notice is given (as an alternative to the calculation taking place at the time that notice of enforcement is given) (s.81(7) of the new Act).

## The effect of a s.81 notice

**7.12.15**    Section 81 has the effect of being a statutory assignment of the sub-tenancy rents. The effect of s.81 is that it:

> transfers to the [superior] landlord the right to recover, receive and give a discharge for any rent payable by the sub-tenant under the sub-lease, until –
>
> (a)    the notified amount has been paid . . . or
> (b)    the notice is replaced or withdrawn.

**7.12.16**    The transfer means that the superior landlord has the entire benefit of the sub-rent until the notified amount has been paid. This means that the superior landlord can choose any remedy to recover the rent (he is not limited to CRAR). In practice (as with s.6 notices) the majority of sub-tenants will simply pay the amount due under the sub-lease to the superior landlord (perhaps after taking legal advice). However if the sub-tenant defaults the superior landlord can utilise any appropriate debtor remedy including CRAR.

**7.12.17**    From that point onwards a superior landlord can recover the sums from the sub-tenant (which have not been paid prior to the service of the notice to the immediate tenant) by an action for rent or by the use of CRAR. There is nothing to stop the superior landlord from concurrently pursuing his claim against the immediate tenant for the rent or taking any other remedy (e.g. liquidation or bankruptcy) (*Re a Debtor (number 549 of 1928)* [1929] 1 Ch 170, CA).

**7.12.18**    The effect of the notice continues until the notified amount has been paid (by payments under the notice or otherwise) or the notice is replaced or withdrawn.

**7.12.19** Under s.84(1) of the new Act for the purposes of the recovery of the sums payable by a sub-tenant following the service of a s.81 notice, the sub-tenant is deemed to be the immediate tenant of the superior landlord and the sums paid are treated as rent. Therefore if the sub-tenant makes payment to superior landlord, the immediate landlord has no remedies against the sub-tenant (*Rhodes v. Allied Dunbar Pension Services Ltd* [1989] 1 All ER 1161, CA).

## Off-setting payments under a notice

**7.12.20** Naturally the sub-tenant only has to pay the superior landlord. He does not also have to pay his immediate landlord. The sub-tenant is permitted to deduct the amounts he pays under the notice to the superior landlord from the rents that would be due under the sub-lease (s.82(1) of the new Act).

**7.12.21** If there is a hierarchy of tenancies and the superior landlord served notices on the sub-tenant together with an under-sub-tenant, then each level of sub-tenant has the right to, in effect, pay its rent only once. Each level of sub-tenant is able to deduct an equal amount of any rents due to its immediate landlord to his immediate landlord under his sub-lease.

**7.12.22** The sub-tenant has the right to make this deduction even if the monies payable by the sub-tenant are not due because the immediate landlord has subsequently paid the rent or the notice has been replaced by a notice served on another sub-tenant (unless the sub-tenant had notice that the payment had already been made).

## Withdrawal and replacement of notices

**7.12.23** If a landlord serves further notices under s.81 this can have the effect of withdrawing and replacing the original notices. The landlord can only serve a notice on one level of sub-tenant at one time (unless for different rents).

**7.12.24** So, if the landlord serves a notice on a sub-tenant and subsequently serves a notice on an under-sub-tenant, the second notice will have the effect of replacing the original notice served on the sub-tenant, which will be deemed to be withdrawn. This principle does not prevent the landlord from serving notices on different sub-tenants and under-sub-tenants in relation to distinct and different parts of the rent. This is providing that there is no overlap between the rents which have been demanded (s.82) from various levels of tenant.

**7.12.25** Accordingly, any payment received by the landlord from a sub-tenant is to be treated as if the sub-tenant had paid his rent to his immediate landlord. If there has been overpayment (because more than one tenant pays) then the landlord must repay and is subject to a potential claim for repayment by the immediate tenant (s.84(3) of the new Act).

## 7.13   TENANT REMEDIES

**7.13.1**   Under s.78 of the Act, if notice of enforcement is given as a commencement of the CRAR process by a landlord of commercial premises, then the tenant can make an application to the court to set the notice aside or to freeze the CRAR process without further order in relation to the rent claimed. The new Act is currently silent about the grounds upon which the tenants will be able to make such an application. However, this remedy may be seen as a process which complements the remedies available to debtors generally (see **12.4**) and also the remedies created by the new Act in relation to Debt Management and Relief (see **Chapters 19–23**).

## 7.14   IS CRAR WORTHWHILE?

**7.14.1**   Whether it is worthwhile exercising CRAR in most cases will, of course, be a commercial decision. To some extent this will depend upon the financial circumstances of the case together with the action being taken by other creditors. If the ultimate objective of CRAR is to sell the goods in order to satisfy the debt then the realisation value of the goods will be an important consideration.

**7.14.2**   However, it is unlikely that an enforcement agent will be able to realise the full market value for goods of which it has taken control. Sales of this nature (sometimes called forced sales) often realise a restricted resale price. Whether there are sufficient goods to make CRAR a useful remedy will often depend upon the nature of the tenant's business.

**7.14.3**   There is likely to be more merit in exercising CRAR in the case of industrial or retail premises. In the case of office premises there may be very little by way of stock and much of the equipment might be rented from third parties. The proportion of goods in the premises which belong to third parties has always been an important factor affecting the success of the law of distress. The CRAR process is unlikely to be significantly different. Third parties will enjoy significant rights (enhanced by the provisions of Sched.12).

**7.14.4**   Even in cases where the sale of goods is not a viable option, the use of CRAR may be beneficial in other ways. CRAR may still prevent an administrator from using the goods in the course of business. CRAR may induce a payment of rent shortly before an insolvency. Additionally if a landlord is tempted to negotiate a surrender the CRAR process may speed up the process of negotiation and give the landlord bargaining strength.

**7.14.5**   The CRAR system will not be as flexible and powerful as the law of distress. However it is likely to remain an essential remedy for landlords. Through CRAR landlords retain their right to instruct enforcement agents without any court process. They remain as one of the only forms of creditor with the power to do this, without first commencing court proceedings and obtaining a court judgment or liability order.

# 8 INSOLVENCY OF TENANT/DEBTOR

## 8.1 INTRODUCTION

**8.1.1** In some situations where the debtor is insolvent, the court's permission is required before the Sched.12 procedure for taking control of the goods can be utilised. The new Act unifies distress (now commercial rent arrears recovery (CRAR)) and execution. However, these remedies have been treated differently and distinguished.

## 8.2 RECEIVERSHIP

### Pre-Act position and the new Act position

**8.2.1** The appointment of a receiver in respect of the debtors' property has little effect on the right to use the enforcement process in the new Act. There is no statutory moratorium preventing creditors from taking action to recover the debt due.

**8.2.2** There are two forms of receiver:

1. Receivers appointed under the terms of a fixed charge (often referred to as an LPA receiver under the provisions of the Law Property Act 1925).
2. Administrative receivers appointed under the terms of a debenture (where the charge is over the whole of the company's assets or substantially the whole of the assets). Administrative receivers are in the process of being phased out. An administrative receivership can only be appointed under a charge granted before 15 September 2003 following the coming into force of the Enterprise Act 2002.

**8.2.3** Where the debtor is a company it is likely that goods which the creditor wishes to take control of will be subject to charge or charges in favour of a third party (e.g. a lender such as a bank or a major creditor). Often the goods will be the subject of a floating charge which the debtor has given over its assets (or over a substantial part of its assets). The charge holder can appoint an administrative receiver, but only if the charge was created before 15 September 2003. The receiver has the capacity of acting as an agent of the debtor. He uses the assets to discharge the debt owed to charge holder.

**8.2.4**   There is no restriction on levying distress for rent. The rights of creditors are unaffected by the receivership (*Re Roundwood Colliery* [1897]).

**8.2.5**   However, once a floating charge has been crystallised over goods, the rights of the floating charge become a fixed charge and have preference over the proceeds of any sale of the assets. This is the case even where the enforcement agent had already bound and seized goods. This is set out in Lord Justice Buckley's judgment in the Court of Appeal case of *Cretanor Maritime Co Ltd* v. *Irish Marine Management Ltd* [1978] 3 All ER 164:

> the debenture holder is now an equitable assignee of the deposited fund, that the[enforcement] gives the owners no present rights against the deposited fund but was made merely with a view to the retention of that fund in England so as to be available in the event of the owners becoming able to levy execution on it, and that, if the owners were hereafter to attempt to levy execution on it, their rights as execution creditors would have to give way to prior rights in the fund, including the rights of the debenture holder . . .

**8.2.6**   There is uncertainty as to whether the remedy of distress would be affected by the crystallisation of a floating charge.

**8.2.7**   Now that the law of distress has been unified with execution and combined into the new Act process of taking control of goods under Sched.12, there is little restriction on enforcement. However the position of taking control in relation to receivership will be subject to the crystallisation of a floating charge as set out above. CRAR will also be subject to the crystallisation.

## 8.3   COMPULSORY LIQUIDATION

### Pre-Act position and new Act position

**8.3.1**   Where a debtor is in a compulsory liquidation the success of enforcement depends upon when the process commenced and when it was completed.

### *Enforcement commenced after petition is presented but before Winding-Up Order is made*

**8.3.2**   After a winding-up petition has been presented, but before the order is made, any enforcement action which is commenced is void under s.128 of the Insolvency Act 1986.

**8.3.3**   Section 128 also currently binds a landlord from commencing the process of distress (or now CRAR) which would be rendered void. Schedule 13 to the new Act (s.85) makes any reference to 'distress' under the Insolvency Act 1986 include the use of the procedure in Sched.12.

**8.3.4**   However, creditors have the power to make an application for permission to bring any action or proceeding against the company or its property under s.130(2) of the Insolvency Act 1986.

## When would an application to use enforcement succeed?

**8.3.5**  If rent fell due prior to the date of the petition then the court would generally not give permission to levy distress (or now CRAR) since to do so would put the landlord in a better position than ordinary creditors. In a similar way the court is unlikely to give permission for any creditor to enforce the debts falling due prior to the dates of the winding-up petition under the terms of the new Act.

**8.3.6**  It is likely that an application for permission will only be successful to allow enforcement under the new Act and the use of the Sched.12 process in relation to unpaid debts which have been incurred during the period of the liquidation (from the date of the petition). If rent arrears (or other liabilities) are incurred during the period of a liquidation, the creditor may have a reasonable argument that permission should be given. A liquidator should pay rent if he has the use of the premises. This is a long-standing principle which flows from the 19th century distress case of *Re Lundy Granite Co* [1871] 6 Ch App 462. Liquidators have the ability to disclaim a lease or any other onerous contract pursuant to s.178 of the Insolvency Act 1986. Accordingly there is an argument that if the liquidator does not expeditiously disclaim an onerous lease he should pay the ongoing rent (post winding-up petition rents) in full. This argument was advanced in the case of *Re Linda Marie Ltd* [1989] BCLC 46 and *Exeter City Council v. Bairstow and others* [2007] EWHC 400 (Ch) and *Re Toshoku Finance UK plc* [2002] 1 WLR 671.

**8.3.7**  As consequence of this, where the liquidator is making use of the premises (e.g. before a sale of the business together with the assignment of a lease as a going concern) then the agreement is reached with the landlord that the ongoing rents for the period of occupation will be paid as an expense of the liquidation.

**8.3.8**  Under the pre-Act regime the insolvency restrictions did not apply to third party goods which landlords could in limited circumstances distrain upon. As CRAR can only be used against the goods of a debtor (i.e. the tenant) then this issue can be seen as effectively closed.

## Where enforcement begins prior to petition

**8.3.9**  Where a creditor has commenced the enforcement process and subsequently a winding-up petition is presented against the debtor then the creditor is not entitled to retain the benefit of the enforcement process.

**8.3.10**  Under Insolvency Act 1986, s.183:

> where a creditor has issued execution against the goods or land of a company or has attached any debt due to it, and the company is subsequently wound up, he is not entitled to retain the benefit of the execution or attachment against the liquidator unless he has completed the execution or attachment before the commencement of the winding up.

**8.3.11**    Under Insolvency Act 1986, s.184, where a company's goods are taken in execution and, before their sale, notice is served on the enforcement officer that:

- a provisional liquidator has been appointed; or
- a winding-up order has been made; or
- a resolution for voluntary winding up has been passed.

**8.3.12**    The enforcement agent is obliged to deliver the goods and any money seized or received to the liquidator. However the costs of execution are a first charge on the goods or money, and the liquidator may sell the goods, or a sufficient part of them to settle his costs.

**8.3.13**    Even where the enforcement agent is not aware of a liquidation, he is required to retain the proceeds of sale for a period of 14 days. If he receives the notification during that period he should pay the sale proceeds to the liquidator (less the costs of enforcement). This rule only applies if the judgment debt is more than £500.

**8.3.14**    This provision does not currently apply to distress for rent. However following the unification of the two processes this provision may be held to apply to CRAR.

## Application for stay

**8.3.15**    Where an enforcement agent has commenced the process (including distress/CRAR) and then a winding-up petition is presented the company or any other creditor may apply to the court under Insolvency Act 1986, s.126 to stay the process.

**8.3.16**    However once a Winding Up Order is made where the distress has been commenced, prior to the petition, the creditor must make an application to continue.

**8.3.17**    The court's usual policy is to allow the distress to continue if it was commenced prior to the date of the petition, unless there were specific reasons to make the distress inequitable (such as fraud). In *Venner's Electrical Cooking and Heating Appliances Limited* v. *Thorpe* [1915] 2 Ch 414, CA. Cozens Hardy MR stated:

> No equitable ground has ever been made out for restraining the Landlord from levying the distress, unless there have been some circumstances outside the levying, such as fraud, or unfair dealing, which would entitle the tenant to an injunction.

**8.3.18**    However the enforcement would still be subject to the charge in favour of preferential debts under Insolvency Act 1986, s.176 (see below).

## The position after a Winding-Up Order is made

**8.3.19**   A Winding-Up Order has the effect of staying all processes without the court's permission under Insolvency Act 1986, s.130. The remedy of the distress was held to be an *action or proceeding* in the meaning of ss.126 and 130 in *Menco Engineering Limited* [1986] Ch 86 although there is some criticism of this decision as distress did not involve a court process (neither would CRAR under the new Act), the principle has prevailed.

**8.3.20**   Now that distress has been abolished and the replacement process of CRAR is unified with enforcement generally, under Sched.12, some may argue that the two procedures should be seen as identical processes. However the fact remains that commercial landlords are able to continue with a process or enforcement by taking control of goods without a court order. Whether enforcement takes place in the county court, the High Court or the magistrates' court some legal process remains and accordingly in relation to insolvency there may continue to be a distinction in relation to the two processes.

## Where enforcement is concluded prior to the petition

**8.3.21**   Where, during the three months prior to a winding up, order goods or effects of the company have been distrained upon by a landlord the goods (or the proceeds of sale) are charged with the benefit of the company with the preferential debts to the extent that the company has insufficient assets to pay its preferential debts (Insolvency Act 1986, s.176(2)).

## Can a creditor seek the court's permission to proceed with enforcement in a compulsory liquidation?

**8.3.22**   A creditor has the right to make an application to the court to allow the execution to continue (under Insovency Act 1986, s.130) and to retain the proceeds of sale. However, the starting point is that commercial landlords and other judgment creditors do not have priority as creditors and rank *pari passu* with other unsecured creditors.

**8.3.23**   In the case of *Re Caribbean Products (YAM importers) Ltd* [1996] Ch 331, CA it was thought that an application may be worth while where the enforcement had been delayed by undue influence or misrepresentation by the debtor. For example, please see *Redman (Builders) Ltd* [1964] 1 All ER 851.

## Landlords

**8.3.24**   Landlords exercising the right to distrain sometimes have a better argument to allow the distress to continue. Liquidators may want the debtor company to retain occupation of the demised premises to facilitate a sale of the business or an asset sale. Where this happens the landlord is in a position where he remains in danger of being forced to continue to supply the property. Other creditor suppliers usually have the right to stop supply. It is not so easy for landlords because the right to forfeit is restricted. None of the restrictions in the Insolvency Act 1986 prevent other suppliers from turning off the tap and refusing to supply any more goods or services.

**8.3.25**   If the lease is not disclaimed by the liquidator and the property is retained for the benefit of the liquidation then the landlord should receive the ongoing rents as an expense of the liquidation under Insolvency Rules 1986, r.4.218. If there is a dispute about this then the landlord has the right to ask the court to allow distress to be levied.

## 8.4   VOLUNTARY LIQUIDATION

### Pre-Act position and the new Act position

**8.4.1**   If a corporate tenant is in voluntary liquidation there is no immediate restriction upon a landlord's rights to levy distress, or to take enforcement action. The position will be the same under the new Act in relation to taking control of the goods under Sched.12 and exercising CRAR. If there is a voluntary liquidation, no permission of the court is required to take action. However, a liquidator may apply to the court and request that the restrictions which apply to enforcement in the compulsory liquidation be applied to this voluntary liquidation. This application would be made under Insolvency Act 1986, s.112 (i.e. an application for a direction).

**8.4.2**   However, in the absence of such an application in a voluntary liquidation there is no provision which automatically makes enforcement (whether execution or distress) void if it commenced after the liquidation started.

**8.4.3**   However, the provisions of Insolvency Act 1986, ss.183 and 184 apply (see **8.3.9** above). Section 176 (CRAR/distress) does not apply to a voluntary winding up (see **8.3.21**).

## 8.5   ADMINISTRATION

Rent is the life blood for commercial landlords and the ability to effectively enforce payment from a defaulting tenant is essential to the commercial property industry. The growing trend for companies to go into the new form of administration creates a significant problem for the future and will inevitably lead to an increasing risk that default will occur.

Iain Blakeley – Dawnay, Day Property Investments Ltd

The 'new' administration procedure has quickly become the dominant insolvency procedure in the battle to rescue and restructure failing companies. The enterprise culture provides a much needed shield against the slings and arrows of outrageous financial fortune. Without the instantaneous moratorium which can be put in place under the new procedure there would often be no business left to save. I am not surprised by the popularity of this procedure. It will dominate the commercial insolvency industry for the next generation . . .

Anthony Murphy – licensed insolvency practitioner

**8.5.1**   When a debtor is a company in administration then all enforcement is subject to a detailed and comprehensive moratorium (Insolvency Act 1986, Sched.B1, paras.43 and 44). The moratorium was redrafted by the Enterprise Act 2002 which came into force in September 2003 to effect all new administrations. All forms of enforcement are bound by the moratorium which does not render the enforcement void, but merely prevents the enforcement continuing (or being commenced if it has not yet started) during the currency of the administration period.

## Effect of moratorium

**8.5.2**   No enforcement step can be commenced or continued (including distress and CRAR) without the:

- consent of the administrator; or
- permission of the court.

Therefore if enforcement is commenced prior to the administration then there is no reason why the enforcement cannot be reactivated after the administration comes to an end. This might depend on the exit route from administration. If the company enters into a voluntary arrangement then the debt subject to the enforcement may be compromised.

## When will the court's permission be granted

**8.5.3**   In *Re Atlantic Computer Systems plc* [1992] 1 All ER 476 Lord Justice Nicholl, giving the lead judgments in the Court of Appeal, set out a number of guidelines as to when enforcement in relation to fixed term contracts (such a leases of equipment and plant) should be allowed. The court took into account the following factors:

- the creditor must make out the case for permission to be given;
- the debtor company's financial position – its ability to pay ongoing rents etc.;
- the administrator's proposals – including whether ongoing debts such as accruing rents will be paid as an expense of the administration;
- the effect on the administration if permission were given;
- the effect on the debtor if permission were refused;
- the prospects of a successful outcome in the administration if permission is refused;
- the conduct of the parties.

## 8.6    BANKRUPTCY

### Pre-Act position and new Act position

**8.6.1**    Surprisingly, the presentation of a bankruptcy petition does not act as an automatic moratorium on enforcement. Under Insolvency Act 1985, s.285:

> At any time when proceedings on a bankruptcy petition are pending or an individual has been adjudged bankrupt the court may stay any action, execution or other legal process against the property or person of the debtor or, as the case may be, of the bankrupt.
>
> Any court in which proceedings are pending against any individual may, on proof that a bankruptcy petition has been presented in respect of that individual or that he is an undischarged bankrupt, either stay the proceedings or allow them to continue on such terms as it thinks fit.

**8.6.2**    A limited moratorium is created by s.285 once the bankruptcy order is made:

> After the making of a bankruptcy order no person who is a creditor of the bankrupt in respect of a debt provable in the bankruptcy shall:
>
> (a)    have any remedy against the property or person of the bankrupt in respect of that debt; or
> (b)    before the discharge of the bankrupt, commence any action or other legal proceedings against the bankrupt except with the leave of the court and on such terms as the court may impose.
>
> This is subject to section 346 (enforcement procedures) and 347 (limited right to distress).

**8.6.3**    If the enforcement commences and a bankruptcy order is then made against the debtor, the enforcement agent must account to the trustee in bankruptcy for the proceeds of sale (once costs have been deducted) under s.346.

**8.6.4**    The court has the discretion to allow the claimant to retain the benefit of the enforcement (Insolvency Act 1986, s.346(6)).

**8.6.5**    Insolvency Act 1986, s.347(9) expressly preserves the right to distrain (or use CRAR) against property comprised in the bankrupt's estate notwithstanding that the bankrupt's assets automatically vest in the trustee.

**8.6.6**    The right to levy distress (or use CRAR) is restricted by the Insolvency Act 1986, s.347(1), which provides that landlord's right to distrain (now exercise CRAR) upon the goods and effects of an undischarged bankrupt for rent due to him is limited to a maximum of six months' rent accrued due before the commencement of the bankruptcy. If the landlord has distrained after presentation of a petition but before the bankruptcy order and an order is subsequently made any sum recovered in excess of six months' rent is to be held for the bankrupt or his estate (Insolvency Act 1986, s.347(2)).

**8.6.7**    This restriction in relation to six months relates only to the period end-ing with the date that the bankruptcy petition has been presented to the court. Accordingly, if the tenancy continues (and the trustee in bankruptcy effectively retains possession of the premises) then distress can be still levied.

**8.6.8**    These provisions are expressly retained by Sched.13 to the new Act which provides that for the purposes of the Insolvency Act 1986:

> 'Distress' includes the use of the procedure in Schedule 12 to the Tribunals Courts Enforcement Act 2007 and references to levying distress, seizing goods and related expression shall be construed accordingly.

**8.6.9**    Accordingly CRAR can be exercised during a bankruptcy in an identical way.

**8.6.10**    However, the creditor may still lose the benefit of the execution for any part of the proceeds exceeding the prescribed amount which is the sum of £1,000 (Insolvency Proceedings (Monetary Limits) Order 1986, SI 1986/1996).

**8.6.11**    The petitioning creditor is required to serve a notice on the enforcement agent that the winding up process has been commenced.

## Distress and CRAR v execution

**8.6.12**    Under the pre-Act regime, where a debtor's good are seized in execution by an enforcement agent, they cannot be removed from the premises unless the execution creditor pays the landlord any rent arrears up to a maximum of one year, Landlord and Tenant Act 1709, s.1 and County Courts Act 1984, s.102. Section 347(6) limits this right to six months. This is often established where a landlord attempts to levy distress (now CRAR) and establishes that enforcement has already been commenced by another creditor. These provisions have been abolished by the new Act, landlords have lost this right.

## 8.7    VOLUNTARY ARRANGEMENTS

**8.7.1**    Insolvency Act 1986, s.252 creates a comprehensive moratorium for the period of the interim order leading up the creditors' meeting in relation to a voluntary arrangement.

**8.7.2**    The same comprehensive moratorium is available for small companies under Insolvency Act 1986, Sched.A1. This moratorium prevents CRAR, distress or any other enforcement commencing and prohibits any existing enforcement to continue.

**8.7.3**    It does not make an existing part completed enforcement void and if the ultimate funds for the arrangement fails, then the enforcement process can ultimately continue.

**Table 8.1** The options for landlords with insolvent tenants

| Type of insolvency/ Type of action | IVA – During Moratorium 14 days | IVA – After Moratorium when IVA approved by creditors | Post IVA new debt | Bankruptcy | CVA – During moratorium small companies only (28 days) | During CVA approved by creditors (all companies) | Post CVA new debt | Administrative/ Law of Property Act receivership | Administration | Members/ Creditors or voluntary liquidation | Compulsory liquidation |
|---|---|---|---|---|---|---|---|---|---|---|---|
| Peaceable re-entry | Not without the leave of the court | Yes, but exceptions | Yes | Yes | Not without the leave of the court | Yes, but exceptions | Yes | Yes | Not without the administrator's consent or the leave of the court | Yes, but liquidator can apply under s.112 IA 1986 | Not without the liquidator's consent or the leave of the court |
| Distress for rent or CRAR | Not without the leave of the court | No | Yes | Yes for the 6 months' rent due before the bankruptcy order only | Not without the leave of the court | No | Yes | Yes | Not without the administrator's consent or the leave of the court | Yes | Not without the administrator's consent or the leave of the court |
| Pursuit of guarantors and/or previous tenants | Yes for the whole of the arrears | Yes for the whole of the arrears | Yes for the whole of the arrears | Yes for the whole of the arrears | Yes for the whole of the arrears | Yes for the whole of the arrears | Yes for the whole of the arrears | Yes for the whole of the rent | Yes for the whole amount of the debt | Yes for the whole amount of the debt | Yes for the whole amount of the debt |
| S.6 notice on sub-tenants or s.81 under the new Act | Yes for the amount of the sub-rent | Yes for the amount of the sub-rent | Yes for the amount of the sub-rent | Yes for the amount of the sub-rent | Yes for the amount of the sub-rent | Yes for the amount of the sub-rent | Yes for the amount of the sub-rent | Yes for the amount of the sub-rent | Yes for the amount of the sub-rent | Yes for the amount of the sub-rent | Yes for the amount of the sub-rent |
| Removal of funds from rent deposit (may depend on nature of deposit) | Not without the leave of the court | Yes | Yes | Yes | Not without the leave of the court | Yes | Yes | Yes | Not without the administrator's consent or the leave of the court | Yes | Not without the leave of Court |
| Can the lease be disclaimed by the insolvency practitioner? | No | No | No | Yes | No | No | No | No | No | Yes | Yes |

# 9 ENFORCEMENT BY TAKING CONTROL OF GOODS

## 9.1 PRE-ACT POSITION

**9.1.1** Where a claimant in the High Court or county court has obtained judgment then, for the purposes of enforcement, they become known as the 'judgment creditor' and the defendant becomes known as the 'judgment debtor'. This terminology has been changed by the new Act (see below).

**9.1.2** In the county court the judgment creditor issues a warrant of execution to commence the process of instructing a county court bailiff to take possession of the goods.

**9.1.3** The procedure in the High Court is distinct and, in some ways, different. However, there is a degree of overlap. In the High Court, the process is commenced by a writ of *fieri facias*. Sometimes this is known as a writ of *fi fa*. Writs of *fi fa* are executed by High Court enforcement officers (HCEO – they used to be called High Court sheriffs).

### Popularity of warrants of execution

**9.1.4** Like Orders to Obtain Information, the number of warrants of execution has declined over the last few years.

Table 9.1    Warrants of execution

| Year | Number of warrants of execution against goods issued |
|------|------------------------------------------------------|
| 1995 | 596,958 |
| 1996 | 420,180 |
| 1997 | 343,208 |
| 1998 | 305,952 |
| 1999 | 261,106 |
| 2000 | 218,118 |
| 2001 | 185,312 |
| 2002 | 165,619 |
| 2003 | 157,158 |
| 2004 | 132,972 |
| 2005 | 123,480 |
| 2006 | 123,120 |

## Financial limits

**9.1.5**   Financial limits are as follows:

- the value of the judgment determining which court has jurisdiction to deal with enforcement;
- a county court bailiff can try to enforce any amount up to £5,000;
- for any amount higher than £5,000, the matter must be transferred to the High Court and the judgment will be enforced by a High Court enforcement officer, even if it is a county court judgment;
- where the money owed is £600 or less, a High Court enforcement officer cannot be instructed to enforce the judgment and a county court bailiff must be used;
- where the amount being enforced is between £600 and £5000 there is a choice between using a county court bailiff and a High Court enforcement officer;
- for debts under the Consumer Credit Act, the limit is under £25,000 for the county court and over £25,000 for the High Court.

## How do I apply for a warrant of execution?

**9.1.6**   Before a court can issue a warrant the defendant must be in arrears of at least part of the debt or at least part of an instalment (County Courts Act 1984, s.86). Section 86 has now been revoked by the new Act and a limit has been set (see later).

**9.1.7**   To issue a warrant in the county court the creditor needs to fill out form N323 (Request to Issue a Warrant of Execution). The fee depends on the amount sought from the debtor.

**9.1.8**   Form N323 and the fee should then be sent to the court where the judgment was entered and within five to 10 working days the court will issue the warrant. The warrant will be given a number and the court staff must record the time the form was filed (under County Courts Act 1984, s.85(3) and County Court Rules (CCR) Order 26, r.1(1A)(b)).

**9.1.9**   In a case where the debtor does not live in that court's area, the court will send the warrant to the county court local to the debtor and the time of the warrant being sent must be recorded (County Courts Act 1984, s.103(1) and CCR Order 26, r.1(1A)(c)).

## Payments in instalments

**9.1.10**   Where the debtor has been ordered to pay in instalments and he defaults on one of the instalments, the creditor can apply for a warrant of execution for the entire amount, not just the amount in default under the instalments, pursuant to CCR Order 26, r.1(2).

## How long does a warrant of execution (now control) last?

9.1.11    Initially a warrant of execution lasts for 12 months but it can be renewed (CCR Order 26, r.1). However, this has been amended by the new Act (see **10.5** below).

## What will the enforcement agent do?

9.1.12    The county court bailiff (now 'enforcement agent') normally (unless ordered otherwise by a District Judge) sends a notice to the debtor saying that a warrant has been issued and that the debtor has seven days within which to pay.

9.1.13    If the debtor pays then the court will send the money to the creditor.

9.1.14    If the debtor does not pay within seven days the enforcement agent will attend the debtor's address within 15 working days of the warrant being issued.

9.1.15    Once at the debtor's address the enforcement agent will try to identify goods which they could sell at auction or collect a payment to prevent the goods from being sold.

9.1.16    Where a number of addresses have been given the enforcement agent will visit each address.

9.1.17    When an enforcement agent executes against goods, he must leave with the debtor, or at the property, a notice of levy (CCR Order 26, r.7).

## Suspension of warrant

9.1.18    The debtor can pay a fee and ask for the warrant to be suspended by form N246A.

9.1.19    If the debtor does not agree to the warrant being suspended an appointment will be arranged at court where both the claimant and the defendant will attend and the judge will decide how the matter will progress.

## Staying execution of a warrant of execution

9.1.20    This is governed by CCR Order 25, r.8 and is commenced by application of the judgment debtor. This remedy is preserved in the new Act procedure and supplemented by new debt relief and debt management remedies (see **Chapters 19–23**).

## Power to stay execution

9.1.21    If a debtor wishes to suspend or stay a judgment or order or stay the execution of any warrant, the rules for doing so are set out in Rules of Supreme Court (RSC) Order 47, r.1 for the High Court or in CCR Order 25, r.8.

**9.1.22**   An application should be made to the District Judge but can be heard by a court officer only in the case of an application to suspend a warrant.

**9.1.23**   A debtor should make a formal application in form N245 stating the grounds on which he wants execution to be stayed and including a signed statement of his means. Where an application is made in the High Court to stay the execution of a writ of control, the debtor will have to show:

■   that there are special circumstances which make it inexpedient to enforce the judgment or order; or
■   that the applicant is unable from any cause to pay the money.

**9.1.24**   If the court is satisfied, it may stay execution for such period and on such conditions as it sees fit.

**9.1.25**   In the case of an application to stay a warrant of control (in the county court), on receipt of the application, the court will send the creditor a copy of the debtor's application and ask the creditor to notify the court, in writing, within 14 days of service whether he objects to the application and giving his reasons for the objection.

**9.1.26**   If the creditor fails to notify the court of an objection within 14 days of service of the application for a stay, the court officer may make an order suspending the warrant on terms of payment.

**9.1.27**   If the creditor does file a notice objecting to the debtor's application to stay execution the court officer may determine the date and rate of payment and make an order suspending the warrant on terms of payment.

**9.1.28**   In this case, any party affected by the order for suspension may, within 14 days of service of the suspension order on him and giving reasons, apply on notice for the suspension order to be reconsidered. In that case a hearing will be set down before a District Judge and the creditor and debtor will be given not less than eight days' notice of the hearing. At the hearing, the District Judge can confirm the order or set it aside and make any new order as he sees fit.

**9.1.29**   In a case where the creditor states in his response to the application to stay execution that he wishes the enforcement agent to execute the warrant the court will fix a hearing before a District Judge and give not less than two days' notice of that hearing.

**9.1.30**   Where a condition, subject to which the warrant was suspended, has not been complied with, the warrant of execution may be reissued by the creditor filing a request and showing that the conditions have not been complied with. Where the District Judge suspends the warrant of control, he may order the debtor to pay the costs of the warrant and any fees or expenses incurred before its suspension. The order also authorises the sale of a sufficient portion of goods seized to cover these costs.

## 9.2   NEW ACT POSITION

**9.2.1**   The new Act unifies the process of the court's power to stay enforcement in relation to the High Court and county court (and creates a similar remedy for CRAR):

■   The new Act gives the High Court the power to stay the execution of a writ of control (s.70) where it is satisfied that the debtor cannot pay. The stay can last until 'it appears that the cause of the inability to pay has ceased'. The provision brings the High Court processes into line with the county court.

■   The county court processes underpinned by County Courts Act 1984, s.17(2) remains unchanged.

■   Section 78 of the new Act allows a commercial tenant (debtor) to make an application to stay the CRAR process on grounds to be set out under the regulations. It remains to be seen whether these grounds are comparable with a court application for a stay.

■   These practices can nullify much of the purpose of applying for a writ of control and it is hoped that the court will not entertain such applications lightly although the requirement of 'special circumstances' still exists in RSC Order 47.

### Effect of appeal on enforcement

**9.2.2**   An appeal does not operate as an automatic stay of execution. An appellant who wants to stay execution of a judgment should make an application to the trial judge at the same time as he makes an application for permission to appeal at the hearing in which judgment is handed down. If he does not, or the application for a stay of execution is refused, the creditor can enforce if payment is not made within the time limit in the order. The appellant can make a further application for a stay of execution when applying to the appeal court for permission to appeal.

**9.2.3**   In making the application to stay execution to the appeal court, the appellant must file, with the notice of appeal, an application under CPR Part 23 and evidence in support of the application for a stay. In making the application, the applicant must show a good reason why the creditor should not be allowed to enforce his judgment, for example that the applicant would suffer extreme financial hardship otherwise, and that he (the appellant) has some prospect of success on appeal.

**9.2.4**   Until a stay of execution is granted, the judgment can be enforced, even if permission to appeal is granted.

## 9.3    WRITS OF *FIERI FACIAS* (CONTROL)

### Pre-Act position

9.3.1    These are now renamed writs of control (s.62(4)(a) of the new Act).

9.3.2    A writ of *fieri facias* provides for the seizure and sale of the debtor's goods and is the High Court equivalent of a county court warrant of execution.

### *Financial limits*

9.3.3    Any High Court judgment or county court judgment for over £600 (except where the judgment is from a regulated agreement under the Consumer Creditor Act 1974) can be enforced in the High Court. County court judgments of over £5,000 which are not covered by the Consumer Credit Act 1974 must be enforced in the High Court.

### *Procedure*

9.3.4    A writ of *fieri facias* can be issued immediately after a court's judgment in relation to the payment or recovery of money. This is in line with Part 40.7(1) of the Civil Procedure Rules which states that a judgment or order takes effect from the date on which it is given or any later date that the court may specify.

9.3.5    The procedure in relation to writs of *fieri facias* is set out in RSC Order 47.

9.3.6    To issue a writ in the High Court the creditor needs a certificate of judgment which has details of the case and says how much is owed. This is requested by form N293A. The form should be sent to the court where the judgment was made. It must state the date of the judgment and the amount for which the order was made including any additional costs and a total of any interest.

9.3.7    Where an order is for the payment of money with costs to be assessed, it is usual for the parties to issue two writs of *fieri facias*, one for the judgment and one of the costs after they have been assessed (RSC Order 47, r.3).

9.3.8    The procedure for writs of *fieri facias*, which are now called writs of control are now set out in Sched.12 to the new Act.

### The new Act position

9.3.9    The new Act modernises the terminology of enforcement and modifies the process so that:

■    County court bailiffs and High Court enforcement officers (HCEOs) have been replaced in the new Act by enforcement agents.

■   The power conferred upon HCEOs and county court bailiffs, which provide for the seizure and sale of a debtor's goods, is replaced by the new Act with a new unified process set out in Sched.12 to the new Act.

■   The law of distress for rent is abolished. Landlords will be able to use the Sched.12 procedure under the new process of commercial rent arrears recovery (see **Chapter 7**).

■   The new Act allows creditors (of all kinds), together with commercial land-lords and public sector bailiffs to operate the Sched.12 procedure. All enforcement officers and bailffs will be known as enforcement agents. The unified system will also apply in relation to all forms of distress and execution.

## The process of taking control of goods under the new Act

**9.3.10**   Taking control of goods can now only be effected through the process set down in Sched.12 to the new Act.

**9.3.11**   Under the new Act:

■   writs of *fieri facias* become renamed writs of control;
■   warrants of execution are renamed warrants of control;
■   warrants of distress are renamed warrants of control.

**9.3.12**   Any power conferred by a writ or warrant of control to recover monies from a debtor can now only be exercised using the procedures set out in Sched.12 to the new Act (s.62(2) of the new Act).

**9.3.13**   The commencement date for the coming into force of Sched.12 has not yet been announced. The current process will apply to distress and execution that has commenced prior to the new Act coming into force. This includes the process in relation to goods which have been made subject to a walking possession agreement (s.66(b) of the new Act).

**9.3.14**   Under the terms of Sched.12 (as it applies to both debtors and other categories of debtors) – such as commercial tenants – the expressions used are creditor and debtor to mean the person liable to pay the debt and person for whom the debt is recoverable.

## 9.4    GOODS WHICH MAY BE TAKEN

### Pre-Act position

#### Court execution

**9.4.1**   High Court and county court enforcement agents are only permitted to seize goods in execution that belong to the debtor. There is no power to seize goods belonging to a third party. This puts court enforcement agents in a weaker position without the powers enjoyed by bailiffs exercising distress for rent.

**9.4.2**    In the High Court only the goods and chattels of the debtor can be taken in execution. This definition was widened by para.9 of Sched.7 to the Courts Act 2003, which extended the definition of 'goods capable of being seized' to include:

(a)    any goods of the execution debtor that are not exempt goods, and
(b)    any money, bank notes, bills of exchange, promissory notes, bonds, specialities or securities for money belonging to the execution debtor.

**9.4.3**    County Courts Act 1984, s.89 has a similar definition for the goods which may be seized by a county court bailiff under a warrant of execution.

**9.4.4**    Third parties can bring claims under the interpleader process. This has been abolished and reformed by the new Act (see **12.2**).

## Landlords

**9.4.5**    Under the law of distress, landlords can levy distress against any goods found on the demised premises (subject to certain categories of goods being exempt). This allowed distress to be taken against goods belonging not only to the debtor (i.e. the tenant) but also goods belonging to a third party (see **12.2**).

**9.4.6**    However, this created a harsh regime where innocent third parties could have their goods seized even where they had little connection with the debtor/tenant. A series of nineteenth century statutes gave third parties rights, culminating in the Law of Distress Amendment Act 1908 which softened the effect of this principle. The 1908 Act provided some degree of protection from distress for lodgers, under tenants and third parties (without any beneficial interest in the tenancy).

**9.4.7**    However, the 1908 Act did not protect all third parties. Landlords can still levy distress and seize the goods on the demised premises belonging to:

- the husband or wife of the tenant;
- a third party who has given permission for the tenant to have the goods in his possession – if the goods are in the reputed ownership of the tenant;
- a business in which the tenant has interest;
- a third party who has stored goods on the premises and has failed to remove them after having been given at least one month's notice to do so;
- a company where the tenant is a director or officer of the company;
- a hire-purchase company unless a default notice has been served.

**9.4.8**    The Law of Distress Amendment Act 1908 has been repealed by the new Act and when it comes into force these extensive rights against third party goods will be lost (see **12.2**).

**9.4.9**    Distress for rent is far more extensive than court based distress.

**9.4.10**    In the research for this book one bailiff commented:

I have levied distress over a wide range of assets over the years. I have seized horses, an executive jet airplane, industrial plant and machinery, the contents of a specialist S&M adult book shop, jewellery, famous works of fine art, vintage cars, fairground rides, stamp collections and a number of yachts. I have also done sheep.

## The new Act position

**9.4.11**    Under Sched.12 all enforcement agents may take control of goods 'only if they are goods of the debtor'. Accordingly landlords have lost the advantage they enjoyed in relation to the wide range of goods that could be taken in distress for rent.

**9.4.12**    The new Act creates a different definition of goods (para.3 of Sched.12 to the new Act):

'Goods' means property of any description, other than land.

### Money

**9.4.13**    This description clearly applies to money (whether Sterling or another currency) and securities (including bills of exchange, promissory notes, bonds, specialities and securities for money) (para.6 of Sched.12).

**9.4.14**    Although the Courts Act 2003 made a distinction between goods and money and securities. The drafting of Sched.12 to the new Act assumes that money and securities are sub-sections of goods.

**9.4.15**    The new Act makes money available to all forms of enforcement (including CRAR). This has been controversial. Some commentators warned of enforcement agents seizing the only cash that a poor family had available. It was also feared that a hunt for money might turn into a search leading to a ransacking of the debtor's property.

**9.4.16**    However, despite these qualms the new Act allows enforcement agents to take control of money. The counterpoint to risks such as these is that enforcement agents will be subject to a higher degree of regulation than ever before.

**9.4.17**    An enforcement agent (whether acting on behalf of the creditor or commercial landlord) may take control of goods only if they are the goods of the debtor. This raises a huge potential for third party claims and debtor remedies, which are dealt with later in this chapter (see **Chapter 12**).

## 9.5    EXEMPT GOODS

**9.5.1**    Referring to Sched.12, para.11, an enforcement agent cannot take control of any goods which are exempt. The regulations to the new Act will define exempt goods.

## Pre-regulation position

**9.5.2**    Until the regulations are published there will be uncertainty as to which goods will be exempt. However, there has been much discussion on what goods should be exempt from being taken into control.

**9.5.3**    The types of goods that may be taken should be set out clearly and be consistent in all cases. The power to exempt goods will be exercisable by the Lord Chancellor in (secondary) legislation, once the regulations are produced. Whilst the onus will be on the debtor to show that goods are exempt, the enforcement agent will also have a general responsibility to direct the debtor to tell him or her which goods are exempt and which can be taken under legal control.

**9.5.4**    In the White Paper *Effective Enforcement* published in March 2003 by the Lord Chancellor's Department, the following were recommended to be exempt (para.168, p.39):

> Such tools, books, vehicles and other items of equipment as are necessary to the debtor for use personally by him in his employment, business or vocation, not exceeding in aggregate value an amount as may be prescribed by the Lord Chancellor; and

> Such clothing, bedding, furniture, household equipment and provisions as are necessary for satisfying his basic domestic needs and those of his family.

**9.5.5**    The White Paper went on to make two generic points in relation to exempt goods, as follows:

> The goods should be those which are used personally by the debtor;

and

> It will be acceptable for very expensive and luxury items, including tools of the trade, to be taken and replaced with similar goods that are necessary to the needs of the debtor (and his family).

**9.5.6**    This description of exempt goods is consistent with the definition adopted in relation to writs of execution by the Courts Act 2003 (Courts Act 2003, Sched.7, para.9).

**9.5.7**    It is highly unlikely that the regulations will encompass the complex system that developed under the common law in relation to a landlord's right to levy distress. At common law, a landlord was entitled to seize goods found in the premises, irrespective of their ownership (*Gorton* v. *Fuller* [1792] Term Rep 565 per Buller J):

> Whether goods be the property of the tenant or a stranger is perfectly immaterial, provided they be on the premises and not be privileged by law from a distress.

**9.5.8**  The common law system in relation to exemptions to distress was established over hundreds of years, but excluded:

- intellectual property rights (*British Muteuo Scope and Biograph Company* v. *Homer* [1901] 1 Ch 671);
- land;
- fixtures (i.e. annexed to the property);
- corn and [sheaves] or stocks (*Griffin* v. *Scott* [1726] No.1 Barn.k.b. 3);
- growing crops (as amended by the Distress for Rent Act 1737, which allowed some crops to be seized);
- wild animals (unless the animal had been tamed or captured);
- raw materials delivered to a person exercising a trade 'to be carried, wrought, worked up or managed in the way of his trade' – this would include customers' goods;
- things in actual use (e.g. a horse, whilst a man is riding it, a machine while it's being used);
- perishables (because, once taken, could not be given back to the debtor in the same condition);
- goods already subject to execution;
- personal effects – under County Courts Act 1984, s.89(1), which mirrors Courts Act 2003, Sched.7, para.9;
- machinery (if hired) under the Agricultural Holding Act 1986 (s.18);
- breeding stock (under the Agricultural Holding Act 1986);
- frames, materials in textile trades (the Hosiery Act 1843, s.18);
- railway rolling stock (if owned by a third party bearing the actual ownership marked by a metal plate or other distinguishing mark);
- utility fittings – gas, electric and water (where owned and marked by the utility companies);
- plough beasts (which work the land) cannot be distrained upon. Also, sheep and cattle cannot be distrained on – but only if there is no other sufficient distress to be found;
- third party goods (see **12.2**).

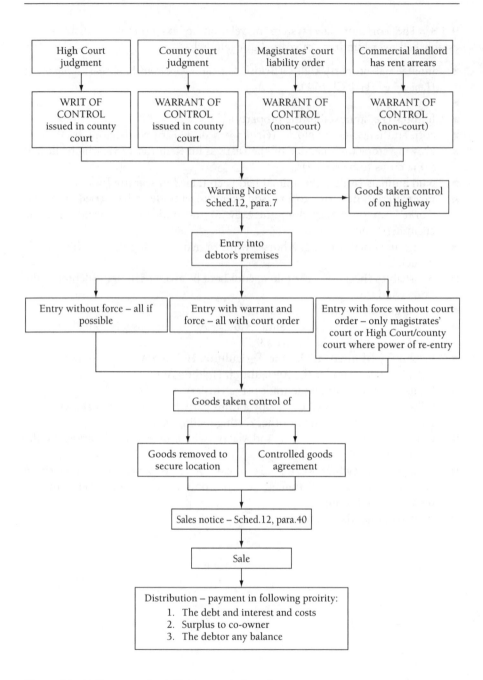

**Figure 9.1**  Enforcement by taking control of goods

# 10 PROCEDURE FOR TAKING CONTROL

## 10.1 PRE-ACT POSITION

10.1.1 The debtor's goods become bound as consequence of the enforcement procedure. This has specific consequences as are set out below:

- In relation to a writ in the High Court, the writ binds the property in the goods from the time it is received from the person who is under a duty to endorse it under Courts Act 2003, Sched.7, para.8. This happens as soon as the High Court enforcement officer receives the writ.
- Where the enforcement is commenced by a warrant in the county court or the magistrates' court then the warrant binds the property and the goods from the time it is received by the county court District Judge/magistrates' court officer ('the person who is under a duty to endorse it'). This happens under County Courts Act 1984, s.99 and Magistrates' Courts Act 1980, s.125ZA.

## 10.2 THE NEW ACT POSITION

10.2.1 The debtors' goods become bound once the procedure commences. This binding takes effect at a very early stage and is comparable to the pre-Act position:

- In relation to a writ of control in the High Court, the writ binds the property in the goods from the time it is received from the person who is under a duty to endorse it: para.4(3) of Sched.12 replaces para.8 of Sched.7 to the Courts Act 2003. The debtors' goods are effectively bound as soon as the High Court enforcement officer (enforcement agents under the new Act) receives the writ of control.
- Where enforcement is commenced by a warrant of control in the county court or the magistrates' court then the warrant binds the property and the goods from the time it is received by the county court/magistrates' court enforcement agent ('the person who is under a duty to endorse it'). Paragraph 4(3) of Sched.12 to the new Act replaces the power conferred by County Courts Act 1984, s.99 and Magistrates' Court Act 1980, s.125ZA. Accordingly, as s.99 has been repealed, this will have limited effect.

10.2.2    In relation to other types of warrants of control (e.g. where commercial rent arrears recovery (CRAR) is being used by a landlord) then goods are bound from the time when the Notice of Enforcement is given (see 10.4).

## 10.3    EFFECT OF BINDING

### Pre-Act position

10.3.1    Under the current regime the process of enforcement has a binding effect on the debtor's goods. The debtor with notice of the enforcement is restricted in law from dealing with his goods. He is not supposed to assign, charge, or sell the goods until the enforcement process has taken its course (or has been withdrawn). The new Act position is similar to the current High Court system (under the Courts Act 2003, Sched.7, para.8) and the County Courts Act 1984.

10.3.2    Although he should not do so, a debtor may pass good title to a purchaser who buys goods in good faith for valuable consideration without notice (an 'innocent purchaser'). If the purchaser is not 'innocent' (i.e. because he had notice or paid an under value for the goods or was not acting in good faith), then the goods continue to remain subject to the enforcement agent's rights.

### The new Act position

10.3.3    The effect of the goods being bound prevents:

■    any assignment of the goods; or
■    any transfer of any interest of the debtor's goods.

10.3.4    If there is an assignment or transfer then it takes place subject to the enforcement power. Regardless of the assignment or transfer the creditor's rights are unaffected (para.4).

#### Innocent purchaser

10.3.5    The exception to this is where a person acquires the goods in good faith for valuable consideration and without notice of the commencement of the enforcement action. This kind of innocent purchaser is able to acquire good title to the debtor's goods free from the enforcement power. The creditor may still have an additional claim against the debtor arising from this breach of the new Act under para.67 and the debtor may have committed an offence under para.68 (see 12.6 below).

10.3.6    The 'innocent purchaser' must purchase without notice. In this context, 'notice' is given a statutory definition. Under para.5(4), the expression 'without notice' means the purchaser has had no notice:

■    that the writ or warrant of control has been received by the person who acts as enforcement agent and that goods remain bound (in relation to High

Court, county court and magistrates' court enforcement i.e. the writ/warrant has been received by the person who is under a duty to endorse the warrant/writ);

■ that a notice of enforcement has been served under para.7 and that goods remain bound under it (in relation to other enforcement, including CRAR).

10.3.7    The innocent purchaser acts in good faith if he has acted honestly (whether or not he has been negligent (para.5(3)). This is a question of fact not belief. The use of the word fact implies an objective test will be applied.

10.3.8    Accordingly an innocent purchaser who with honesty acquires goods without notice and for valuable consideration will acquire good title even where there is negligence.

## How long are the goods bound?

10.3.9    Under para.6 the property in the goods ceases to be bound in the following circumstances:

(a)  when particular goods are sold then the binding stops for the sold goods (but potentially continues for the remaining goods (but see the effect of abandonment if the sale fails at 11.6 below));
(b)  in the case of money, if it is used to pay any of the amount outstanding it stops being bound at the times it is used (but the debtor's remaining goods are bound);
(c)  if the entire amount outstanding is paid and then the binding stops and all the debtor's goods are released;
(d)  the instrument under which the enforcement power is exercisable ceases to have effect or the power ceases to be exercisable (please see time for which a warrant remains capable of being enforced at 10.5.1 and 10.5.6). This could happen following a successful application, under s.78 of the new Act, by a tenant to set aside an enforcement notice for CRAR. This would release all the debtor's goods.

## 10.4    NOTICE OF ENFORCEMENT (PARA.7)

### Pre-Act position

10.4.1    At present there is limited requirement to give notice before taking legal control of a debtor's goods. However, in most cases some form of written notice is given. At common law there is no requirement that notice of this claim be given, but a number of the statutory regimes require the bailiff/enforcement officer to provide a level of notification. Once again, there is no uniformity of approach. Commercial landlords generally gave no information or notice to tenants.

**10.4.2**    During the consultation process the landlords (whom of course, enforce without a judgment of a court) considered that an obligation to give tenants notice of a possible distraint might lead to unscrupulous tenants removing or disposing of assets (even though this constitutes the offence of fraudulent removal). There was limited statistical information as to whether a requirement to inform the debtor that enforcement action was imminent would have a real impact on the ability to recover the debts.

**10.4.3**    County court judgments carry a notification that the claimant has the right make an application for a warrant. County Courts Rules (CCR) 1981, Order 26, r.7 requires notice upon levying execution. This does not require a preliminary warning notice. However, the practice in the High Courts and the county courts is for the courts to send warning letter (unless the court feels that the debtor may dispose of the goods).

**10.4.4**    In recent years it has also become more common for commercial landlords to issue warning notices (although there is no strict need to do so until the new Act comes into force). This was partly a response to the comments of Lightman J in *Fuller v. Happy Shopper* [2001] 1 WLR 1681 who commented:

> a Landlord is bound to take the greatest care before levying distress that there are no claims on the part of the tenant . . . In any ordinary case he would be well advised to give notice of his intention . . .

## Bailiff's example

**10.4.5**    Although giving notice is not a requirement the industry has adjusted to the changing environment. One bailiff reported:

> For the last 10 years I have been operating a process for larger clients. I send a 'bailiff's letter' to defaulting debtors requesting payment to be made within seven days. The letter makes it clear that if payment is not made distress will be levied. The mere fact that the letter is sent helps reduce the number of defaulting tenants. For one client this reduced the level of tenant default from 22 per cent to 3 per cent. This approach also provided comfort to the client that we were operating in compliance with the Human Rights Act. In my experience many landlords now take this action.

## The new Act position (para.7 notice)

**10.4.6**    The new Act introduces a uniform requirement that notice must be given of an impending enforcement of a warrant of control or writ of control. In all cases the debtors' goods will be bound either at the time the notice of enforcement is given or prior to this (see **10.3.9**).

**10.4.7**    The enforcement agent will not be able take control of goods unless the debtor has been given notice. It is therefore a pre-condition of taking control. The regulations to the new Act will state:

- the minimum period of notice;
- the form of the notice;
- what the notice must contain;
- how the notice must be given; and
- who must give the notice.

**10.4.8**   There are likely to be prescribed circumstances that allow shorter notice to be provided (and perhaps no notice). This will depend upon an application to the court and the regulations to the new Act. The court will be able to impose whatever conditions it feels appropriate.

**10.4.9**   The enforcement agent is required to keep a record of the time the notice was given. This is likely to be essential evidence if the debtor claims that he received no notice. As the requirement is a precondition for taking control of goods it will be essential for enforcement agents to be able to demonstrate that notice was properly given in full compliance with the regulations. This is likely to be a subject of a great deal of contested enforcements.

## 10.5   TIME LIMITS FOR TAKING CONTROL

### Pre-Act position

**10.5.1**   The current position in the High Court and county court is that where six years or more have elapsed since the date of the judgment or order a writ or warrant cannot be issued without the court's permission. Under Rules of Supreme Court (RSC) Orders 45–46, the creditor can make an application without notice setting out the reasons for the delay. This is a matter of the court's discretion and not one which is prohibited by the Limitation Act 1980. More than one application can be made if new evidence comes to light (*National Westminster Bank* v. *Powney* [1990] 2 All ER 416, CA).

**10.5.2**   Accordingly it helps to demonstrate that some steps had been taken to attempt to uphold judgments and enforce but had been unsuccessful. If the delay is not the creditors' fault, then the court would make the order (*Lloyds* v. *Jean Pierre Longtin* [2005] EWHC 249).

**10.5.3**   However, the burden is currently on the creditor to show the court that it should exercise its discretion and grant its permission to enforce after a period of delay.

**10.5.4**   Reasons may include:

- negotiations which may have taken place between claimant and defendant;
- information gathering as to the defendant's circumstances;
- repeated (but failed) attempts to enforce in the past;
- lack of good faith in declaring assets by the debtor.

**10.5.5**    In the county court (CCR Order 26, r.5) to obtain the court's permission is subject to similar considerations, where six years or more have elapsed since the date of judgment.

## The new Act position

**10.5.6**    The new Act provides that an enforcement agent will not be able to take control of goods after the prescribed period (para.8(1)). The regulations will set the prescribed period. It is likely that a period of six years will be prescribed and in which case the current regime in the High Court and county court will apply. The case law in relation to the current position is likely to illustrate the circumstances which are likely to be taken account of by the court.

### CRAR

**10.5.7**    As set out above, landlords of commercial premises will only be able to use CRAR in limited circumstances once the lease has come to an end for a limited period of six months.

## 10.6    PLACE WHERE ENFORCEMENT CAN TAKE PLACE

### Pre-Act position

**10.6.1**    Court enforcement agents (either in the High Court or county court) have the ability to seize goods with little restriction in relation to where the goods are located:

- in the county court, execution of a warrant can take place in relation to goods under County Courts Act 1984, s.85(2): 'wherever they may be found within the district of the Court';
- in the High Court, execution of a writ can take place in relation to goods under Courts Act 2003, Sched.7 and at common law 'wherever they may be found'. Each HCEO is able to operate across the jurisdictional area of the High Court, although in practice HCEOs are assigned to particular areas (defined by postcode).

**10.6.2**    Landlords were under a more restricted position in terms of the place where distress could take place. With limited exceptions the landlord can only seize goods which are located on his land. The starting point is that landlords can only levy distress on goods found on premises demised to the tenant. If a tenant has two separate demises, let under two separate leases then the distress can only be made on the land from which the rent issues.

Example

A landlord grants two leases to a tenant, unit A and unit B. The tenant does not pay his rent for unit A and leaves the unit empty. He continues to trade from unit B. Even though it is the same landlord and the same tenant – the landlord can only levy distress for the unit A rent arrears by seizing goods at unit A. He cannot levy distress at unit B for the unit A arrears.

**10.6.3**   Accordingly landlords are only able to levy distress in relation to rent arrears arising from one premises and not take goods from separate premises occupied by the same tenant (even where acting on behalf of the landlord of both demises).

**10.6.4**   Landlords in the pre-Act regime could not levy distress on:

- an adjoining highway (unless the highway forms part of the demised premises);
- other premises occupied by the tenant;
- a common part of a building outside the demised premises;
- land where the tenant had an easement but no demise, e.g. a right of way over an access road to the demised premises.

**10.6.5**   There are limited exceptions to this principle:

- under the Statute of Marlborough 1267 (Chapter 15) the Crown can levy distress outside his fee. The Crown can levy distress for rent on any property where it is the landlord. Therefore the Crown has the right to distrain on any of the properties leased to its tenants even if let under separate leases;
- distress can be levied off the premises where the tenant has fraudulently removed goods to avoid distress;
- the bailiff can follow the goods off the premises where the tenant has committed pound breach.

**10.6.6**   Under the current system where tenants fraudulently remove goods from the demised premises to avoid distress then, under the Distress for Rent Act 1737 (s.7), landlords are allowed to follow the goods and levy distress wherever they are found for a period of 30 days after they have been fraudulently removed. It even allowed landlords to use force to break open the place where goods have been concealed.

**10.6.7**   However, as part of the unifying process, provisions relating to fraudulent removal in the Distress for Rent Act 1737 have been repealed.

## The new Act position

### Where can goods be taken under the new Act?

**10.6.8**   Under the terms of the new Act the place where enforcement agents can take control of goods has been unified so that landlords are brought under the same regime. However, enforcement agents acting on behalf of commercial landlords continue to have a more restricted right to take action which remains linked to the demised premises.

**10.6.9**   Pursuant to para.9 of Sched.12 to the new Act:

An enforcement agent may take control of the goods only if they are –

(a)    on premises that he has power to enter under this Schedule, or
(b)    on a highway.

**10.6.10**    Accordingly, the place where an enforcement agent may take control of goods is defined by the right of entry or where goods are situated on a highway.

**10.6.11**    Accordingly, if the goods are located in a place where the enforcement agent has no right of entry under Sched.12 then they cannot be taken control of unless they are situated on a highway.

**10.6.12**    Court enforcement agents have the right to enter premises where the debtor lives or carries out business.

**10.6.13**    Landlords' enforcement agents only have a right of entry to exercise CRAR at the demised premises. This is similar to the pre-Act position. However, a landlord now has the right to apply to a county court for a warrant of entry to any specified property (see **10.7** below). If the court grants a warrant to enter premises other than the demised premises then this may extend the place where CRAR can be used. For example, a landlord may make an application for a warrant if there has been a fraudulent removal (see pre-Act position above). The regulations will define the form and extent of this kind of application.

## Can landlords now take control of goods on a highway?

**10.6.14**    This is one advantage for commercial landlords. Under the current system there is no right to levy distress on the highway. However, the right to carry out CRAR extend to the highway. There is no distinction that the highway must be adjoining the demised premises.

**10.6.15**    Accordingly, there is no restriction to prevent an enforcement agent acting on behalf of a commercial landlord exercising CRAR:

■    on the highway outside the tenant's domestic premises; or
■    wherever the tenant's goods can be found provided they are on the highway.

**10.6.16**    This conjures up images of an enforcement agent secretly following a defaulting tenant and taking goods from premises (which are not the demised premises) should the tenant ever park his transport lorry on the highway then the enforcement agent can take control of the goods.

## 10.7    ENTRY INTO PLACE WHERE CONTROL OF GOODS CAN BE TAKEN

### The pre-Act position

#### *Dwelling house*

**10.7.1**    Under the current regime enforcement agents are not allowed to use force to obtain entry to a dwelling house (*Vaughan* v. *McKenzie* [1968] 1 All ER 1154).

**10.7.2**    Entry can be achieved by way of:

- an unlocked outer door (a latch can be lifted, a bolt drawn, but a lock cannot be broken);
- an open window (including French windows), but not through a closed window (a window cannot be forced, *Attack* v. *Bramwell* [1863] B&S 520);
- climbing over garden fences or walls;
- crossing a drive or yard or garden area.

**10.7.3**    Lord Denning summed up the rights of an enforcement agent to gain entry in the case of *Southam* v. *Smout* [1968] 1 All ER 104:

> it seems to me that the law now is that, where a landlord enters under a right given by the law to levy a distress or a sheriff's officer enters . . . he may not break the door, in the sense that he may not break it physically. If it is locked, bolted or barred, he must not open it, he is forbidden to do so. But if it is open and ajar, or if it is closed and can be opened by the peaceable means of lifting the latch or turning the knob or just by gently pushing, in those circumstances he can lawfully enter because there he is not breaking. The difference between the two cases is this, that, in the case where a man locks, bolts or bars his door, he makes it clear that no one is to come in, whereas, if he leaves it open, or just shuts it and all that is needed is to turn the handle or lift the latch or give it a push, then he gives an implied invitation to all people who have lawful business to come in . . .

Example

However, enforcement agents are sometimes prevented from carrying out their work by the debtor (aware that there may be an attendance by a bailiff) locking the enforcement agent out of the premises. Enforcement agents often tread a very narrow line. In *Vaughan* v. *McKenzie* [1968] 1 All ER 1154 a county court bailiff pushed past a debtor. The debtor then struck the bailiff with a bottle. However, the entry was held to be illegal. The debtor was held not to have assaulted the bailiff because he had used force to gain entry.

**10.7.4**    At common law, enforcement agents were not entitled to break open the outer door of a dwelling house in order to levy execution. This principle flows from *Semayne's case* (1604) No.5 CO91 which underlined the expression 'an Englishman's home is his castle'.

## Commercial premises

**10.7.5**    Bailiffs levying distress for rent in relation to commercial premises are bound by the same rules set out above for dwelling houses. They cannot use force to gain entry.

**10.7.6**    The position is different for HCEO and county court bailiffs. They can use reasonable force to break into commercial premises.

## Repeated entry

**10.7.7**    Once the bailiff has gained entry if he is subsequently locked out he can break a door open. Lord Justice Morritt stated in the case of *Khazanchi* v. *Faircharm* [1998] 1 WLR 1603, CA:

> if he knew that the bailiff was seeking to re-enter but locked or left the door locked to exclude him then the tenant committed a wrong for he was wilfully obstructing the right of the bailiff to possession of the goods. But if he did not know of the bailiff's intended re-entry at any particular time then to leave his door locked and to absent himself to go about his normal affairs was his right.

## The bailiff's view

**10.7.8**    One bailiff who contributed to this book gave the following example:

> The rules of access are very complex. Bailiffs are required to have an intimate knowledge of the rules.
>
> In one case I attended the property to collect rent under a warrant of distress. When I got to the property access was very difficult because the area was surrounded by high fences and locked gates. However these were not the walls of the building and I am allowed to climb over. I scaled the fence and I was then able to cross the car park and enter the property through an open door. I then levied distress which led to successfully collecting the rent.

## Entry under the new Act

### Rationale for reform

**10.7.9**    The restrictions on using force sometimes led to most hardened debtors developing strategies to stymie the ability of enforcement agents to gain entry and take control of goods. This made certain debts unenforceable. The White Paper *Effective Enforcement* identified this as a problem although it also recognised that some debtors genuinely are unable to pay the amounts due and allowing enforced entry may lead to vulnerable individuals being placed in a situation of unnecessary harassment.

**10.7.10**    The new Act seeks to ensure that:

No debt should be unenforceable; and

Continuous refusal to allow a regulated enforcement agent will not mean that enforcement will not take place – even within a private home. (*Effective Enforcement* White Paper.)

**10.7.11**    There are a small number of hardened debtors which refuse access to enforcement agents. This was seen to undermine the credibility and integrity of the civil courts. Under the new Act there will be a remedy for creditors who are unable to enforce. Continued refusal to open a door or unlock a gate will not stop legitimate enforcement action. It was perceived that new technology has made the bailiff's situation even more difficult. Premises are now often equipped with security cameras and electronic gates so that debtors may effectively be able to decide when to lock out their visitors.

**10.7.12**    Forcible entry in commercial premises is currently allowed for most enforcement agents who undertake civil enforcement on behalf of the High Court and county court. It will continue to be permitted for those who presently have this power. Having failed to gain normal entry, enforcement agents, save for those who are currently officers of the court, may apply to the court for permission to undertake forcible entry in commercial premises with or without notice.

**10.7.13**    Normal entrance of third party premises is permitted. However, enforcement agents need to be certain that goods on the premises are on the premises before attempting to gain entrance. Forceful entry to third party premises will require the court's permission in all cases. The new Act structures methods of entry into entry without warrants and entry under warrants and then sets out the general powers to use reasonable force and where an application can be made to use reasonable force.

## Entry without warrant

**10.7.14**    Under para.14 of Sched.12 to the new Act enforcement agents are able to enter a property without the court's permission to search for and take control of goods, providing the premises are 'relevant premises' (para.40 of Sched.12 to the new Act).

### CRAR – WHICH PREMISES CAN A LANDLORD'S ENFORCEMENT AGENT ENTER?

**10.7.15**    In relation to commercial landlords the relevant premises are restricted to the premises demised to the tenant (para.14(4)). Other than taking control of goods on the highway, enforcement agents can only use an enforcement power on the demised premises. However, an application can be made for a warrant to enter other premises (see **10.7.19**).

### COURT ENFORCEMENT AGENTS

**10.7.16**    Court enforcement agents entry in relation to relevant premises is defined as the place or places where the debtor:

- usually lives; or
- carries on a trade or business (para.14(6) of Sched.12).

10.7.17    The enforcement agents are authorised to make repeated entries into the same premises (although this may be further restricted by the regulations when they are produced).

10.7.18    The enforcement agent can enter premises subject to this definition if he reasonably believes that the debtor usually lives or carries out a trade or business there. Accordingly, the enforcement agent does not have to have certain knowledge. This is a more limited definition than the current system which allows goods to be seized wherever they may be found.

## Entry under warrant

10.7.19    Enforcement agents are also able to make an application to the court for a warrant authorising entry into other premises (para.15 of Sched.12). Before issuing the warrant the court must be satisfied that the following conditions are met:

(a)    an enforcement power has become exercisable;
(b)    there is reason to believe there are goods on the premises that the enforcement power will be exercisable to take control of if the warrant is issued;
(c)    it is reasonable in all the circumstances to issue the warrant.

10.7.20    This provision appears also to be open to commercial landlords. Accordingly, whereas under the current regime commercial landlords are only able to levy distress where goods are found upon the demised premises, if the above conditions are met then the court's permission could be sought by a commercial landlord to exercise CRAR in relation to other premises.

## Re-entry

10.7.21    In a similar way to the current position for enforcement agents, para.16 of Sched.12 authorises repeated entry to the same premises. This can be used by the enforcement agent to inspect the goods or to remove the goods or to remove them for storage or sale.

## Forced entry

### PRE-ACT POSITION

10.7.22    Generally enforcement agents are not allowed to use force. There are limited exceptions. For civil debts it is possible for court enforcement agents to use force in relation to commercial premises (providing no one is inside). It is possible for all enforcement agents to use force to gain re-entry to a property (after goods have already been seized in a first entry). The force which can be used relates to methods of entry (e.g. if necessary breaking a lock). It must be proportionate and does not sanction force against people.

Bailiff example

In one case I had levied distress against the contents of an Indian restaurant. When I returned to the site I could not get access. The doors had been locked and secured with internal bracing. However I noticed that a sky light was open. So to use the least force possible we gained access through the open sky light and removed the contents through the first floor windows.

## THE NEW ACT POSITION

**10.7.23**    The new Act creates a new remedy allowing enforcement agents to use force to gain entry. The use of force was prohibited for most forms of enforcement and so this new right is likely to make a significant difference. Most enforcement agents will first need to obtain the court's permission to use force. However, no court permission will be needed for limited categories.

*Power to use reasonable force without express court permission*
**10.7.24**    An enforcement agent can use reasonable force to gain entry without court sanction in two circumstances:

- *Magistrates' court:* under para.18 of Sched.12, an enforcement agent may if necessary use reasonable force to enter premises if the following conditions are met:

  (a) the enforcement agent has power to enter the premises without a warrant under Sched.12; and

  (b) the agent is acting under a warrant of control under the Magistrates' Court Act 1980; and

  (c) the enforcement agent is acting under a warrant by virtue of s.125A or s.125B of the Magistrates' Court Act 1980.

  This allows reasonable force to be used by an enforcement agent executing a warrant of control in the magistrates' court.

- *Re-entry:* where there is a right to re-enter a property under s.16 (where a first entry has taken place to take control of the goods and the enforcement agent wishes to inspect or remove the goods at a later stage for storage or sale) then para.19 of Sched.12 allow reasonable force to be used to effect the re-entry if the following conditions are met:

  - the enforcement agent reasonably believes that the debtor is carrying on a trade or business on the premises; and
  - he is acting under an enforcement power under any of the following:

    • a writ/warrant of control in the High Court/county court;
    • s.61(1) of the Taxes Management Act 1960;
    • s.121A(1) of the Social Security Administration Act 1992;

- s.51(A1) of the Finance Act 1997;
- para.1A of Sched.12 to the Finance Act 2003.

**10.7.25**    Commercial landlords will not be able to use force to exercise CRAR without the court's permission. This removes a right currently enjoyed by landlords' bailiffs, who can currently use force to re-enter a property (following an earlier levy). Where force is required then an enforcement agent (including those exercising CRAR) can if necessary apply to the court.

*Application to the court for power to use reasonable force*
**10.7.26**    All enforcement agents have the right to make an application to the court to authorise the use, if necessary, of reasonable force to enter the premises to do anything for which entry is authorised. The application can be made:

- as a stand alone application for a warrant to use force where there is a right of entry to the premises; or
- as part of an application under para.15 for a warrant to enter specified premises.

**10.7.27**    In order to succeed the enforcement power must have become exercisable and the enforcement agent must have reason to believe that there are goods on the premises to take control of once a warrant is issued and that it is reasonable in all the circumstances to issue the warrant under para.15 (para.21 to Sched.12 to the new Act).

**10.7.28**    These new remedies will add considerably to the armoury available to enforcement agents:

- an application to use force will be possible when using CRAR, not just for re-entry but also for the initial process (this was not possible under the law of distress);
- when faced with the minority of hardened debtors that are prepared to exploit the weaknesses in the system, simply locking out the agent will result in an enforcement agent making an application

**10.7.29**    Naturally there has to be a balance (see **Chapter 19** in relation to 'can't pay/won't pay' and in relation to the new debt management and relief schemes). Further conditions may be set by the regulations in relation to an application to use reasonable force (para.22).

**10.7.30**    Under para.22 the court can direct that a police constable attend and assist the enforcement agent in gaining entry.

*What constitutes reasonable force?*
**10.7.31**    Paragraph 24 of Sched.12 indicates that the regulations will define in more detail what amounts to reasonable force and impose restrictions on what can and cannot be done (para.24(1)). In any event a power to use force will not include a power to use force against persons (para.24(2)).

**10.7.32**    The report produced by the Lord Chancellor's Department (*An Independent Review of Bailiff Law* by Professor J Beatson QC) distinguished between normal entry and entry using reasonable force. However, it is clear from the consultation process that the amount of force to be used will be limited particularly in relation to domestic premises. The regulations are likely to lay down the same levels of evidence and scrutiny that the police must satisfy in criminal cases to obtain entry. The relevant factors may include:

- demonstrating a reasonable belief that the debtor will refuse voluntary access;
- the reason that valuable goods were on the premises which could be the subject of a writ/warrant of control;
- the debtor's credit record;
- the debtor's history in relation to evasion of enforcement proceedings;
- whether the premises are used for business purposes or as a dwelling house;
- the enforcement agent's proposals for how the forced entry will be achieved.

Case example

The regulations are likely to be heavily influenced by the Court of Appeal decision in *Khazanchi* v. *Faircharm Investments Limited* and *McLeod* v. *Butterwick* [1998] 2 All ER 901, CA. The Court of Appeal reviewed the case law in relation to forcible entry and bailiff action in relation to the court process and also the law of distress for rent. Lord Justice Morris giving the leading judgment that the question of whether an enforcement agent is being obstructed depends on the debtor's knowledge of whether he knew there was going to be an attendance:

> If he knew that the bailiff was seeking to re-enter but locked or left the door locked to exclude him then the tenant committed a wrong for he was wilfully obstructing the right of the bailiff to possession of the goods. But if he did not know of the bailiff's intended re-entry at any particular time then to leave his door locked and to absent himself to go about his normal affairs was his right.

**10.7.33**    The new statutory regime in Sched.12 is designed to provide clarity as to when reasonable force can be used. The regulations are likely to provide that a warning notice be first served on the debtor making it clear that reasonable force will be used.

*Reasonable force in relation to goods on a highway*
**10.7.34**    An enforcement agent may make an application to the court if he wishes to use force when seizing goods located on a highway (para.31(1) of Sched.12 to the new Act).

**10.7.35**    Once again regulations are likely to prescribe conditions as to when such an application can be made (para.31(2) of Sched.12 to the new Act).

**10.7.36**    The regulations may be more flexible in relation to enforcement on a highway as there is less danger of breaching someone's human rights, as such force would not involve an intrusion into a domestic residence (it may be that the conditions are more relaxed than those which apply to applications to use reasonable force to obtain entry into other premises).

## 10.8    THE PROCESS OF TAKING CONTROL

### Time of day

*Pre-Act position*

**10.8.1**    The general common law is that distress should not occur between sunset and sunrise. This has been a longstanding principle in relation to distress for rent. It leaves enforcement agents in a weak position in relation to businesses which operate only at night.

> Bailiff's example
>
> When I attempted to execute a warrant against a nightclub this involved monitoring the business for several nights to establish whether the club was ever open after sunrise. At first it appeared that we would be unable to enforce the warrant because the club always shut before sunrise. After much persistence we established that they had applied for a late licence for a particular event and on that evening the club was still operating (clearing up after the night before at 6.30am the next morning. This was after sunrise and we then levied.

*New Act position*

**10.8.2**    Paragraph 13(3) of Sched.12 provides that regulations will make provision determining the time when control is taken. In addition, para.25(1) of Sched.12 provides that the regulations will set prescribed times of the day when an enforcement agent may enter and remain on the premises. The regulations are likely to provide a right to make an application to the court to remain on the premises or enter the premises at other times.

**10.8.3**    In the consultation process there has been some debate as to whether the sunset and sunrise rule should be replaced by a more generalised rule allowing reasonable times. Others have suggested fixed times be used. Various organisations have made suggestions:

- Association of Certified Enforcement Agents and the Inland Revenue: 6.00am to 9.00pm;
- the Sheriff's Association and the Under Sheriff's Association: 7.00am to 10.00pm;
- Money Advice Association: 8.00am to 5.00pm.

**10.8.4**    The regulations may create a distinction between residential and commercial premises. In principle there is no reason why a late night opening retail premises should be protected from enforcement whereas the argument would be stronger in relation to a domestic premises. The recommendation made in the

*Independent Review of Bailiff Law* report produced for the Lord Chancellor in June 2000 recommended fixed times between 8.00am and 8.00pm to commence the process and allowing the process to continue after hours until the levy was completed.

**10.8.5**    The rules are also likely to prohibit distress on certain public and religious holidays and perhaps Sundays. Once again there is a case for a different rule in relation to the position for businesses and commercial premises as opposed to residential premises.

## 10.9   HOW GOODS MAY BE TAKEN UNDER CONTROL

### Pre-Act position

**10.9.1**    In order to take control there must be a seizure of goods (*Evans* v. *South Ribble Borough Council* [1992] 2 All ER 695). The seizure may be actual or constructive:

- a seizure is deemed actual if the enforcement agent physically touches an item and specifically identifies an item and expressly declares that item seized;
- constructive seizure depends on the circumstances, the enforcement agent must see an item and make it clear that the item has been seized.

Bailiff's example

In practice an enforcement agent will not physically touch or control each and every item which is subject to the distress. The process is often done by way of summarising broad categories and informing either the debtor/tenant what has been distrained upon. Accordingly a constructive seizure may take place by the enforcement agent entering the premises and walking around them and leaving notice that certain identified goods have been seized. But it is bad practice to simply declare that the contents of a building have been seized without a proper inspection and assessment taking place, in fact unless a clear inventory is created after an inspection then the distress will fail.

**10.9.2**    In the case of *Lloyds and Scottish Finance* v. *Modern Cars and Caravans (Kingston)* [1964] 1 QB 764 it was held that the act of preventing the removal of an article from a property may amount to a seizure but the position must be clear.

**10.9.3**    However, no seizure can take place without an entry into the premises. (Although see the case of *Evans* v. *South Ribble Borough Council* [1992] 2 All ER 695 where a seizure was allowed even though no entry was achieved.)

### New Act position

**10.9.4**    In order to take control of the goods an enforcement agent must do one of the following (para.13 of Sched.12):

- secure the goods on the premises where they are found;
- if the goods are on a highway to secure them on the highway where he finds them or within a reasonable distance;
- remove the goods and secure them elsewhere;
- enter into a controlled goods agreement with the debtor.

10.9.5    The provisions which govern how these steps can be taken to secure goods are dealt with below.

10.9.6    The emphasis provided by the new Act is 'securing' or 'removing' goods rather than 'seizure'. The word removal self-evidently requires the goods to be uplifted. The concept of securing suggests that the idea of a constructive seizure will not be enough to demonstrate that control has been taken.

10.9.7    The regulations may make further provision about how goods are to be taken into control. The regulations are likely to set conditions which will prohibit certain uses of the goods subject to the seizure. The regulations may stipulate what amounts to an actual securing of the goods and may make some provision for securing in a way which is equivalent to a constructive seizure. However it is more likely that the industry practice of enforcement in this way will be consigned to history (*Cramer* v. *Mott* (1870) LR 5 QB 357).

## 10.10    NOTICES AND INVENTORY

### Inventory

10.10.1    The position under the new Act is unchanged. Under para.34 of Sched.12 if an enforcement agent takes control of goods he must provide the debtor with an inventory of the goods. This is often provided as soon as the enforcement takes effect; it is part of the process. The enforcement agent will typically list the goods as he decides what is to seized. However the requirement under para.34 is that the inventory must be provided 'as soon as reasonably practicable'.

10.10.2    The regulations will state the form and contents of the inventory.

### Notices

10.10.3    During the process the enforcement agent must serve the following notices at the following times:

- Notice warning of enforcement before process is commenced under para.7 (see 10.4).
- List of goods taken away under para.29. This is different to the inventory and is designed to give notice to other occupiers of the premises (in occupation with the debtor) as to what has been taken. The list must be left at the premises.

- Notice giving information as to the process under para.28 after entering the premises. Notice to be served by:

  - giving it to the debtor at the time of enforcement, if he is there; or
  - leaving the notice in a conspicuous place on the premises (in a sealed envelope addressed to the debtor).

- Notice under para.33 to the debtor giving information in relation to any goods taken on the highway. The notice is to be served:

  - if the debtor is there, giving it to the debtor at the time of enforcement, if he is there; or
  - delivering the notice to the debtor's premises (in a sealed envelope addressed to the debtor).

- Sale notice under para.40 giving the date, time and place of sale (see **11.3**).

## 10.11    IMPOUNDING

### Pre-Act position

**10.11.1**    At common law goods could be impounded on the premises or taken away and kept in a pound elsewhere. A pound is effectively a secure safe or prison for the goods. Goods are only 'impounded or otherwise secured' if it is a distinct act such as appointing a security guard to keep the goods in close possession on the premises or entering into agreement with the debtor (walking possession agreement – now replaced by a controlled goods agreement – see below).

**10.11.2**    The act of impounding goods on the debtor's premises does not give a landlord the right to require keys to the premises or have possession of the premises (*Planned Properties* v. *Ramsdens Commercials* (1984) *The Times*, 2 March). The use of CRAR by keeping the goods in close possession on the premises has to complement the tenant's right to possession and enjoyment of the demised premises. The tenancy still continues. The landlord cannot simultaneously exercise CRAR and forfeit. CRAR would be a waiver of the right to forfeit (on the ground of rent arrears which is a 'once and for all' breach). Therefore the tenant must be allowed usual access to the building and permitted to use the premises so far as this does not interfere with the pound.

**10.11.3**    If the goods are wrongfully removed from the pound (without the enforcement agent's consent) then the debtor may have committed pound breach (see **12.5.1** relating to pound breach and rescue). This principle also applied where goods were removed wrongfully after a walking possession agreement ('pound breach').

## The new Act position

**10.11.4**    The position is broadly the same under the new Act. The regulations may have an impact on this but no radical changes are expected.

**10.11.5**    In order to take control of the goods an enforcement agent must either secure the goods or remove the goods or enter into a controlled goods agreement (see **10.12**). Accordingly the goods can still be secured on the premises or removed and secured else where.

**10.11.6**    Paragraph 35 of Sched.12 provides that:

> An enforcement agent must take reasonable care of controlled goods that he removes from the premises or highway where he finds them.

**10.11.7**    Although pound breach has been abolished, if the debtor interferes with the process or the secured goods he commits an offence under para.68 of Sched.12 (see below).

## 10.12    CONTROLLED GOODS AGREEMENTS

### Pre-Act position

**10.12.1**    Perhaps the most common form of seizure under the current regime is by way of a walking possession agreement. This is where the enforcement agent and the debtor enter into a formal agreement not to remove seized goods from the premises in consideration for the enforcement agent not leaving a security guard in close possession. This reduced the expense of the process and also reduces the cost to the debtor. The Distress for Rent Rules 1988 prescribe a form for walking possession (form 9) whereby the debtor promises to:

- pay the enforcement agent's fees;
- allow the enforcement agent to re-enter; and
- not to interfere with, sell or remove the goods and respect the fact that the goods have been impounded on the premises.

However, form 9 is not compulsory. An agreement can be reached orally and providing it can be properly evidenced it is enforceable.

**10.12.2**    Once the goods have been properly impounded in the premises, sub- ject to a walking possession agreement, the enforcement agent is not entitled to use force to re-enter the premises unless there had been a deliberate exclusion. In other words, force could be used where the debtor/tenant had deliberately locked the bailiff out of the premises to try to defeat the distress (*Khazanchi* v. *Faircharm Investment* [1998] 1 WLR 1603).

**10.12.3**    Accordingly enforcement agents acting prudently would notify the debtor/tenant that they intend to come back to the premises at a specified time and date in order to collect the goods or inspect the goods which had been distrained upon.

**10.12.4**   It was in this limited circumstance where there had been an intentional lockout by the debtor that reasonable force could be contemplated. This has now been reviewed and codified by the Act (see **10.8** above).

## The new Act position

**10.12.5**   Walking possession agreements have been replaced by controlled goods agreements. A controlled goods agreement pursuant to para.13(4) of Sched.12 is an agreement between the debtor and enforcement agent whereby the debtor:

- is permitted to retain custody of the goods;
- acknowledges that the enforcement agent is taking control of them; and
- agrees not to remove or dispose of them, nor to permit anyone else to, before the debt is paid.

**10.12.6**   A controlled goods agreement is essentially a compromise. The enforcement agent agrees that the debtor can retain possession of the goods without a security guard being left to guard them. In return the debtor undertakes not to remove the goods (or allow another to remove them) and agrees that the enforcement agent may return at a later time to complete the enforcement process.

**10.12.7**   Under the current system there is a degree of tolerance in the system in that an informal walking possession can be created by oral agreement. Provided the consent of the debtor has been obtained, it is not strictly necessary for a formal written walking possession agreement on form 9 to be completed (*McLeod* v. *Butterwick* [1996] 1 WLR 995).

**10.12.8**   Although the regulations may require a formal prescribed form of a controlled goods agreement this degree of tolerance is replicated. Paragraph 13 merely requires an agreement to be reached. Naturally it will be in the enforcement agent's best interest to ensure that the terms of the agreement are clear and, of course, the best way of achieving this will be by way of some form of agreement in writing.

**10.12.9**   Where there is a controlled goods agreement, then whilst this is effective against the debtor, it is unlikely to bind a third party who is not aware that the goods have been impounded (*Abingdon RDV* v. *O'Gorman* [1968] 2 QB 811) (see **12.2**).

# 11

# BETWEEN SEIZURE AND SALE

## 11.1 CARE OF GOODS REMOVED

### Pre-Act position

**11.1.1** An enforcement agent is in the position of being a bailee of the goods which have been seized. As such he owes a duty of care. This is limited by the circumstances. For example the duty under an arrangement of walking possession is less than the duty which arises to ensure that the goods (if uplifted) are impounded in a suitable place.

### The new Act position

**11.1.2** Under the new Act a statutory duty of care is imposed by para.35 of Sched. 12 in relation to the goods removed. The duty is to take reasonable care of controlled goods.

**11.1.3** The regulations may make detailed provision about how goods are to be kept.

## 11.2 VALUATION

### Pre-Act position

**11.2.1** Law of Distress Amendment Act 1888, s.5 allows an enforcement agent to sell goods without an appraisement or valuation. The debtor has a right under the Act to require an appraisement to take place prior to the sale. He must do this by making the request in writing.

### The new Act position

**11.2.2** Enforcement agents are now required by the new Act to obtain a valuation of the goods under their control. This valuation must take place before the sale takes place (i.e. prior to the expiry of the minimum period – see **11.3.8** below).

**11.2.3**   The debtor must also be given an opportunity to obtain an independent valuation. It is anticipated that this opportunity will be notified to the debtor as part of the process giving notice of sale (see **11.3.9** below).

## 11.3   SALE PROCESS

### Best price

#### *Pre-Act position*

**11.3.1**   It has been a long established principle that an enforcement agent has a duty to obtain the best price for the goods. This was set out in the Distress for Rent Act 1689. The best price has been held to be the best net proceeds of sale. This is not the same as the best-selling price. The focus on realising the best net proceeds prevents the enforcement agent from electing to use a very expensive sale process.

**11.3.2**   The fact that goods have been sold at public auction does not automatically mean the best price has been obtained (*Khazanchi* v. *Faircharm Investments* [1998] 1 WLR 1603). The enforcement agent has to show the auction has been properly advertised and conducted. If the goods are of a specialist nature, then the enforcement agent should take advice from an appropriate person in relation to the valuation and manner of sale (*American Express* v. *Hurley* [1985] 3 All ER 564).

#### *The new Act position*

**11.3.3**   Under para.37 of Sched.12 to the new Act, an enforcement agent must sell or dispose of the goods 'for the best price that can be reasonably obtained in accordance with this Schedule'. Accordingly, the position is relatively unchanged, and the old case law illustrates how this provision is likely to be interpreted.

### Time of sale

#### *Pre-Act position*

**11.3.4**   Enforcement agents levying distress for rent cannot sell the goods distrained upon for at least five days after seizure. The period is calculated not counting the day the distress commences or the day of sale (Distress for Rent Act 1689).

**11.3.5**   This time was designed to allow the debtor/tenant time to pay the sum due and 'replevy' the goods (i.e. free from distress). However, the debtor has a statutory right to request, in writing, an extension of this right to 15 days. If this is the case, then the enforcement agent cannot sell for this prolonged period. If the enforcement agent breaches this rule, then it does not automatically result in a liability for damages. The debtor would have to demonstrate loss (e.g. the goods had been sold at an undervalue) (*Rodgers v. Parker* [1856]).

**11.3.6**   There is no requirement for landlords to give notice of a sale.

**11.3.7**   In the county court the court will notify the debtor of the sale giving at least four days' notice. The notice states the date, time and place of the sale (County Court Rules (CCR) Order 26, r.12).

## The new Act position

**11.3.8**   The new Act creates a minimum period for which the goods are required to be held prior to an enforcement sale (para.39). This period can be shortened with the consent of the debtor (and any co-owner).

**11.3.9**   Before the sale takes place, the enforcement agent must give a notice under para.40 providing the date, time and place of the sale.

**11.3.10**   The regulations must state (NB the regulations are required to do this):

■   the minimum period of the notice;
■   the form of the notice;
■   what the notice must contain;
■   how the notice must be given.

**11.3.11**   If the arrangements for the sale are changed then there will be prescribed circumstances where the para.40 notice can be replaced with another notice.

**11.3.12**   The notice must be given within 12 months beginning with the day on which control was taken over the goods, although the creditor and debtor can agree in writing to extend the period (para.40). This constitutes the permitted period for the sale. If a sale has not taken place within the permitted period then the enforcement process may be deemed to have been abandoned (see **11.6** below).

## Manner of sale

### Pre-Act position

**11.3.13**   As set out in **11.3.1**, enforcement agents have a duty to obtain the best price. They do not have to achieve this necessarily through a public auction, although the position varies:

■   High Court: the general rule is that sales take place in a public auction but an enforcement agent can apply to the court for an order that a sale by private treaty takes place under Rules of Supreme Court (RSC) Order 47, r.6. An application for permission would have to set out the grounds relied on. This could include:

- the goods being of a rare or specialist nature;
- there is a special buyer who is offering a high price for a speedy transaction;
- the goods are of a perishable nature (but see exempt goods at 9.5.8).

- County court: the position is similar to the High Court under CCR Order 26, r.15.
- Distress: there is no requirement, however the enforcement agent's duty to realise the best price prevails.

### The new Act position

**11.3.14**   Under para.41 of Sched.12, the sale must be by public auction. However, like the current High Court process the enforcement agent can apply for the court's permission to sell in a different way. The court will not make an order until notice has been given to other creditors who have an enforcement power.

**11.3.15**   Notice would have to be given to a landlord if a para.7 notice had been served (see 10.4).

**11.3.16**   The regulations are likely to make further provision about the manner of sale including:

- advertising;
- conduct of the sale;
- types of sale the court may order.

### Place of sale

**11.3.17**   Under paras.43–6 of Sched.12, the sale can take place:

- on the premises where the goods were found (with the occupier's consent);
- at any other place permitted by the regulations (likely to be a recognised public auction property).

## 11.4    APPLICATION OF SALE PROCEEDS

**11.4.1**   Under para.50 of Sched.12, once the sale has taken place then the enforcement agent must distribute the proceeds and make payments in the following priority:

- the amount outstanding (para.50(1)): this is the amount of the debt, interest, and costs (under para.62); then,
- any surplus must first be used to pay a co-owner (his share proportionate to his interest); then,
- the debtor.

**11.4.2**  The regulations will set out the procedure for resolving a dispute between the co-owner and the debtor as to what their respective entitlement should be.

## 11.5  PASSING OF TITLE

**11.5.1**  The enforcement agent can give good title to a purchaser unless:

- the purchaser, the creditor or the enforcement agent has notice that the goods are not the debtor's at the time of sale; or
- a lawful claimant has made a claim to the court claiming title.

**11.5.2**  This does not apply to a third party who has acquired his interest whilst the goods have been bound under paras.4 and 5 of Sched.12.

**11.5.3**  This provision is contained in para.51. It does not protect an innocent purchaser who acquired an interest for value, without notice of the enforcement (see 10.3.6). Under this provision, the third party lawful claimant must have acquired his interest prior to the goods being bound by the effect of para.4.

## 11.6  ABANDONMENT OF GOODS

**11.6.1**  As set out in 11.3.12 above the enforcement agent has a permitted period of 12 months to serve a notice under para.40 giving the date, time and place of sale to the debtor and any co-owner. This period may be extended pursuant to para.40(5).

**11.6.2**  However, if no notice is served in the permitted period (including extensions) then the controlled goods are deemed to be abandoned by the enforcement agent (para.52).

**11.6.3**  If the controlled goods are abandoned, then the enforcement power ceases to be exercisable. Where the enforcement agent has removed the goods from the debtor's premises, then they must be made available for collection by the debtor (or co-owner). There is no obligation on the enforcement agent to deliver the goods back to the debtor or co-owner. If the goods are uncollected, then the regulations may make provision about how the enforcement agent can dispose of the goods after the end of the permitted period.

### Torts (Interference with Goods) Act 1977

**11.6.4**  After the statutory abandonment takes place the enforcement agent will be in the position of being a bailee of the goods until the debtor collects them. At this point as an, involuntarily, the enforcement agent will still owe a duty of care for the safe custody of the goods. However the enforcement agent can fall back on the protection of the Torts (Interference with Goods) Act 1977. Under s.12 of the Act an involuntary bailee can discharge this duty of care by serving a notice on the owner of goods. The notice invites the owner to collect the goods within a reasonable time after which the bailee has the right to sell or dispose of the goods pursuant to the Act.

Enforcement agent example

One of the difficulties with the s.12 process is that sometimes the whereabouts of the owner are unknown and therefore it is not possible to serve the notice. There have been examples in the industry where this has led to a significant burden. For example, a well known tobacco company sold a batch of high quality cigars for personal use to a wealthy private individual for a sum in excess of £200,000. The purchaser paid the amount due, requested that the company store the goods and then was never heard from again. I advised about the disposal of the goods. However we had no address for service. We eventually had to seek redress from the court so that the cigars could be disposed of. The costs of storage of such items quickly becomes a burden on the bailee and the Act is effectively deficient in prescribing a remedy in those circumstances.

**11.6.5**   Where there has been an abandonment of goods by the enforcement agent if he remains in possession then he is under a duty of care in relation to the goods.

## Where sale does not take place

**11.6.6**   If an enforcement agent does serve a para.40 notice within the permitted period, but the goods remain unsold after the sale process, then once again the goods are automatically deemed abandoned. At first glance this appears to be a very harsh rule, which will create a significant operational problem:

- the enforcement agent is obliged to sell the goods at the best price (see **11.3.3** above and para.37);
- in order to demonstrate that the best price is obtained in an auction, the enforcement agent is likely to want to sell subject to a reserve price. Accordingly it would seem sensible that the sale would take place subject to a floor, below which the sale price can not fall. The enforcement agent is likely to want to target the reserve price within a spectrum of what may be considered to be a reasonably obtainable best price. However, if a reserve price is set and the goods are not sold, then they are deemed automatically abandoned.

**11.6.7**   Where the enforcement power arose under a writ or warrant, the abandonment does not stop the enforcement agent from issuing a further writ or warrant. Accordingly, in the High Court and county court this problem may be resolved by the judgment creditor expeditiously commencing the procedure afresh.

**11.6.8**   If there are circumstances where a reserve price has been utilised it may be prudent for the judgment creditor to have prepared and the application forms ready to go, to put fresh enforcement proceedings in place so that the enforcement agent can take control again of the goods if the sale fails.

**11.6.9**   Commercial landlords do not expressly have this right. Schedule 12 is silent as to whether a landlord's enforcement agent could simply re-open the CRAR process and take back control of the goods on the failure of the sale. These problems are unlikely to be resolved by the regulations. Paragraphs 52–4 of Sched.12 indicate that the regulations may prescribe further circumstances where abandonment takes place. The indication is that abandonment may take place on occasions which are additional to the ones already specified in Sched.12.

**11.6.10**   In relation to abandonment of securities, see **11.10.14**.

## 11.7   PAYMENT OF AMOUNTS OUTSTANDING – TENDER

### Pre-Act position

**11.7.1**   The general principle in all current forms of distress is that the payment of the debt and costs will bring the enforcement process to an end. However, under the current regimes, there is a variance as to the requirement to pay costs. The debtor needs to know whether the costs of enforcement should be paid, in addition to the principal amount.

**11.7.2**   Generally speaking, the debtor is only liable to pay the principal amount due before an entry to the premises has been made. Where payment is made after entry to bring the enforcement to an end, the debtor must also pay a sum towards the costs (incurred by the time the debtor tenders payment). The position is set out across the different statutory regimes including:

■   Section 54(11) of the Magistrates' Court Rules 1981 states that:

> if any person pays or tenders to the constable or other person charged with the execution of [the warrant] . . . the sum mentioned in the warrant . . . and also pays the amount of the costs and charges of the distress up to the time of the payment or tender . . . the constable or other person [charged with the execution of the warrant] shall not execute the warrant or shall cease to execute it.

■   Regulation 14 of the Non-Domestic Rating (Collection and Enforcement) (Local List) Regulations 1989 distinguishes between payment made or tendered before 'any goods are seized' and payment or tender 'where an authority has seized goods'. In the former 'the levy shall not be proceeded with' and in the latter 'the sale shall not be proceeded with and the goods shall be made available for collection to the debtor'.

**11.7.3**   From the debtor's perspective, he needs to know how much to pay in order to bring the enforcement to an end. This may be an easy calculation at certain stages of the process:

■   before entry;
■   immediate period after entry.

The enforcement agent is likely to know what costs have been incurred after entry and control has been effected but prior to the sale process being commenced.

**11.7.4**    However, the sum due is likely to be more difficult to ascertain if the debtor seeks to pay mid-process. Accordingly, if a debtor attempts to pay to bring the enforcement to an end whilst the enforcement agent is continuing, the amount of costs will be uncalculated. The costs will only be known after the enforcement agent (having started the process) has concluded the process of inspecting the stock, compiling an inventory and attempting to establish whether the goods need to be removed. At this stage it will be difficult to provide the debtor with a precise figure in relation to costs.

## The new Act position

**11.7.5**    In the *Independent Review of Enforcement Agent Law* (Prof J Beatson QC, June 2000). The recommendation was that the legislation:

> Should provide that the [distraint] should cease if the debtor tenders the amount owed and the costs either before the distrainer takes legal control of the goods (the replacement proposed for seizure and impounding) or at any time before sale save during the process of taking legal control or removing the goods for the premises.

**11.7.6**    Paragraph 58 of Sched.12 deals with this issue by stating that if the debtor pays:

> the amount outstanding in full . . . after the enforcement agent has taken control of the goods and . . . before they are sold or abandoned [then] . . . no further step may be taken under the enforcement power concerned.

Accordingly the debtor must pay the *amount outstanding* which is calculated in accordance with the definition in para.50(3), which provides that the amount outstanding is the amount of the debt which remains unpaid together with costs.

**11.7.7**    This provision does not give the debtor the right to make payment at any time. However the debtor will have the right to pay the amount outstanding and bring the process to an end:

■    In all enforcement, the debtor has the right to pay during the period of the warning notice served pursuant to para.7 of Sched.12 which gives a minimum period of notice (the prescribed period). So during the prescribed period the debtor must pay:

  –    In relation to CRAR, a sum so as to bring the amount outstanding to below the minimum amount of outstanding rent (to include a payment for costs if that is necessary to bring the amount outstanding to a sum which is below the minimum amount). This arises if the debtor [is] a commercial tenant and makes payment to reduce the amount of unpaid rent to below the minimum amount (as provided by s.77). If the amount

outstanding is less than the minimum amount, then the right to exercise CRAR will be removed.
- In relation to all other enforcement, the full amount outstanding (i.e. a figure which includes costs).
- The debtor has the right to pay the amount outstanding in full and bring the process to an end (under para.58).
- After the enforcement agent has taken control of goods.
- Before they are sold or abandoned (see paras.40 and 52).

**11.7.8**   If a tender is made pursuant to para.58, then no further step can be taken under the enforcement power concerned and the controlled goods must be made available for collection by the debtor (Sched.12, para.58(2)).

**11.7.9**   If the enforcement agent has seized money, then the debtor is to be given credit for this in relation to payment of the amount outstanding which will be reduced accordingly (Sched.12, para.58(4)).

**11.7.10**   However, if the enforcement agent does not have notice that payment has been made by the debtor he is not liable for any further steps taken, even where the amount has been paid in full (Sched.12, para.59(2)).

**11.7.11**   Accordingly, an enforcement agent acting without notice can sell and pass good title to a purchaser even where an amount outstanding has been paid. However, if either the purchaser or the enforcement agent were on notice, or would have found out about the payment if reasonable enquiries had been made, then this position is reversed and the enforcement agent may be liable and good title will not have passed.

**11.7.12**   Where the enforcement agent has innocently sold the goods without notice that the debtor has paid the creditor, then the debtor may have a claim against the creditor. Where the creditor has been paid the amount outstanding in full then he may be liable if he fails to notify the enforcement agent of the position and further steps are taken. Paragraph 58(6) of Sched.12 expressly reserves the right of a debtor or any co-owner to any remedy they may enjoy against any other person (including the creditor) or any related party.

## 11.8   COSTS

### Pre-Act position

**11.8.1**   There is currently a degree of inconsistency as to the circumstances where enforcement agents are able to recover their costs and charge fees and as to the amount which may be charged to the debtor. In the High Court, the judgment creditor is able to:

> Levy the poundage, fees and expenses of execution over and above the sum recovered and the High Court enforcement officer has a right to recover the amount

incurred in securing the goods even where a sale does not take place (*Mortimer* v. *Cragg* [1978] 3 CPD 216).

**11.8.2**    An enforcement officer is entitled to a percentage of the money recovered where he has actually obtained the money through the enforcement process (*Re Leadmore* [1884] 13 QBD 415, 417). If the judgment is set aside then the enforcement officer is not allowed to make a sale of the seized goods in respect of his fees and costs. If the debtor makes an application for a stay of execution then the court can order that the enforcement process be frozen and make provision as to what will happen in relation to costs.

**11.8.3**    However, if the debtor tenders the money prior to the enforcement officer making his sale then the costs incurred by the enforcement officer are still payable by the debtor. This principle was enunciated by Lord Lindley MR in *Re Thomas* [1899] 1 QB 460, 462:

> The sheriff has seized no doubt but he has not sold. It has been by law settled for years that he is not entitled to poundage. I am aware there has been a qualification on that where the sheriff has seized but has not sold in consequence of a compromise between the parties; there the law regards him as having secured the money for the creditor and gives him poundage.

**11.8.4**    In the law of distress the level and amount of costs recoverable by an enforcement agent is prescribed by the Distress for Rent Rules 1988. This sets out table of costs recoverable in different situations.

## The new Act position

**11.8.5**    Paragraph 62 of Sched.12 deals with the issue of costs of enforcement. The amount recoverable will be calculated on the same basis whether the process is High Court, county court, magistrates' court or CRAR.

**11.8.6**    The new Act contains no details and this has been wholly reserved to the regulations. The regulations will make provision for the assessment of costs, fee scales and which amounts can be recovered from the proceeds of sale. The regulations will govern costs in relation to all enforcement related services. This will include anything done under or in connection with an enforcement power or any services used in accordance with Sched.12.

**11.8.7**    The White Paper *Effective Enforcement,* published in March 2003, put forward 10 recommendations in relation to costs. The recommendations were designed to balance fairly the twin objectives of:

- rewarding enforcement agents for their work; and
- ensuring that costs are proportionate and affordable by the debtor.

**11.8.8**    *Effective Enforcement* recommended principles be set for costs to be enshrined within the primary legislation. This has not happened. The Act relies almost exclusively on what the regulations would contain in relation to all issues of costs. However, the regulations are likely to adopt the recommendations which included (White Paper: *Effective Enforcement*, March 2003, p.54):

1.  There should be an up-front fee payable by the creditor to initiate the enforcement action (this may be a fixed fee or one which is negotiated within a prescribed band).
2.  The initial payments should cover all initial actions up to the act of entrance and seizure.
3.  The initial fee should be recoverable from the debtor when enforcement is successful [this is perhaps unfair if the enforcement is unsuccessful].

    [The up-front fee is to include taking up the case, setting up of a file, the use of licensed and reputable enforcement staff, initial actions or investigations which may lead to the provision of a probability report to be supplied by the agent to the creditor indicating the likelihood of debt recovery.]

4.  Following the up-front fee, the preparation of an initial action report that covers a range of activities that may be undertaken by the enforcement agent for which fixed fees would be charged for the following actions:

    –   enquiries;
    –   letter;
    –   visit;
    –   securing goods (including levy, seizure, walking and closed possession).

5.  Fees for the following activities would not be fixed and might include charges to cover hourly attendance rates by enforcement agents. Enforcement agents would be required to inform the debtor at an early stage of the fees for these activities (to be monitored by a future regulatory body):

    –   removal;
    –   storage;
    –   valuation;
    –   auction.

6.  There would be no fixed abortive removal visit fee.
7.  Enforcement agents should be able to charge a fee for establishing and administering a repayment plan. This fee, which should be proportionate to the size of the debt, would be recoverable from the debtor.
8.  The fees for enforcing the judgment of a large amount (which exceeds a threshold to be determined by the regulator) would be negotiable between the creditor and the enforcement agent.
9.  Any future regulatory body charged with the responsibility of advising the Lord Chancellor on a detailed fee structure would have investigative powers to obtain any relevant information they require from those providing enforcement services.

## 11.9    LIMITATION OF LIABILITY FOR SALE OR PAYMENT OF PROCEEDS

### Re-entry and second distress

*Second distress*

**11.9.1**    Under the law of distress, a landlord cannot undertake a second distress save for in exceptional circumstances.

**11.9.2**    However, there is no restriction in Sched.12 preventing an enforcement agent (including where CRAR is being exercised) from returning to the relevant premises and seizing more goods. This may happen where the enforcement agent receives intelligence that the debtor has further goods on the premises which were not there originally.

*Re-entry*

**11.9.3**    Paragraph 16 of Sched.12 authorises an enforcement agent to re-enter the premises to inspect goods or remove them to storage or sale. This right applies where goods have been taken control of and have not been removed by the enforcement agent (see 10.7 in relation to the circumstances when an enforcement agent can use reasonable force in relation to a re-entry).

## 11.10    GOODS ON THE HIGHWAY

**11.10.1**    Schedule 12 allows all enforcement agents (even those exercising CRAR) to seize goods on a highway. This broadens the existing regime. In the consultation process to the new Act, there was some debate as to whether enforcement agents would be able to use wheel clamps in relation to vehicles parked on a highway. Schedule 12 does not give an express power to use wheel clamping. However, if a person is lawfully entitled to seize and impound a vehicle then use of clamps would surely flow from this right in any event. It is also possible to seize goods situate on a highway (presumably when inside a vehicle).

**11.10.2**    It may be necessary to use force to break open a vehicle and seize goods contained within it. The question arises where a vehicle is seized together with the goods inside as a job lot. In that circumstance arguably reasonable force is not being used to seize the goods (which can take place without force).

**11.10.3**    Under para.35 of Sched.12, an enforcement agent must take reasonable care of the control of goods that he removes from the premises or highway where he finds them. Having seized the vehicle (with goods inside) it might be then reasonable under para.35 to use force to break open the vehicle to inspect and deal with the goods inside. The reasonableness may depend upon whether the debtor has refused to provide keys to the vehicle and whether it is necessary to open the vehicle to inspect, appraise and sell the goods. Where, for example, the goods are perishables, this would be an easier case to maintain.

**11.10.4**   However, there may be circumstances where reasonable force is required in the actual seizure of the vehicle. In this case an application to use force can be made to the court under para.31. The application must satisfy the prescribed conditions which will be set by the regulations. Any power or authority to use force will not include a power to use force against persons (although the regulations may alter this principle).

**11.10.5**   Perhaps strangely, there is no general power to use force to seize goods on a highway (unlike the limited circumstances where there is a general power to enter premises under paras.17–19). The court may require a constable to assist an enforcement agent to execute it when using reasonable force (Sched.12, para.31(4)).

## Time of enforcement on highway

**11.10.6**   The regulations will prescribe fixed times of the day (and perhaps days of the year) when goods can be seized on a highway. The times prescribed are likely to be in line with the times prescribed by the rules in relation to when an enforcement agent can enter a building to take control of goods. Any such restriction will be subject to the right of the enforcement agent to make an application to seize goods on the highway at other times, provided grounds can be shown that this is the only way of obtaining control (Sched.12, para.32(2)).

**11.10.7**   Where goods are left in a vehicle on a highway, there is obviously a greater danger that the debtor will not be aware that the goods have been taken control of. Accordingly, para.33 of Sched.12 obliges the enforcement agent to provide a notice to the debtor giving information about what he is doing. The form and content of the notice will be prescribed by the regulations. The enforcement agent must have a copy of a notice with him at the time that enforcement takes place. This is because if the debtor is there then the enforcement agent is obliged to give him the notice there and then.

## The holding and disposal of securities

**11.10.8**   The word 'securities' is given a statutory definition in Part 1 of Sched.12 as follows:

> 'Securities' includes bills of exchange, promissory notes, bonds, specialties and securities for money.

**11.10.9**   In the High Court and county court there is currently authorisation for enforcement agents to seize securities (as defined by Courts Act 2003, Sched.7, para.9 and County Courts Act 1984, s.89). Securities are defined in broadly the same way under Sched.12 to the new Act. The new statutory provision authorising the seizure of money, bank notes, bills of exchange, promissory notes, bonds, specialties and securities for money, now extends to all forms of enforcement (including enforcement on behalf of commercial landlords). However, the White Paper *Effective Enforcement* (March 2003) recognised that dedicated specific training was necessary to ensure that those taking legal control of securities were fully aware of the need firstly to recognise the true value of such items and secondly, to recognise that some debtors are in a vulnerable position. The suggestion is that an enforcement agent will only be given permission to seize securities if they are qualified and experienced in that kind of enforcement (White Paper: *Effective Enforcement* March 2003, para.172).

**11.10.10**    Accordingly, the regulations are likely to make this a requirement for enforcement agents contemplating taking control of securities. However, where an enforcement agent is permitted to take control of securities, then they will be able:

- to dispose of the security;
- to realise the sums secured or that are payable to the debtor under the security;
- to take action (including the ability to issue proceedings) for the recovery of those sums; or
- to assign the right to sue for their recovery.

**11.10.11**    In this regard not only the enforcement agent but also the creditor may sue in the name of the debtor or in the name of any person in whose name the debtor might have been sued for the recovery of any sums secured or made payable. This is obviously subject to payment being due under the terms of the security.

**11.10.12**    However, before this action is taken, a notice must be served on the debtor, pursuant to para.49 of Sched.12 to inform him that this action is being taken. The debtor will be entitled to receive a minimum period of notice. The period together with the form of content of the notice will be prescribed by the regulations (para.49 of Sched.12 to the new Act).

**11.10.13**    In line with the principles regarding sale of goods, a para.49 notice must be served within 12 months of the securities being taken control of. This period may be extended by agreement. Any such agreement must be in writing (para.49(6) of Sched.12 to the new Act). An unlimited number of extensions is permitted.

## Abandonment of securities

**11.10.14**    If a para.49 notice has not been served on the debtor within the permitted period (or on any co-owner), then securities will be automatically abandoned. In addition to this, the securities will be abandoned if, following a para.49 notice of disposal, the disposal does not actually take place. Further instances of abandonment may be specified by the regulations (para.56 of Sched.12 to the new Act).

**11.10.15**    The effect of the abandonment is comparable to the effect of abandonment of goods other than securities under paras.52–4 of Sched.12. If there has been abandonment the enforcement power ceases to be exercisable and the securities must be made available for collection. Naturally the securities will be in paper form and therefore the potential problems of storage pending collection may not be as onerous as the position which arises in relation to the abandonment of goods. However, the enforcement agent might once again find himself in the position of being an involuntary bailee with a limited duty of care (see **11.6** in relation to abandonment of goods).

**11.10.16**    The regulations may make provision for this potential liability. One problem which is likely to arise in relation to securities is whether the enforcement agent will be responsible for bringing action before the expiry of any limitation periods in relation to the recoverability of sums under the securities. Where the limitation period expires during the period of control (or abandonment prior to the debtor collecting the security) compliance will fall within the enforcement agent's duty of care.

**11.10.17**    The regulations are likely to regulate the position carefully in relation to securities. This is presumably why they are dealt with in separation statutory provisions in Sched.12. Although securities form part of the definition of 'goods' they are dealt with in a distinct way. In accordance with this principle, the new Act makes provision for a distinct set of regulations to be set to regulate their control and disposal.

# 12 LIABILITY AND REMEDIES

## 12.1 INTRODUCTION

**12.1.1** The enforcement industry currently deals with the complaint process largely through applications to the court. The majority of the complaints relating to enforcement agents stem from the issue of fees and costs. The consultation process identified a general feeling that some enforcement agents do not give a clear message to the debtor as to their right to information about the process. The National Association of Citizens Advice Bureaux reported:

> . . . the complexity of the current system not only perpetuates the potential for genuine mistakes but also provides the perfect environment for the unscrupulous in the sector to break the rules without any real fear of challenge or correction . . . However, CAB experience suggests that bailiffs are not good at informing people clearly about the processes they are carrying out or about their individual situation – how much they have paid, how much they still owe, and how the amounts for costs have been made up. In some cases this may be due to administrative procedures . . . some firms of bailiffs may have a deliberate policy of non co-operation with debtors . . .
>
> Undue Distress – NACAB

**12.1.2** Many of the complaints which are made relate to over-charging fees which are not appropriate (e.g. van charges where the goods are not uplifted and the bailiff took walking possession). Once a new regulatory body is in place (whether this is the SIA or otherwise) then this will be empowered to deal with complaints. However, where the enforcement is illegal a complaint through the court process might still be the preferred option. In relation to the complaint process there will be a number of options:

- a complaint in relation to an enforcement agent's certificate (currently made to the county court through the Distress for Rent Rules 1988 and as to the new Act position see **Chapter 6**);
- a challenge to the validity of the enforcement process either through the provisions of Sched.12 or through an action for trespass.

**12.1.3**    This chapter deals with the remedies available to the parties arising from the Sched.12 process.

## 12.2    THIRD PARTY CLAIMING GOODS

### Pre-Act position

#### *Landlords*

**12.2.1**    As set out in 9.4, enforcement agents are generally not authorised to take control of third party goods. The most significant exceptions to this are the limited rights for landlords to levy distress against certain categories of third party. Landlords were able to levy distress against goods belonging to third parties at first instance. Thereafter some third parties had the right to serve a statutory declaration under Law of Distress Amendment Act 1908, s.1 claiming protection. However this protection was not available to closely connected parties (e.g. the husband or wife of the tenant, a business partner of the tenant, and a company where the tenant is a director (Law of Distress Amendment Act 1908, s.2(4))).

**12.2.2**    One important exception was that the protection given by the Law of Distress Amendment Act 1908 did not protect goods which were in the possession of the tenant with the consent of the true owner under circumstances where the tenant could be considered the reputed owner. Accordingly even where a third party seemingly fitted the description of one of the protected categories there was no protection if they had allowed the tenants use of the goods in circumstances where they could be considered the reputed owner. Where a third party has the protection of the 1908 Act then the Act sets out a procedure for the matter to be dealt with by the magistrates' court. If the landlord proceeds with the distress after receiving a valid declaration under s.1 of the 1908 Act then it is an illegal distress.

#### *Other creditors – interpleader*

**12.2.3**    Enforcement agents do not have the right to seize third party goods when acting for a judgment creditor.

**12.2.4**    If an enforcement agent inadvertently seizes goods belonging to a third party then the third party is able to give notice of his claim to the enforcement agent. The enforcement agent will then seek relief from the court through an interpleader application:

- in the High Court under Civil Procedure Rules (CPR) Schedule 1 (Rules of Supreme Court (RSC) Order 17); and
- in the county court under CPR Schedule 2 (County Court Rules (CCR) Order 33).

**12.2.5**    When the third party claim is received the High Court enforcement officer or county bailiff gives notice of the claim to the judgment creditor on whose behalf the goods were seized. This notice requires the judgment creditor to state whether he admits or disputes the claim. If the claim is admitted, the enforcement agent withdraws from possession of the goods which were the subject of the claim.

**12.2.6**   Where the creditor disputes the third party claim, the High Court enforcement officer, or county court bailiff, proceeds with the application to the court for interpleader relief. The court will give directions to the third party and the creditor for the disposal of the application.

## The new Act position

**12.2.7**   The Law of Distress Amendment Act 1908 has been abolished by the new Act and now third party claims are dealt with under a unified regime under Sched.12. The regime set out by para.60 of Sched.12 will also replace the rules on interpleader in the High Court and county court.

**12.2.8**   Under the new Act enforcement agents are only able to take control of goods which belong to the debtor (see 9.4). Accordingly where a third party claims the goods which were taken belong to him and not the debtor then he is able to make an application under para.60 of Sched.12.

### *Paragraph 60 procedure*

**12.2.9**   Once the application is made and notice is given to the enforcement agent the goods must not be sold or disposed of unless directed by the court (para.60(2) of Sched.12) in a way that is similar to the interpleader process the court may direct the enforcement agent to sell or dispose of the goods. However, the third party claimant may be required by the court to make required payments into court of:

(a)   An amount equal to the value of the goods or to a proportion of it as directed by the court.
(b)   Any amounts prescribed in respect of the enforcement agent's costs of retaining the goods.

**12.2.10**   This principle is designed to alleviate the problem which an enforcement agent sometimes finds, where a third party makes a claim in relation to goods and the enforcement agent is in an onerous position because the goods may have to be stored expensively for a protracted period of time. Sometimes the costs of storage become disproportionate to the value of the goods being held.

**12.2.11**   It would seem that making the required payment does not provide the third party with the right to recover the goods straight away. The required payment simply prevents the enforcement agent from making the sale. This may seem harsh in circumstances where the third party applicant is effectively paying the full value of the goods into court together with an amount in relation to costs.

**12.2.12** Even where a required payment has not been ordered the court may still direct the enforcement agent to sell or dispose of the goods before the court determines the claim where this is considered to be appropriate (Sched.12, para.60(6)).

**12.2.13** Where a required payment is ordered, if there is a dispute as to the value of the goods this is to be determined by reference to an independent valuation. The regulations will set out how this valuation will take place. If the third party claim has already made a payment into court then the rules will prescribe the time when the balance is to be paid into court. The presumption will be that this will take place once an independent valuation has determined whether there has been an underpayment (Sched.12, para.60(5)).

**12.2.14** Where the court directs the sale to take place even where a third party claim is being made then the usual sale provisions of paras.38 to 49 of Sched.12 apply (although the court can alter and modify the sale provisions). The sale proceeds must be paid into court. If the enforcement process has commenced in the High Court or county court then the complaint process is dealt with by that court. Otherwise the third party claimant can elect to bring his claim in the High Court or county court (Sched.12, para.60(8)).

## The balance between innocent third parties and unscrupulous debtors

**12.2.15** It is not uncommon for unscrupulous debtors to claim the goods belong to a third party. It should be noted that it is not the debtor that can make the third party claim (it is not unknown for debtors to mistakenly attempt to do this). If the goods are owned by a third party then the third party (not the debtor) has the right to make the application claiming that the goods which had been taken control of are his and not the debtors. In contested distress cases third party claims are very common. This is particularly so where associated companies trade from a single premises. One company may be the tenant whilst a related company trades and is in occupation. A landlord exercising CRAR might not be aware of the position until the enforcement agent is in the property attempting to take control of goods. It is at this stage that the third party position becomes relevant. The reforms under the new Act allow an enforcement agent only to take the goods belonging to the tenant.

**12.2.16** Accordingly even in circumstances where:

■ a third party is in occupation of a landlord's premises with the tenant's consent; and
■ in breach of the terms of the tenant's lease,

the goods of the third party will not be subject to the Sched.12 process and the landlord will not be able to exercise CRAR.

**12.2.17** However, this behaviour may constitute an offence contrary to para.68 of Sched.12 (see **12.6**).

## 12.3   LIMITATION OF LIABILITY FOR SALE OR PAYMENT OF PROCEEDS

### Pre-Act position

*Liability prior to sale*

12.3.1   In common law where a landlord levies distress he is personally responsible for all irregular acts committed by the bailiff in the making of the distress. This includes any breach of the process of taking control of goods or the sale process.

12.3.2   High Court enforcement officers and county court bailiffs are also liable for any wrongful act, committed prior to sale. However, they have a degree of protection in relation to the sale of seized goods (pursuant to para.11 of Sched.7 to the Courts Act 2003 and County Courts Act 1984, s.98).

*Liability for sale*

12.3.3   Where landlords have seized more goods in value than the rent that was owing, then the tenant has a remedy in damages under the Statute of Marlborough 1267 (i.e. had taken an unreasonably large quantity of goods than was necessary to satisfy the unpaid rent and costs) – see *Concorde* v. *Andromeda Investments SA* (1983) 265 EG 86. This is known as excessive distress.

12.3.4   The landlord can seize what would be reasonable to satisfy the claim. If the landlord has no option but to seize an item which is of too high a value he can do this if no other items are available of sufficient value.

### The new Act position

12.3.5   Pursuant to para.63 of Sched.12, any liability of an enforcement officer for sale of controlled goods is excluded except where:

(a) At the time of the sale the enforcement agent had notice that the goods were not the debtor's, or not his alone.
(b) Before the sale the lawful claimants had made an application to the court claiming an interest in the goods.

12.3.6   In this context a lawful claimant is a person who has an interest in the goods at the time of sale. This does not include the position where any such interest was assigned or transferred to him after the goods were bound (see **10.3** and **11.5.2**).

12.3.7   This protection for enforcement agents is extended by para.64 which excludes liability for enforcement agents for paying over proceeds except where:

(a) he had notice that the goods were the debtors and not his alone;

(b) before payment is made the lawful claimant had made an application to the court claiming interest in the goods;

(c) in relation to para.64 a lawful claimant is simply one who has an interest in the goods at the time of sale.

**12.3.8**    Paragraph 64 is not dependent upon whether there has been an assignment or transfer after the goods were bound. Accordingly where an assignment or transfer has taken place the enforcement agent may bear a liability if the proceeds are not paid in accordance with true ownership of the goods (i.e. where after the sale there is enough to pay the debt and costs and there is a surplus to pay back to the debtor).

**12.3.9**    The enforcement agent is expected to make reasonable enquiries before he can avail himself of the protection of paras.63 and 64.

**12.3.10**    The protection is also extended to related parties of enforcement agents. A related party is any person who assists in the exercising of an enforcement power.

**12.3.11**    Where a third party has taken a transfer or assignment of the goods after the goods are bound for the purposes of enforcement power pursuant to para.5 of Sched.12, then the sale can take place free of the assignee's interest. This is so even where the assignees/transferee has made an application to the court. The enforcement agent has no liability in relation to the sale.

## 12.4    REMEDIES AVAILABLE TO DEBTOR

**12.4.1**    Paragraph 66 of Sched.12 creates a new category of remedy available to debtors in relation to breaches of the provisions of Sched.12. The remedies are also available where an enforcement agent is acting under a defective writ or warrant or other instrument which creates the enforcement power. Any such breach or defect does not make the enforcement agent the trespasser. But the debtor has a right to the remedies provided by para.66. The remedy in effect has to be brought:

- in the High Court (where the enforcement power arises under a writ of the High Court);
- in the county court (where the enforcement power arose under a warrant issued by a county court);
- in all of the cases where the debtor has the choice of the High Court or county court (subject to the court limits in relation to quantity of damages).

### Damages claim for breach of Schedule 12

**12.4.2**    The debtor can claim damages as a consequence of the breach or defect.

**12.4.3**    The breach or defect does not make the enforcement agent or person he is acting for, a trespasser (Sched.12, para.66(2)).

**12.4.4**   The debtor has a right to bring proceedings for an order that the goods be returned or can bring a claim for damages in respect of loss suffered as a result of the breach or anything done under the defective instruments.

**12.4.5**   There is a further limitation of liability in para.66(a), which provides the right to claim damages does not apply where the enforcement agent acted in the reasonable belief that he was not breaching a provision of Sched.12 or that the instrument was not defective.

## Damages continuing enforcement after payment

**12.4.6**   The debtor or a co-owner also has a remedy where the amount out-standing has been paid in full pursuant to para.58 of Sched.12, and the enforcement officer or related party takes a further step contrary to para.58(3). This liability only arises where the enforcement agent had notice, when the step was taken, that the amount outstanding had been paid in full (Sched.12, para.59(2)).

**12.4.7**   These provisions replace the principles of debtors' remedies in relation to all types of defective and irregular distress including excessive distress.

## CRAR

**12.4.8**   Under s.78 of the new Act a debtor (tenant) can apply to the court for a court order to set aside a para.7 (Sched.12) notice to stay the CRAR process. The regulations will set out the basis of the application.

## 12.5   CREDITORS' REMEDIES

### Pre-Act position

**12.5.1**   Under the current system landlords have the right to pursue goods which have been removed from the demised premises by tenants in order to avoid distress. This is the principle of fraudulent or clandestine removal under the Distress for Rent Act 1737 which authorised landlords to follow and distrain upon the goods within 30 days after removal. The landlord's bailiff had the right to use force to break open places of concealment.

**12.5.2**   This remedy was important to landlords as they did not have the right to levy the distress at first instance in any place other than demised premises. High Court enforcement officers and county court bailiffs enjoy the right to seize goods wherever they find them.

## The new Act position

**12.5.3**    Under Sched.12 this remains the case. A landlord's right to take control of goods at a place other than a demised premises remains limited, whereas, enforcement agents acting on behalf of judgment creditors are able to take goods wherever they find them. Section 7 of the Distress for Rent Act 1737 has been repealed by the new Act and so has the remedy associated with fraudulent removal.

### Wrongful interference

**12.5.4**    Paragraph 67 of Sched.12 creates a general remedy for all creditors as follows:

> If a debtor wrongfully interferes with controlled goods and the creditor suffers loss as a result, the creditor may bring a claim against the debtor in respect of the loss.

**12.5.5**    This remedy only applies to controlled goods. It does not apply to goods which are bound pursuant to para.4 of Sched.12 prior to the goods being taken control of.

**12.5.6**    For commercial landlords the goods will be bound when notice of enforcement is given. But if the goods are then removed from the demised premises the remedy in para.67 does not apply.

**12.5.7**    Where there has been a removal to avoid CRAR, the enforcement agent could potentially apply for a warrant under para.15 of Sched.12 to enter specified premises other than the demised premises.

## 12.6    OFFENCES

### Intentional obstruction

**12.6.1**    Where a person intentionally obstructs an enforcement agent he is guilty of an offence under para.68 of Sched.12. There is a further offence where the person intentionally interferes with controlled goods without lawful excuse.

**12.6.2**    On prosecution and conviction the person is liable to imprisonment to a term not exceeding 51 weeks or a fine not exceeding level 4 on the standard scale or both (Sched.12, para.68(3)).

### Assignment/transfer while goods are bound

**12.6.3**    Where there has been an assignment or transfer in good faith for valuable consideration and without notice then the assignee/transferee has all the benefits of the provisions relation to co-owners. The assignee is entitled to receive an inventory, take part in the valuation process, receive all the information relating to the sale and enjoy the remedies that co-owners have under para.59(6) of Sched.12.

**12.6.4**    However, where the assignee or transferee acquired their interest not in good faith for valuable consideration and without notice their only true right is to receive any surplus payable once a sale has taken place pursuant to para.50(5) of Sched.12.

# PART III ENFORCEMENT AGAINST THIRD PARTIES

# 13 ATTACHMENT OF EARNINGS ORDERS

## 13.1 OVERVIEW

**13.1.1** An Attachment of Earnings Order is an order by the court that a debtor's employer must pay some of the debtor's earnings into court. The court then releases those monies to the creditor in part payment of the debt. This continues on a regular basis until the debt is paid in full.

**13.1.2** The idea is that the judgment debt 'attaches' to the debtor's wages.

### Popularity of Attachment of Earnings Orders

**13.1.3** As an enforcement method, an Attachment of Earnings Order is extremely popular as it is an easily made, low cost and effective application.

**13.1.4** The disadvantage of an Attachment of Earnings Order is that it can take a long time to pay off the debt and the level of payment depends both on the level of earnings and of course whether the party is in employment to start with.

**13.1.5** Attachment of Earnings Orders have always been, and remain, a popular method of enforcement.

Table 13.1

| Year | Attachment of Earnings Order applications | Attachment of Earnings Orders made |
|------|------------------------|------------------------|
| 1995 | 74,786 | 70,560 |
| 1996 | 65,863 | 74,651 |
| 1997 | 63,541 | 65,545 |
| 1998 | 64,975 | 60,275 |
| 1999 | 56,897 | 59,844 |
| 2000 | 80,276 | 62,451 |
| 2001 | 77,991 | 71,228 |
| 2002 | 79,602 | 68,484 |
| 2003 | 79,942 | 68,719 |
| 2004 | 76,051 | 70,105 |
| 2005 | 92,560 | 71,091 |
| 2006 | 85,328 | 66,475 |

**13.1.6**    The above figures have been extracted from the Business Management System (1995–1999) and from the main Civil Law Case Management System from 2000 onwards. These figures include priority Maintenance Orders from early 1998 onwards and are estimates. They have been provided by the Economics and Statistics Division of the Ministry of Justice.

## Types of Attachment Order

**13.1.7**    This book concentrates solely on civil debts. There are other Attachment of Earnings Orders that can be made for other types of debt but they are not the focus of this book. The different types of Attachment Order for England and Wales are set out in the Table 13.2.

Table 13.2

| Order type | Issued by | Debt type | Payable to | Legislation |
|---|---|---|---|---|
| AEO | High Court | Maintenance | CAPS | AEA 1971 and Courts Act 2003 |
| CAEO | County court | Civil debts | CAPS | AEA 1971 |
| AE on AO | County court | Civil debts | CAPS | AEA 1971 |
| AEO | County court | Maintenance Civil debts | CAPS | AEA 1971 |
| AEO | Magistrates' court | Fines Maintenance Orders | Local authority | AEA 1971 |
| Council Tax AEO | Local authority | Council tax | Local authority | Local Government Finance Act 1992 |
| DEO | CSA | Child maintenance | CSA | Child Support (Collection and Enforcement) |
| Income Payment Orders | High Court or county court | Bankruptcy | Official receiver or trustee in bankruptcy | Insolvency Act 1986 |
| Income Support Deduction Notice | Jobcentre Plus | Income Support | Department for Work and Pensions | Social Security Contributions and Benefits Act 1992 |

AEO – Attachment of Earnings Order
CAEO – Consolidated Attachment of Earnings Order
AEA – Attachment of Earnings Act
AE – Attachment of Earnings
AO – Admin Order
DEO – Deductions from Earnings Order
CSA – Child Support Agency
CAPS – Centralised Attachment of Earnings Payment System

*Source*: HMCS *Attachment Orders Guide for Employers*

## Effect of the new Act

**13.1.8**   The implications of the new Act will be set out later in this chapter. In brief, they do not affect the procedure for applying for an Attachment of Earnings Order. The new Act introduces:

- a system of deductions at fixed rates – this system is likely to be similar to the fixed table deductions that already exist for council tax Attachment of Earnings Orders and for fines Attachment of Earnings Orders from 5 April 2004 (the fixed table deductions for fines being introduced by the Courts Act 2003);
- a system whereby it is easier for creditors to track employees who change jobs.

**13.1.9**   The amendments brought in by the new Act follow the recommendations of the Civil Enforcement Review which suggested the introduction of:

- fixed tables for Attachment of Earnings Orders, such tables being based on a percentage of salary; and
- an information gateway which would create a link between the civil courts and Her Majesty's Revenue and Customs (HMRC) to enable debtors to be traced to their new jobs.

**13.1.10**   When setting out the government's rationale for enhancing enforcement powers at the second reading debate of the new Act in the House of Lords, the Lord Chancellor, Lord Falconer, said of the new procedures for Attachment of Earnings Orders that they:

> will simplify and streamline the arrangements for deducting payment of a judgment debt direct from a debtor's salary. In future, deductions from salary will be made according to fixed rates, as they are for Council Tax debtors, rather than on an individual case by case basis. A further difficulty which Part 4 seeks to address is the lapse of these orders where debtors change employers. Currently, the court depends on the debtor to provide up to date information. This is unsatisfactory so Clause 84 [now s.92 of the new Act] will allow Her Majesty's Revenue and Customs to provide the court with new employer's details in such cases.

## Jurisdiction

**13.1.11**   Courts that can make the different types of Attachment of Earnings Orders are set out in Attachment of Earnings Act 1971, s.1. This book concentrates on civil debts, although see Table 13.2 above on types of Attachment of Earnings Orders.

**13.1.12**   An application for an Attachment of Earnings Order for a civil debt can be made only in a county court.

**13.1.13**   Judgments or orders obtained in the High Court will firstly have to be transferred to the county court if the creditor wants to enforce the civil judgment by means of an Attachment of Earnings Order.

**13.1.14**    The power to transfer proceedings from the High Court to the county court is provided under County Courts Act 1984, s.40(6). Having transferred the High Court judgment, it can be enforced as if it were a county court judgment.

## Transfer from High Court to county court

**13.1.15**    This is dealt with fully in **Chapter 4**. If a creditor wants to enforce a High Court judgment in the county court he must first apply to the High Court for the proceedings to be transferred to the county court.

**13.1.16**    Having done that, he must then apply to the county court where enforcement is to take place and enclose, with his application:

- a copy of the judgment or order;
- a certificate verifying the amount due under the judgment or order;
- if a writ of execution has previously been issued in the High Court, a copy of the relevant enforcement officer's return to the writ; and
- a copy of the order transferring the proceeding to the county court.

## When are Attachment of Earnings Orders used?

**13.1.17**    Attachment of Earnings Orders can be made when an employee:

- is ordered by a court to pay a debt or fine (this book will concentrate on civil debts);
- has been ordered to pay maintenance to support a spouse or child; or
- is in arrears with a council tax bill.

## Procedure

**13.1.18**    The county court governs the procedure for obtaining an Attachment of Earnings Order.

**13.1.19**    In a similar way to charging orders, Attachment of Earnings Orders are governed by the Civil Procedure Rules (CPR) (CCR Order 27, found in Sched.2 to the CPR), which sets out the procedure, and an Act of Parliament (in this case the Attachment of Earnings Act 1971) which sets out the rules.

## Venue

**13.1.20**    Under CCR Order 27, r.3 (which can be found in Sched.2 to the CPR) an application for an Attachment of Earnings Order is made in the court local to the debtor.

**13.1.21**    If the debtor does not reside in England or Wales or the creditor does not know where he resides, the application should be made in the court where the order being enforced was obtained (CCR Order 27, r.3(3)).

**13.1.22**    Where an application for an Attachment of Earnings Order is made for two or more debtors who are jointly liable under an order, the application can be made to the court local to any of the debtors.

## Filing and serving application

**13.1.23**    A creditor applying for an Attachment of Earnings Order should file an application in form N337. The application must certify the amount of money remaining due under the order and that the whole or part of any instalment due remains unpaid.

**13.1.24**    When the application documents are filed, the court officer will issue form N55 (notice of application) and, in the case of a maintenance order will fix a day for the hearing of the application.

**13.1.25**    The application and a reply form (form N56) must be served on the debtor.

## Debtor's reply

**13.1.26**    Within eight days of service of the documents the debtor must file with the court officer a reply in form N56. The reply is a basic statement of earnings. This requirement is under Attachment of Earnings Order Act 1971, s.14(4).

**13.1.27**    Alternatively, the debtor can, within eight days after service pay to the creditor the money remaining due under the judgment and must inform the court officer that he has done so.

**13.1.28**    The debtor's reply should contain:

- the name and address of any person paying him earnings;
- details of his earnings and anticipated earnings;
- details of his resources and needs;
- details to enable his employer to identify him (such as national insurance number); and
- any other matters relevant to deciding the normal deduction rate and the protected earnings rate.

**13.1.29**    Once the court officer receives the debtor's reply, he will send a copy to the applicant.

**13.1.30**    At any stage during the proceedings the court officer may send a notice to anybody he believes may be the debtor's employer. That notice will ask the alleged employer to provide a statement of the debtor's earnings and anticipated earnings.

## Failure to reply

**13.1.31**   Where a debtor does not file a reply within eight days after service on him of the application, or does not make payment in full to the creditor, the court officer may issue an order under Attachment of Earnings Order Act 1971, s.14(1). This order will be served on the debtor personally and if the debtor fails to obey it or to file a statement of his means or make payment, the court officer will issue a notice 'calling on that person to show good reason why he should not be imprisoned' (CCR Order 27, r.7A). This notice must be served on the debtor personally not less than five days before the hearing.

**13.1.32**   The procedure is similar in relation to orders to obtain information.

**13.1.33**   If the debtor does not attend an adjourned hearing and a committal order is made pursuant to s.23(1) the judge has the power to order that the committal order be suspended so long as the debtor attends at a time and place specified in the committal order (CCR Order 27, r.7B). If the committal order is suspended and the debtor still fails to attend, a warrant of committal will normally be issued. The debtor can be imprisoned for up to 14 days and fined.

## Notice to employer

**13.1.34**   As well as the committal powers under Attachment of Earnings Act 1971, s.14, if a court officer believes a party may be the debtor's employer, he can send a notice to that party, asking the purported employer to give a statement of the debtor's current and anticipated earnings. The purported employer must respond 'within such period as may be specified in the notice' (CCR Order 27, r.6). A notice can be sent to a purported employer at any time during the attachment of earnings procedure.

**13.1.35**   In practice, a creditor who believes he knows the identity of the debtor's employer will make an application, in form N338, at the time of applying for the Attachment of Earnings Order, for the notice (form N55) also to be served on the purported employer. That way, if the debtor fails to reply in form N56, but the employer does, the District Judge can make the Attachment of Earnings Order based on the information provided by the employer, rather than spending further time in trying to force the debtor into replying.

## Making the order

**13.1.36**   As soon as the court officer receives the debtor's reply, if he has sufficient information he may make an Attachment of Earnings Order straightaway without a hearing and of his own motion. If he does so, a copy of the Attachment of Earnings Order will be sent to the parties and to the debtor's employer.

**13.1.37**   In that case, the creditor or the debtor may, within 14 days of service of the Attachment of Earnings Order, apply for the Attachment of Earnings Order to be reconsidered at a hearing. Reasons for requiring a hearing must be set out in the application notice. The reasons could include that the debtor is considering making an application for relief under the new debt management provisions under Part V of the new Act. If this application is made, the court officer will fix a day for the hearing of the application and the creditor and debtor must be given not less than two days' notice.

**13.1.38** At this application, which will be held before a District Judge, the District Judge may confirm the Attachment of Earnings Order or set it aside and make a new Attachment of Earnings Order.

**13.1.39** If, on receipt of the debtor's reply, the court officer does not make an Attachment of Earnings Order he will refer the papers to the District Judge. If the District Judge considers that he has sufficient information to make an Attachment of Earnings Order without the parties attending court then he will do so. If the District Judge does not make an immediate Attachment of Earnings Order, he will fix the hearing of the application and the creditor and the debtor will be given not less than eight days' notice of that hearing date.

**13.1.40** Again, where a District Judge makes an order without the parties attending, they can apply to have the order reconsidered.

**13.1.41** The creditor does not need to attend the hearing but if he does not plan on attending the hearing he should provide a witness statement or request, in writing, that the court proceeds without him. Without either of these, the court will not hear the application.

## Conditions for an Attachment of Earnings Order application

**13.1.42** The following conditions apply:

- the judgment debt must be not less than £50 (CCR Order 27, r.7(9));
- the debtor must have an employer who can be identified; and
- the debtor must have failed to pay at least one of the relevant payments (pursuant to s.3(3) and (3)(a) of the Attachment of Earnings Act 1971).

## Contents of order

**13.1.43** The Attachment of Earnings Order will be in form N60. Provided that the court knows these details, an Attachment of Earnings Order shall contain:

- the debtor's full name and address;
- the debtor's place of work; and
- the nature of work and his work number.

**13.1.44** Once an Attachment of Earnings Order is granted, it must be served on the debtor and on the employer (CCR Order 27, r.10(2)).

## What will the Attachment of Earnings Order state?

**13.1.45**    An Attachment of Earnings Order served on an employer will tell the employer:

- the total debt owed by the employee (unless the order is for ongoing maintenance);
- how often the employer should make a deduction;
- the normal deduction amount (i.e. the amount that should usually be deducted each week or each month); and
- the protected earnings level (i.e. the amount below which a deduction should not be made).

**13.1.46**    Attachment of Earnings Orders can only be applied to attachable earnings (see **13.1.54**).

## Effect of Attachment of Earnings Order

**13.1.47**    The process of actually attaching the debtor's earnings is governed by the Attachment of Earnings Act 1971 and run by the court, with the employer paying a certain amount to the court, which is then released to the creditor.

**13.1.48**    Under Attachment of Earnings Act 1971, s.6(5) a rate is determined by the court, being the maximum amount per month which can be deducted from the employee ('the normal deduction amount').

**13.1.49**    The court then works out the minimum amount that must be paid to the employee ('the protected earnings level').

**13.1.50**    Once past the protected earnings level, the employer must pay to the court any additional monies up to the normal deduction amount. Anything earned above the normal deduction amount will then be released to the employee (debtor), over and above what he has already received as protected earnings.

**13.1.51**    This leaves a situation where the employee is guaranteed a certain amount of money and, once that is paid, the debtor gets up to a certain other amount.

**13.1.52**    As an example, using random figures, if an employee earns £225 per month, his protected earnings are £100 and the normal deduction amount is £50 then the employee would be paid his £100, £50 would be released to the creditor and a further £75 would be released to the employee.

**13.1.53**    The system of deductions has been reformed by the new Act, which seeks to move towards a system of fixed rate deductions. This is dealt with later in this chapter (see **13.2.2**).

## What earnings can be subject to an Attachment of Earnings Order?

**13.1.54** Only 'earnings' can be the subject of an Attachment of Earnings Order. 'Earnings' are defined in Attachment of Earnings Act 1971, s.24. What can be attached depends on the type of Attachment of Earnings Order made (see Table 13.2 at **13.1.7** for the different types of Attachment of Earnings Orders).

**13.1.55** For example, with a council tax Attachment of Earnings Order, a pension or redundancy payment cannot be attached; whereas for an Attachment of Earnings Order in relation to maintenance, fines and civil debts, pension and redundancy pay can be attached.

**13.1.56** For Attachment of Earnings Orders in relation to civil debts (the same rules apply to maintenance and fines), earnings that can be attached by an Attachment of Earnings Order are:

- wages or salary (including any fees, bonuses, commission, overtime pay or other emoluments payable in addition to wages or salary payable under a contract of service);
- pension; and
- statutory sick pay (the ability to attach to statutory sick pay was added to the Attachment of Earnings Order Act 1971 by Sched.4 to the Social Security Act 1984).

**13.1.57** Excluded from any earnings (and therefore unable to be the subject of an Attachment of Earnings Order) are:

- a tax credit (within the meaning of the Tax Credits Act 2002);
- pension or allowances in respect of disablement or disability;
- pay or allowances to a member of Her Majesty's Forces, unless payable as a special member of a reserve force within the meaning of the Reserve Forces Act 1996;
- except in relation to a Maintenance Order, wages payable to a person as a seaman, other than wages payable to him as a seaman of a fishing boat;
- sums payable by any public department of the Government of Northern Ireland or of a territory outside the United Kingdom; and
- pension, allowances or benefit payable under any enactments relating to social security (e.g. statutory maternity pay, statutory paternity pay and statutory adoption pay, guaranteed minimum pension (within the meaning of the Pension Schemes Act 1993)).

**13.1.58** The amount of income that is attachable is therefore calculated by deducting from the earnings (as defined above):

- income tax;
- Primary Class 1 Contributions under Part 1 of the Social Security Contributions and Benefits Act 1992 (national insurance);
- amounts deductible under any enactment following pursuance of a request in writing by the debtor, for the purposes of a superannuation scheme,

namely any enactment, rules, deed or other instrument providing for the payments of annuities or lump sums:

- – to the persons with respect to whom the instrument has effect on their retirement at a specified age or on becoming incapacitated at some earlier age; or
- – to the personal representatives or the widow's relatives or dependants of such persons on their death or otherwise whether with or without any further or other benefit. This does not include freestanding additional voluntary contributions.

## Applications to determine whether payments are earnings

**13.1.59**    Under Attachment of Earnings Act 1971, s.16, any of the following parties can apply to court for guidance as to whether payments being made fall within the category of earnings and so whether they fall within the Attachment of Earnings Order. The parties who can make this application are:

- ■ the employer;
- ■ the debtor;
- ■ the creditor;
- ■ the collecting officer (for magistrates' court Maintenance Orders).

**13.1.60**    This application should be made in writing to the District Judge. On receipt of this application, the court officer will list a hearing and will notify the employer, the creditor and the debtor of the time and date of the hearing.

## What should an employer do when receiving an Attachment of Earnings Order?

**13.1.61**    Employers with questions can call the Centralised Attachment of Earnings Payment System (tel: 08454 085312), the court or local authority that issued the order, or the Child Support Agency.

**13.1.62**    If the employer does not employ the person named in the Attachment of Earnings Order, he must write to the court within 10 days of receiving the Attachment of Earnings Order. Similarly he must write to the court within 10 days of the employee leaving employment. This notification must be made in writing.

**13.1.63**    If, on receipt by the employer of an Attachment of Earnings Order, the debtor is employed by the employer, the employer must take all reasonable steps to comply with the Attachment of Earnings Order.

**13.1.64**    In practice, on each payday the employer should:

- ■ calculate the debtor's attachable earnings;
- ■ set aside (and pay to the employee) the debtor's protected earnings;

- deduct (where possible) the amount specified in the Attachment of Earnings Order;
- send the deduction to the address stated in the Attachment of Earnings Order (cheques should be made payable to HMCS). Most civil debts will require the employer to pay the amount to the Centralised Attachment of Earnings Payments System whose address is PO Box 404, Northampton NN1 2ZY, fax: 08454 085315, email: **customerservice.caps@hmcourts-service.gsi.gov.uk**, tel: 08454 085312;
- pay to the debtor the protected earnings and the balance following deduction (if there are no other deductions to be made).

## Notification to employee

**13.1.65**   The employee/debtor must be notified in writing by the employer about each deduction when he is given his pay statement. This can be done within the pay statement itself.

## When does an Order come into force?

**13.1.66**   The Attachment of Earnings Order comes into force on the day on which the employer receives it. The employer should start making deductions on the first payday after he receives the Attachment of Earnings Order and on each future payday after that.

## Employer's failure to comply

**13.1.67**   If the employer fails to do so, he may be fined.

**13.1.68**   The exception is that an employer has seven days to act on the Attachment of Earnings Order and so cannot be fined if he does not make a deduction on the first payday where that first payday falls within seven days of the date on which the order was received. Practically though, as soon as an employer receives an Attachment of Earnings Order, he should act.

## Can the employer change the rate of deductions?

**13.1.69**   The employer can ask the court to recalculate and amend the Attachment of Earnings Order so that deductions are made weekly or monthly (to coincide with the frequency of paydays for the employee).

## Employer's expenses

**13.1.70**   For every deduction, the employer is allowed to deduct £1 from the debtor's earnings towards administrative costs relating to the Attachment of Earnings Order.

## Priority of orders

**13.1.71**   If an employer receives more than one Attachment of Earnings Order for the same employee, the orders are dealt with in priority. Attachment of Earnings Orders for maintenance or fines have priority over Attachment of Earnings Orders for civil debts.

## More than one order for the same employee

**13.1.72**   If an employer receives two or more Attachment of Earnings Orders for civil judgment debts for the same employee, he can ask that the court grant a combined (or consolidated) Attachment of Earnings Order which will allow the employer to make a single deduction each payday.

**13.1.73**   Where a consolidated Attachment of Earnings Order is granted, the court will recalculate the protected earnings level and the normal deduction amount and send a new Attachment of Earnings Order to the employer.

## Variation of the Attachment of Earnings Order

**13.1.74**   The court may change the normal deduction amount or the protected earnings level at any time and will send a copy of the varied Attachment of Earnings Order to the employer.

**13.1.75**   The court or the Centralised Attachment of Earnings Payments System will also notify the employer in writing when an order has been paid in full, is cancelled, or no longer has effect.

**13.1.76**   Under the new Act, a party can also apply to the county court for the suspension of a fixed rate deduction order if the fixed rates are too high/low or the payments under the fixed rates are too frequent or not frequent enough. This is governed by the new Attachment of Earnings Act 1971, s.9A(1) and is dealt with at **13.2.11** below.

## What if the debtor leaves employment before the Attachment of Earnings Order is paid?

**13.1.77**   Under the current system, if the debtor leaves employment, the Attachment of Earnings Order lapses from the payday following termination of employment.

**13.1.78**   In relation to this, the new Act has introduced procedures to assist where employees change jobs. Employers should be aware of the new procedures about to be introduced by the new Act.

**13.1.79**   If an employee does leave employment, the employer must write to the court or the Centralised Attachment of Earnings Payments System within 10 days.

## 13.2   NEW ACT POSITION

**13.2.1**   The pre-Act position for Attachment of Earnings Orders was criticised for being unduly complicated and allowing debtors to change employment to avoid the effect of the Attachment of Earnings Order. The new Act has therefore introduced a fixed rate scheme for deductions and a system whereby employees can be 'followed' more easily to their new employment.

## Deductions

**13.2.2**   The new Act changes the way in which deductions are made in relation to all civil judgment debts.

### New fixed rate deduction scheme

**13.2.3**   Section 91 of the new Act introduces a new system whereby deductions under certain orders are now to be made in accordance with a fixed rate deduction scheme, rather than in accordance with Part 1 of Sched.3 to the 1971 Act (the current system).

**13.2.4**   There are now therefore two methods of deductions:

- *Fixed rate deductions* – The new system of deductions at fixed rates will, once the new Act comes into force, replace the usual procedure and will (pursuant to the new Attachment of Earnings Act 1971, s.6(1)(A)) apply to all Attachment of Earnings Orders issued by a court to secure a judgment debt.
- *Schedule 3 deductions* – The alternative method will be deductions under the old system of Part 1 of Sched.3 to the 1971 Act and will only apply where the fixed rate scheme does not apply (Attachment of Earnings Act 1971, s.6(1), (1B)).

**13.2.5**   Schedule 15 to the new Act makes amendments to the Attachment of Earnings Act 1971 to bring this new scheme into force.

### Fixed rate scheme

**13.2.6**   Once the new Act is in force, there will be no discretion in relation to the new fixed rate scheme. All Attachment of Earnings Orders for judgment debts issued by a court must be under the new fixed deduction scheme and any Attachment of Earnings Order made under the fixed deduction scheme is now called Fixed Deductions Orders.

**13.2.7**   The new Act introduces a new s.6A into the Attachment of Earnings Act 1971. It states that the fixed deduction scheme is:

> any scheme that the Lord Chancellor makes which specifies the rates and frequencies at which deductions are to be made under Attachment of Earnings Orders so as to secure the repayment of judgment debts.

**13.2.8**    The level and frequency of deductions under the fixed rate deduction scheme are therefore to be set down in regulations made by the Lord Chancellor. Those regulations are not yet in force.

**13.2.9**    As an idea of the form the new regulations might take, below is a table of fixed deductions already in force.

## Attachment of Earnings Orders for magistrates' courts and fines

**Table 13.3**    Deductions from weekly earnings

| Net earnings | Deduction rate (%) |
| --- | --- |
| Not exceeding £55 | 0 |
| Exceeding £55 but not exceeding £100 | 3 |
| Exceeding £100 but not exceeding £135 | 5 |
| Exceeding £135 but not exceeding £165 | 7 |
| Exceeding £165 but not exceeding £260 | 12 |
| Exceeding £260 but not exceeding £370 | 17 |
| Exceeding £370 | 17 in respect of the first £370 and 50 in respect of the remainder |

**Table 13.4**    Deductions from monthly earnings:

| Net earnings | Deduction rate (%) |
| --- | --- |
| Not exceeding £220 | 0 |
| Exceeding £220 but not exceeding £400 | 3 |
| Exceeding £400 but not exceeding £540 | 5 |
| Exceeding £540 but not exceeding £660 | 7 |
| Exceeding £660 but not exceeding £1,040 | 12 |
| Exceeding £1,040 but not exceeding £1,480 | 17 |
| Exceeding £1,480 | 17 in respect of the first £1,480 and 50 in respect of the remainder |

**Table 13.5**    Deductions from daily earnings:

| Net earnings | Deduction rate (%) |
| --- | --- |
| Not exceeding £8 | 0 |
| Exceeding £8 but not exceeding £15 | 3 |
| Exceeding £15 but not exceeding £20 | 5 |
| Exceeding £20 but not exceeding £24 | 7 |
| Exceeding £24 but not exceeding £38 | 12 |
| Exceeding £38 but not exceeding £53 | 17 |
| Exceeding £53 | 17 in respect of the first £53 and 50 in respect of the remainder. |

*Deduction tables for council tax Attachment of Earnings Orders made on or after 1 April 2007*

**Table 13.6**   Deductions from weekly earnings:

| Net earnings | Deduction rate (%) |
|---|---|
| Not exceeding £75 | 0 |
| Exceeding £75 but not exceeding £135 | 3 |
| Exceeding £135 but not exceeding £185 | 5 |
| Exceeding £185 but not exceeding £225 | 7 |
| Exceeding £225 but not exceeding £355 | 12 |
| Exceeding £355 but not exceeding £505 | 17 |
| Exceeding £505 | 17 in respect of the first £505 and 50 in respect of the remainder |

**Table 13.7**   Deductions from monthly earnings:

| Net earnings | Deduction rate (%) |
|---|---|
| Not exceeding £300 | 0 |
| Exceeding £300 but not exceeding £550 | 3 |
| Exceeding £550 but not exceeding £740 | 5 |
| Exceeding £740 but not exceeding £900 | 7 |
| Exceeding £900 but not exceeding £1,420 | 12 |
| Exceeding £1,420 but not exceeding £2,020 | 17 |
| Exceeding £2,020 | 17 in respect of the first £2,020 and 50 in respect of the remainder |

**Table 13.8**   Deductions based on daily earnings:

| Net earnings | Deduction rate (%) |
|---|---|
| Not exceeding £11 | 0 |
| Exceeding £11 but not exceeding £20 | 3 |
| Exceeding £20 but not exceeding £27 | 5 |
| Exceeding £27 but not exceeding £33 | 7 |
| Exceeding £33 but not exceeding £52 | 12 |
| Exceeding £52 but not exceeding £72 | 17 |
| Exceeding £72 | 17 in respect of the first £72 and 50 in respect of the remainder. |

**13.2.10** It is not certain, but deductions at a fixed rate under the new Act are likely to be in line with these current fixed deductions.

## What if the fixed rates are too high/low or too often/not often enough?

**13.2.11**   Although it may seem harsh that fixed rates, which may not take into account a debtor's individual circumstances, have been introduced, this is mitigated by the fact that a party can apply to the county court for the suspension of a Fixed Rate Deduction Order.

**13.2.12**    The term 'Suspension Order' is somewhat of a misnomer in that it does not actually suspend payments. Either the creditor or the debtor can apply for a Suspension Order. Its effect is to suspend the Fixed Rate Order while at the same time replacing it with new payments under the Suspension Order. All the Suspension Order does, therefore, is temporarily replace the Fixed Rate Order. The new payments under the Suspension Order may in fact be higher or more frequent than the payments under the Fixed Deductions Order.

**13.2.13**    Under the new s.9A(1) of the Attachment of Earnings Act 1971, a county court must make an order suspending a fixed rate deduction order if it is satisfied:

- that the Fixed Deductions Order requires periodical deductions to be made at a rate which is not appropriate; and/or
- that the Fixed Deductions Order requires periodical deductions to be made at times which are not appropriate.

**13.2.14**    In that situation, the county court will make a Suspension Order either specifying the rate at which the debtor must make repayments (this can be either at a higher or lower rate as it is open to the creditor to claim that the payments are not enough) or specify the times at which the debtor must make repayments (again this can be more or less frequent).

**13.2.15**    The court can also order any additional terms as it thinks appropriate.

**13.2.16**    An employer who is given notice of the Suspension Order must stop making deductions under the Fixed Deductions Order and must instead make the deductions under the Suspension Order.

## Revocation of Suspension Order

**13.2.17**    Under the new s.9A(4) of the Attachment of Earnings Act 1971, a county court must revoke the Suspension Order if any of the terms of the Suspension Order are broken.

**13.2.18**    A county court also has the discretion to revoke the Suspension Order in any other circumstances if the court thinks it is appropriate to do so.

**13.2.19**    The aim of the suspension provisions in the new Act are to simplify the position for employers.

## Schedule 3 scheme

**13.2.20**    Under the new s.6(1B) if a court makes 'any other Attachment of Earnings Order' the payments are to be made 'in accordance with Part 1 of Schedule 3' which are payments made under the current scheme.

**13.2.21**    The new Act is designed to phase out Sched.3 payment schemes:

- a Sched.3 Judgment Debt Order (under the old system) can be varied to become a Fixed Deductions Order either on an application to the county court or by the court deciding of itself to make the change;
- where a Sched.3 Judgment Debt Order lapses, for example because the debtor has changed employment, then the court must change it to a Fixed Deductions Order if the Attachment of Earnings Order is redirected to the debtor's new employer; and
- the Lord Chancellor can also specify a 'changeover date' when all existing Sched.3 Judgment Debt Orders must become Fixed Deduction Orders. On that changeover date 'all Sched.3 Judgment Debt Orders are to be treated as if a county court had varied them by changing the basis of deductions'.

**13.2.22**    Part 2 of the new Sched.3A to the Attachment of Earnings Act 1971 deals with changing from the fixed deduction scheme by way of an Administration Order.

## Moving jobs

**13.2.23**    The paper *Effective Enforcement* found that a weakness of the current system relating to Attachment of Earnings Orders was that if a debtor changed jobs and did not inform the court of his new employer's details (despite his obligation to do so under s.15 which was introduced in 2006), the Attachment of Earnings Order would lapse under s.9(4) of the Attachment of Earnings Act 1971 and the creditor would have to track down the debtor and make a new application.

**13.2.24**    The new Act seeks to streamline the process in the favour of the creditor. Under the new Act, 'lapsed' Attachment of Earnings Orders can now be redirected more easily than the pre-Act procedure under CCR Order 27, r.13.

**13.2.25**    To help with this, the new ss.15A–15D, inserted into the Attachment of Earnings Act 1971 by the new Act, enable information to be provided to the courts by Her Majesty's Revenue and Customs (HMRC) for the purpose of redirecting a lapsed Attachment of Earnings Order. With that information, the court can then redirect the Attachment of Earnings Order.

### Debtor's obligation to notify change of employment

**13.2.26**    Under the new s.15A of the 1979 Act, an employee/debtor is under an obligation to notify the court where he changes employment. If he does not do so, the court can now 'chase him down' via HMRC.

## Court's new powers

**13.2.27**   Where the debtor fails to notify the court that he has changed employment and the Attachment of Earnings Order lapses under s.9(4) then the 'proper
authority' (i.e. the court that made the Attachment of Earnings Order) may
request the Commissioners for HMRC to let them know whether it appears to
them that the debtor has a current employer and to disclose the name and address
of that employer.

**13.2.28**   A request cannot be made of HMRC, however, until regulations are in
force governing the use and supply of debtor information. Those regulations have
not yet been drafted.

## Commissioners' disclosure obligations

**13.2.29**   The Commissioners are entitled to provide information to the court to
enable a creditor to chase down a debtor who has changed jobs.

**13.2.30**   Section 15B gives the Commissioners protection in relation to this disclosure. Disclosure is such information as the Commissioners consider necessary
to comply with the court's request.

## Offences of unauthorised use or disclosure

**13.2.31**   Parties who receive this information must be careful, however, as to
how they use it. Section 15B makes it an offence for a person to whom the
Commissioner discloses information about a debtor to use the information in a
way that is not authorised by the Act.

**13.2.32**   Ways that are authorised by the Act are:

■   for a purpose connected with the enforcement of the lapsed Attachment of
    Earnings Order and with the consent of the Commissioners;
■   in accordance with an enactment or an order of court or for the purpose of
    any proceedings before a court and it is in accordance with regulations;
■   the information has previously been lawfully disclosed to the public; or
■   in accordance with rules of court that comply with regulations.

**13.2.33**   Again, these regulations are not yet in force and will only be brought
into force with the agreement of the Commissioners and once a draft statutory
instrument has been approved by each of the Houses of Parliament.

**13.2.34**   It is a defence for a person charged with an offence of unauthorised use
or disclosure to prove that he reasonably believed that the disclosure was lawful
but if found guilty then on conviction on indictment the offender is liable to
imprisonment for a term not exceeding two years and/or to a fine and on summary conviction to imprisonment for a term not exceeding 12 months and/or to
a fine not exceeding the statutory maximum.

**13.2.35**   It is therefore important to ensure that any party to whom information about the debtor is disclosed is fully aware of the limits under which this information can be used.

**13.2.36**   The new ability to track employees to new jobs via HMRC should result in yet further rises in the use of Attachment of Earnings Orders and in the enforceability of judgment debts.

## Transitional period

**13.2.37**   The new sections (ss.15A–15D) apply to any Attachment of Earnings Order as soon as the new Act is in force, whether the Attachment of Earnings Order was made before or after the commencement of the new Act.

## 13.3    OVERVIEW FLOWCHART

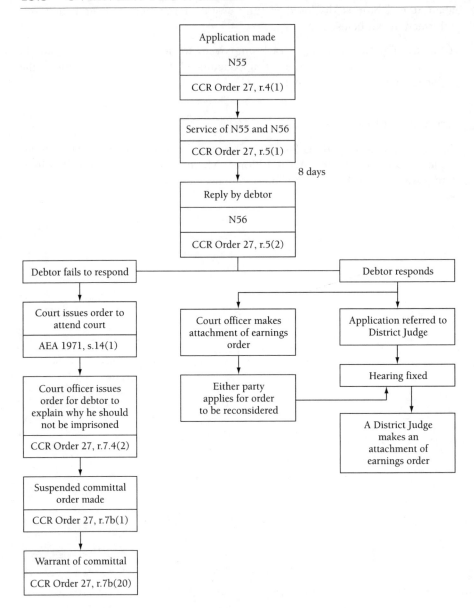

## 13.4   FORMS

N55      Notice of application for Attachment of Earnings Order

N55A     Notice of application for Attachment of Earnings Order (maintenance)

N56      Reply to attachment of earnings application – statement of means

N58      Order for debtor's attendance at adjournal hearing of attachment of earnings application – maintenance

N59      Warrant of committal under Attachment of Earnings Act 1971, s.23(1)

N60      Attachment of Earnings Order – judgment debt

N61      Order for production of Statement of Means

N61A     Notice to employer for production of statement of earnings

N62      Summons for offence under Attachment of Earnings Act 1971

N63      Notice to show cause under Attachment of Earnings Act, s.23

N64      Suspended Attachment of Earnings Order

N64A     Suspended Attachment of Earnings Order – maintenance

N65      Attachment of earnings order – (priority maintenance)

N65A     Attachment of earnings arrears order

N66      Consolidated Attachment of Earnings Order

N66A     Notice of application for consolidated Attachment of Earnings Order

N112A    Power of arrest Attachment of Earnings Act 1971, s.23

N118     Notice to defendant where committal order made but suspended under Attachment of Earnings Order 1971

N336     Request for search in Attachment of Earnings Order

N337     Request for an Attachment of Earnings Order

N338     Request for statement of earnings

N339     Discharge of Attachment of Earnings Order

N340     Notice as to payment under Attachment of Earnings Order made by the High Court

N341     Notice of intention to vary Attachment of Earnings Order under Attachment of Earnings Act 1971, s.10(2)

N448     Request to defendant for employment details – attachment of earnings

N449     Notice to employer – failure to make deductions under Attachment of Earnings Order

# 14 THIRD PARTY DEBT ORDERS

## 14.1 OVERVIEW

**14.1.1** Third Party Debt Orders are governed by Part 72 of the Civil Procedure Rules (CPR).

**14.1.2** CPR rule 72.1 defines a Third Party Debt Order, as an order by which a third party who owes money to the debtor, is ordered to pay that money to the creditor in part or full satisfaction of the judgment debt.

**14.1.3** Third Party Debt Orders are most often used against bank accounts.

### Popularity of Third Party Debt Orders

**14.1.4** Third Party Debt Orders are, of all the enforcement methods, the least used method. In 1995 there were only around 5,000 applications made and in 2006 this had only risen to 6,500 applications, compared to in excess of 92,000 applications for a charging order in 2006.

Table 14.1

| Year | Third Party Debt Order applications | Third Party Debt Orders made |
|------|-------------------------------------|------------------------------|
| 1995 | 5,054 | 2,941 |
| 1996 | 4,847 | 2,800 |
| 1997 | 3,996 | 2,459 |
| 1998 | 3,596 | 1,658 |
| 1999 | 3,347 | 1,233 |
| 2000 | 2,847 | 1,018 |
| 2001 | 3,999 | 1,373 |
| 2002 | 5,277 | 1,513 |
| 2003 | 5,999 | 1,723 |
| 2004 | 6,299 | 1,806 |
| 2005 | 6,522 | 1,789 |
| 2006 | 6,506 | 1,806 |

*Source*: The figures from 2000 onwards have been extracted from the main Civil Law Case Management System, and the figures prior to 1999 extracted from the Business Management System. The figures have been provided by the Economics and Statistics Division of the Ministry of Justice.

**14.1.5**    One reason for the lack of popularity of Third Party Debt Orders may be that it appears from the figures that only around one-third of applications result in an order being made. In fact, over the last 10 years, the success rate of applications for Third Party Debt Orders has fallen from 58 per cent to 27 per cent.

**14.1.6**    Compared to the 92,560 Attachment of Earnings Order applications made in 2005, a mere 6,522 Third Party Debt Order applications were made. In 2005, even for the unpopular Orders to Obtain Information, there were still over 31,000 made.

**14.1.7**    It is quite probable that the relatively low number of applications for Third Party Debt Orders that are made has something to do with the fact that very few debtors are owed monies by third parties. If, for example, a debtor had money in the bank, by the stage of enforcement he would more than likely have paid the debt and so, although useful where a person is simply refusing to pay a debt ('won't pay'), where the person cannot pay the debt and it has to be fixed against other assets, such as property, then Third Party Debt Orders are of limited use.

**14.1.8**    The infrequent use of Third Party Debt Orders could equally be a product of the impotence of Orders to Obtain Information (which rarely assist in providing information about bank accounts with money in them). This is being addressed in the new Act by the introduction of Departmental Information Requests and Information Orders (see 5.4).

**14.1.9**    In the 31,000 Orders to Obtain Information in 2005, it was shown that hardly any of the judgment debtors had money in the bank, whether because of lack of funds or untruthful responses by the debtor. Again, this may have more to do with the limited usefulness of Orders to Obtain Information than Third Party Debt Orders.

**14.1.10**    The likelihood of a judgment debtor actually having enough funds in an account to justify an application is another factor.

**14.1.11**    A further reason is that the applicant must provide evidence that the judgment debtor has an account. This may be hard to do, although the new Act has introduced measures to counter this.

## Identity of third party

**14.1.12**    An application for a Third Party Debt Order can be made against any third party within the jurisdiction (except the Crown) but is usually made against a bank or building society. CPR rule 72.1(1) states that the third party must be 'within the jurisdiction'.

## Banks or building societies

**14.1.13**    Banks or building societies are defined as a 'deposit taking business' under Banking Act 1987, s.6.

**14.1.14**   One anomaly is the National Savings Bank. This is seen as under the control of the Crown and, under CPR rule 66.7(1)(a), a Third Party Debt Order cannot be made against any money due from the Crown. CPR rule 66.7(3), however, allows an application to be made against the Crown (and so also against the National Savings Bank) with a similar procedure to the procedure in CPR Part 72.

**14.1.15**   Conditions may be placed on withdrawals from banks, such as a notice period before money can be taken out. In this context, Supreme Court Act 1981, s.40 and County Court Act 1984, s.108 allow certain conditions to be ignored.

**14.1.16**   Banks or building societies can deduct a fixed level of expenses from the balance of the money they hold as an administrative fee for dealing with an interim Third Party Debt Order (Supreme Courts Act 1981, s.40A or County Courts Act 1984, s.109).

## Debt

**14.1.17**   CPR rule 72.2 allows a Third Party Debt Order to apply to 'any debt due or accruing due to the judgment debtor from the third party'.

**14.1.18**   Certain principles apply:

- until the debt becomes due, it cannot be the subject of a Third Party Debt Order. The Third Party Debt Order cannot accelerate the time for payment of the debt;
- rent can be the subject of a Third Party Debt Order, but only when it becomes payable by the tenant;
- a Third Party Debt Order can apply to an unascertained sum;
- wages cannot be the subject of a Third Party Debt Order, they must be the subject of an Attachment of Earnings Order (see **Chapter 13**); and
- the Crown cannot be the subject of a Third Party Debt Order, but an application can be made against the Crown under CPR rule 66.7(3).

## Procedure

**14.1.19**   The procedure for obtaining a Third Party Debt Order is a two-stage process: first by obtaining an interim Third Party Debt Order and then by obtaining a final Third Party Debt Order.

## Venue

**14.1.20**   An application for a Third Party Debt Order may be made without notice. It must be issued in the court which made the judgment being enforced unless the proceedings have been transferred to a different court, in which case it must be issued in that court.

**14.1.21**   The application does not have to be made in the court local to the debtor or the third party and there is no provision for automatic transfer to their local courts.

## Contents of application notice

**14.1.22**   The application notice must be in form N349 and must contain the following information:

Section 1: The name and address of the debtor
Section 2: Details of the judgment or orders being enforced:

- the amount of the judgment or order;
- the amount of money remaining due under the judgment or order;
- if the judgment debt is payable by instalments, the amount of any instalments which have fallen due and remain unpaid.

Section 3: Confirmation that, to the best of the creditor's knowledge or belief, the third party is within the jurisdiction; and owes money to or holds money to the credit of the debtor:

- If the third party is a bank or building society:

  1. Its name and address of the branch at which the debtor's account is believed to be held; and
  2. The account number or, if the debtor does not know all or part of this information, that fact.

- Otherwise, the name and address of the third party.

Section 4: The name and (if known) address of any person that the creditor knows or believes has any claim to the money, including such information as is known to the creditor about his claim.
Section 5: Sources or ground of the judgment creditor's knowledge or belief of the matters referred to in sections 3 and 4.
Section 6: Details of any other applications for Third Party Debt Orders issued by the creditor in respect of the same judgment debt.

**14.1.23**   A court will not grant speculative applications to creditors. A court will only make an interim Third Party Debt Order against, for example, a bank or building society if a creditor's application notice 'contains evidence to substantiate his belief that the judgment debtor has an account with the bank or building society in question' (but not necessarily that the account is in credit) (paragraph 1.3 Practice Direction to CPR Part 72).

**14.1.24**   Although this was a failing under the pre-Act position, where the debtor might not be as truthful as he could be about bank accounts he had that were in credit (even pursuant to an Order to Obtain Information), the new Act has covered this by the introduction of Information Orders.

**14.1.25**   Under an Information Order, the court can now ask a bank or building society directly whether the debtor has an account and can ask the bank to provide details of that account.

**14.1.26**   The ability to obtain information direct from a bank is likely to see a rise in the popularity of Third Party Debt Orders.

## Interim Third Party Debt Order hearing

**14.1.27**   An application for a Third Party Debt Order will initially be dealt with by a judge without a hearing (CPR rule 72.4). The application should be placed before a Master or District Judge on the same day it is made.

**14.1.28**   The judge has the power to make an interim Third Party Debt Order in form N84. At the same time, he will list a hearing to consider whether to make a final Third Party Debt Order.

**14.1.29**   The interim Third Party Debt Order will specify the amount of money which the third party must retain. This will be the total of the amount of money remaining due to the creditor under the order and an amount for the creditor's fixed costs of the application. The party subject to the Third Party Debt Order cannot make payments that reduce the amount he owes to below the amount he has been ordered by the court to retain.

## Service of interim Third Party Debt Order

**14.1.30**   It is in the creditor's interests to serve the interim Third Party Debt Order on the third party as soon as possible because the third party is obliged to comply with the order as soon as he is served with it. It is also advisable to serve the interim Third Party Debt Order on the third party before serving it on the debtor.

**14.1.31**   In relation to bank accounts (and especially solicitors' client accounts), if the creditor knows that a large deposit is about to be made, he could wait to serve the interim Third Party Debt Order until immediately after the deposit has been made because the order only restricts the amount in the account at the time of service. If money is subsequently paid in, a further interim order is needed (*Heppenstall v. Jackson & Barclays Bank Limited (Garnishees)* [1939] 1 KB 585).

**14.1.32**   Copies of the interim Third Party Debt Order, the application notice and any documents filed in support, must be served on the third party in any event not less than 21 days before the date fixed for the hearing and on the judgment debtor not less than seven days after a copy has been served on the third party and seven days before the date fixed for the hearing.

**14.1.33**   Having served the interim Third Party Debt Order, the creditor either has to file a certificate of service not less than two days before the hearing or produce a certificate of service at the hearing.

## What to do if served with an interim Third Party Debt Order

**14.1.34**   A third party (e.g. bank or building society) served with an interim Third Party Debt Order must carry out a search to identify all accounts held with it by the debtor and must disclose to the court and to the creditor, within seven days of being served with the order:

■   the number of the account;
■   whether the account is in credit;
■   if the account is in credit:

   (a)   whether the balance of the account is sufficient to cover the amount specified in the interim Third Party Debt Order;
   (b)   the amount in the account at the date the third party was served with the interim Third Party Debt Order, if it is less than the amount specified in the interim Third Party Debt Order; and
   (c)   whether the bank or building society asserts any right to the money in the account (either pursuant to right of set off or otherwise) and, if so, giving details of the grounds for that assertion.

These obligations of the third party are set out in form N84.

**14.1.35**   Under CPR rule 72.6, the bank or building society must provide this information for each and every account held by the debtor. If the debtor does not hold an account with the bank or building society they must inform the court and the creditor within seven days of being served with the interim Third Party Debt Order.

**14.1.36**   If the bank or building society cannot comply with the interim Third Party Debt Order for any other reason (e.g. they cannot identify to which account the order applies), they must inform the court and the creditor within seven days of being served with the order.

**14.1.37**   If the bank fails to do this, the court may make a final Third Party Debt Order, but it depends on the facts and the evidence as to whether the court will do so.

**14.1.38**   A Third Party Debt Order can be used against anybody who owes money to the debtor, not just a bank or building society. Where the interim Third Party Debt Order is served on a third party other than a bank or building society, that person must notify the court and the creditor in writing within seven days of being served the order if he claims not to owe any money to the debtor or to owe less than the amount specified in the order.

**14.1.39**   If a third party other than a bank or a building society does not respond after service with an interim Third Party Debt Order, the court is entitled to assume that the third party owes the money and so make a final Third Party Debt Order.

## Effect of interim Third Party Debt Order

**14.1.40**   Once served with an interim Third Party Debt Order the bank or building society must not reduce the amount in the account to below the amount it is ordered to retain (CPR rule 72.4(2)(b)).

**14.1.41**   An interim Third Party Debt Order served on a bank or building society therefore effectively freezes the account in the amount set out in the order.

**14.1.42**   The amount the third party is ordered to retain will include the applicant's fixed costs (CPR rule 72.4(3)(b)). The amount of fixed costs, mentioned in the interim Third Party Debt Order, and allowed to the creditor, is set out in CPR rule 45.6 as if the whole balance of the debt were recovered.

**14.1.43**   An interim Third Party Debt Order only acts, however, as an equitable charge on the debt. The third party should therefore wait until a final Third Party Debt Order before releasing the money to the creditor.

## Joint names

**14.1.44**   Where a bank or building society is served with an interim Third Party Debt Order, unless the order states otherwise, it is only required to retain monies in accounts held solely by the debtor.

**14.1.45**   It is made specifically clear in paragraph 3.2 of the Practice Direction to CPR Part 72 that the bank or building society is not required to retain money in accounts in the joint names of a debtor and another party who is not affected by the interim Third Party Debt Order.

**14.1.46**   Where there are joint debtors, the interim Third Party Debt Order can apply to accounts held jointly by them or solely by either of them.

## Partnerships

**14.1.47**   Where debts are due to a creditor from a partnership, an interim Third Party Debt Order must be served on either a member of the partnership within the jurisdiction or a person authorised by a partner or some other person having the control or management of the partnership business.

## Hardship Payment Orders

**14.1.48**   These only apply where the debtor is an individual.

**14.1.49**   Where a debtor is prevented from withdrawing money from his bank or building society account because the bank or building society has been served with an interim Third Party Debt Order and he or his family is suffering hardship in meeting ordinary living expenses because of this, the debtor can make an application to court in which the court may permit the bank or building society to make a payment or payments out of the account.

**14.1.50**    This is known as a Hardship Payment Order. See also **Chapters 19–23** on debt management schemes, Debt Relief Orders and Administration Orders, introduced by the new Act.

## Application for Hardship Payment Order

**14.1.51**    An application for a Hardship Payment Order may be made where it is High Court proceedings at the Royal Courts of Justice or to any District Registry or where it is county court proceedings to any county court, but a debtor may only apply to one court for a Hardship Payment Order.

**14.1.52**    The application does not need to be made in the same court as made the interim Third Party Debt Order.

## Contents of a Hardship Payment Order

**14.1.53**    The application notice seeking a Hardship Payment Order has to include detailed evidence explaining why the debtor needs a payment of the amount requested and be verified by a statement of truth.

**14.1.54**    The application notice must be served on the creditor at least two days before the hearing but does not need to be served on the third party.

**14.1.55**    The Hardship Payment Order can permit the third party to make one or more payments out of the account and can specify to whom the payments should be made.

## Final hearing of a Third Party Debt Order

**14.1.56**    The date of the hearing to consider the application for a Third Party Debt Order will be not less than 28 days after the interim Third Party Debt Order is made (CPR rule 72.4(5)).

**14.1.57**    It will take place before a Master or a District Judge.

**14.1.58**    At the final hearing the judge will decide whether to make a final Third Party Debt Order or whether to dismiss the application and discharge the interim Third Party Debt Order. Alternatively, the court may decide any issues in dispute between the parties or direct a trial of these issues and give directions (CPR rule 72.8(6)).

**14.1.59**    If the debtor wishes to file evidence in response to the interim Third Party Debt Order, this evidence must be filed and served on each party as soon as possible and in any event not less than three days before the hearing. This usually only happens where the debtor objects to a final Third Party Debt Order.

**14.1.60**   Where the court is notified that some person other than a debtor may have a claim to the money in the interim order, it will serve on that person notice of the application and the hearing.

## Effect of final Third Party Order

**14.1.61**   While an interim Third Party Debt Order operates merely as an equitable charge, a final Third Party Debt Order is enforceable as an order to pay money under CPR rule 72.9(1).

**14.1.62**   Once the third party pays money to the debtor pursuant to the final Third Party Debt Order, it acts as a discharge of the third party's liability to the debtor to the amount of the payment.

**14.1.63**   It is important, however, that the third party waits until the final third party debt Order is granted before paying the creditor and does not pay following the interim Third Party Debt Order. If the third party pays the creditor before he is ordered to, and a final Third Party Debt Order is not granted, the payment will not act as a discharge of the third party's debt to the debtor and the third party may end up paying twice, once to the creditor and once to the debtor.

**14.1.64**   If, following a Third Party Debt Order, the third party refuses to release the money he had been ordered to retain, despite the fact that it is now enforceable as an order to pay money, the creditor can take enforcement action against the third party.

**14.1.65**   If the third party disagrees with the final Third Party Debt Order he can:

- appeal it (if he was at the hearing); or
- apply for it to be set aside (if he was not at the hearing or new information becomes available).

## Money in court

**14.1.66**   Third Party Debt Orders do not apply to money in court.

**14.1.67**   Where money owned by the debtor is in court, the creditor can apply for an order that the money in court be paid to him to cover the judgment order and the costs of the application. An application notice seeking this order under CPR rule 72.10 must be served on the judgment debtor and the Accountant General at the Court Funds Office.

## Balance in account

**14.1.68**   Where a final Debt Order is made, it cannot reduce the amount in a judgment debtor's building society account to less than £1.

## 14.2    OVERVIEW FLOWCHART

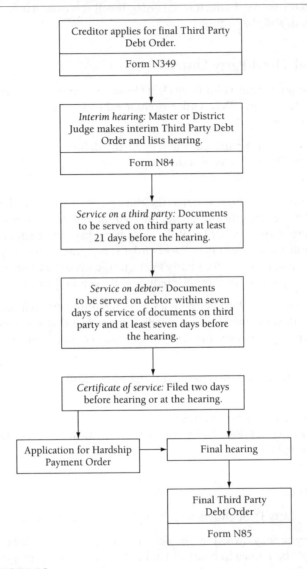

| Creditor applies for final Third Party Debt Order. |
| Form N349 |

| *Interim hearing:* Master or District Judge makes interim Third Party Debt Order and lists hearing. |
| Form N84 |

| *Service on a third party:* Documents to be served on third party at least 21 days before the hearing. |

| *Service on debtor:* Documents to be served on debtor within seven days of service of documents on third party and at least seven days before the hearing. |

| *Certificate of service:* Filed two days before hearing or at the hearing. |

| Application for Hardship Payment Order | → | Final hearing |

| Final Third Party Debt Order |
| Form N85 |

## 14.3    FORMS

N349    Application for Third Party Debt Order

N84     Interim Third Party Debt Order

N85     Final Third Party Debt Order

# PART IV  ENFORCEMENT OVER PROPERTY

# 15 CHARGING ORDERS

## 15.1 OVERVIEW

**15.1.1** Charging Orders are a commonly used enforcement tool. They are, however, not technically a method of enforcement in that they do not extract payment from the debtor. Charging Orders are simply a means of securing a judgment debt. Only once the asset is sold does the debt become discharged, and even then, depending on the value of the asset and any other charges that may have priority, the debt may not be discharged in full or even at all.

**15.1.2** Actually to enforce the debt, an Order for Sale is needed (once a Charging Order has been obtained).

### Popularity of Charging Orders

**15.1.3** Unlike warrants of execution (**Chapter 9**) and Orders to Obtain Information (**5.3**), the popularity of Charging Orders has risen over the last 10 years.

**15.1.4** The number of applications for Charging Orders, and actual orders, made since 1995 has risen dramatically. In 1996, there were 15,842 applications and 13,261 orders granted. This remained relatively constant until 2000 when there was a rise to 25,521 applications and 15,158 orders granted in 2001. This jumped again in 2002 and has risen every year since, until 2006 when over 92,000 applications were made and over 66,000 orders were granted.

**15.1.5** The rise in the number of Charging Orders coincides with the drop in numbers of Orders to Obtain Information (see **5.3.4**). Details about a debtor's house and other property can be found in other ways (not least of which, the claim form) and his interest in that property can be verified by a search at the Land Registry.

Table 15.1

| Year | Charging Order applications | Charging Orders made |
|------|------|------|
| 1995 | 21,081 | 18,515 |
| 1996 | 15,842 | 13,261 |
| 1997 | 14,002 | 11,422 |
| 1998 | 13,481 | 10,652 |
| 1999 | 13,527 | 9,749 |
| 2000 | 15,574 | 9,418 |
| 2001 | 25,521 | 15,158 |
| 2002 | 30,390 | 21,140 |
| 2003 | 34,681 | 24,963 |
| 2004 | 45,163 | 32,978 |
| 2005 | 65,437 | 48,985 |
| 2006 | 92,584 | 66,813 |

*Source*: The figures were obtained from the Economics and Statistics Division of the Ministry of Justice.

**15.1.6**    The increase in popularity of Charging Orders is largely due to the recent state of the property market in the UK. In a rising market, there is more chance of equity in a debtor's house than cash in his bank account and so Charging Orders become more effective than other methods of enforcement.

## Amounts

**15.1.7**    Even though the number of Charging Orders has risen dramatically over the last few years, the average amount charged on a property has remained relatively constant at somewhere between £11,000 and £12,000 per Charging Order.

Table 15.2

| Year | Charging Orders from which estimates obtained | Total amount fixed under Charging Orders | Average amount fixed under Charging Orders |
|------|------|------|------|
| 2000 | 15,500 | £176,900,000 | £12,000 |
| 2001 | 19,900 | £211,500,000 | £11,200 |
| 2002 | 27,000 | £302,000,000 | £11,200 |
| 2003 | 31,300 | £258,700,000 | £11,400 |
| 2004 | 41,200 | £481,500,000 | £11,700 |
| 2005 | 60,300 | £675,100,000 | £11,200 |
| 2006 | 85,700 | £976,100,000 | £11,400 |

*Source*: These figures were extracted from the Economics and Statistics Division of the Ministry of Justice and are estimates.

## Why change?

**15.1.8**    It might be worth asking why the new Act is introducing changes to such a popular post-judgment procedure. In short, it is to make them even more popular. In some ways, a Charging Order is a less draconian method of enforcement than, for example, sending round an enforcement agent or bankruptcy, and should be encouraged, not just for its efficiency for creditors but also for the relatively minimal impact for debtors as well.

**15.1.9**    The rationale behind the change was introduced by the new Act as first set out in the Department for Constitutional Affairs' Civil Enforcement Review. One of the proposals in that review was to widen access to Charging Orders.

**15.1.10**    The new Act is therefore designed to encourage use, and increase the availability, of Charging Orders, although some new measures (such as introducing a financial limit) will not have that effect.

## 15.2    PRE-ACT CURRENT POSITION

**15.2.1**    The new Act makes changes in relation to:

- instalments; and
- financial limits.

These are dealt with below.

**15.2.2**    The pre-Act position remains unchanged for the procedure in relation to obtaining Charging Orders.

**15.2.3**    Charging Orders are most commonly used where the debtor's only asset is a legal and/or beneficial interest in property (usually a house).

**15.2.4**    Charging Orders are, in the vast majority of cases, sought against property (land/buildings) but can also be sought against Stock Orders (Civil Procedure Rules (CPR) Part 73, section II) and against stock notices (CPR Part 73, section III).

**15.2.5**    As Charging Orders are mainly used against real property, any examples in this chapter will be for a house. Stock Orders will be dealt with at the end of the chapter.

### Effect of Charging Order

**15.2.6**    A Charging Order acts in the same way as a mortgage. The loan (or, in this case, judgment debt) is secured against property and is paid off when the property is sold before any equity in the property is paid to the seller/debtor.

**15.2.7**    A Charging Order will take effect subject to any pre-existing mortgage or charge already on the property.

**15.2.8**    A single Charging Order can be made to secure more than one judgment or order against the same debtor.

## What can be charged?

**15.2.9**    Under Charging Orders Act 1979, s.2, the following can be the subject of a Charging Order:

- land;
- securities (various forms of stock);
- funds in court;
- any interest under a trust.

**15.2.10**    For other assets, a writ or warrant of execution may be more appropriate.

## Why use Charging Orders?

**15.2.11**    Initially it is difficult to see why Charging Orders are so popular.

### *Disadvantage*

**15.2.12**    The problem with a Charging Order is that there is no immediate payment for the creditor. All a Charging Order does is to secure the judgment (not the debt) so that when the debtor (the owner of an interest in the property) comes to sell the property, the Charging Order bites with the effect that the creditor is paid off before any equity in the property is paid to the debtor.

**15.2.13**    Without an Order for Sale, there is no guarantee of when that sale might be. This would seem to make other methods of enforcement, where the money is received straightaway, far more attractive.

**15.2.14**    A Charging Order is therefore, in some respects, a long-term investment in that it does not guarantee immediate payment. In fact, some creditors use it just as that, letting a Charging Order remain on a house with little equity until its value rises sufficiently to cover the debt.

**15.2.15**    Once a Charging Order is obtained, the creditor needs to obtain an Order for Sale against that property in order to realise that judgment debt but does not need to do it straightaway. There are a number of competing interests in relation to an Order for Sale, especially where the Charging Order is over a party's home.

**15.2.16**    A Charging Order, and any subsequent Order for Sale, is effective where there is equity in the property. However, it is one of the least rapid methods of enforcement.

### *Advantage*

**15.2.17**    One of the reasons for the popularity of Charging Orders over the last five to 10 years is the buoyancy of the housing market.

**15.2.18**    In a falling market, where debtors are unlikely to have any equity left in their house after payment of the mortgage (a situation commonly known as 'negative equity'), a Charging Order becomes a less attractive method of enforcement. This is because a Charging Order takes effect subject to any prior mortgages or charges over the property.

**15.2.19**    However, in a rising market, as has been the case in the UK over the past 10 years, the equity in the debtor's home may be the only asset left to the debtor and may be substantial to the extent that, without it, the debtor may have considered insolvency.

**15.2.20**    It can also be beneficial for the debtor in that the effect of a Charging Order over a home is a relatively painless way to postpone payment. Repayment is delayed (often for a long period). The creditor has to wait for the payment, but is compensated at a relatively high interest rate (currently 8 per cent per annum as the standard court rate).

**15.2.21**    Charging Orders are also a low-cost method of securing the judgment debt.

## How to obtain a Charging Order

**15.2.22**    Charging Orders are governed by:

- Charging Orders Act 1979, which sets out the rules; and
- CPR Part 73 (which came into force in March 2002), which sets out the procedure.

**15.2.23**    The procedure for obtaining a Charging Order is at least a two-stage process, although it is advisable for it to be a three-stage process. Only stages 1 and 3 are obligatory.

### Stage 1 – interim application

**15.2.24**    Under Charging Orders Act 1979, s.2, a charge may be imposed by a Charging Order only on:

- any interest held by the debtor beneficially; or
- any interest held by a person as trustee of a trust, if the interest is in such an asset or is an interest under another trust and:
  - the judgment or order in respect of which a charge is to be imposed was made against that person as trustee of the trust; or
  - the whole beneficial interest under the trust is held by the debtor unencumbered and for his own benefit.

**15.2.25**    The use of the word 'may' in s.2 means that that there is a judicial discretion in each case in deciding whether to grant a Charging Order. The District

Judge hearing the application will consider all the circumstances of the case before exercising his discretion.

**15.2.26**    An application for a Charging Order may be made without notice (CPR rule 73.3(1)) and will initially be dealt with by a judge without a hearing (CPR rule 73.4(1)).

## FORMS REQUIRED

**15.2.27**    The creditor will make an application to court in form N379 where the application relates to land or form N380 where the application relates to securities.

**15.2.28**    Under paragraph 1.2 of the Practice Direction to CPR Part 73, the application notice must contain:

- the debtor's name and address;
- details of the judgment or order sought to be enforced;
- the amount of money remaining due under the judgment or order (see below in relation to unascertained sums);
- if the judgment debt is payable by instalments the amount of any instalments which have fallen due and remain unpaid;
- if the creditor knows of the existence of any other creditors of the debtor, their names and (if known) their addresses;
- identification of the asset or assets which it is intended to charge;
- details of the debtor's interest in the asset; and
- the names and addresses of the persons on whom an interim Charging Order must be served under CPR rule 73.1(1).

## VENUE

**15.2.29**    Under CPR rule 73.3(2) an application for a Charging Order must be issued in the court that made the judgment unless:

- the proceedings have since been transferred to a different court (in which case the application must be issued in that court);
- the application is made under the Council Tax (Administration and Enforcement) Regulations 1992, in which case it must be issued in the county court for the district in which the relevant dwelling (as defined in reg.50(3)(b) of those regulations) is situated;
- the application is for a Charging Order over an interest in a fund in court, in which case it must be issued in the court in which the claim relating to that fund is, or was, proceeding; or
- the application is to enforce a judgment or order of the High Court and it is required by s.1(2) of the 1979 Act to be made to a county court.

**15.2.30**    Where the application is not in relation to the 1992 regulations or funds in court, Charging Orders Act 1979, s.1(2) sets out the rules about which court to use.

**15.2.31**    The appropriate court is therefore generally the county court unless the judgment to be enforced is a judgment or order of the High Court for a sum exceeding the county court limit or the party is enforcing a maintenance order of the High Court or in a case where the property to be charged is a fund in court.

### INTERIM CHARGING ORDER

**15.2.32**    Following the application, if the court awards an interim Charging Order under CPR rule 73.4 a charge will be placed on the debtor's property (most commonly the debtor's house) and a hearing will be set down to decide whether to make a final Charging Order.

**15.2.33**    The interim Charging Order itself will set down a hearing date, giving the debtor an opportunity to attend and put his case to the court.

**15.2.34**    A Charging Order or interim Charging Order may be made against any property within the jurisdiction belonging to a debtor even where the debtor is a partnership.

### SERVICE

**15.2.35**    The interim Charging Order (together with the application notice and any documents filed in support) must then be served on the debtor by the creditor (CPR rule 73.5). Service is not effected by the court. Service must be not less than 21 days before the final Charging Order hearing.

**15.2.36**    The court will send to the creditor the forms that need to be served (i.e. the interim Charging Order (which itself sets down a date for the final hearing), the application notice and any documents filed in support).

## Stage 2 – registration

**15.2.37**    Having obtained the interim Charging Order, it should be registered.

**15.2.38**    An interim Charging Order is registerable under s.3 of the Charging Orders Act 1979:

> The Land Charges Act 1972 and the Land Registration Act 2002 shall apply in relation to Charging Orders as they apply in relation to other orders or writs issued or made for the purpose of enforcing judgments.

**15.2.39**    It is highly advisable to register the interim Charging Order against the title to the property as soon as it is obtained and prior to any hearing for a final Charging Order.

**15.2.40**    Registration will, as with any registered charge, prevent the interim Charging Order from being defeated by a sale to a bona fide purchaser for value without notice (such sale taking place between the interim Charging Order being made and the final Charging Order hearing). What this means is that registering the Charging Order effectively stops the debtor from defeating the charge by selling the house to a third party before the final Charging Order hearing.

**15.2.41**    The procedure for registering a Charging Order is set out below.

## Stage 3 – final hearing

**15.2.42**   Having served, and in most cases registered, the interim Charging Order, the final hearing will then take place. The court will, at the time of issuing the interim Charging Order, have set down a date for a final hearing.

### DEBTOR'S EVIDENCE

**15.2.43**   Under CPR rule 73.8, a party wanting to object to a final Charging Order must file written evidence to the court and also serve that evidence on the applicant at least seven days before the date of the final hearing.

### FINAL HEARING

**15.2.44**   At the final hearing, the court will want to see that the interim Charging Order has been served and will consider the evidence of both parties.

**15.2.45**   Pursuant to rule 73.8(2), the court may:

- make a final Charging Order, which is basically maintaining the position under the interim Charging Order;
- discharge the interim Charging Order and dismiss the application; or
- decide any issues or direct a trial of any issues.

**15.2.46**   In deciding whether to make a Charging Order, the court should consider all the circumstances in the case, any evidence before it as to the personal circumstances of the debtor and whether any other creditor of the debtor would be likely to be unduly prejudiced by the making of the order (Charging Orders Act 1979, s.1(5)).

**15.2.47**   The court may refuse to make a final Charging Order if insolvency or bankruptcy proceedings are imminent, because the effect of the order would be to give the creditor priority over other unsecured creditors (*Robert Petroleum Limited* v. *Bernard Kennedy Limited* [1983] AC 192).

### POSSIBLE ORDERS

**15.2.48**   At the final hearing, the following orders may be made by the court:

- Final Charging Order – this is an order continuing the interim Charging Order either with or without modification;
- discharge the interim Charging Order and dismiss the application;
- decide any issues and disputes between the parties (and any other person who objects to the court, e.g. another creditor of the debtor) and make a final Charging Order; or
- direct a trial of any issues and give directions.

**15.2.49**   It will only be in exceptional circumstances that a trial will be directed to determine any issues (CPR rule 73.8(2)(d)).

## What is charged

**15.2.50**   To register a Charging Order, the parties need to take into account:

- the way in which the property is held; and
- whether the debtor is co-owner of the property with a third party who does not owe a judgment debt.

**15.2.51**   Where the debtor is the sole owner of the land, the Charging Order will impose a charge over the entire legal and beneficial interest in the property. Where there are joint debtors who are co-owners, then the entire legal (but not beneficial) interest is charged.

**15.2.52**   Where there are co-owners, only one of whom is a debtor under the Charging Order, only the debtor's beneficial interest is charged.

## Does the final Charging Order need to be registered?

**15.2.53**   If a final Charging Order is obtained, it needs to be served on all persons on whom the interim Charging Order had to be served (CPR rule 73.8(4)).

**15.2.54**   Although it is good practice to register the final Charging Order, technically, and so long as the interim Charging Order has been correctly registered, it is not necessary to register the final Charging Order. This is because the charge takes effect (albeit conditionally) as soon as the interim Charging Order is made. The final Charging Order does not create a new charge; it simply makes the charge unconditional.

**15.2.55**   Therefore, where the interim Charging Order has been properly registered, it need not be re-registered when made final. If an interim Charging Order is discharged, however, its registration must be removed.

## Procedure for registering a Charging Order

### Unregistered land

**15.2.56**   In all cases, a caution is placed on the title by filing at Land Registry form CT1 and form K4.

**15.2.57**   A fee is payable.

### Registered land

**15.2.58**   In cases where the debtor is either sole owner of the property, joint owner with a party also jointly liable under the judgment debt or a company, a notice is placed on the title by filing at Land Registry either form AN1 or form UN1.

**15.2.59**   In cases where the debtor jointly owns the property with a third party not liable under the judgment debt, a restriction is placed on the title by filing at Land Registry a form RX1. The restriction will be in form K.

**15.2.60**   A fee is payable.

## Varying the Charging Order

**15.2.61**   Pursuant to CPR rule 73.9, an interested party can apply to discharge or vary a Charging Order. An application to discharge or vary a Charging Order must be made to the court that made the Charging Order. The court has jurisdiction to discharge or vary the order at any time under Charging Orders Act 1979, s.3(5).

**15.2.62**   The procedure for varying or discharging a Charging Order is set out in CPR rule 73.9.

## Order for sale

**15.2.63**   In the event that a final Charging Order is made, the creditor may decide not to take the matter any further and simply wait until the property is sold (which may of course be many years).

**15.2.64**   With a final Charging Order, a creditor could, however, apply to court for an Order for Sale to realise his judgment debt. This is governed by CPR rule 73.10.

**15.2.65**   Only the person who has the benefit of a final Charging Order may enforce that Charging Order by an application for an Order for Sale.

**15.2.66**   In doing so, the creditor is basically asking the court to order the debtor to sell his property and pay off the charges over the property (including the final Charging Order) in order of priority.

**15.2.67**   Again, there is still no guarantee that the judgment debt will be paid in full as it all depends on the amount achieved by the sale and the amount of the prior charges.

### Mechanics of sale

**15.2.68**   If a final Charging Order is granted, the creditor can apply at any time for an Order for Sale.

**15.2.69**   The procedure is set out in CPR rule 73.10. The creditor has to issue a new claim form under CPR rule 8. The claim (which will be asking for an Order for Sale) should be issued in the court that made the Charging Order, unless that court does not have jurisdiction to order a sale e.g. if the amount owing under the charge is above the county court limit (County Courts Act 1984, s.23(a) sets out the extent of the county court's jurisdiction).

**15.2.70**   If a sale is ordered, the net proceeds (after deduction of sale costs) are paid to the court.

## Venue

**15.2.71**   An application for an Order for Sale involving a sum of over the county court limit (currently £30,000) must be started in the High Court, Chancery Division.

**15.2.72**   Any other applications for Order for Sale are in the county court, usually the county court with jurisdiction over that property (paragraph 4 of the Practice Direction to CPR Part 73).

## Procedure for applying for an Order for Sale

**15.2.73**   The creditor with the benefit of a final Charging Order who wishes to apply for an Order for Sale needs to issue a new Part 8 claim and send to the court:

■   Part 8 claim form;
■   claimant's written evidence;
■   copy of the Charging Order; and
■   the appropriate fee.

**15.2.74**   The requirements of the written evidence are set out in the Practice Direction to CPR rule 73.10. The written evidence in support of the claim for an Order for Sale must:

■   identify the Charging Order and the property sought to be sold;
■   state the amount in respect of which the charge was imposed and the amount due at the date of the issue of the claim;
■   verify, so far as is known, the debtor's title to the property charged;
■   state, so far as the claimant is able to identify:

  –   the names and addresses of any other creditors who have a prior charge or other security over the property;
  –   the amount owed to each such creditor;

■   give an estimate of the price which would be obtained on sale of the property;
■   if the claim relates to land, give details of every person who (to the best of the claimant's knowledge) is in possession of the property;
■   if the claim relates to residential property, state whether a registration has been made of:

  –   a class F land charge;
  –   a notice under Family Law Act 1996, s.31(10) or under any provision of an Act which preceded that section and if so state:

- on whose behalf the land charge or notice has been registered; and
- that the claimant will serve notice of the claim on that person.

**15.2.75**   A claimant must take all reasonable steps to obtain the above information before issuing the claim.

## Hearing

**15.2.76**   In deciding whether to grant an Order for Sale, the court is balancing the interests of the creditor on one hand (who has obtained judgment against the party and is entitled, at some point, to realise that judgment) and the interests of the debtor and in particular any of his dependants or joint owners of the property. The court will be acutely aware that until the Order for Sale is granted, the creditor is not receiving the money he is due.

**15.2.77**   The debtor may argue, for example, that the sale would be pointless because there is negative equity in the house. The claimant should have evidence to counter this.

**15.2.78**   Where a property is owned and occupied solely by the debtor, the court will be likely to order a sale but if the judgment debt could be paid by other means within a reasonable time or hardship will be caused, then the court may refuse to make an Order for Sale or may postpone or suspend it.

## Joint ownership

**15.2.79**   Where the property is owned by more than one person, Trusts of Lands and Appointment of Trustees Act 1996, s.15 applies.

**15.2.80**   If the property is in the sole name of the debtor or is owned jointly by parties who are both debtors then the charge will be against land itself. Where, however, the property is owned jointly with a third party but the third party (e.g. spouse) is not a debtor then the Charging Order will only affect the debtor's equitable interest in the land, rather than the full legal and beneficial title. Where the debtor is a joint owner with another party who is not a debtor, the creditor will be able to make an application for an Order for Sale under Land and Appointment of Trustees Act 1996, s.14.

## Suspending Order

**15.2.81**   It is possible that a sale may be suspended, for example, until the debtor's children are 18. In *Austin-Fell v. Austin-Fell Midland Bank plc* [1990] All ER 445 the order was suspended for 10 years for this reason.

## Interest

**15.2.82**   Once a Charging Order is obtained, it does not affect interest payable on that judgment debt, pursuant to County Courts (Interest on Judgment Debt) Order 1991, s.4(2). Therefore if the judgment debt remains unpaid, even after the Order for Sale is obtained, interest still accrues, even where a sale is more than six years later (*Ezekiel v. Orakpo* [1997] 1 WLR 340). This contrasts with applications to enforce the judgment where interest is not payable if six years is waited (*Lowsley v. Forbes* [1999] 1 AC 329).

## Human rights

**15.2.83**   Article 8 of the European Convention on Human Rights provides firstly that everyone has the right to respect for his private and family life, his home and his correspondence and secondly that there should be no interference by a public authority with the exercise of this right except such as in accordance with the law and as is necessary in the interests of national security, public safety or the economic well-being of the country.

**15.2.84**   It was held in *Wells v. Pickering* [2002] 2 FLR 798 that a creditor's right to be paid was to be protected and the sale of a person's house by an Order for Sale was not a breach of Article 8 of the European Convention on Human Rights.

## Securities/funds in court

### Effect of interim Charging Order on securities

**15.2.85**   Under CPR rule 73.6(1), once an interim Charging Order is obtained against securities, if the debtor then disposes of his interest in those securities (once the interim Charging Order has been served on him) the sale of those securities shall not (so long as the order remains in force) be valid as against the creditor and the creditor can enforce against those securities.

**15.2.86**   However, a person served with an interim Charging Order (see below for service) must not permit any transfer of any of the securities or pay any dividend interest or redemption payment relating to those securities without the court's permission. If he does, that party will be liable to pay to the creditor to the value of the securities transferred or the amount of the payment made or the amount necessary to satisfy the debt in relation to which the interim Charging Order was made pursuant to CPR rule 73.6(3).

## Service

**15.2.87**   Service of the interim Charging Order in relation to securities is covered by CPR rule 73.5(1)(d) which states that:

■   in the case of stock for which the Bank of England keeps the register, the Bank of England must be served;

- in the case of government stock to which the section above does not apply, the keeper of the register;
- in the case of stock of any body incorporated within England and Wales, that body;
- in the case of stock of any body incorporated outside England and Wales or of any state or territory outside the United Kingdom which is registered in a register kept in England and Wales, the keeper of that register; or
- in the case of units of any unit trust in respect of which a register of the unit holders is kept in England and Wales the keeper of that register.

## Effect of interim Charging Order in relation to funds in court

**15.2.88**    Service of an interim Charging Order in relation to funds in court is set out in CPR rule 73.5(1)(e) which states that the Accountant General at the Court Funds Office must be served, as well as the debtor.

**15.2.89**    If a debtor disposes of his interest in funds in court while subject to an interim Charging Order which has been validly served on him and the Accountant General, that disposition shall not, so long as the Charging Order remains in force, be valid as against the creditor (CPR rule 73.7).

## Stop Orders and stop notices

**15.2.90**    Stop Orders relate to funds in court or securities specified in the Stop Order. Stop notices relate to securities not held in court.

### Stop Orders

**15.2.91**    If the court makes a final Charging Order which charges securities (other than securities held in court), the order will include a stop notice unless the court orders otherwise (CPR rule 73.8(3)). Where the securities are funds in court, a Stop Order will be made.

**15.2.92**    Stop Orders are covered by CPR rules 73.11–73.15.

**15.2.93**    Pursuant to rule 73.11 a Stop Order is:

> an order of the High Court not to take, in relation to funds in court or security specified in the order, any steps listed in section 5(5) of the 1979 Act.

**15.2.94**    Section 5(5) of the Charging Orders Act 1979 lists the steps as:

- the registration of any transfer of the securities;
- in the case of funds in court, the transfer sale delivery out payment or other dealing with the funds or of the income thereon;
- the making of any payment by way of dividend, interest or otherwise in respect of the securities; or

- in the case of a unit trust, any acquisition of or other dealing with the units by any person or body exercising functions under the trust.

**15.2.95**   CPR rule 73.12(1)(a), (3) states that a creditor of a person entitled to an interest in funds in a court office can make an application for a Stop Order.

**15.2.96**   An application for a Stop Order is made either by an application notice in existing proceedings or by a rule 8 claim form if there are no existing proceedings in the High Court.

### SERVICE

**15.2.97**   The application notice or claim form must be served on every person whose interest may be affected by the order and either the Accountant General at the Court Funds Office (in the case of funds in court) or the persons specified in CPR rule 73.5(1)(d) (if the application relates to securities other than the securities held in court). The persons specified in that rule are set out above.

**15.2.98**   Once a Stop Order is made in relation to funds in court it prevents the transfer, sale, delivery, payment or other dealing with the funds or any income on the funds (CPR rule 73.13).

**15.2.99**   Where the Stop Order relates to securities other than the securities held in court it prohibits registration of any transfer, the making of any payment by way of payment interest or other payment and in the case of units in the unit trust any acquisition of or other dealing with the units by any person or body exercising functions under the trust (CPR rule 73.14).

## Stop notices

**15.2.100**   A stop notice is a notice issued by the court requiring a person not to take any of the steps listed in s.5(5) of the 1979 Act without first giving notice to the person who obtained the stop notice. A stop notice does not relate to securities held in court.

**15.2.101**   The High Court, on the request of any person claiming to be beneficially entitled to an interest in those securities, may issue a stop notice. A stop notice may also be included in a final Charging Order either by the High Court or by the county court under CPR rule 73.8(3).

### PROCEDURE

**15.2.102**   A request for a stop notice is made by filing a draft stop notice and written evidence. The written evidence must identify the securities in question, describe the applicant's interest in the securities and give an address for service for the applicant (CPR rule 73.17(2)). Under rule 73.17(3), if a court officer considers that the request complies with paragraph 2 he will issue a stop notice.

## SERVICE

15.2.103    The applicant must serve copies of the stop notice and his written evidence in support on the person to whom the stop notice is addressed.

## EFFECT OF STOP NOTICE

15.2.104    A stop notice only takes effect when it is properly served. It remains in force unless it is withdrawn or discharged in accordance with CPR rule 73.20 or rule 73.21.

15.2.105    While a stop notice is in force the person on whom it is served cannot register a transfer of the securities described in the notice or take any other step restrained by the notice without first giving 14 days' notice to the person who obtained the stop notice.

15.2.106    Stop notices can be amended under CPR rule 73.19 and are usually used where securities are incorrectly described in a stop notice.

## WITHDRAWAL OF STOP NOTICE

15.2.107    If the person who has obtained a stop notice wishes to withdraw it he must serve a request for its withdrawal on the person on whom the stop notice was served and the court which issued the stop notice. This is pursuant to CPR rule 73.20. The formalities are that the request must be signed by the person who obtained the stop notice and his signature must be witnessed by a practising solicitor under CPR rule 73.20(2).

## DISCHARGE OR VARIATION OF STOP NOTICE

15.2.108    On an application by the person affected by the stop notice the court may make an order discharging or varying the notice.

## 15.3    THE NEW LAW

### Judgment in instalments

15.3.1    The new Act in relation to Charging Orders relates primarily to where the judgment being enforced provides that the debtor is to pay in instalments. This may be ordered by the court or when a party makes an admission, for example, they can make an offer to pay in instalments.

15.3.2    The new Act is designed to close a loophole in the pre-Act position that prevents a Charging Order from being granted over property if the debtor is not in default of payments under an Instalment Order.

15.3.3    This is all part of the rationale behind the new Act, as Lord Falconer put it, 'to ensure that creditors receive the money to which they are properly entitled'.

## Pre-Act position for instalments

**15.3.4**    Under the old law, a creditor with the benefit of an order to pay a judgment in instalments would have to rely on Charging Orders Act 1979, s.1(1), which allowed the court to order a charge 'for securing the payment of any money due or to become due' under a judgment or order. This meant that the court had power to make a Charging Order to secure the whole judgment debt, not just any arrears in relation to instalments.

**15.3.5**    The difficulty with the old law was that under County Courts Act 1984, s.86(1), a Charging Order could not be obtained until after default in payment of one or more instalments:

> Where the court has made an order for payment of any sum of money by instalments, execution on the order shall not be issued until after default in payment of some instalment according to the order.

**15.3.6**    Similarly, in the High Court, the court would most likely use their discretion to refuse a Charging Order where instalments were not yet in arrears.

**15.3.7**    It was recognised that the court's inability to grant a Charging Order where instalments under a judgment debt were not in arrears could cause prejudice to the creditor. For example, the debtor could keep paying instalments, and in the meantime sell his property (which may be his only asset). If the debtor stopped paying instalments under the order at a later date, the creditor would no longer be able to enforce against the property, it having been sold while the instalments were up to date.

**15.3.8**    This was denying the Charging Orders of their intended effect – to act as security for payment.

## New law for instalments

**15.3.9**    The new Act has changed that position. Under s.93 of the new Act, a new s.1(6), (7) and (8) of the Charging Orders Act 1979 will apply in cases where 'a debtor is required to pay a sum of money by instalments'.

**15.3.10**    The effect of these new sections in the Charging Orders Act 1979 is that a creditor can now obtain a Charging Order where the judgment debt is ordered to be paid in instalments even where there has been no default in payment under those instalments (Charging Orders Act 1979, s.1(7)). However, the creditor will be unable to obtain an Order for Sale unless the debtor is in default of one of those instalments (s.1(8)).

**15.3.11**    This reinforces the premise that a Charging Order is a method of security, not enforcement. It allows security against the property but does not allow enforcement until default, just as with a mortgage.

**15.3.12**   The new Act also allows the Lord Chancellor to set financial limits below which a court cannot grant a Charging Order and an Order for Sale cannot be obtained (Charging Orders Act 1979, s.3A). This is designed as a safeguard to ensure that Charging Orders are not used to secure disproportionately small judgment debts. This is dealt with later.

### DO I HAVE TO WAIT FOR AN INSTALMENT TO BE UNPAID:

*(a) to get a Charging Order?*

**15.3.13**   Under the new s.1(7) of the Charging Orders Act 1979, even with no default in payment of the instalments, a creditor can still obtain a Charging Order in respect of that sum.

**15.3.14**   This power is unfortunately not as strong as it could be. The wording of s.1(7) makes it clear that the power to obtain a Charging Order is still at the court's discretion:

> the fact that there has been no default in payment of the instalments does not prevent a Charging Order from being made in respect of that sum.

**15.3.15**   Also, under the new s.1(8), the fact that payments are not in arrears is a factor that the court will take into account when exercising its discretion under s.1(5) as to whether or not to grant a Charging Order.

**15.3.16**   How the courts will exercise that discretion remains to be seen, and it is hoped that Charging Orders will be granted even where instalments are not in default as, combined with the new s.3(4)(c), this would allow a creditor to secure his debt while protecting a non-defaulting debtor from the sale.

**15.3.17**   The starting point is that even if instalments are being paid on time, the court does have jurisdiction to order a Charging Order to secure the debt and the future instalments.

*(b) to get an Order for Sale?*

**15.3.18**   Under the new s.3(4C) of the Charging Orders Act 1979 (introduced by s.93(3) of the new Act), where a party has obtained a Charging Order for payment in instalments, they cannot enforce that Charging Order unless there has been a default in payment of an instalment.

**15.3.19**   Further, the court will not order enforcement of the Charging Order unless, at the time of enforcement, at least part of an instalment that had become due remains unpaid (Charging Orders Act 1979, s.3(4E)).

**15.3.20**   It is therefore a two-stage test. To obtain an Order for Sale for a judgment in instalments, there must be arrears under the instalments both:

- at the time of the application, in order to trigger the application to enforce; and
- at the time of enforcement.

**15.3.21**  Effectively, the Charging Order can be used, as it is currently used, as security or a guarantee in relation to the judgment, but while instalments are being paid, it cannot be enforced. This is only natural as until a party is in default of payment by instalments, a debt has effectively not arisen and the Charging Order carries out its role of securing the judgment, just as with a mortgage.

## When a debtor fails to pay an instalment

**15.3.22**  Once a party is in default of payment of an instalment, the creditor who has a Charging Order securing payment of those instalments can ask for enforcement of the whole sum by way of an Order for Sale.

**15.3.23**  Under the new s.3(4D), there may be limits as to when a court is prepared to do that and also the amounts for which it is prepared to order a sale although the court does have jurisdiction, under the new s.3(4E)(a) to order that the charge be enforced for the full sum once there is default.

**15.3.24**  Although at first glance it would seem harsh to order that the full sum be paid, it would destroy the security of the Charging Order to order that the property be sold and only part of the charged sum be paid, with the remainder being paid later under instalments (which by then would no longer have any security, the property having been sold).

## New limits on Charging Orders

**15.3.25**  Under the new s.3(A) of the Charging Orders Act 1979 there may be a minimum limit on:

- the amount that can be charged; and
- the amount that has to be outstanding before there can be an Order for Sale.

**15.3.26**  This will be introduced by way of statutory instrument and at the date of publication, these limits are not yet known and are to be introduced by regulations from the Lord Chancellor. They are however likely to be higher than the limit of £1,000 in relation to a Charging Order on non-payment of council tax.

**15.3.27**  It is hoped that the limit will not be made unrealistically high as it should be borne in mind that the average amount due in Charging Order applications is only £11,000 to £12,000.

**15.3.28**  The new limits mean that a Charging Order cannot be used for small amounts and that Orders for Sale will not be granted where only small amounts are outstanding.

**15.3.29**  The justification for placing a limit on the exercise of these powers is that in cases of small debts, where a court is highly unlikely to exercise its discretion to order a sale of the property (and effectively make a party homeless), a rule setting a limit would assist the parties both in knowing whether it was worth making an application to court (and thereby saving legal costs) and whether the debtor could enforce by other methods.

15.3.30   The limit introduced by the new Act gives statutory effect to the already common judicial practice that 'the Order is likely to be refused if it would be oppressive for example if the debt appears too small to justify the remedy . . .' (CPR rule 73.4.2).

15.3.31   The difficulty with this approach is where the debtor's only asset is the property. This approach may leave the debtor without a method of enforcement and, until the judgment debt is awarded, there is no guarantee of exactly how much the order for the judgment debt will be. Where the creditor has a debt that falls below the threshold, and the debtor's only asset is property, the creditor will have to consider various insolvency options to realise the debt.

15.3.32   A more appropriate change under the new Act may have been to allow a Charging Order even where there is no default in instalments (as the new Act currently does), but only to put a limit on the ability to apply for an Order for Sale, not on the ability to apply for a Charging Order. That would stop homes being sold where only small sums were due but would still allow a creditor to use the Charging Order as a form of long-term security over the debt.

## Charging Order over costs to be assessed

15.3.33   Under Charging Orders Act 1979, s.1(1), a Charging Order can be obtained 'for securing the payment of any money due or to become due under the judgment or order'.

15.3.34   At first glance, it appears that this makes it possible to obtain a Charging Order to secure costs where the court has ordered that the debtor pays costs, to be assessed if not agreed. As long as the applicant can show that some costs will become due in the future (which will be possible where a party has a Costs Order in their favour but may be more difficult where an interim payment on account of costs has been ordered by the court) the beneficiary of that Costs Order should, in theory, be able to argue under Charging Orders Act 1979, s.1(1) that once the costs are assessed they will 'become due' under the order and therefore a Charging Order is appropriate. However, this is not the case.

15.3.35   A Charging Order cannot be obtained on costs that have yet to be assessed because unassessed costs are an unascertained sum and do not 'become due' until they are ascertained.

15.3.36   The new Act does not change this position. Even under the new Act, it is not possible to obtain a Charging Order in relation to costs where the court has ordered that the debtor pay costs but those costs have not yet been assessed or agreed. Only once the costs are assessed do they become due under the order and therefore only at that time an application for a Charging Order be made.

**15.3.37** In *A & M Records Inc* v. *Darakejian and another* [1975] All ER 1983 it was held that the court has no power under Administration of Justice Act 1958, s.35(1) to impose a charge on the land of a debtor for an unascertained sum.

**15.3.38** In that case, the claimants were awarded two sets of costs against the defendants, such costs to be assessed (or taxed in those days) if not agreed.

**15.3.39** While costs were being assessed, the claimants applied to court for a Charging Order under the then relevant section, being s.35(1) of the Administration of Justice Act 1956. The reason for applying for this was that the debtors were concerned that the property might be sold, leaving them without any prospect of recovering their costs.

**15.3.40** Unfortunately for the debtors (and this is an issue that is not addressed by the new Act) the court found that it did not have the power to impose a Charging Order where the sum was unascertained:

> . . . it seems to me that when that subsection talks about 'any monies due or to become due' if one is imposing a charge for an uncertain amount, those are not monies due nor, I think, do they become due.

**15.3.41** This case was before the Charging Orders Act 1979 came into force. However, the wording of the old 1956 Act, on which the case was decided, included identical wording to the 1979 Act, that is to say the court has the power to impose a 'charge for securing the payment of any monies due or to become due under the judgment or order'.

**15.3.42** Walton J held that costs are included in 'payment of any monies due' but that it is not possible to impose a charge to secure those costs before there is an ascertained sum (so in the case of costs, a Charging Order cannot be obtained before those costs have been assessed).

**15.3.43** The rationale behind this decision was that this section of the 1979 Act was for the enforcement of judgments and was not a section designed to impose a penalty on the debtor because he has sums to pay.

**15.3.44** Although clearly good law, the position does seem too 'defendant friendly'.

**15.3.45** In a position where a party is ordered to pay costs, that is a sum that will 'become due' once the formalities of assessment have been complied with. To prevent the Charging Order being imposed (and bearing in mind that a Charging Order is not strictly speaking a means of enforcing the debt but simply a means of securing its payment) is potentially denying the claimant a sum (albeit as yet unascertained) that the court has already ordered should be his. An unscrupulous defendant, especially where he has not been ordered to pay an interim payment in relation to costs, may dispose of his property in an attempt to avoid payment of a costs liability. He could delay that costs liability, and gain time to sell his property, by seeking the bill of costs be assessed.

**15.3.46**   With no evidence that this is the defendant's intention, an injunction preventing the sale would not be possible and it would be left to the claimants to seek the court's redress again, in seeking to have the transaction set aside, which is by no means guaranteed.

**15.3.47**   The new Act could have made it clear that the phrase 'to become due' includes where money is to be paid at a future date (as in the case of a Costs Order) but that sum has not yet been ascertained.

**15.3.48**   If this change had been introduced, any prejudice to the defendant brought about by the claimant's delay in seeking to ascertain the amount of costs due could be mitigated either by:

- the interim Charging Order being discharged for failure to take reasonable steps; or
- imposing in the interim Charging Order itself conditions relating to progressing the assessment of the costs; and in either case
- not allowing an Order for Sale on an unascertained sum.

**15.3.49**   In those circumstances, each party's rights would be properly protected. That is, however, not the case under the current law, either pre-Act or under the new Act.

**15.3.50**   As Walton J said:

> it seems to me, however one dresses it up, one would be imposing a penalty on the debtor, because one would be putting on his land for however short a time, and in some cases it would be a very long time indeed, a Charge which would prevent him from freely dealing with the interest in the land which he undoubtedly, at the end of the day, would be found to have.

> Moreover it seems to be that although section 35(1) uses the words 'for securing the payment for any monies due or to become due under the judgment or order' that means all monies due or to become due under the judgment or order. One cannot say: 'I must at least get £500 on inquiry as to damages. Therefore I want a Charging Order for £500.' It seems to me that the Charging Order was intended to be a simple method or procedure designed to deal with the simple situation – that is to say an order saying 'A shall pay B £x'.

Walton J found reinforcement for this point by the terms of the Rules of the Supreme Court Order 50, rule 1(4) (the relevant rules at the time) which required an application for a Charging Order to be supported by an affidavit stating the amount remaining unpaid. The CPR have a similar current obligation in paragraph 1.2(3) of the Practice Direction to Part 73.

**15.3.51**   Despite the new Act, therefore, the position remains that until costs are assessed, a creditor cannot obtain a Charging Order for those unassessed costs.

**15.3.52**   An exception to this general rule that a Charging Order cannot be obtained for unassessed costs is in *Holder and others* v. *Superstore and others* [2000] 1 All ER 473. In that case, it was held that where a person already holds a Charging Order, he can add the costs incurred by him of enforcing the Charging Order to the sum already secured by the charge, even where those costs were not yet assessed. The basis for this decision is that the costs of enforcing the Charging Order are an equitable charge and so can be added to the security conferred by the Charging Order under Attachment of Earnings Act 1979, s.3(4). This is distinguished from other legal costs (not incurred in enforcing the Charging Order), which fall under s.1(1) of the 1979 Act and which can only be secured under a Charging Order once ascertained by agreement or assessment (as set out above).

**15.3.53**   The *Holder* case only applies where a person already holds a Charging Order and wishes to add costs incurred by him, in enforcing the Charging Order, to the secured judgment debt (in which case it is allowed).

## Transitional periods

**15.3.54**   The new Act does not apply to cases where a creditor was required to pay a sum of money by instalments before the coming into force of this section. This means the order to pay by instalments, rather than the default.

## Reaction to the new Act

**15.3.55**   Some, for example Citizens Advice, are concerned that making it easier to obtain a Charging Order may encourage parties to issue proceedings rather than accept an affordable payment plan from a party having trouble paying a debt.

**15.3.56**   Having said that, if a party is prepared to offer a payment plan but not offer the comfort of a charge which they would realistically have to offer to anybody loaning them the money, there is no reason why a claimant should not issue proceedings. The new Act also closes a loophole allowing some parties to escape payment.

## 15.4    OVERVIEW FLOWCHART

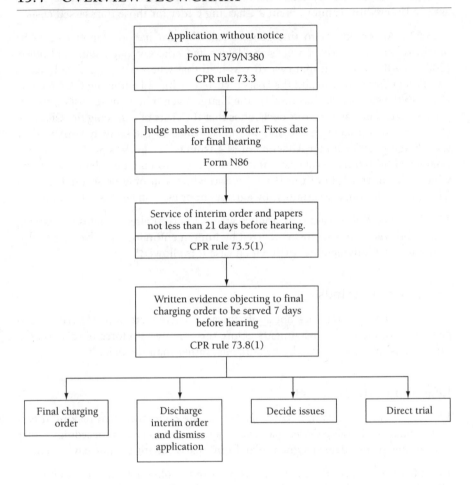

## 15.5    FORMS

N379       Application for Charging Order/land/property

N380       Application for Charging Order (securities)

N86        Interim Charging Order

N87        Final Charging Order

No.79      Stop Order

No.80      Witness statement and stop notice

No.81      Order on claim to restrain transfer of stock

# 16 OBTAINING POSSESSION OF COMMERCIAL PREMISES

## 16.1 INTRODUCTION

**16.1.1** A commercial lease can be terminated in a number of ways:

- *By effluxion of time* – This is where the term of the lease is to end on a certain date and it does so. Once the term ends, unless the tenant enters into a new lease or the lease is not excluded from the Landlord and Tenant Act 1954, the tenant is a trespasser and can be evicted.

  It is important to remember that if the lease is not excluded from the Landlord and Tenant Act 1954 (either by court order or by statutory declaration, depending on when it was entered into), then the lease does not end on the contractual termination date. On the contractual termination date, a lease within the 1954 Act would continue as a statutory extension under s.24 of that Act until terminated by, for example, a s.25 notice or a s.26 request.

- *Break notice* – The requirements of a break notice are usually very strict and need to be complied with fully. Only where the lease contains a break clause can a party serve a break notice.

- *Forfeiture* – In order to be able to forfeit there must firstly be a right to forfeit in the lease (which there will be in almost all cases) but otherwise by common law. To exercise the right to forfeit requires a breach by the tenant.

- *Surrender* – This is where the landlord acquires the tenant's lease, either by deed or by operation of law.

- *Disclaimer* – By the original tenant's liquidator or trustee in bankruptcy.

- *Other methods* – For example, repudiation or frustration.

## 16.2 FORFEITURE

**16.2.1** This is a means of terminating a lease prior to the contractual termination date because of a breach in the lease terms by the tenant. The effect of forfeiture is that the lease ends from the date of forfeiture and all future obligations under the lease fall away.

## Right to forfeit

**16.2.2**   The lease should contain a right to forfeit. Virtually all commercial leases will.

**16.2.3**   Without a contractual right to forfeit in the lease, a landlord would have to rely on a common law right to forfeit which will require the landlord to prove a breach of a condition of the lease or will require the tenant denying the landlord's title. In the vast majority of cases, forfeiture is pursuant to a contractual right to forfeit, found within the lease.

## Type of breach

**16.2.4**   If the breach is anything but non-payment of rent, a s.146 notice needs to be served prior to exercising the right to forfeit.

**16.2.5**   If the breach is non-payment of rent (or items reserved as rent under the lease) a s.146 notice is not required and a landlord or enforcement agent (acting as the landlord's agent) can enter the property and forfeit the lease by peaceable re-entry although a landlord must first wait until the right to forfeit has arisen (there is usually a 21-day grace period in the lease).

**16.2.6**   Peaceable re-entry is available for all breaches, although if it is done for a breach other than non-payment of rent, there is a risk that a 'reasonable amount of time' has not elapsed (see later for what constitutes a 'reasonable time').

**16.2.7**   Peaceable re-entry is not generally available on residential premises pursuant to Protection from Eviction Act 1977, s.2 (see **17.2.7**).

## Section 146 notices

**16.2.8**   A landlord must serve a s.146 notice for any breach other than non-payment of rent. Law of Property Act 1925, s.146 states that the notice must:

- specify the particular breach complained of;
- if the breach is capable of remedy require the lessee to remedy the breach; and
- require the lessee to make compensation in money for the breach.

Section 146 goes on to state that if the lessee fails within a reasonable time to remedy the breach and to make reasonable compensation in money to the satisfaction of the landlord, then forfeiture may take place.

**16.2.9**   The s.146 notice does not have to specify what a 'reasonable time' is, but if the landlord tries to forfeit the lease before a reasonable time has elapsed, or before the tenant has shown that he does not intend to comply with the notice, the forfeiture will be unlawful.

## Reasonable time

**16.2.10** Generally, where there is no real commercial harm to the landlord being caused by the breach, a longer time may be more reasonable.

**16.2.11** In effect, the reasonableness of the time given depends on the breach. If forfeiture take place before a reasonable time has elapsed, however, the forfeiture will be unlawful.

## Relief from forfeiture

**16.2.12** This involves the tenant complying with conditions to remedy the breach and the lease then being handed back as if it had not been forfeited.

**16.2.13** If forfeiture is obtained, the tenant is entitled to apply for relief from forfeiture. Relief from forfeiture, if granted, would reinstate the lease, which has ended by the act of forfeiture.

**16.2.14** Relief from forfeiture is usually only granted on certain conditions. These conditions are usually that the tenant has to pay the landlord's legal costs of the forfeiture and relief, sometimes on an indemnity basis, or any other condition that the court thinks fit to prevent future breaches. These conditions are designed to put the landlord into the position he would have been in had the tenant not been in breach.

**16.2.15** To obtain relief from forfeiture where the breach is non-payment of rent, a tenant need not pay all of the rent prior to the hearing or even be capable of paying it immediately after the hearing. He simply has to show that he can pay the rent arrears within a fixed and fairly short period of time after the hearing.

## Procedure for peaceable re-entry

**16.2.16** The enforcement agent has to attend the property and serve a forfeiture notice.

**16.2.17** It is said that peaceable re-entry only has to be peaceable 'to the person, not to the property'. That means that an enforcement agent can break in if the property is empty but must not breach of Criminal Law Act 1977, s.6 (see **18.6.3**), where a person is on the property who is opposed to the enforcement agent's entry.

**16.2.18** Peaceable re-entry involves an enforcement agent changing the locks to the premises. The enforcement agent will enter, change the locks, and fix a notice to the premises.

**16.2.19** In practice, an enforcement agent will attend site, remove the tenant and change the locks. If the tenant does not want to leave, the enforcement agent can forcibly evict him provided that the enforcement agent does not need to use force to gain entry to the premises. For most commercial premises, an enforcement agent will attend at dawn, when no one is there, and will change the locks.

## Peaceable re-entry in relation to residential property

16.2.20    Protection from Eviction Act 1977, s.2 prevents a landlord or enforcement agent from forfeiting a property by peaceable re-entry where the property has been 'let as a dwelling':

> Where any premises are let as a dwelling on a lease which is subject to a right of re-entry or forfeiture it shall not be lawful to enforce that right otherwise than by proceedings in the court while any person is lawfully residing in the premises or any part of them.

This is dealt with fully in **Chapter 17**. It means that where somebody is living at the property the locks cannot be changed without a court order.

16.2.21    'Let as a dwelling' is defined in s.75(3) of the new Act as:

> let on terms permitting only occupation as a dwelling or other use combined with occupation as a dwelling.

16.2.22    Where the occupation as a dwelling is in breach of lease or any superior lease the premises will not be treated as let as a dwelling (s.75(5) of the new Act), which may cause concern for residential tenants who did not realise that their immediate landlord needed consent.

16.2.23    Where a landlord wishes to take possession of a property that has been let as a dwelling, he needs to issue forfeiture proceedings. He cannot forfeit the lease of a dwelling by peaceable re-entry because of Protection from Eviction Act 1977, s.2.

## What if the premises are part commercial and part dwelling?

16.2.24    Peaceable re-entry not being available for premises let as a dwelling has caused problems where the premises let by the landlord are mixed use premises.

16.2.25    A particular example is in the retail industry where the freeholder may let premises to a retail tenant that consist of a ground floor retail unit with a residential flat (typically above).

16.2.26    As the lease is of the whole premises, i.e. both the commercial unit and the residential flat, the lease is of mixed used premises.

16.2.27    *Pirabakaran* v. *Patel* [2006] 3 EGLR 23 decided the position in relation to forfeiture by peaceable re-entry for mixed used premises.

**16.2.28**   The Court of Appeal had to decide whether 'let as a dwelling' under Protection from Eviction Act 1977, s.2 meant 'let wholly or partly as a dwelling' or 'let exclusively as a dwelling'. The Court of Appeal decided that it meant 'let wholly or partly as a dwelling'.

**16.2.29**   The main reason is that people should not be locked out of their homes without due process simply because there is a place of business below.

**16.2.30**   A landlord wanting to forfeit by peaceable re-entry therefore needs to check that no part of the premises have been let as a dwelling, otherwise he will have to issue forfeiture proceedings and will not be allowed to forfeit by peaceable re-entry. To do so would be a criminal offence pursuant to Protection from Eviction Act 1977, s.2.

## Effect of new Act on forfeiture by peaceable re-entry of mixed use premises

**16.2.31**   The new Act has added further guidance to forfeiture of mixed use premises, under s.75(1)–(3) of the new Act, with the following definitions:

(1)   The lease (A) is of commercial premises if none of the demised premises is –

  (a)   let under lease A as a dwelling,
  (b)   let under an inferior lease (B) as a dwelling, or
  (c)   occupied as a dwelling.

(2)   The 'demised premises' in this section include anything on them.
(3)   'Let as a dwelling' means let on terms permitting only occupation as a dwelling or other use combined with occupation as a dwelling.

**16.2.32**   The definitions under the new Act take a wide view of what classifies as a dwelling, and the use of the phrase 'or other use combined with occupation as a dwelling' puts the already existing case law in *Pirabakaran* v. *Patel* into statutory effect.

**16.2.33**   The position remains, therefore, that if any part of the property is used for residential purposes, the landlord can only forfeit by court proceedings, not by peaceable re-entry.

## Waiver of right to forfeit

**16.2.34**   The right to forfeit is lost by a landlord where:

- the breach is a once and for all breach;
- the landlord knows about the breach; and
- the landlord does an act which recognises the continuing relationship of landlord and tenant (the classic example being the demand or acceptance of rent by the landlord, distraining on rent (pre-Act) or taking control of goods (new Act) or giving consent under the lease).

**16.2.35**    Examples of once and for all breaches (that can be waived) are:

■    insolvency;
■    failure to apply for consent for alterations;
■    failure to apply for consent for sub-letting or assignment; or
■    failure to pay rents and other sums due.

**16.2.36**    Examples of continuing breaches (that cannot be waived) are:

■    breach of repairing covenant;
■    breach of keep open clause; or
■    breach of user clause.

## Reform of law of forfeiture

**16.2.37**    There is talk of replacing breaches and forfeiture clauses with a 'tenant default' which would state positions in which a landlord may seek to terminate a lease before the end of the term.

**16.2.38**    Waiver of the right to forfeit would also be abolished.

**16.2.39**    Talk of reforming the law of forfeiture has been going on for some time but does not form part of the new Act.

## What if the tenant breaks back in?

**16.2.40**    Having forfeited the lease by peaceable re-entry and having changed the locks, if the tenant breaks back into the property, he would be guilty of criminal damage (Criminal Damage Act 1971, s.1).

**16.2.41**    Proving it may be a problem, although if the tenant admits to the police that he broke in (because a tenant frequently does not recognise the landlord's right to forfeit) this should be sufficient for the police to arrest the tenant.

**16.2.42**    In breaking back in, the enforcement agent is entitled to use reasonable force to remove the tenant. However, as one enforcement agent explained:

> I was instructed to forfeit the lease of an Indian restaurant.
>
> I attended the premises whilst closed with a locksmith and obtained peaceable possession of the premises, changed all the locks and displayed notices.
>
> When the tenant arrived at the premises they broke in, removed the notices and changed the locks and continued to trade.
>
> It was decided by the landlord and their lawyers that I would re-attend whilst the premises were open and trading, place security guards on the doors to prevent access by members of the public, and notify the tenants that the landlord was continuing his right to possession subsequent to the forfeiture. The tenant was allowed to occupy the premises.
>
> The enforcement agent and security continued the landlord's possession whilst the tenant took legal advice.

The tenant subsequently accepted that the lease had been terminated and removed his assets from the premises.

## What happens to goods left on site by the tenant following forfeiture?

**16.2.43**   When a landlord takes possession of premises following forfeiture he may be left with some of the tenant's goods on site. This can be a major problem for landlords. In this position the landlord becomes an involuntary bailee and has a duty of care to the tenant in relation to his custody of the goods.

**16.2.44**   There is no automatic right to seize the goods (or take control of the goods). Following a forfeiture the right to levy distress (pre-Act) is lost and under the new Act there is no right to exercise CRAR (see **7.9.2**).

**16.2.45**   A remedy available to the landlord arises under the Torts (Interference with Goods) Act 1977 which enables the landlord as enforcement agent to serve a notice on the tenant (bailor) in order to discharge his obligations. The notice is served under s.12 of the Act.

**16.2.46**   The tenant has a right to collect his goods by prior arrangement from the landlord, following forfeiture, but no obligation to do so.

**16.2.47**   If the landlord sells the tenant's goods without serving a torts notice, the tenant could sue the landlord for conversion or unlawful interference with goods. In practice, a landlord could make a commercial decision to run that risk and, if sued, counterclaim for unpaid rent or dilapidations.

## Content of torts notice

**16.2.48**   The notice should ask that the (now former) tenant collect his goods from the premises. The notice should tell the tenant that if the tenant does not collect his goods by a certain date (giving the tenant reasonable time to collect), the tenant's goods will be sold and any storage costs will be deducted from the proceeds of sale.

## Effect of notice

**16.2.49**   If the former tenant does not collect the goods, the landlord can sell the goods. Any proceeds not claimed by the landlord can be paid into court.

**16.2.50**   A s.12 notice should be served on tenants in the following circumstances:

■   after forfeiture of lease or any repossession of a property (although there is debate whether the 1977 Act applies in forfeiture but a notice in the same form would have an identical effect);

- when a tenant vacates the premises at the end of the tenancy term and abandons goods on site;
- when a tenant absconds leaving goods on site; or
- where, after a surrender, goods are left on site.

## Inventory

**16.2.51**    In practice, goods left by tenants is one of the major problems faced by landlords following forfeiture. It is essential that landlords take a proper inventory of the goods on site so that a comprehensive record of the goods is taken. The inventory must be accurate and if necessary record the condition of the goods.

**16.2.52**    On the importance of inventories, one enforcement agent reported:

> I would advise that when attempting a forfeiture the enforcement agent should take a full inventory and photos of assets on site. Some enforcement agents are members of the National Association of Valuers and Auctioneers and can provide full appraisals.

> It is recommended that on completion of the forfeiture a torts notice is served and an insurance policy taken out by the landlord whilst the assets are in his custody. It has become apparent over the last few years that tenants have broken back into their premises after forfeiture and removed their own assets and subsequently made a claim against the landlord for theft of the assets, claiming that the goods were in the custody of the landlord and he had a duty as to their security.

Another enforcement agent reported:

> In one case I was asked to forfeit a lock-up storage garage. The tenant had seemingly disappeared not paying her rent. The garage was full of antiques of questionable value. I conducted a detailed inventory supported by photographic and video evidence. A tort notice was served. The tenant subsequently reappeared on the scene (she was a singer in a well known 1970s pop group) claiming she had been on tour in America. She claimed that the garage had contained an original painting by Picasso of substantial value. She issued proceedings, however the court accepted the evidence provided by the comprehensive inventory and she lost.

**16.2.53**    Enforcement agents have been known to use the s.12 procedure in a wide range of circumstances. One enforcement agent has, for example, implemented the use of Torts (Interference with Goods) Act 1977 on horses illegally placed on privately owned land.

**16.2.54**    In that case, notices are served on the land in the same way that notices are served under CPR rules. They are staked to the land and tied to fencing in prominent positions all around the land. The notice gives the owner of the livestock a reasonable period of time to remove their livestock from the land. If the horses are not removed within the allocated time they can be removed and sold under the provisions of the Act. Costs incurred in the removal and sale may be deducted from the proceeds of the sale.

**Table 16.1** Taking possession of premises – overview

|  | Commercial | Residential | Trespassers |
|---|---|---|---|
| Can they be evicted without a court order at end of lease? | Yes, provided the landlord can gain entry without force | No (PEA 1977, s.3) | Yes, provided the landlord can gain entry without force |
| Can there be forfeiture by peaceable re-entry midlease? | Yes | No (PEA 1977, s.2) | No lease to forfeit |

# 17 OBTAINING POSSESSION OF RESIDENTIAL PREMISES

## 17.1 INTRODUCTION

**17.1.1** Although unaffected by the new Act, this is a major area of enforcement.

**17.1.2** Before obtaining possession, an enforcement agent (or those instructing him) needs to decide under what sort of tenancy the tenant is occupying. Nowadays, this tends to be an assured shorthold tenancy but could be, for example, an assured tenancy or a Rent Act tenancy.

**17.1.3** In the case of an assured shorthold tenancy, the landlord will need to serve a s.8 notice or a s.21 notice pursuant to the Housing Act 1988 and, on expiry of the notice, will apply to court for a Possession Order.

**17.1.4** That is, of course, a brief overview of the procedure leading up to enforcement.

**17.1.5** If the tenant does not want to leave, after an order for possession, the landlord will have to obtain a warrant of possession and then evict the tenant by an enforcement agent.

**17.1.6** Residential landlords need to be careful that they comply with the correct procedure, otherwise they could find that they commit a criminal offence. To evict a trespasser without a court order is a criminal offence pursuant to the Protection from Eviction Act 1977.

## 17.2 PROTECTION FROM EVICTION ACT 1977

**17.2.1** Under Protection from Eviction Act 1977, s.1 a residential occupier is:

> a person occupying the premises as a resident, whether under a contract or by virtue of any enactment or rule of law giving him the right to remain in occupation or restricting the right of any other person to recover possession of the premises.

This term is construed widely.

**17.2.2**    Section 1(2) of the Protection from Eviction Act 1977 prevents a party from unlawfully depriving a residential occupier of his occupation of premises and makes it a criminal offence to try to do so.

**17.2.3**    It is also a criminal offence under Protection from Eviction Act 1977, s.1(3) to interfere with the peace or comfort of the residential occupier in an attempt to get him to give up occupation of the premises, even where the acts themselves are not civil wrongs.

**17.2.4**    In R v. *Helen Yuthiwattana* (1985) 80 Cr App R 55, the Court of Appeal held that a landlord's refusal to replace a key to a bed-sit room was, in the circumstances of the case which included threats of eviction and confiscation of belongings:

> an act calculated to interfere with the occupier's peace and comfort and was 'an act intended to cause him to give up his occupation of the premises' and so was an offence under section 1(3).

It was an offence even where the tenant was in arrears of rent, and the landlord had no contractual obligation to replace the key and the tenant was found to be 'clearly a difficult lodger'.

**17.2.5**    The landlord was fined £150 and ordered to pay costs for contravening s.1(3).

**17.2.6**    Similarly, in R v. *Burke* [1990] 2 WLR 1313, the landlord padlocked the door to a toilet, deliberately disconnected the front door bells and made gestures to suggest the tenant should seek rehousing. It was held that these were acts 'calculated to interfere with the peace or comfort of the residential occupier . . . with the purpose or motive of causing the occupier to give up his occupation of the premises' and were an offence under s.1(3), for which the landlord was fined and ordered to pay costs.

## Peaceable re-entry not available

**17.2.7**    Protection from Eviction Act 1977, s.2 also provides that a landlord cannot only use a right of forfeiture by peaceable re-entry for a premises that are 'let as a dwelling'. If a tenant is 'lawfully residing' forfeiture can only be by court proceedings (and not by peaceable re-entry). See **16.2.24** for the position where premises are partly let as a dwelling, s.2 still applies. The fact that the tenant must be lawfully residing means that unauthorised sub-tenants are not afforded the protection of s.2. If a landlord evicts a person lawfully residing in a dwelling without a court order, he commits a criminal offence. A landlord could argue that premises have been abandoned (in which case no court order is needed) but without strong proof, this is not advisable.

## Protection of expiry of tenancy

**17.2.8** Under Protection from Eviction Act 1977, s.3, where premises have been 'let as a dwelling' and the tenancy expires but the tenant lawfully residing does not vacate, the owner has to issue court proceedings to obtain possession. The landlord cannot evict a residential occupier of a dwelling house, even peaceably, unless he has a writ or warrant of possession.

**17.2.9** The effect of the Protection from Eviction Act 1977 is that:

- residential occupiers cannot be evicted without a court order and a warrant/writ of possession;
- residential occupiers cannot be harassed into leaving; and
- residential premises cannot be forfeited except by court order.

The effect is that, unlike with commercial premises, even if an enforcement agent can gain entry peaceably, there is little he can do without a writ/warrant of possession.

## Exceptions

**17.2.10** Exceptions to this are in Protection from Eviction Act 1977, s.3A, which provides that the following tenancies or licences are not subject to s.3, where:

- the occupier shares the accommodation with the landlord/licensor or any member of the landlord's/licensor's family;
- immediately before the tenancy/licence was granted and at the time it ends, the landlord/licensor occupied the premises of which the shared accommodation forms part; and
- where the occupier is sharing with a member of the landlord's/licensor's family, the landlord/licensor must have occupied the premises of which the shared accommodation forms part both immediately before the tenancy/licence was granted and at the time it ends.

**17.2.11** The following tenancies also do not have the protection of s.3:

- holiday-only occupation;
- trespassers;
- rent-free occupation; and
- hostels.

## 17.3 CRIMINAL LAW ACT 1977

**17.3.1** A landlord is also subject to Criminal Law Act 1977, s.6, which prevents a landlord from using force to gain entry to premises where a person is on the premises who is opposed to their entry. This is dealt with fully in **18.6.3**.

## 17.4   ORDER FOR POSSESSION

**17.4.1**    To obtain an Order for Possession, the person with an immediate right to occupy must issue a claim in court. The papers required and the procedure used is the same as for trespass and is set out in **18.7**.

**17.4.2**    Once an Order for Possession is obtained and possession is ordered at some time either forthwith or up to 40 days later, the landlord can then enforce the Possession Order. A court order is required because under Protection from Eviction Act 1977, s.2, it is illegal to evict a person occupying a property as a dwelling without a court order.

**17.4.3**    Once the court order is obtained, if the tenant still does not vacate, the landlord will have to apply for a warrant of possession. This can be done either in the county court or in the High Court. A claimant cannot enter into possession of a dwelling house, even if he can do so peaceably or with a court order, unless he has a writ of possession or a warrant of possession. To re-take possession without a warrant/writ (even peaceably or even if the landlord has a court order for possession) would be a criminal offence under Protection from Eviction Act 1977, s.3. Under County Court Rules (CCR) Order 26, rule 17(1) a landlord cannot enforce a Possession Order in the county court except by warrant of possession.

**17.4.4**    The procedure for applying for a warrant of/for possession is set out in CCR Order 26, rule 17 for the county court and in Rules of the Supreme Court (RSC) Order 45, rule 3.

## 17.5   COUNTY COURT PROCEDURE

**17.5.1**    Warrants of possession are governed by CCR Order 26. A claimant cannot use an order for possession to evict a tenant. The claimant, even with an order for possession, still has to apply for a warrant of possession in the county court.

**17.5.2**    A request for warrant of possession is made in form N325. The warrant of possession itself is form N49.

**17.5.3**    A bailiff enforcing a warrant of possession is entitled to evict any person found on the premises even though that person is not a party to the proceedings for possession.

**17.5.4**    A claimant must apply for a warrant of possession within three months of obtaining the Possession Order (CCR Order 24, rule 6(2)). Once a warrant of possession is obtained, it remains in force while unexecuted for a year (County Courts Act 1984, s.111(2)) but can be renewed year by year. Once executed, however, if it needs to be reused against the same people the claimant must apply for a warrant of restitution under CCR Order 26 r.17(4) and (5).

**17.5.5**   To transfer a county court order to the High Court for enforcement, the claimant must apply to the county court which made the order for possession for a certificate of judgment in form N293a. The form is completed and sealed and returned to the claimant who completes the reverse and the writ of possession is then completed using form 66a and is sent to the High Court for sealing. The High Court then sends it on to the local High Court enforcement officer for enforcement.

## 17.6   HIGH COURT PROCEDURE

**17.6.1**   The High Court procedure for enforcing Possession Orders is set out in RSC Order 45 r.3. It is done by applying for a writ of possession or, in rare cases, an order for committal or a writ of sequestration. The latter two are only available where the Possession Order specifies a time by which possession is to be given and the defendant refuses or neglects to do it within time.

**17.6.2**   A writ of possession cannot be issued without permission from the court unless (as in most cases):

- every person in actual possession of the whole or any part of the land has received sufficient notice to enable him to apply for relief; or
- Landlord and Tenant Act 1954, s.16(2) does not apply.

**17.6.3**   An application for permission is made in the Queen's Bench Division without notice and supported by evidence.

## 17.7   FORMS

**17.7.1**   A writ of possession is in form 66. If it is combined with a writ of *fieri facias* (now a writ of control), it will be in form 53.

## 17.8   CONSENT ORDERS

**17.8.1**   Claimants should be careful not to agree a Consent Order for possession. These cannot be enforced by a writ of possession as the court will not have considered whether it was reasonable to make the order.

# 18 OBTAINING POSSESSION FROM TRESPASSERS/ SQUATTERS

## 18.1 INTRODUCTION

**18.1.1** The expressions 'trespasser' and 'squatter' have the same meaning and are interchangeable. A trespasser or squatter is a party who enters onto, or remains on, property without lawful authority or permission from the party with an immediate right to occupation of that property.

**18.1.2** The law treats residential squatters differently to squatters of commercial premises. However, there has been a rise in the number of instances of commercial premises being used for residential purposes. This chapter deals with each form.

## 18.2 WHEN IS A COURT ORDER REQUIRED?

**18.2.1** Usually a court order is required in order to secure possession from a trespasser.

**18.2.2** However, there are some important exceptions to this principle:

- displaced residential occupiers;
- all forms of commercial premises where force is not needed/used to gain entry;
- where outside premises are used by trespassers (e.g. to park caravans) and reasonable force can be used in this instance.

**18.2.3** In the vast majority of cases though, a court order is needed.

## 18.3 DISPLACED RESIDENTIAL OCCUPIERS/PROTECTED INTENDING OCCUPIERS

**18.3.1** Where a trespasser enters a person's home the owner who is a 'displaced residential occupier' or a 'protected intending occupier' can rely on criminal sanctions to evict the trespasser immediately. This is a powerful remedy which is actively supported and enforced by the police. It is automatically an offence not to leave when asked to by a 'displaced residential occupier' or a 'protected intending occupier', hence the strength of the provision and its right to immediate use.

**18.3.2**    The criteria for deciding whether a person is a 'displaced residential occupier' are set out in Criminal Law Act 1977, s.12. A 'displaced residential occupier' is:

- any person;
- occupying any premises;
- as a residence;
- immediately before being excluded from those premises by a trespasser.

This applies equally to access.

**18.3.3**    An exception is that if a party was occupying as a trespasser and he is excluded from the premises by another trespasser. That does not make the original trespasser a displaced residential occupier (Criminal Law Act 1977, s.12(4)).

**18.3.4**    If a person is allowed onto the premises by a trespasser, that person is still a trespasser (s.12(6)) who will be displacing the residential occupier.

**18.3.5**    The criteria for deciding whether a person is a 'protected intending occupier' are set out in Criminal Law Act 1977, s.12A. Under s.12A, there are three types of 'protected intending occupier':

- freeholder (s.12A(2)) – this applies where:
  - an individual;
  - has a freehold interest or a leasehold interest in premises with not less than two years still left to run;
- tenant/licensee (s.12A(4)):
  - the same position applies to a person who has a tenancy or licence of the premises. If he fulfils the criteria, he will be a protected intending occupier;
- local authority tenant:
  - the same position applies to a person who has a tenancy or licence of the premises granted by a local authority, housing corporation or registered social landlord. If he fulfils the criteria, he will be a protected intending occupier.

**18.3.6**    The criteria for each of these parties to fulfil to become protected intending occupiers are:

- he requires those premises for his own occupation as a residence;
- he has been excluded from the premises by a trespasser; and
- he (or his agent) has a statement sworn by him (the freeholder/leaseholder) before a justice of the peace or a commissioner for oaths and that statement confirms:

- his interest in the premises;
- that he requires the premises for occupation as a residence for himself; and
- the relevant requirements as to the statement have been fulfilled.

Technically, it is only once the party obtains the statement referred to above that he attains the status of protected intending occupier.

**18.3.7** The key difference between a displaced residential occupier and a protected intending occupier is that a displaced residential occupier must be occupying 'immediately before being excluded'.

**18.3.8** If a 'displaced residential occupier' or 'a protected intending occupier' asks a trespasser to leave their premises and the trespasser fails to leave, the trespasser commits a criminal offence under Criminal Law Act 1977, s.7.

**18.3.9** Because the matter becomes criminal, rather than civil, the trespasser can be arrested and so the residential occupier can regain possession immediately.

**18.3.10** The trespasser has various defences to the offence under s.7(2) and (3), such as:

- if he can prove that he believed that the person requiring him to leave the premises was not a displaced residential occupier or protected intending occupier of the premises (or a person acting on their behalf); or
- if he can prove that the premises are (or form part of) premises used mainly for non-residential purposes; and
- that he was not on any part of the premises used wholly or mainly for residential purposes.

The rationale behind these defences is that s.7 is designed to protect people who are evicted from their own homes and so is only available in those circumstances.

**18.3.11** Even if the squatter is eventually shown to have a defence to the offence, it does not prevent him from being arrested at the time of the trespass and from the occupier regaining possession immediately.

**18.3.12** A person found guilty under Criminal Law Act 1977, s.7 is liable on summary conviction to up to six months imprisonment and/or a fine not exceeding level 5 on the standard scale.

## 18.4   COMMERCIAL PREMISES (WITHOUT USE OF FORCE)

**18.4.1** Possession can be obtained in relation to all forms of commercial premises without a court order, providing:

- the occupier is not a residential tenant (or a former residential tenant) of any part of the building;
- no force is required to obtain entry into the premises.

18.4.2    In relation to force, the important factor is whether it is being used in relation to 'entry' (Criminal Law Act 1977, s.6). This is dealt with below (see 18.6.3).

## 18.5    OUTSIDE AREAS

18.5.1    With outside areas of premises, even with trespassers, where trespassers are in occupation of any external areas (e.g. car parks, fields etc.), reasonable force can be used.

## 18.6    FORCIBLE ENTRY

18.6.1    In cases not involving a displaced residential occupier or a protected intending occupier, the Criminal Law Act 1977 applies.

18.6.2    To use force to enter onto premises is a criminal offence pursuant to the Criminal Law Act 1977.

### Criminal Law Act 1977

18.6.3    Under Criminal Law Act 1977, s.6 it is a criminal offence to:

- use or threaten violence to try to gain entry into premises where there is someone present on those premises at the time who is opposed to the entry of that person; and
- the person using the violence knows that this is the case.

18.6.4    Well-practised (or well advised) squatters will use what has now become known as a 's.6 notice'. It involves placing a notice at the boundary fence or points of entry to the land stating that they are occupying it and a court order is needed to evict them.

18.6.5    Although such a notice is not essential to invoke the protection of s.6, the purpose of this notice is to give notification to anybody trying to enter the premises that there is someone present on the premises who is opposed to the entry. Under Criminal Law Act 1977, s.6(1)(b) this would then make it a criminal offence for that person to go onto the land and use violence to secure it, meaning the owner has to get a court order which costs him time and money.

18.6.6    This section does not apply to a displaced residential occupier or a protected intending occupier, although this does not mean that they can use anything more than reasonable force to seek an eviction.

18.6.7    It was held in *Hemmings* v. *Stoke Poges* that the force used must be 'no more force than is necessary'. The amount of force necessary depends directly on the level of resistance.

**18.6.8**    Other than a displaced residential occupier or a protected intending occupier, even if the person is the lawful owner of the property, this does not permit him to use force to secure entry.

**18.6.9**    However, these rules are narrowly construed. If enforcement agents can obtain entry without force, then once they are in the property they can gain possession without a court order. One bailiff reported the following episode by way of example:

> I attended a commercial warehouse premises in south east London on instruction of the landlord after reports of persons unknown occupying the premises.
>
> On attendance at the premises I identified myself as the landlord's agent and requested access to the premises. I informed the occupiers that I was there on instruction of the landlord to inspect the premises. The occupiers opened the door to the premises and invited me in.
>
> Once inside the premises I was asked by the occupiers what I intended to do. I informed the occupiers I was the landlord's bailiff and asked the occupiers to leave.
>
> I explained to the occupiers that because they had opened the premises and allowed me entry without opposition that I now had legal occupation of the building.
>
> The occupiers began to pack their belongings and the landlord was handed back a vacant building within three hours.

**18.6.10**    This tactic can work because the effect of s.6 is merely to prevent the threat or actual use of violence to gain entry. Where violence/force can be avoided or is unnecessary to gain entry, s.6 has no effect. Section 6 does not create a right of occupation.

**18.6.11**    A person found guilty under Criminal Law Act 1977, s.6 is liable on summary conviction to imprisonment for a term of up to six months or to a fine not exceeding level 5 on the standard scale or both.

**18.6.12**    This is what trespassers sometimes refer to as 'squatters' rights' (although this phrase is often also used for the entirely different area of adverse possession). In reality though, the only 'rights' that squatters actually enjoy are the right to prevent a landlord from entering with force and, in that case, not to be evicted without a court order. The effect of this is dealt with below.

## 18.7    OBTAINING AN ORDER FOR POSSESSION

**18.7.1**    Although not technically 'enforcement', obtaining an Order for Possession is an integral part of removing a trespasser which is enforcing the owner's right to possession.

**18.7.2**    Knowledge of the procedure should be helpful to all enforcement agents who should be involved in a possession action right from the start (service of papers) to the end (eviction).

## Procedure

**18.7.3**    Part 55 of the Civil Procedure Rules (CPR) applies to all trespasser possession claims.

**18.7.4**    Part 55.1 defines 'a possession claim against trespassers' as:

> a claim for the recovery of land which the claimant alleges is occupied only by a person or persons who entered or remained on the land without the consent of a person entitled to possession of that land but does not include a claim against a tenant or sub-tenant whether his tenancy has been terminated or not.

**18.7.5**    In a possession claim against trespassers, the claimant has the choice of either proceeding under section I of Part 55 (normal Possession Orders) or under section III of Part 55 (interim Possession Orders).

**18.7.6**    Peter Mooney, as an enforcement agent, describes best practice as follows:

> I usually attend the site and ascertain the number of persons and vehicles in occupation. I then prepare a comprehensive witness statement detailing all the information, which can be used by the solicitor in support of the possession claim. This often includes when the squatters arrived, how many dogs they have, the quantity and type of vehicles in occupation, the area being occupied, what the site is being used for (e.g. raves, underground art exhibitions, new-age gatherings, residential etc.). The statement also details such matters as anti-social behaviour and any damage being caused to the property.

> Once the application for possession has been drafted by the solicitor, I take the application to the court for issue and wait for the papers to be processed. I then attend the premises with the notice of hearing and serve upon persons unknown in accordance with the CPR Rules [Part 55]. I then prepare a statement of service. Service must be carried out very carefully, strictly in accordance with the CPR. If I cannot get inside the grounds because of high fencing and gates I fix a number of copies of the notices to gates, fences and any other prominent positions. I would also post copies (in sealed envelopes addressed 'to the occupiers') through the railings. I would also try to obtain the attention of the occupiers through the railings and attempt to serve them personally.

> Once the hearing has taken place and the Order for Possession has been granted I attend court to collect sufficient sealed copies of the order. I then attend the premises and serve the order in the same way as the claim.

> If an Order for Possession has been granted ordering the occupiers to vacate the premises forthwith the agent is able to prevent any further persons from entering the premises and prevent the re-entry of persons after they have left.

**18.7.7**    Current legislation provides only for the order to be enforced by the county court bailiff (or High Court enforcement officer for High Court orders). The court bailiffs can take anywhere from two to eight weeks to enforce the Possession Order. They must carry out a health and safety assessment and organise the eviction. They also have guidelines which state that squatters must be given prior notice of the eviction, this notice being 10 days for residential premises and two days for commercial premises.

**18.7.8** A practical procedure for enforcement of the order is for the landlord to arrange all necessary manpower to prevent further occupiers entering the premises and prevent the re-entry of persons after they have left, until the court bailiff can attend to evict. In most cases the squatters will vacate the premises because they no longer enjoy peaceful possession. This is usually achieved within 72 hours.

## Venue

**18.7.9** The claim must be issued in the county court nearest to the property unless the matter is referred to the High Court (CPR rule 55.3(1)). The matter should, however, only be started in the High Court in exceptional circumstances.

**18.7.10** If the claimant wishes to issue in the High Court, he must file a statement of reasons with the claim form. Possible reasons are:

- there are complicated disputes of fact;
- there are points of law of general importance; or
- the claim is against trespassers and there is a substantial risk of public disturbance or of serious harm to persons or property which properly require immediate determination.

**18.7.11** The value of the property and the amount of any financial claim being brought at the same time as the possession claim may be relevant to whether the matter should be referred to the High Court but these factors on their own will not normally be valid reasons for starting the claim in the High Court.

**18.7.12** It is a real risk to start a claim in the High Court because if the High Court decides that the possession claim should have been started in the county court, the High Court can decide on its own volition either to strike the claim out or to transfer it to the county court. This will result in delay and additional costs which, even if they were recoverable (see below to the general recoverability of costs), would normally be disallowed where they were the costs of starting the claim in the High Court and the costs of any transfer.

## Papers

**18.7.13** The papers needed to issue the claim are:

- Claim form – in form N5.
- Particulars of claim.
- In a possession claim the particulars of claim must:
  - identify the land to which the claim relates;
  - state whether the claim relates to residential property (this is relevant in relation to service);
  - state the ground on which possession is claimed (in this case, usually trespass);
  - give full details about any mortgage or tenancy agreement; and

- give details of every person who, to the best of the claimant's knowledge, is in possession of the property.

■ Where the claim relates to non-payment of rent on residential property let on a tenancy (for residential tenants, see earlier **Chapter 17**), the particulars of claim must also set out:

- the amount due at the start of the proceedings;
- in schedule form, the date and amounts of all payments due and payments made under the tenancy agreement for a period of two years immediately preceding the date of issue, or if the first date of default occurred less than two years before the date of issue from the first date of default and a running total of the arrears;
- the daily rate of any rent and interest;
- any previous steps taken to recover the arrears of rent with full details of any court proceedings; and
- any relevant information about the defendant's circumstances, e.g. whether the defendant is in receipt of social security benefits and whether any payments are made on his behalf directly to the claimant under the Social Security Contributions and Benefits Act 1992.

■ If the possession claim is against trespassers the particulars of claim must state the claimant's interest in the land or the basis of his rights to claim possession and the circumstances in which it has been occupied without licence or consent:

- witness statement – a witness statement is not essential but, for best practice, especially where the claimant is a company, it is useful to have evidence before the judge that the claimant is the party who has an immediate right to possession of the property, i.e. that they are the correct party to be the claimant. The person giving the evidence will not be required to attend court (CPR rule 55.8(3)).
- cheque – as a court fee for issuing. Fees can be checked at **www.hmcourts-service.gov.uk**.

## Types of claim

18.7.14    A person bringing a possession claim (whether against trespassers or other occupiers whose interest has expired) is faced with an immediate choice as to the type of claim to bring. The choices are:

■ normal possession claim (CPR Part 55);
■ interim possession claim (CPR Part 55, section III);
■ online possession claim;
■ accelerated possession procedure (CPR Part 55, section II).

18.7.15    The accelerated possession procedure applies solely to landlords who have served a notice on tenants pursuant to Housing Act 1988, s.21 and is not relevant for trespassers.

**18.7.16**   In a claim against trespassers, the usual choice is between the normal possession claim and the interim possession claim.

**18.7.17**   The majority of cases tend to be brought under the normal possession procedure as an interim possession claim requires two hearings and so tends to be more expensive in legal costs.

**18.7.18**   The interim Possession Order's advantage is that it does not require an enforcement agent to enforce the warrant of possession/writ of possession. Not to comply with an interim Possession Order is a criminal offence.

**18.7.19**   If the current trend continues, of squatters not leaving on service of the Possession Order but waiting for an eviction, interim Possession Orders may be used more frequently.

## Normal possession claims

**18.7.20**   The following process applies to normal possession claims:

- *Issuing papers* – the claimant must send to court four copies of the claim form, the particulars of claim, and the witness statement and also the cheque for the court fee. One copy will be kept by the court for the file, and three copies will be returned to the claimant, one for the claimant to keep and two to be served on the defendants (or more if there are more defendants). In the case of trespassers (or 'persons unknown'), it is advisable to obtain at least three for service, to allow the enforcement agent to be able to comply with the rules of service.

  On issuing the papers, the court will set down a date for a hearing. It will be printed on the front of the claim form.

  The date fixed for the hearing must allow time for service of the papers (i.e. at least two working days for commercial property and five working days for residential property). Weekends and bank holidays are not counted; it must be two or five working days. The rules of calculating days are set out in CPR rule 2.8.

  The court will then return the papers to the claimant for service. In the case of trespassers, it is advisable for the enforcement agent to attend court to issue the papers and then attend site to serve the papers straightaway.
- *Service of papers* – there are specific rules for service of the claim where it has been issued against 'persons unknown'. These are set out in CPR rule 55.6 and require all papers to be attached to the main door and (where possible) posted, or placed in clear sealed envelopes and placed in clearly visible places on the land by stakes.

  For claims against tenants, the usual methods of service can be used (CPR rule 6.4).

  One bailiff reported the rising problem of language problems on service:

  > It is becoming more and more common to find that the people we are trying to serve have no knowledge of English. Some individuals have no concept of the

workings of the court system and have not been able to understand the effect of any warning notices they have been given. Where I am aware of such a problem I make sure that I take along an appropriate translator so that I can explain the position to the trespassers and answer any questions they might have in relation to the process.

Proof of service, in the form of an affidavit of service by the enforcement agent who served the papers, must be produced at court for the hearing.

- *Defendant's response* – in relation to a possession claim an acknowledgement of service is not required and a defendant need not file a defence. Even if he does not file a defence he can still turn up and take part in the hearing but his failure to file a defence may be taken into account when deciding an order in relation to costs. There is no procedure for default judgment in possession claims.
- *Hearing* – at the hearing the court may either decide the claim or give case management directions.
- *Enforcement* – having obtained a Possession Order, a county court bailiff or High Court enforcement officer must enforce it.

## Possession claim online

**18.7.21**  On 30 October 2006 an online possession claim procedure was launched. It applies to claims for possession of residential property.

**18.7.22**  The procedure allows the forms to be filled out online and fees to be paid by credit card, debit card or direct debit. The claims are issued immediately and the hearing dates are listed automatically.

**18.7.23**  The claim can be tracked online by both parties and once the Possession Order has been ordered, the claimant can arrange for a warrant to be issued online. Full details of how claims can be brought online are set out in CPR, Practice Direction B to Part 55.

## Interim possession claims

**18.7.24**  This procedure is available only where:

- the claimant is seeking just possession (i.e. not also a claim for rent or mesne profits). In a claim against 'persons unknown' a claim for rent has in any event no real effect as there is no person named against whom the judgment can be enforced;
- the claimant has an immediate right to possession and has had this right throughout the squatters' occupation;
- the claim is made within 28 days of the date on which the claimant first became aware (or should have become aware) of the trespass. The procedure is designed as a fast track to possession and so is not available to parties who delay more than 28 days; and
- the defendant did not commence his occupation with the consent of the person who, at the time of the defendant entering occupation, had an immedi-

ate right to occupation. This basically means that the procedure is reserved for trespassers. It cannot be used against tenants or licensees, even if their tenancy or licence has expired and they are now trespassers.

18.7.25   The following procedure applies:

- *Issuing papers* – the claim form and the defendant's form of witness statement must be as set out in the practice direction. This requires the claim form to be in form N5, the application for an interim Possession Order to be in form N130 and the defendant's witness statement to be in form N133.

  On filing the claim form the claimant must also file an application notice and written evidence which must be given by the claimant personally or by a duly authorised officer where the claimant is a company.

  On issue the court will set down a date for the hearing which will be as soon as practical but not less than three days after the date of issue.

- *Service of papers* – there are specific rules for service of the claim where an interim Possession Order is sought. These are set out in CPR rule 55.23. The claimant must serve on the trespassers the claim form, the application notice, written evidence in support and a blank form for the defendant's witness statement in form N133 within 24 hours of issue of the application and must provide a certificate of service at the hearing.

  The defendant may file a witness statement in response at any time before the hearing

- *Hearing* – because an interim Possession Order is effectively an interim injunction the court will consider whether the claimant is prepared to give an undertaking that if, after the interim Possession Order, the court subsequently decides that the claimant was not entitled to the interim Possession Order the claimant will reinstate the defendant and will pay such damages as the court may order, and also whether the claimant will undertake, before the claim for possession is finally decided, not to damage the premises, grant a right of occupation to any other person and damage or dispose of any of the defendant's property.

  Where the premises were vacant for a fit-out, the claimant needs to be careful that any fit-out between the interim and final Possession Order will not be seen as damage to the premises.

  In the event that those undertakings are given and the claimant has filed a certificate of service of the requisite documents and proves service of those documents and the conditions for an interim Possession Order are satisfied, then the court will order an interim Possession Order.

  On making an interim Possession Order the court will set a date for the final hearing of the claim for possession which will be not less than seven days after the date on which the interim Possession Order is made.

  If the court does not make an interim Possession Order then it will set a date for the final hearing of the claim and may give directions for the future conduct of the claim and, subject to those directions, the claim will proceed in the same way as with a normal possession claim.

Once an interim Possession Order has been made, it must be served within 48 hours after it is sealed together with the copies of the claim form and the written evidence in support.

Before the final hearing, the claimant must file a certificate of service in relation to the documents specified in CPR rule 55.26(2), i.e. the claim form and evidence in support.

An application can be made to set aside an interim Possession Order.

At the final hearing, the court may make any order it considers appropriate which may include making a final Order for Possession, dismissing the claim for possession, giving directions for the claim for possession to continue under section 1 or enforce any of the claimant's undertakings.

■ *Enforcement* – following the hearing, if an interim Possession Order is granted, the squatters have 24 hours to leave, after which they can be arrested. This is an advantage over the normal possession procedure, that the police become involved much quicker

## What arguments might trespassers raise in court?

**18.7.26**   The court has no discretion for interim Possession Orders. If the relevant papers are filed and properly served, an interim Possession Order must be granted.

**18.7.27**   For normal possession claims though, trespassers may raise any number of arguments to seek to adjourn the matter and spend more time in the property. A quick search of the internet will raise numerous websites dedicated to assisting squatters in fighting their corner. There is some very questionable advice given:

> as long as no one sees you break in, no one can accuse you of criminal damage. Once in, a Possession Order is needed for eviction. [For this reason, a typical response when a squatter is asked how he gained entry to a property is to say he climbed in through an open window.]
>
> if the police arrive, tell them it is a civil (not criminal) matter
>
> notify the legal owner of the squatters having taken possession (to take the benefit of section 6 so that they cannot use violence to obtain entry), but give as little detail as possible so as not to help with drafting of the possession proceedings
>
> try to delay matters by asking for an adjournment, either to help prepare a complicated case or to rectify any technical errors in the claimant's papers
>
> challenge ownership [All well-prepared possession actions should, as a matter of course, prove ownership.]
>
> send a letter to yourself at the property to convince the police that you live there

**18.7.28**   Some other tricks frequently used by squatters are to claim that the property is residential in that it has a shower and cooking facilities (as most office buildings tend to). The reason for arguing that the property is residential is that the service requirements for residential property are five working days before the hearing, rather than two working days and that the trespassers were therefore not served within time.

**18.7.29**    One bailiff reported:

Squatters use various tactics to delay an inevitable eviction including:

- providing false names when attending court;
- claiming that they are now occupying an additional unit or premises which was not served with the original notice;
- barricading themselves into the premises;
- obtaining support of the local community;
- offer themselves as 'security' for the premises;
- claiming health and social issues.

**18.7.30**    Subject to proper service of the claim under CPR, section III of Part 55, the court has no discretion to award anything other than possession.

## Costs

**18.7.31**    Costs of possession proceedings are recoverable, but in a claim against trespassers they are rarely actually recovered, as the action is usually brought against 'persons unknown'.

**18.7.32**    In addition, if the possession hearing is uncontested, the claimant would in any event only be entitled to fixed costs.

## 18.8    ENFORCEMENT OF POSSESSION ORDER

**18.8.1**    Once an order is obtained, it needs to be served and then, if necessary, executed by an enforcement agent. Enforcement of a Possession Order is either via the county court or the High Court. As most possession proceedings are brought in the county court, most enforcements by the High Court follow a transfer from the county court. **Chapter 4** deals with transfers between courts.

**18.8.2**    Where the enforcement takes place in the High Court, the claimant applies for a writ of possession. Where the enforcement takes place in the county court, the claimant applies for a warrant of possession.

**18.8.3**    These are unaffected by the new Act.

## High Court

**18.8.4**    This is governed by Rules of Supreme Court (RSC) Order 45, rule 3. A writ of possession is enforced by a High Court enforcement officer. This changed the previous position (on 1 April 2004) by which the High Court sheriff enforced writs of execution. The position was changed by Courts Act 2003, s.99 and Sched.7.

**18.8.5**    A writ of possession is in form 66. Where it is combined with a writ of *fieri facias* (now known as a warrant of control under the new Act), it is in form 53.

**18.8.6**    An Order for Possession can also be enforced not just by a writ of possession but also by an order for committal or a writ of sequestration. In that case, where the order states that possession must be given by a certain time, then possession can be enforced by a writ of sequestration under RSC Order 45, rule 5 which allows a procedure for committal of a person disobeying the order.

**18.8.7**    High Court enforcement officers are regulated by the High Court Enforcement Officers Regulations 2004, SI 2004/400. It is the creditor who makes the decision as to which High Court enforcement officer to use. A search for High Court enforcement officers can be made at **www.hceoa.org.uk**.

**18.8.8**    Permission from the court is required to issue a writ of possession except in a mortgage action (RSC Order 45, rule 3(2)). An application for permission to issue a writ of possession is made without notice.

## County court

**18.8.9**    If the trespasser does not leave, having been served with the Order for Possession, the claimant who wants to enforce the order in the county court must make a request for a warrant of possession. A claimant is not allowed to enforce an Order for Possession without a warrant of possession (CCR Order 26, rule 17(3)).

**18.8.10**    The procedure for obtaining a warrant of possession is governed by County Court Rules (CCR) Order 26, rule 17.

**18.8.11**    The request for a warrant of possession is made on form N325 and must certify that the land has not been vacated as ordered by the court. The warrant of possession itself will be in form N49.

**18.8.12**    A warrant of possession can include the enforcement of a money judgment.

**18.8.13**    Where a trespasser resists the enforcement of a warrant of possession, the claimant can apply to court for the trespasser to be arrested for contempt.

**18.8.14**    A court bailiff will generally serve a notice prior to eviction. Comment on this was given by an enforcement agent:

> Providing prior notice of the time of eviction to the squatters, can cause problems for the eviction.

> I served notice on squatters to vacate occupied premises. The notice gave the squatters 48 hours to vacate, if they did not comply the notice gave the squatters the date and time the eviction would take place.

On arrival at the premises to enforce the eviction I was met with twice as many squatters in the premises as had previously been there, members of the local community and members of the press.

The squatters had taken up position on the roof of the building as well as having barricaded themselves in the premises.

The police were on site for the eviction to prevent a breach of the peace, and after lengthy discussions it was decided that we would have to withdraw from the premises as it was unsafe to proceed because specialist tactical climbing teams would need to be drafted in, in order to ensure the safety of the rooftop protestors.

The police were of the opinion that the notice given to the squatters to vacate the premises had been counter-productive to the enforcement agents as it had given the squatters the time to prepare and take up positions on the roof, knowing that an effective enforcement would be highly unlikely on the day for safety reasons.

## Police intervention

18.8.15   Whenever dealing with squatters, the co-operation of the police is crucial. They will often assess the situation as regards a potential breach of the peace and, without a court Order for Possession, are unlikely to intervene and, in some cases, will try to prevent the enforcement agent from taking action, to avoid a potential breach of the peace.

18.8.16   One bailiff reported:

I was instructed by the landlord of a commercial premises in east London to attend the premises after reports of the building being occupied.

I was supplied with keys to the premises by the landlord. On attendance at the premises two of my bailiffs gained access to the building via the front door with the keys provided. On entry to the building we were confronted by two people claiming to be occupying the premises under s.6 of the Criminal Justice and Public Order Act although no notices were displayed in any part of the premises.

I informed the occupiers that we had entered legally and peaceably with the use of the keys to the premises and informed the occupiers that should they not leave peacefully, we had the legal right to remove them using reasonable force. The police were called to the premises and I called in additional personnel to deal with the removal of the occupiers. The occupiers also called other squatters who occupied nearby premises (who they were in contact with) to attend the premises.

By the time of the police arrival on site there were in the region of 50 squatters outside the premises along with 30 of my security officers. The police informed me that they did not have the resources to police the action and prevent any breach of the peace and allowed the squatters to enter the premises freely. However, they would not allow my security personnel entry to the premises because, according to the police, it may cause a breach of the peace.

The police informed my security officers positioned at the entrances to the premises that if they refused access to any persons they would be arrested.

The senior officer on site informed me that should the bailiffs not withdraw their personnel and cease their actions she would have no alternative than to arrest me in order to bring my actions to an end by removing me from the situation.

We were in physical occupation of the premises at all times during the eviction but eventually decided to withdraw due to the lack of support from the police.

The client eventually obtained a court Order for Possession which, frustratingly, took another six to eight weeks.

**18.8.17**    Other criminal offences that may be committed but are rarely enforced in these situations by the police are:

- theft of electricity and gas;
- breaking and entering;
- criminal damage.

**18.8.18**    A summary of an enforcement agent's view of the current squatting position in the UK is:

Over the last two years there has been major criminal activity. Squatters have been taking up occupation of commercial premises and claiming protection under s.6 of the Criminal Justice and Public Order Act 1994.

These squatters are occupying the premises for financial gain rather than for a place to live. There has been an increase in the instances of criminal damage and theft from buildings after they have been occupied. Central heating systems, air con systems, wiring, cabling and pipe work are removed from the premises and sold.

The occupiers also hold raves and so-called art exhibitions at the premises, where the building itself is used as a canvas. There is often a charge for entrance to these events and the organisers are usually gone long before the authorities arrive.

## Criminal Justice and Public Order Act 1994, Part V, s.61

**18.8.19**    This makes it an offence to remain on the land when asked to leave by a police officer.

**18.8.20**    The conditions for s.61 to apply are that there must be:

- two or more people;
- intending to reside;
- who have been asked to leave by the owner; and
- they have caused damage; or
- there are more than six cars.

**18.8.21**    Under s.61:

If the senior police officer present at the scene reasonably believes that two or more persons are trespassing on land and are present there with the common purpose of residing there for any period, that reasonable steps have been taken by or on behalf of the occupier to ask them to leave and –

(a)    that any of those persons has caused damage to the land or to property on the land or used threatening, abusive or insulting words or behaviour towards the occupier, a member of his family or an employee or agent of his, or

(b)   that those persons have between them six or more vehicles on the land,

he may direct those persons, or any of them, to leave the land and to remove any vehicles or other property they have with them on the land.

**18.8.22**   If they do not leave when directed to do so, or return within three months, that becomes an offence and they can be arrested without a warrant.

**18.8.23**   Possible defences are for the accused to show that he was not trespassing on the land, or that he had a reasonable excuse for failing to leave the land as soon as reasonably practicable or for again entering the land as a trespasser.

**18.8.24**   It must be stressed that this requires co-operation from the police and, in the vast majority of cases, the police refuse to exercise their powers. Theoretically though, all that is required is for the squatters to be abusive when asked to leave, and the police can arrest them.

## *Drugs*

**18.8.25**   The Anti-Social Behaviour Act 2003 gives the police the power to issue a closure notice on premises where class A drugs are present and there is a serious public nuisance.

**18.8.26**   A closure notice lasts for three months. Any squatters entering during that period commit an offence.

## 18.9   SQUATTERS' RIGHTS

**18.9.1**   Unless they leave voluntarily, and if the landlord or his agents cannot peaceably enter the property, the squatters cannot be evicted without a court order. Criminal Law Act 1977, s.6 describes the squatters' only rights. There is nothing to stop the owner from preventing access to further trespassers.

**18.9.2**   Issuing proceedings and having a hearing listed for seven days later does not mean the trespassers have a right to stay for seven days. Their rights (being the right to prevent access to the property by the landlord by force) remain unchanged.

**18.9.3**   This means that the owner can, quite legally:

- stop any more trespassers from entering; and
- stop a trespasser who has left the property from re-entering, just as he would have been perfectly in his rights to stop the original trespassers from entering had he been on the property at the time of the original trespass.

**18.9.4**   Neither of these is obtaining possession without a court order or accessing the property with force.

## 18.10    ALTERNATIVE METHOD FOR HIGH STREET SQUATTERS

18.10.1    Although not just limited to retail premises, and applicable to all non-residential premises, if a bailiff can enter a property peacefully (usually during opening hours), he can use reasonable force to evict. An example given by a bailiff is:

> For many years landlords have had the problem of commercial squatters gaining access to high street retail units and trading from the premises.
>
> Landlords have usually been advised to obtain an Order for Possession in the county court. This process is not only expensive but over recent years has become more and more time consuming as the court bailiffs are undertaking more work and the enforcement of a Possession Order can take anywhere between four and 12 weeks.
>
> Landlords have also had the right to attend and obtain peaceable possession of the premises, much as would be done in the case of forfeiture, by attending and changing the locks when the premises are closed.
>
> The problem with this of course is that if a squatter is residing in the premises the landlord or agent acting for the landlord must cease his action for possession and hand any new keys to the occupier and obtain possession through the courts.
>
> Enforcement agents today can attend the premises when they are open and trading. By walking peacefully into an open premises the enforcement agent has the legal right to occupy the premises (with the landlord's consent) and prevent any persons from entering who do not have the authority of the legal owner.
>
> Once the enforcement agents are in occupation of the premises they are able to deny access to members of the public, thus preventing the occupier from carrying on his trade. The occupier is then requested to remove all his belongings from the premises, failure to do so could result in the bailiff removing the goods from the premises. The bailiff has a right to remove the goods from the premises onto a public highway on the basis that they have been placed there with the full knowledge and in sight of their rightful owner (i.e. the squatter).
>
> The police are aware of this common law right. The enforcement officer is able to use reasonable force to remove the squatters and their possessions from the premises provided the enforcement agent has not used force to gain entry.

## 18.11    RAVES

### What if my property is about to be used for a rave?

18.11.1    A 'rave' has now long entered the English language and was defined (in a rather long-winded way) in the Criminal Justice and Public Order Act 1994 as:

- a gathering of 100 or more persons;
- on land in the open air;
- at which amplified music is played during the night; and
- which is likely to cause serious distress to the inhabitants of the locality.

**18.11.2** Criminal Justice and Public Order Act 1994, ss.63–6 relate to the police's powers in relation to raves. Section 63 gives the police power to remove persons attending or preparing for a rave. Section 63 applies to trespassers as well as non-trespassers but it does not apply to gatherings licensed by an entertainment licence.

**18.11.3** The definition has been extended by the Anti-Social Behaviour Act 2003 to include gatherings in a building and the number has been reduced from 100 to 20.

**18.11.4** If a police officer (he must be ranked superintendent or higher) reasonably believes that:

■ two or more persons are making preparations to hold a rave on any land (in the open air);
■ 10 or more persons are waiting for a rave to begin on the land; or
■ 10 or more persons are actually attending a rave in progress;

then the superintendent may order those persons and anybody else who arrives to leave the land and remove any vehicles or other property from the land.

**18.11.5** Quite sensibly this need not be communicated to them by the superintendent himself but can be communicated by a police officer at the scene.

**18.11.6** Under s.63(4) not every person has to be told. Providing reasonable steps have been taken to bring it to their attention they shall be treated as having been notified.

## Offence

**18.11.7** Anybody being notified must leave the land as soon as reasonably practicable and must not return for seven days. If they do not leave the land as soon as reasonably practicable or re-enter the land within seven days, they commit an offence and are liable on summary conviction to imprisonment of a term for up to three months or a fine not exceeding level 4 on the standard scale or both pursuant to Criminal Justice and Public Order Act 1994, s.63(6).

## Arrest without warrant

**18.11.8** Police on the scene can arrest people who are guilty of this offence without a warrant.

## Defence

**18.11.9** It is a defence to show that the person ordered to leave had a reasonable excuse for failing to leave the land as soon as reasonably practicable or has a reasonable excuse for again entering the land under s.63(7).

## Rights of occupiers

**18.11.10**    Criminal Justice and Public Order Act 1994, s.63 applies to trespassers and non-trespassers alike. It does not however apply to the occupier, any member of his family and any employee or agent of them and any person whose home is situated on the land. This stops people being evicted from their own land but does not stop guests from being evicted.

## Access to land

**18.11.11**    The police have the right to enter land to ascertain whether a rave is about to take place or is taking place and to exercise any of their powers under s.63. They can do so without a warrant.

## Seizure of equipment

**18.11.12**    If a trespasser fails to remove any vehicle or sound equipment on the land, this may be seized and removed by the police under Criminal Justice and Public Order Act 1994, s.64(4). Once again, the vehicle or sound equipment of an occupier, any member of his family and any employee or agent of them and any person whose home is situated on the land cannot be seized.

## Persons travelling to a rave

**18.11.13**    The police also have the power, within a five mile radius of the site, to stop people that they reasonably believe are on their way to a rave and order them not to head towards the rave. If those people do not comply, they commit an offence and are liable on summary conviction to a fine not exceeding level three on the standard scale. They can also be arrested at the scene without a warrant.

## Forfeiture of sound equipment

**18.11.14**    Under Criminal Justice and Public Order Act 1994, s.66, the court may make an order for forfeiture of sound equipment seized under s.64(4).

**18.11.15**    If the real owner of the sound equipment comes forward within six months, he can apply to the magistrates' court for the property to be delivered to him if he can show ownership but in doing so he must show that he had not consented to the offender having possession of the equipment or that he did not know and had no reason to suspect that the equipment was likely to be used at a rave.

**18.11.16**    After six months, the Secretary of State can make regulations for the disposal of the property and for the application of the proceeds of sale of the forfeited property.

**18.11.17**   It has been very helpful in the past to encourage the police to exercise their powers to show that stereo equipment has been taken onto the property and that a rave may take place. Not wanting all their resources (usually on a Friday or Saturday night) to be used up policing an illegal rave, they may use these powers earlier in the day to effect immediate possession.

**18.11.18**   An example of the usefulness of this section is explained by a bailiff:

> The landlord of a vacant office building situated within a residential area received reports on a Friday morning that the premises had been occupied by squatters. The landlord instructed me to attend the premises and report back on the situation. I attended the premises at 3pm on that afternoon. On attendance at the premises I witnessed a number of vehicles in the car park along with a large number of people in and around the building. On the railings surrounding the premises there were banners advertising a free art exhibition over the course of the weekend.

> We placed security personnel around the entrances to the site in order to prevent members of the public and further squatters from entering the premises and causing substantial criminal damage. We informed the police that the premises had been illegally occupied and that an illegal event was being advertised for that weekend and also informed them of the landlord's intention to prevent further occupation of the premises. We also informed the police that we had witnessed music equipment including speakers being taken into the premises from the vehicles that were already in the car park.

> The police supported our proposed action and assisted the security personnel by cordoning off a number of roads surrounding the property. Over the course of 36 hours over 1,000 people attended the site and were refused entry, occupiers who left the premises were also refused entry back into the premises. Several people were removed by the police for breach of the peace and later released without charge. The last of the occupiers of the premises had vacated by 10am on the Monday morning and we entered the premises to inspect any damage.

> There was an estimated £100,000 worth of damage caused to the building, however it was estimated that without the landlord's intervention the damage would have been in excess of £250,000.

> Landlords should speak with their insurers prior to executing these procedures as the insurance company may decide to pay for this expensive operation rather than indemnify the loss caused by the damage as the savings could be substantial.

## 18.12   TRAVELLERS

**18.12.1**   Private landowners have available to them common law rights over trespassers on land. Reasonable force may be used to obtain possession providing the force used is not excessive. If excessive force is used then this may amount to a criminal offence (assault) or create a tortious liability (trespass against a person).

**18.12.2**    A summary of the procedures employed by enforcement officers are set out below:

■    On receipt of instructions from a landowner the enforcement officers will attend site and assess the situation and serve notice, under common law, upon all vehicles and persons on site, requesting the trespassers to vacate the site within the designated time span. This time span is dependent on the conduct of the trespassers, although it usually gives them until the morning following service.

■    If the trespassers fail to vacate site within the prescribed period, enforcement agents will re-attend site to remove the trespassers. The enforcement officer has no duty and care for the vehicles and may remove the said vehicles from the land and place them safely on the highway without causing an obstruction. Police are always willing to attend site on eviction in order to ensure there is no breach of the peace. It has been recognised by the police that the vehicles may be placed on a highway. The police would treat the vehicles as abandoned after a period time. It is extremely rare that an enforcement agent has to physically remove the vehicles as trespassers are aware of a landowner's rights and usually move them of their own accord.

      Private landowners are under no obligation to consider social and welfare issues of the trespassers, whereas local authorities have strict guidelines they must adhere to when enforcing against trespassers.

**18.12.3**    There has been a trend over the last 12 months for groups of travellers to occupy vacant commercial premises under Criminal Law Act 1977, s.6, affording them the same protection as squatters and causing the same problems for landowners. These squatters/travellers are occupying the premises for financial gain rather than for a place to live. There has been an increase in the instances of criminal damage and theft from buildings such as the removal of wiring cabling, copper piping and lead from the premises.

**18.12.4**    If faced with this problem, landowners should take the same procedures as they would when faced with squatters by obtaining a Possession Order from the county court or High Court:

■    The enforcement agent will attend site and ascertain whether he is able to enter the premises peaceably and carry out a common law eviction. If not, he will ascertain the number of persons and vehicles on occupation. A witness statement will be provided detailing all the information, which can be used by the solicitor in support of a claim for possession application.

■    The enforcement agents will take the application to the court for issue and wait for the papers. The enforcement agent will then attend the premises with the notice of hearing and serve upon persons unknown in accordance with CPR Part 55. A witness statement of service will be provided.

■  Once the hearing has taken place and the Order for Possession has been granted the enforcement agent will attend court to collect sufficient sealed copies of the order. The enforcement agent will then attend the premises and serve the order in accordance with CPR.

18.12.5    If an Order for Possession has been granted ordering the occupiers to vacate the premises forthwith the agent is able to prevent any further persons from entering the premises and prevent the re-entry of persons after they have left.

## 18.13    CHECKLIST FOR DEALING WITH SQUATTERS

### Prevention

1.  Regular visits.
2.  Locks.

### Action

3.  Have deeds ready.
4.  Instruct a solicitor immediately. Although you will not get the property back straight away, it is usually with a court order that the police co-operate and the squatters move.
5.  Instruct an enforcement agent to attend site.

## 18.14    FORMS

| | |
|---|---|
| N5 | Claim form for possession of property |
| N5B | Claim form – accelerated possession |
| N11 | Defence |
| N11B | Defence – accelerated possession |
| N11R | Defence – rented residential premises |
| N26 | Order for Possession |
| N26A | Order for Possession – accelerated procedure |
| N119 | Particulars of claim – rented residential premises |
| N121 | Particulars of claim – trespassers |
| N130 | Application for interim Possession Order |
| N133 | Defendant's witness statement (interim possession procedure) |
| N134 | Interim Possession Order |
| N136 | Order for Possession (following interim Possession Order) |
| N206A/B | Notice of issue |

PART V  **DEBT MANAGEMENT AND RELIEF**

# 19 INTRODUCTION TO DEBT MANAGEMENT AND RELIEF

## 19.1 INTRODUCTION

**19.1.1**  Part 5 of the new Act makes changes to two statutory debt management schemes: Administration Orders and Enforcement Restriction Orders. The new Act also amends the Insolvency Act 1986 to allow for the introduction of a new form of personal insolvency procedure. This allows the Official Receiver to make a Debt Relief Order in relation to individual debtors.

**19.1.2**  The effect of these provisions is stay enforcement by creditors whilst the debts are comprised or discharged over a period of time.

**19.1.3**  Part 5 of the new Act allows the Lord Chancellor to approve debt management schemes (DMSs). Approved scheme operators will be able to arrange debt repayment plans.

**19.1.4**  These schemes will allow providers of debt management advice to help debtors put in place procedures which compel creditors to accept a repayment plan.

**19.1.5**  The new procedures are:

- Administration Orders (AOs) for individuals (a modified version of the existing procedure);
- Enforcement Restriction Orders (EROs);
- Debt Relief Orders (DROs);
- debt management schemes (DMSs).

DROs and DMSs will complement the existing statutory schemes such as AOs and individual voluntary arrangements.

**19.1.6**  The measures are designed to assist the 'can't pay' group of debtors (see 6.2.3).

## 19.2 BACKGROUND

**19.2.1**  In 2002 net lending by individuals rose by almost £10 billion per month. It was estimated that each adult in the United Kingdom owed an average of

£18,000 each. This might not in itself lead to debtors who cannot pay their debts. However, the concern is that if there should be an economic downturn or recession with rising interest rates, then this would put a large number of people at risk. In the report to the Department of Trade and Industry, *Over-Indebtedness in Britain* (November 2002) it was estimated that:

- 5 per cent of adults spent 25 per cent or more of their income repaying consumer debt;
- 6 per cent of adults spend more than half their income on consumer credit and mortgage repayments.

The National Association of Citizens Advice Bureaux estimate that they deal with 24 per cent more debt-related problems now than they did in 2000.

**19.2.2**   High levels of debt problems can be caused by a range of factors, including marriage breakdown, redundancy, sickness and reduced work for the self-employed. Over-indebtedness can affect people of all incomes either because people on middle-to-high incomes borrow large sums or people on low incomes borrow amounts which represent a large proportion of their income. The new procedures are designed to counteract over-indebtedness and alleviate the associated problems such as social exclusion, homelessness, and damage to health and family relationships (Consultation Paper: *A choice of paths, better options to manage over-indebtedness and multiple debt*, 20 July 2004).

**19.2.3**   The provisions of the new Act are designed to bring benefits for debtors and creditors. However the aspirations of the Act are even more ambitious. In the White Paper: *Effective Enforcement*, the government's overall objectives were:

> To minimise the number of people who become over indebted by promoting affordable credit and responsible lending and borrowing e.g. through a better financial education and access to advice on handling money.

> To improve services for those who have fallen into debt and their creditors. This includes promoting financial rehabilitation for debtors, e.g. through debt relief in appropriate cases; and ensuring that debt problems are resolved fairly, effectively and speedily e.g. through promoting best practice and access to information, advice and assistance with debtors, and through providing efficient court services and effective enforcement.

**19.2.4**   The debt relief provisions of the new Act are designed to assist the category of people who have fallen into debt and that have great difficulty in recovering from the position. The procedures assist those debtors with no surplus income available after they have met ordinary living expenses. These are the people who cannot afford to make payments in full to their creditors, the debtors that have no assets that can be sold in order to defray the debt and even those people who have insufficient funds to afford to pay the fee to petition for their own bankruptcy.

**19.2.5**   There has been a general rise in bankruptcies, Income Payments Orders (a post-bankruptcy process) and individual voluntary arrangements (IVAs). The

Enterprise Act 2002 introduced a new regime for personal insolvency on 1 April 2004. There has been a major increase in personal insolvency. The number of personal insolvencies increased by more than 400 per cent between 1998 and 2006 (the number of IVAs by more than 800 per cent).

**19.2.6**    The Insolvency Service paper entitled *Relief for the Indebted – An alternative to bankruptcy* (March 2005) estimated that 70 per cent of people who became bankrupt could be described as a consumer bankrupt. In 1996 only 40 per cent of people who became bankrupt could be described in this way.

**Table 19.1**    Personal involvency by year

| Year | Percentage of bankrupts on the basis of non-trading debt | Bankruptcy Orders | Individual voluntary arrangements |
|------|------|------|------|
| 1996 | 40% | | |
| 1997 | 42% | | |
| 1998 | 48% | 19,647 | 4,902 |
| 1999 | 50% | 21,611 | 7,195 |
| 2000 | 54% | 21,550 | 7,978 |
| 2001 | 58% | 23,477 | 6,298 |
| 2002 | 62% | 24,292 | 6,295 |
| 2003 | 69% | 28,021 | 7,583 |
| 2004 | | 35,898 | 10,752 |
| 2005 | | 47,291 | 20,293 |
| 2006 | | 62,956 | 44,332 |

**19.2.7**    In addition to this, the number of people who present their own bankruptcy petitions has grown dramatically. In the mid-1990s the number of debtor petitions and creditor petitions for bankruptcy were approximately the same. Today twice as many people petition for their own bankruptcy as are made bankrupt pursuant to a creditor petition.

**19.2.8**    The current position in relation to Administration Orders is that 74 per cent of people who apply for an Administration Order do not own their own home, in contrast to 31 per cent of the population generally and 55 per cent of other people who are in arrears with their payments.

**19.2.9**    Of those with county court Administration Orders, 38 per cent are lone parents, compared to 6 per cent of the population generally, and about 70 per cent of them are of working age but are not working, compared with 18 per cent of the general population.

**19.2.10**    Some creditors suspect that people apply for an Administration Order to avoid repaying monies and to avoid their liabilities. The Insolvency Service report *Relief for the Indebted – An alternative to bankruptcy* (March 2005) stated that it had not found any evidence to support this view. However, creditors often have a cynical view as to the motives of debtors in making such applications.

# 20 ADMINISTRATION ORDERS

## 20.1 PRE-ACT POSITION

**20.1.1** Administration Orders are governed by ss.112–17 of the County Court Act 1984. Administration Orders (AOs) are a court administered debt management scheme for those with multiple debts totalling no more than £5,000. In order to obtain an Administration Order one of the debts must be a judgment debt. There is currently no time limit on the order so that under some orders debtors are given a very long period in which to make a payment.

**20.1.2** Section 13 of the Court and Legal Services Act 1990 was supposed to have introduced changes so that:

■ the need for a judgment debt was removed;
■ the debt limit increased and a three-year limit to the order introduced.

**20.1.3** For the first time, an explicit power was given to the court to grant an order restricting enforcement where it considered that this would be more appropriate than an Administration Order.

**20.1.4** However s.13 was widely criticised and has never been brought into force. The new Act flows from the changes which were supposed to originate from s.13.

**20.1.5** The new Administration Orders:

■ will be opened up to a higher level of debt;
■ will be open for a longer period; and
■ it will not be necessary to be a judgment debtor.

## 20.2 THE NEW ACT POSITION

### When an Administration Order can be made

**20.2.1** A county court can make an Administration Order on behalf of an individual who is a debtor where there are two or more qualifying debts.

**20.2.2**    The expression 'qualifying debt' relates to all debts which are unsecured. Further exclusions may be made by the regulations (County Court Act 1984, s.112AB).

**20.2.3**    However, the AO process is designed for consumer debt only. The individual must not be a debtor under any business debt. A business debt is any debt:

> (Whether or not a qualifying debt) which is incurred by a person in the course of the business (County Court Act 1984, s.112AB, as amended by the new Act)

## When it cannot be made

**20.2.4**    An AO cannot be made in the following circumstances:

- if the individual already has a current AO or has had an AO in place in the last 12 months (beginning with the day when the previous order ceased to have effect);
- if a debtor is currently bound by an individual voluntary arrangement approved under Part 8 of the Insolvency Act 1986 (or during the currency of an interim order under Insolvency Act 1986, s.252 in respect of a proposal for a voluntary arrangement);
- the debtor is excluded from having an AO if there is already a pending bankruptcy petition which is presented to the court or if he is an undischarged bankrupt.

## Debt limit

**20.2.5**    The debtor must have at least two qualifying debts and be unable to pay at least one of them (County Court Act 1984, s.112B, as amended by the new Act). However an order can only be made where the debtor's qualifying debts are less than the prescribed minimum. At present the minimum is £5,000 (under the existing scheme).

**20.2.6**    The new limit will be prescribed in due course. However, it is highly likely that the limit will be raised substantially. The setting of the limit may be controversial. There has already been a significant degree of consultation on the issue.

**20.2.7**    The debtor must have some ability to make repayments. This is defined by the fact that the debtor's surplus income must be more than the prescribed minimum (County Court Act 1984, s.112B, as amended by the new Act) (this will be set by the regulations).

## Requirements imposed by the order

**20.2.8**    When an AO is made the court imposes a repayment requirement on the debtor. The court determines the repayment requirement which may provide for the debtor to repay different scheduled debts to different extents. This suggests that creditors can be treated differently (County Court Act 1985, s.112E(4), as amended by the new Act). The court may also decide that in the case of a new debt that is scheduled to the order, no repayment is to be made until the debtor has made all repayments in respect of the original declared debt.

20.2.9    Repayments can be made by an Order for Instalments pursuant to s.112E(6). The court decides when the instalments are to be made and how much they are to be. The District Judge will be required to act in accordance with repayment regulations which have not yet been set. The regulations make provisions for instalments to be determined by reference to the debtor's surplus income. The repayments are made to the court. The fund is used firstly to pay costs and then to begin to repay the creditors (i.e. the scheduled debts).

## New debt

20.2.10    An AO applies to existing debt. However, pursuant to s.112D, it can also apply to new debt (i.e. debt incurred after the date of the order). So where a consumer has incurred debt he can go on incurring further debt (for which he may not be able to repay) in the hope that this becomes scheduled to the order. This may appear to be a rogue's charter but the provisions attempt to reduce the risk of abuse. The debtor is obliged to provide the court with full information about his goods and means (see **20.2.22**). However, he is not obliged to provide new creditors (i.e. post AO creditors) with information.

20.2.11    Creditors are able to search the County Court Register of Judgment Orders and Fines (see **Chapter 3**). From 6 April 2006 this was extended to cover AO.

20.2.12    In relation to new debt it can be added to the schedule providing that the total amount and the debtor's qualifying debts remains less than the prescribed maximum.

20.2.13    The court can order that the original creditors are paid prior (either in whole or proportionately) to the new debt being paid.

## Bankruptcy petitions and other remedies against the debtor – moratorium

20.2.14    Once the AO has been made then it will impose a requirement during the currency of the order that:

- no creditor of the debtor is to present a bankruptcy petition in respect of a qualifying debt (i.e. unsecured) unless the creditor has permission of the court (s.112F);
- no qualifying creditor of the debtor is to pursue any remedy for the recovery of a qualifying debt without the court's permission;

- no creditor under a scheduled debt is to charge any sum by way of interest, fee or other charge in respect of the debt (s.113H);
- no domestic utility provider is to stop the supply of gas or electricity or the supply of any associated services (without the court's permission) (s.112I);
- pursuant to s.112, if an AO is made then a county court must stay any court proceedings in relation to a qualifying debt. If this happens the court may allow the costs incurred already by the creditor and may add these costs to the debt and to the amounts scheduled to the AO.

**20.2.15**   In relation to utilities the supplier can stop supply if the debtor fails to pay further charges incurred after the making of the order (unless they have become scheduled to the order or if the creditor has forced to disconnect for other reasons (s.112I(5)).

## The making of the order

**20.2.16**   A county court may make an AO on the debtor's application pursuant to s.112J. The debtor no longer has to be a judgment debtor prior to the application being made. The position on this has been relaxed so that any debtor may make an application for an AO whether or not he is involved in other proceedings in respect of any of his debts (s.112J).

**20.2.17**   A court can, of its own volition, suggest to the debtor that an AO be made. This can be suggested following an application for an Order to Obtain Information.

**20.2.18**   The court will not make the order without first considering representations made by creditors and interested parties.

## Duration of the order

**20.2.19**   The court has a degree of flexibility as to how long the order will last. However, pursuant to s.112K, the maximum permitted period is five years beginning with the day on which the order is made. The court is empowered to set a day on which the order will cease to have effect. Strangely the court does not have to specify a date (the expression used under s.112K is that 'a county court *may* . . . specify a day on which the order will cease to have effect' (emphasis added)). This leaves it open to the court to set perhaps an initial period for the AO and for it to be brought back before the court for review.

**20.2.20**   The period for the AO set by the court is subject to permitted variations under the terms of s.112S and the possibility that the order may be revoked under s.112W (see **20.2.25** and **20.2.26**).

## Effect of the order on other schemes

**20.2.21**   Once the order is made then any other debt management arrangement automatically ceases to be in force. This includes Enforcement Restricting Orders, Debt Relief Orders and debt repayment plans.

**20.2.22**   The debtor must at prescribed times provide the court with particulars of his:

■   earnings;
■   income;
■   assets;
■   outgoings (s.112M).

**20.2.23**   Information given in relation to these issues also has to take into account what the debtor expects to happen in the near future. The period of 'expectation' will be prescribed by the regulations. The debtor must within a prescribed period provide the court with details of any disposals of property or assets he plans to make (s.112M(4)). It is an offence to fail to provide information pursuant to s.112M. The offence attracts a fine of up to £250 or imprisonment for a period up to 14 days (s.112N).

## Discharge

**20.2.24**   Once a debtor repays the scheduled debt to the extent provided for by the AO then the debtor is discharged from that debt and the debt is removed from the schedule. This allows the debtor to work through the list of debts pursuant to the terms and conditions of the order. Once all the scheduled debts have been repaid (to the extent provided) then the AO is revoked.

## Variation

**20.2.25**   If a debtor finds that he cannot comply with the terms of the order then he can make an application for a variation. In addition to this a creditor can make an application or the court can make a decision of its own motion. The power to vary includes:

■   the power to specify a new termination date (providing this falls on or before the last day of the maximum permitted period) (s.112S(2));
■   the power to de-schedule a debt (only if it appears that it is just and equitable to do so (s.112T)).

## Revocation

**20.2.26**   The court must revoke the AO in the following circumstances:

■   where it becomes apparent that the debtor did not have two or more qualifying debts when the order was made (s.112U(1)(a));

- where it becomes apparent that the debtor had business debts when the order was made (s.112U(2)(a));
- where the debtor subsequently becomes a debtor under a business debt and is still a debtor under that debt;
- where it becomes apparent that the debtor had a voluntary arrangement or was bankrupt or subject to a bankruptcy petition or an AO (s.112U(3)) – either before the current AO or afterwards;
- where it becomes apparent that the debtor was in fact able to pay the qualifying debt at the time of the AO or has subsequently become able to pay them (s.112U(5));
- where it becomes apparent that the debtor's qualifying debts were in fact more than the prescribed maximum or have subsequently become more than the prescribed maximum (s.112U(6));
- where it becomes apparent that the debtor's surplus income is less than or the same as the prescribed minimum or has subsequently become so (s.112U(7)).

## Business debt

20.2.27   These provisions may preclude the debtor from taking part in any business activity after the time the AO is made. It is very difficult to take part in business without incurring some kind of business debt (even if this is only by way of overdraft). A business debt is defined by s.112AB as any debt which is incurred during the course of a business.

20.2.28   On this basis it would seem that, for example, self-employed people will be excluded from this process unless they can show they have absolutely no business debt.

20.2.29   The court also has a power to revoke the AO on the basis of non-compliance:

(a)  if a debtor fails to make two payments (whether consecutive or not); and
(b)  where a debtor has failed to provide the information required at the prescribed times pursuant to s.112N.

20.2.30   If there has been non-compliance then a court can revoke the AO of its own motion or following an application a qualifying creditor (s.112V). A court is able to revoke on terms and ultimately the AO will cease to have effect in accordance with those terms. Creditors are entitled to receive notice when the order is made, varied or revoked pursuant to ss.112X–112Y.

## S.112AC – inability to pay debts

20.2.31   A debtor is to be regarded as an unable to pay the debt only if:

(a)  the debt has become due;
(b)  the debtor has failed to make a single payment (or one or more payments);
(c)  the debtor is unable to make that payment.

# 21 ENFORCEMENT RESTRICTION ORDERS

## 21.1  INTRODUCTION

**21.1.1**   Enforcement Restriction Orders (EROs) follow a very similar structure to Administration Orders (AOs). They are a new device available to a debtor that is suffering from a:

> Sudden and unforeseen deterioration in his financial circumstances

However, the debtor must also show:

> a realistic prospect that the debtor's financial circumstances will improve within the period of 6 months beginning when the order was made.

**21.1.2**   EROs offer temporary respite to a debtor, a breathing space during which the creditors are restricted from taking action. This could be relevant for someone who is facing redundancy and a gap between jobs.

**21.1.3**   The order is made where it is fair and equitable to do so having regard to any representations made by any person about why the order should not be made.

**21.1.4**   In a similar way to an AO the debtor must not:

- have any debts which are business debts; or
- be subject to an individual voluntary arrangement (or an interim order pursuant to Insolvency Act 1986, s.252); or
- be subject to a Bankruptcy Order or a bankruptcy petition; or
- be subject to an existing ERO.

A debtor must be a debtor under two or more qualifying debts. The debts do not include business debts or debts secured against assets (County Court Act 1984, s.117B).

## 21.2    OVERVIEW

### Effect of order

**21.2.1**    When an ERO is made the following provisions apply:

- no creditor is able to present a bankruptcy petition in respect of a qualifying debt without the court's permission (s.117C);
- no creditor is able to pursue any remedy for the recovery of a qualifying debt without the court's permission;
- utility companies are not able to stop the supply of gas or electricity or supply of associated services (there are common sense exceptions to this principle in relation to non-payment of new supplies or other connected reasons) (s.117E);
- if other debt management arrangements are in force in respect of the debtor then they cease to be in force on the making of an ERO including an AO, a Debt Relief Order or a debt repayment plan;
- county court proceedings are stayed once an ERO is made in respect of a qualifying debt pursuant to s.117L.

### Duration

**21.2.2**    When the order is made the court specifies the day on which it will come to an end and set the period. However, the maximum permitted period is 12 months beginning with the day on which the order was made (s.117H).

### Repayment requirements

**21.2.3**    An ERO may impose a repayment requirement on the debtor (although this is not an absolute requirement). However, it cannot alter the amount which is to be repaid. An ERO will not reduce the debt. This is because an ERO anticipates that there is a realistic prospect that the debtor's financial circumstances will improve (s.117B(7)).

**21.2.4**    Accordingly EROs work to allow a debtor to make repayment over a period of time.

### Application

**21.2.5**    Only the debtor can make an application for an ERO and this application can be made whether or not he is judgment debtor.

### Discharge

**21.2.6**    EROs do not discharge debt (other than through repayment in full).

## Duty to provide information

**21.2.7**   Pursuant to s.117J, the debtor has to provide information at prescribed times in relation to his:

- earnings;
- income;
- assets;
- outgoings.

This is a similar requirement and works in a similar way to the provisions relating to AOs. The information provided must reflect the current position and how the debtor expects his affairs to be at such times in the future as may be prescribed. The debtor must also provide the court with information in relation to property intent to disposal (although this requirement does not extend to exempt goods of the new Act, i.e. goods which are capable of being taken control of under Sched.12).

**21.2.8**   Failure to comply with the requirements to provide information is an offence under s.117K and carries identical consequences as those set out for AOs (see **20.2.23**).

Table 21.1

| | Moratorium | Available for consumers or businesses | Requirement to repay | Duration | Creditors' support needed | Discharge | Debt limit | Income |
|---|---|---|---|---|---|---|---|---|
| **Administrative orders** | √ | Not business, consumer only | Yes but flexible as to proportion | Max 5 years | No | Yes following payment of the proportion of debt ordered | Currently £5,000. Likely to increase | Must be above prescribed minimum |
| **Enforcement restriction orders** | √ | Not business, consumer only | Yes but no reduction of debt level | Max 1 year | No | No discharge | No limit | Must be realistic prospect income will improve within 6 months |
| **Debt relief orders** | √ | Both consumer and business | No requirement to repay | Max 1 year + 3 months (with extension) | No | Discharge at end of moratorium | There will be a prescribed limit | No surplus income available to repay |
| **Debt management schemes** | √ | Not business, consumer only | Depends on terms of scheme | Depends on terms of scheme | Depends on terms of scheme | Yes after payment under a debt repayment plan | Depends on terms of scheme | Depends on terms of scheme |
| **IVAs** | √ | Both consumer and business | Depends on terms of arrangement | Flexible | Yes + 75% in value | Discharge if IVAs complied with | No limit | Flexible |

# 22 DEBT RELIEF ORDERS

## 22.1 BACKGROUND

**22.1.1** Debt Relief Orders (DROs) were originally proposed in a paper published by the Insolvency Service: *Relief for the Indebted – An Alternative to Bankruptcy* (March 2005).

**22.1.2** DROs were designed to assist consumer debtors who have little or no prospect of paying their debts. The Insolvency Service outlined the type of debtors their proposals were aimed at:

> The profile of the type of person entering bankruptcy has changed, and we have found that more and more people who get into debt have financial difficulties that are not related to a failed business. They are what could be described as 'consumer' debtors. Often their affairs are not particularly complicated, they have run into financial difficulty as a result of a 'life accident' such as loss of employment or relationship breakdown and bankruptcy was their last resort . . .

> We think that the people who would use our proposed debt relief scheme are those who are the very poorest. They are not people who look for an easy route to avoid paying their debts, they are simply unable to pay, or unlikely to be able to within any sort of realistic timetable.

## 22.2 AN OVERVIEW OF DEBT RELIEF ORDERS

- The scheme entails making (administratively) a Debt Relief Order that results in the debtor being discharged from his debts after a period of one year.
- The scheme requires little court intervention.
- The scheme is operated by the Insolvency Service (the Official Receiver attached to the court).
- Creditors can make a valid objection to the making of the order on specified grounds (such as the failure to disclose information about assets, income or debts) but not otherwise.
- The number of times a person can apply for an order is restricted.
- The entry fee to cover the costs of administering the scheme will be minimal and do not involve paying a court fee. The imposition of a fee at all is designed to deter frivolous applications.

- The scheme will operate through an approved intermediary such as Citizens Advice, which would enable the Official Receiver's costs of administering the scheme to be kept as low as possible.
- The scheme is not intended to be a 'debtor's charter' that grants an easy way out to people who owe money and have made no attempt to meet their obligations. Consequently, the debtor is required to demonstrate to the intermediary (e.g. by copy correspondence) that he has made an attempt to deal with his creditors without success.

## 22.3   PROCEDURE

22.3.1   The procedure is set out in Sched.17 to the new Act which inserts a new Part 7A into the Insolvency Act 1986.

### Making the application

22.3.2   An application for a DRO must be made to the Official Receiver through an approved intermediary. The approved intermediary is likely to be an organisation such as the Citizens Advice Bureaux. The regulations will set out the formal content of the application but it must include:

- a list of debts for which the debtor is subject to at the date of the application;
- details of any security held;
- general information about the debtor's affairs, including identity of creditors, income and assets.

22.3.3   The application must be submitted with the prescribed fee (s.251B of Part 7A of the Insolvency Act 1986).

### The role of the Official Receiver

22.3.4   The application is considered by the Official Receiver who must be satisfied that the debtor is unable to pay his debts. This consideration is framed by conditions set out in Part 1 of Sched.4ZA (a new schedule to the Insolvency Act 1986 inserted by Sched.18 to the new Act).

22.3.5   Under Sched.4ZA, the Official Receiver considers the debtor's previous insolvency history to ensure that at the determination date:

- he is not an undischarged bankrupt;
- he is not subject to an interim order or voluntary arrangement;
- he is not subject to a Bankruptcy Restriction Order or a Debt Relief Restriction Order;
- he is not subject to any bankruptcy petition which has been presented against him (or he has not presented his own bankruptcy petition) – unless the petitioning creditor consents to the application;

- a DRO has not been made in relation to the debtor in the period of six years ending with the determination date;
- the total amount of the debtor's debt does not exceed the prescribed amount;
- the debtor's monthly income does not exceed the prescribed amount;
- the total value of the debtor's property does not exceed the prescribed amount;
- the debtor has not entered into a transaction with any person at any under value (Part II of Sched.4ZA);
- the debtor has not given a preference to any person during the period of two years ending with the application date and the determination date (para.10 of Sched.4ZA to the Insolvency Act 1986).

**22.3.6** The Official Receiver cannot make an order unless the debtor has at least one qualifying debt. This means a liquidated sum, which is payable immediately and is unsecured. The debt must also not be one of the excluded debts under the terms of the rules.

## Presumptions

**22.3.7** The Official Receiver is compelled by s.251D to presume that the information provided to him by the approved intermediary is correct. This is the case unless it is obvious there are deficiencies in the application or the information provided.

## Effect on other debt management arrangements

**22.3.8** Where a DRO is made then it has the effect of terminating all other debt management arrangements (including Administration Orders, Enforcement Restriction Orders and debt repayment plans arranged in accordance with a debt management scheme) (s.251F).

## Moratorium

**22.3.9** When the DRO is made then moratorium takes effect.

**22.3.10** The moratorium only affects creditors in relation to their 'specified qualifying debts'. Therefore it does not affect the right of a secured creditor in relation to the enforcement of security (s.251G(5)).

**22.3.11** Whilst the moratorium is in place a creditor:

- cannot have any remedy in respect of the debt (s.251G(2)(A)); and
- may not:
  - commence a creditor's petition in respect of the debt; or
  - otherwise commence any action or other legal proceedings against the debtor for the debt.

**22.3.12**    Action can be taken with permission of the court. The court has the discretion to impose terms. If there is a pending bankruptcy petition (which commenced prior to the DRO) then this is not automatically caught by the moratorium; however, the courts may stay the proceedings (on terms) or allow them to continue.

**22.3.13**    The moratorium lasts for a period of one year (unless varied or extended under the terms of Part 7A of the Insolvency Act 1986).

**22.3.14**    The power for the Official Receiver to extend the moratorium period is limited by any evidence 'which materialises of the debtor's misconduct. The Official Receiver may carry out an investigation which results in a decision . . .' to revoke the order (for investigations see **22.3.20**). In any event, the moratorium period cannot be extended beyond the end of three months after the initial period of one year has expired.

## Discharge

**22.3.15**    At the end of the moratorium period, the debtor is discharged from all the qualifying debts specified in the order (including all interest, penalties and other sums which may have become payable in relation to those debts (s.251I)).

## When does discharge not take place?

**22.3.16**    Under s.251J the debtor has an ongoing obligation to provide assistance to the Official Receiver and provide information as to his affairs. As a consequence of this the Official Receiver can take matters further by considering creditors' objections and investigating the behaviour of the debtor.

**22.3.17**    The Official Receiver may revoke the DRO on the ground that he should not have been satisfied the debts were qualifying debts or that the conditions set out in Sched.4ZA had been met. However, providing the debtor complies with his obligations to provide information then at the end of the moratorium period he is able to walk away from the debt as all the qualifying debts specified in the order will be discharged.

## Remedies of creditors and others

**22.3.18**    Creditors (or the debtor) can make an application to the court on the basis that the Official Receiver is dissatisfied by any act, omission or decision of the Official Receiver (s.251M).

**22.3.19**    The Official Receiver can make an application for directions under s.251M. This is likely to happen if he receives strong representations from creditors.

**22.3.20**    The court has a wide discretion as to allow the Debt Relief Order to continue or to revoke it (s.251(6)).

**22.3.21**   If the Official Receiver is unhappy with the behaviour of the debtor then he can apply to the court for an order that there be a formal inquiry (together with a public examination) of the debtor and his circumstances (s.251M(2)).

**22.3.22**   This is an extensive power. The court can order not just the debtor, but also his spouse (or former spouse or civil partner or former civil partner) to attend court. Also any person appearing to the court to be able to give information or assistance concerning the debtor or his dealings, affairs and property can be summonsed (s.251N).

**22.3.23**   If the debtor or person summonsed does not appear, then a warrant can be issued for their arrest and the seizure of any records or documents in that person's possession (s.251N).

## Offences

**22.3.24**   It is a criminal offence:

- under s.251O, if the debtor makes false representations, omissions, conceals assets or falsifies documents;
- if property is fraudulently disposed of (s.251Q); or
- if after the DRO (during the term of the order) property is obtained on credit and fraudulently disposed of (s.251R).

## Effect of DRO

**22.3.25**   A DRO has the following effects:

- whilst the DRO is in place, the debtor cannot obtain credit (unless he declares his status);
- likewise the debtor is not allowed to engage directly or indirectly in any business activity in any other name other than in which the order was made, without disclosing the DRO.

## Registry of DROs

**22.3.26**   Under s.251W the Secretary of State will maintain a register of:

- Debt Relief Orders;
- Debt Relief Restriction Orders;
- debt relief restrictions and undertakings.

This may be combined with the Register of Judgments, Orders and Fines (see **Chapter 3**).

## Debt relief restrictions and undertakings (Sched.4ZB to the Insolvency Act 1986)

22.3.27   If a debtor's behaviour is sufficiently bad, then the court can impose a Debt Relief Restriction Order. In deciding whether to make an order, the court takes into account the debtor's conduct including:

- failing to keep records during the two year period prior to the application for a DRO;
- failing to produce records on demand to the Official Receiver;
- entering into a transaction at an undervalue in the period beginning two years before the application date;
- giving a preference during the same period;
- making an excessive pension contribution during this period;
- a failure to supply goods or services that were wholly or partly paid for;
- wrongfully trading: trading at a time when the debtor knew or ought to have known that he was unable to pay his debts (before the DRO is made);
- the court also takes into account whether the debtor was an undischarged bankrupt at the time during the period of six years ending the debt of the application for the Debt Relief Order;
- gambling, rash and hazardous speculation;
- failing to account for a loss of property;
- neglect of business affairs which increased the debtor's inability to pay his debts;
- fraud or fraudulent breach of trust;
- failing to co-operate with the Official Receiver.

## Sched.19 (Sched.4ZB to the Insolvency Act 1986)

22.3.28   An application for a Debt Relief Restriction Order can be made at any time:

- during the moratorium period; or
- after the end of that period but only with the permission of the court (Sched.4ZB, para.3).

The effect of the Debt Relief Restriction Order lasts for a minimum period of two years and can last up to 15 years from the date of the order. A provision for an undertaking to be given in lieu of the order is contained at para.7 of Sched.4ZB.

## Effect of the restriction

22.3.29   If a Debt Relief Restriction Order is made (or undertaking given) then a Debt Relief Order cannot be made (para.2 of Sched.4ZA to the Insolvency Act 1986).

## Interim order: under para.5 (Sched.4ZB)

**22.3.30**   If the circumstances justify rapid action the court can make an interim order which has immediate effect and lasts until the determination of the main proceedings for a full restriction. An application for an interim order can be made by the Official Receiver or the Secretary of State on the grounds of public interest. The effect is the same as a full order (i.e. it prevents a DRO being made).

## Debt relief restriction undertakings

**22.3.31**   The debtor is able to propose an undertaking (to the Secretary of State) to avoid the proceedings. This process is comparable to the undertakings which can be given in relation to Bankruptcy Restriction Orders and directors proceedings under the Company Directors Disqualification Act 1986.

**22.3.32**   When deciding whether to accept an undertaking the Secretary of State must have regard to the debtor's behaviour (as set out above).

# 23 DEBT MANAGEMENT SCHEMES

## 23.1 OVERVIEW

**23.1.1**   The final measure for debt management comes in the form of debt management schemes (DMSs). This allows an authorised operator (e.g. this might be Citizens Advice) to operate an approved scheme. The scheme will be open to all debtors (in relation to non-business debts) or certain categories of debtors (as defined by the particular scheme). Each debtor is likely to be subject to a debtor repayment plan and the regulations will specify how DMSs will work.

**23.1.2**   Where a properly constituted DMS has been set up, then this will restrict creditors during the currency of a debtor repayment plan for the currency of a period of protection.

**23.1.3**   The DROs are likely to be registered with the Register of Judgments, Orders and Fines (see **Chapter 3**).

**23.1.4**   It remains to be seen as to the role the schemes will play in the expanded armoury of debt relief measures created by the new Act.

Appendix
# TRIBUNALS, COURTS AND ENFORCEMENT ACT 2007

*Reproduced below are Parts 3–5, ss.139–40, 146–9, Scheds.12–22, Sched.23 Parts 3–5.*

## 2007 CHAPTER 15

## CONTENTS

*\*\*\*\*\**

## CHAPTER 2   ENFORCEMENT RESTRICTION ORDERS

## CHAPTER 3   DEBT RELIEF ORDERS

## CHAPTER 4   DEBT MANAGEMENT SCHEMES

\*\*\*\*\*

# PART 7   MISCELLANEOUS

\*\*\*\*\*

# PART 8   GENERAL

\*\*\*\*\*

\*\*\*\*\*

\*\*\*\*\*

\*\*\*\*\*

# TRIBUNALS, COURTS AND ENFORCEMENT ACT 2007

## 2007 CHAPTER 15

An Act to make provision about tribunals and inquiries; to establish an Administrative Justice and Tribunals Council; to amend the law relating to judicial appointments and appointments to the Law Commission; to amend the law relating to the enforcement of judgments and debts; to make further provision about the management and relief of debt; to make provision protecting cultural objects from seizure or forfeiture in certain circumstances; to amend the law relating to the taking of possession of land affected by compulsory purchase; to alter the powers of the High Court in judicial review applications; and for connected purposes.

[19th July 2007]

Be it enacted by the Queen's most Excellent Majesty, by and with the advice and consent of the Lords Spiritual and Temporal, and Commons, in this present Parliament assembled, and by the authority of the same, as follows: –

\*\*\*\*\*

## PART 3    ENFORCEMENT BY TAKING CONTROL OF GOODS

### CHAPTER 1    PROCEDURE

**62  Enforcement by taking control of goods**

(1)  Schedule 12 applies where an enactment, writ or warrant confers power to use the procedure in that Schedule (taking control of goods and selling them to recover a sum of money).

(2)  The power conferred by a writ or warrant of control to recover a sum of money, and any power conferred by a writ or warrant of possession or delivery to take control of goods and sell them to recover a sum of money, is exercisable only by using that procedure.

(3)  Schedule 13 –

    (a)  amends some powers previously called powers to distrain, so that they become powers to use that procedure;

    (b)  makes other amendments relating to Schedule 12 and to distress or execution.

(4)  The following are renamed –

    (a)  writs of fieri facias, except writs of fieri facias de bonis ecclesiasticis, are renamed writs of control;

    (b)  warrants of execution are renamed warrants of control;

    (c)  warrants of distress, unless the power they confer is exercisable only against specific goods, are renamed warrants of control.

**63  Enforcement agents**

(1)  This section and section 64 apply for the purposes of Schedule 12.

(2)  An individual may act as an enforcement agent only if one of these applies –

    (a)  he acts under a certificate under section 64;

    (b)  he is exempt;

    (c)  he acts in the presence and under the direction of a person to whom paragraph (a) or (b) applies.

(3)  An individual is exempt if he acts in the course of his duty as one of these –

    (a)  a constable;

    (b)  an officer of Revenue and Customs;

    (c)  a person appointed under section 2(1) of the Courts Act 2003 (c. 39) (court officers and staff).

(4)  An individual is exempt if he acts in the course of his duty as an officer of a government department.

(5)  For the purposes of an enforcement power conferred by a warrant, an individual is exempt if in relation to the warrant he is a civilian enforcement officer, as defined in section 125A of the Magistrates' Courts Act 1980 (c. 43).

(6)  A person is guilty of an offence if, knowingly or recklessly, he purports to act as an enforcement agent without being authorised to do so by subsection (2).

(7)  A person guilty of an offence under this section is liable on summary conviction to a fine not exceeding level 5 on the standard scale.

### 64  Certificates to act as an enforcement agent

(1)  A certificate may be issued under this section –

    (a)  by a judge assigned to a county court district;

    (b)  in prescribed circumstances, by a district judge.

(2)  The Lord Chancellor must make regulations about certificates under this section.

(3)  The regulations may in particular include provision –

    (a)  for fees to be charged for applications;

    (b)  for certificates to be issued subject to conditions, including the giving of security;

    (c)  for certificates to be limited to purposes specified by or under the regulations;

    (d)  about complaints against holders of certificates;

    (e)  about suspension and cancellation of certificates;

    (f)  to modify or supplement Schedule 12 for cases where a certificate is suspended or cancelled or expires;

    (g)  requiring courts to make information available relating to certificates.

(4)  A certificate under section 7 of the Law of Distress Amendment Act 1888 (c. 21) which is in force on the coming into force of this section has effect as a certificate under this section, subject to any provision made by regulations.

### 65  Common law rules replaced

(1)  This Chapter replaces the common law rules about the exercise of the powers which under it become powers to use the procedure in Schedule 12.

(2)  The rules replaced include –

    (a)  rules distinguishing between an illegal, an irregular and an excessive exercise of a power;

    (b)  rules that would entitle a person to bring proceedings of a kind for which paragraph 66 of Schedule 12 provides (remedies available to the debtor);

    (c)  rules of replevin;

    (d)  rules about rescuing goods.

### 66  Pre-commencement enforcement not affected

Where –

    (a)  by any provision of this Part a power becomes a power to use the procedure in Schedule 12, and

(b)    before the commencement of that provision, goods have been distrained or executed against, or made subject to a walking possession agreement, under the power,

this Part does not affect the continuing exercise of the power in relation to those goods.

### 67  Transfer of county court enforcement

In section 85(2) of the County Courts Act 1984 (c. 28) (under which writs of control give the district judge, formerly called the registrar, power to execute judgments or orders for payment of money) for 'the registrar shall be' substitute 'any person authorised by or on behalf of the Lord Chancellor is'.

### 68  Magistrates' courts warrants of control

In the Magistrates' Courts Act 1980 (c. 43) after section 125 insert –

#### '125ZA  Warrants of control

(1)    This section applies to a warrant of control issued by a justice of the peace.
(2)    The person to whom it is directed must endorse the warrant as soon as possible after receiving it.
(3)    For the purposes of this section a person endorses a warrant by inserting on the back the date and time when he received it.
(4)    No fee may be charged for endorsing a warrant under this section.'

### 69  County court warrants of control etc.

For section 99 of the County Courts Act 1984 substitute –

#### '99  Endorsement of warrants of control etc.

(1)    This section applies to –
      (a)    a warrant of control issued under section 85(2);
      (b)    a warrant of delivery or of possession, but only if it includes a power to take control of and sell goods to recover a sum of money and only for the purposes of exercising that power.
(2)    The person to whom the warrant is directed must, as soon as possible after receiving it, endorse it by inserting on the back the date and time when he received it.
(3)    No fee may be charged for endorsing a warrant under this section.'

### 70  Power of High Court to stay execution

(1)    If, at any time, the High Court is satisfied that a party to proceedings is unable to pay –
      (a)    a sum recovered against him (by way of satisfaction of the claim or counterclaim in the proceedings or by way of costs or otherwise), or
      (b)    any instalment of such a sum,
      the court may stay the execution of any writ of control issued in the proceedings, for whatever period and on whatever terms it thinks fit.
(2)    The court may act under subsection (1) from time to time until it appears that the cause of the inability to pay has ceased.
(3)    In this section a party to proceedings includes every person, whether or not named as a party, who is served with notice of the proceedings or attends them.

## CHAPTER 2   RENT ARREARS RECOVERY

### *Abolition of common law right*

#### 71  Abolition of common law right

The common law right to distrain for arrears of rent is abolished.

### *Commercial rent arrears recovery*

#### 72  Commercial rent arrears recovery (CRAR)

(1)  A landlord under a lease of commercial premises may use the procedure in Schedule 12 (taking control of goods) to recover from the tenant rent payable under the lease.
(2)  A landlord's power under subsection (1) is referred to as CRAR (commercial rent arrears recovery).

#### 73  Landlord

(1)  In this Chapter 'landlord', in relation to a lease, means the person for the time being entitled to the immediate reversion in the property comprised in the lease.
(2)  That is subject to the following.
(3)  In the case of a tenancy by estoppel, a person is 'entitled to the immediate reversion' if he is entitled to it as between himself and the tenant.
(4)  If there are joint tenants of the immediate reversion, or if a number of persons are entitled to the immediate reversion as between themselves and the tenant –

  (a)  'landlord' means any one of them;
  (b)  CRAR may be exercised to recover rent due to all of them.

(5)  If the immediate reversion is mortgaged, 'landlord' means –

  (a)  the mortgagee, if he has given notice of his intention to take possession or enter into receipt of rents and profits;
  (b)  otherwise, the mortgagor.

(6)  Subsection (5) applies whether the lease is made before or after the mortgage is created, but CRAR is not exercisable by a mortgagee in relation to a lease that does not bind him.
(7)  Where a receiver is appointed by a court in relation to the immediate reversion, CRAR is exercisable by the receiver in the name of the landlord.
(8)  Any authorisation of a person to exercise CRAR on another's behalf must be in writing and must comply with any prescribed requirements.
(9)  This Chapter applies to any other person entitled to exercise CRAR as it applies to a landlord.

#### 74  Lease

(1)  'Lease' means a tenancy in law or in equity, including a tenancy at will, but not including a tenancy at sufferance.
(2)  A lease must be evidenced in writing.
(3)  References to a lease are to a lease as varied from time to time (whether or not the variation is in writing).
(4)  This section applies for the purposes of this Chapter.

#### 75  Commercial premises

(1)  A lease (A) is of commercial premises if none of the demised premises is –

  (a)  let under lease A as a dwelling,
  (b)  let under an inferior lease (B) as a dwelling, or

(c)   occupied as a dwelling.

(2)   The 'demised premises' in this section include anything on them.

(3)   'Let as a dwelling' means let on terms permitting only occupation as a dwelling or other use combined with occupation as a dwelling.

(4)   Premises are not within subsection (1)(b) if letting them as a dwelling is a breach of a lease superior to lease B.

(5)   Premises are not within subsection (1)(c) if occupying them as a dwelling is a breach of lease A or a lease superior to lease A.

(6)   This section applies for the purposes of this Chapter.

## 76   Rent

(1)   'Rent' means the amount payable under a lease (in advance or in arrear) for possession and use of the demised premises, together with –

(a)   any interest payable on that amount under the lease, and

(b)   any value added tax chargeable on that amount or interest.

(2)   'Rent' does not include any sum in respect of rates, council tax, services, repairs, maintenance, insurance or other ancillary matters (whether or not called 'rent' in the lease).

(3)   The amount payable for possession and use of the demised premises, where it is not otherwise identifiable, is to be taken to be so much of the total amount payable under the lease as is reasonably attributable to possession and use.

(4)   Where a rent is payable under or by virtue of Part 2 of the Landlord and Tenant Act 1954 (c. 56), the amount payable under the lease for possession and use of those premises is to be taken to be that rent.

(5)   This section applies for the purposes of this Chapter except sections 71 and 85.

## 77   The rent recoverable

(1)   CRAR is not exercisable except to recover rent that meets each of these conditions –

(a)   it has become due and payable before notice of enforcement is given;

(b)   it is certain, or capable of being calculated with certainty.

(2)   The amount of any rent recoverable by CRAR is reduced by any permitted deduction.

(3)   CRAR is exercisable only if the net unpaid rent is at least the minimum amount immediately before each of these –

(a)   the time when notice of enforcement is given;

(b)   the first time that goods are taken control of after that notice.

(4)   The minimum amount is to be calculated in accordance with regulations.

(5)   The net unpaid rent is the amount of rent that meets the conditions in subsection (1), less –

(a)   any interest or value added tax included in that amount under section 76(1)(a) or (b), and

(b)   any permitted deductions.

(6)   Regulations may provide for subsection (5)(a) not to apply in specified cases.

(7)   Permitted deductions, against any rent, are any deduction, recoupment or set-off that the tenant would be entitled to claim (in law or equity) in an action by the landlord for that rent.

## 78   Intervention of the court

(1)   If notice of enforcement is given in exercise (or purported exercise) of CRAR the court may make either or both of these orders on the application of the tenant –

(a)   an order setting aside the notice;

    (b)   an order that no further step may be taken under CRAR, without further order, in relation to the rent claimed.

(2)   Regulations may make provision about –

    (a)   the further orders that may be made for the purposes of subsection (1)(b);
    (b)   grounds of which the court must be satisfied before making an order or further order.

(3)   In this section 'the court' means the High Court or a county court, as rules of court may provide.

### 79  Use of CRAR after end of lease

(1)   When the lease ends, CRAR ceases to be exercisable, with these exceptions.
(2)   CRAR continues to be exercisable in relation to goods taken control of under it –

    (a)   before the lease ended, or
    (b)   under subsection (3).

(3)   CRAR continues to be exercisable in relation to rent due and payable before the lease ended, if the conditions in subsection (4) are met.
(4)   These are the conditions –

    (a)   the lease did not end by forfeiture;
    (b)   not more than 6 months has passed since the day when it ended;
    (c)   the rent was due from the person who was the tenant at the end of the lease;
    (d)   that person remains in possession of any part of the demised premises;
    (e)   any new lease under which that person remains in possession is a lease of commercial premises;
    (f)   the person who was the landlord at the end of the lease remains entitled to the immediate reversion.

(5)   In deciding whether a person remains in possession under a new lease, section 74(2) (lease to be evidenced in writing) does not apply.
(6)   In the case of a tenancy by estoppel, the person who was the landlord remains 'entitled to the immediate reversion' if the estoppel with regard to the tenancy continues.
(7)   A lease ends when the tenant ceases to be entitled to possession of the demised premises under the lease together with any continuation of it by operation of an enactment or of a rule of law.

### 80  Agricultural holdings

(1)   This section applies to the exercise of CRAR where the premises concerned are an agricultural holding.
(2)   CRAR is not exercisable to recover rent that became due more than a year before notice of enforcement is given.
(3)   For the purposes of subsection (2), deferred rent becomes due at the time to which payment is deferred.
(4)   'Deferred rent' means rent the payment of which has been deferred, according to the ordinary course of dealing between the landlord and the tenant, to the end of a quarter or half-year after it legally became due.
(5)   The permitted deductions under section 77(7) at any time include any compensation due to the tenant in respect of the holding, under the 1986 Act or under custom or agreement, that has been ascertained at that time.
(6)   In this section –

the '1986 Act' means the Agricultural Holdings Act 1986 (c. 5);
'agricultural holding' has the meaning given by section 1 of the 1986 Act.

## Right to rent from sub-tenant

### 81  Right to rent from sub-tenant

(1)  This section applies where CRAR is exercisable by a landlord to recover rent due and payable from a tenant (the immediate tenant).

(2)  The landlord may serve a notice on any sub-tenant.

(3)  The notice must state the amount of rent that the landlord has the right to recover from the immediate tenant by CRAR (the 'notified amount').

(4)  When it takes effect the notice transfers to the landlord the right to recover, receive and give a discharge for any rent payable by the sub-tenant under the sub-lease, until –

  (a)  the notified amount has been paid (by payments under the notice or otherwise), or

  (b)  the notice is replaced or withdrawn.

(5)  A notice under this section takes effect at the end of a period to be determined by regulations.

(6)  Regulations may state –

  (a)  the form of a notice under this section;

  (b)  what it must contain;

  (c)  how it must be served;

  (d)  what must be done to withdraw it.

(7)  In determining for the purposes of this section whether CRAR is exercisable, section 77 applies with these modifications –

  (a)  if notice of enforcement has not been given, references to that notice are to be read as references to the notice under this section;

  (b)  if goods have not been taken control of, section 77(3)(b) does not apply.

(8)  In this section and sections 82 to 84 –

  (a)  'sub-tenant' means a tenant (below the immediate tenant) of any of the premises comprised in the headlease (and 'sub-lease' is to be read accordingly);

  (b)  'headlease' means the lease between the landlord and the immediate tenant.

### 82  Off-setting payments under a notice

(1)  For any amount that a sub-tenant pays under a notice under section 81, he may deduct an equal amount from the rent that would be due to his immediate landlord under the sub-lease.

(2)  If an amount is deducted under subsection (1) or this subsection from rent due to a superior sub-tenant, that sub-tenant may deduct an equal amount from any rent due from him under his sub-lease.

(3)  Subsection (1) applies even if the sub-tenant's payment or part of it is not due under the notice, if it is not due because –

  (a)  the notified amount has already been paid (wholly or partly otherwise than under the notice), or

  (b)  the notice has been replaced by a notice served on another sub-tenant.

(4)  That is subject to the following.

(5)  Subsection (1) does not apply if the landlord withdraws the notice before the payment is made.

(6)  Where the notified amount has already been paid (or will be exceeded by the payment), subsection (1) does not apply (or does not apply to the excess) if the sub-tenant has notice of that when making the payment.

(7)  Subsection (1) does not apply if, before the payment is made, payments under the notice at least equal the notified amount.

(8)  Subsection (1) does not apply to a part of the payment if, with the rest of the payment, payments under the notice at least equal the notified amount.

(9)  Where the notice has been replaced by one served on another sub-tenant, subsection (1) does not apply if the sub-tenant has notice of that when making the payment.

### 83  Withdrawal and replacement of notices

(1)  A notice under section 81 is replaced if the landlord serves another notice on the same sub-tenant for a notified amount covering the same rent or part of that rent.

(2)  A notice under section 81 served on one sub-tenant is also replaced if –

(a)  the landlord serves a notice on another sub-tenant for a notified amount covering the same rent or part of that rent, and

(b)  in relation to any of the premises comprised in the first sub-tenant's sub-lease, the second sub-tenant is an inferior or superior sub-tenant.

(3)  The landlord must withdraw a notice under section 81 if any of these happens –

(a)  the notice is replaced;

(b)  the notified amount is paid, unless it is paid wholly by the sub-tenant.

### 84  Recovery of sums due and overpayments

(1)  For the purposes of the recovery of sums payable by a sub-tenant under a notice under section 81 (including recovery by CRAR), the sub-tenant is to be treated as the immediate tenant of the landlord, and the sums are to be treated as rent accordingly.

(2)  But those sums (as opposed to rent due from the immediate tenant) are not recoverable by notice under section 81 served on an inferior sub-tenant.

(3)  Any payment received by the landlord that the sub-tenant purports to make under a notice under section 81, and that is not due under the notice for any reason, is to be treated as a payment of rent by the immediate tenant, for the purposes of the retention of the payment by the landlord and (if no rent is due) for the purposes of any claim by the immediate tenant to recover the payment.

(4)  But subsection (3) does not affect any claim by the sub-tenant against the immediate tenant.

## Supplementary

### 85  Contracts for similar rights to be void

(1)  A provision of a contract is void to the extent that it would do any of these –

(a)  confer a right to seize or otherwise take control of goods to recover amounts within subsection (2);

(b)  confer a right to sell goods to recover amounts within subsection (2);

(c)  modify the effect of section 72(1), except in accordance with subsection (3).

(2)  The amounts are any amounts payable –

(a)  as rent;

(b)  under a lease (other than as rent);

(c)  under an agreement collateral to a lease;

(d)  under an instrument creating a rentcharge;

(e)  in respect of breach of a covenant or condition in a lease, in an agreement collateral to a lease or in an instrument creating a rentcharge;

(f)  under an indemnity in respect of a payment within paragraphs (a) to (e).

(3)  A provision of a contract is not void under subsection (1)(c) to the extent that it prevents or restricts the exercise of CRAR.

(4)  In this section –

'lease' also includes a licence to occupy land;

'rent' and 'rentcharge' have the meaning given by section 205(1) of the Law of Property Act 1925 (c. 20).

## 86 Amendments

Schedule 14 makes minor and consequential amendments (including repeals of powers to distrain for rentcharges and other amounts within section 85(2)).

## 87 Interpretation of Chapter

In this Chapter –

'landlord' has the meaning given by section 73;
'lease' has the meaning given by section 74 (subject to section 85(4));
'notice of enforcement' means notice under paragraph 7 of Schedule 12;
'rent' (except in sections 71 and 85) has the meaning given by section 76;
'tenant', in relation to a lease, means the tenant for the time being under the lease.

# CHAPTER 3   GENERAL

## 88 Abolition of Crown preference

Crown preference for the purposes of execution against goods is abolished.

## 89 Application to the Crown

(1)  This Part binds the Crown.
(2)  But the procedure in Schedule 12 may not be used –

   (a)  to recover debts due from the Crown,
   (b)  to take control of or sell goods of the Crown (including goods owned by the Crown jointly or in common with another person), or
   (c)  to enter premises occupied by the Crown.

## 90 Regulations

(1)  In this Part –

'prescribed' means prescribed by regulations;
'regulations' means regulations made by the Lord Chancellor.

(2)  The following apply to regulations under this Part.
(3)  Any power to make regulations is exercisable by statutory instrument.
(4)  A statutory instrument containing regulations under paragraph 24(2) or 31(5) of Schedule 12 may not be made unless a draft of the instrument has been laid before, and approved by a resolution of, each House of Parliament.
(5)  In any other case a statutory instrument containing regulations is subject to annulment in pursuance of a resolution of either House of Parliament.
(6)  Regulations may include any of these that the Lord Chancellor considers necessary or expedient –

   (a)  supplementary, incidental or consequential provision;
   (b)  transitory, transitional or saving provision.

(7)  Regulations may make different provision for different cases.

## PART 4   ENFORCEMENT OF JUDGMENTS AND ORDERS

### *Attachment of earnings orders*

#### 91  Attachment of earnings orders: deductions at fixed rates

(1)  Schedule 15 makes amendments to the Attachment of Earnings Act 1971 (c. 32).

(2)  Those amendments are about the basis on which periodical deductions are to be made under an attachment of earnings order.

(3)  In particular, they provide that deductions under certain orders are to be made in accordance with a fixed deductions scheme made by the Lord Chancellor (rather than in accordance with Part I of Schedule 3 to the 1971 Act).

#### 92  Attachment of earnings orders: finding the debtor's current employer

(1)  After section 15 of the Attachment of Earnings Act 1971 insert –

##### '15A Finding the debtor's current employer

(1)  If an attachment of earnings order lapses under section 9(4), the proper authority may request the Commissioners –

   (a)  to disclose whether it appears to the Commissioners that the debtor has a current employer, and

   (b)  if it appears to the Commissioners that the debtor has a current employer, to disclose the name and address of that employer.

(2)  The proper authority may make a request under subsection (1) only for the purpose of enabling the lapsed order to be directed to the debtor's current employer.

(3)  The proper authority may not make a request under subsection (1) unless regulations under section 15B(5) and (8) are in force.

(4)  The proper authority may disclose such information (including information identifying the debtor) as it considers necessary to assist the Commissioners to comply with a request under subsection (1).

(5)  The Commissioners may disclose to the proper authority any information (whether held by the Commissioners or on their behalf) that the Commissioners consider is necessary to comply with a request under subsection (1).

(6)  A disclosure under subsection (4) or (5) is not to be taken to breach any restriction on the disclosure of information (however imposed).

(7)  Nothing in this section is to be taken to prejudice any power to request or disclose information that exists apart from this section.

(8)  The reference in subsection (5) to information held on behalf of the Commissioners includes a reference to any information which –

   (a)  is held by a person who provides services to the Commissioners, and

   (b)  is held by that person in connection with the provision of those services.

##### 15B  Offence of unauthorised use or disclosure

(1)  This section applies if the Commissioners make a disclosure of information ("debtor information") under section 15A(5).

(2)  A person to whom the debtor information is disclosed commits an offence if –

   (a)  he uses or discloses the debtor information, and

   (b)  the use or disclosure is not authorised by subsection (3), (5), (6) or (7).

(3)  The use or disclosure of the debtor information is authorised if it is –

   (a)  for a purpose connected with the enforcement of the lapsed order (including the direction of the order to the debtor's current employer), and

   (b)  with the consent of the Commissioners.

(4)   Consent for the purposes of subsection (3) may be given –

    (a)   in relation to particular use or a particular disclosure, or

    (b)   in relation to use, or a disclosure made, in such circumstances as may be specified or described in the consent.

(5)   The use or disclosure of the debtor information is authorised if it is –

    (a)   in accordance with an enactment or an order of court, or

    (b)   for the purposes of any proceedings before a court,

and it is in accordance with regulations.

(6)   The use or disclosure of the debtor information is authorised if the information has previously been lawfully disclosed to the public.

(7)   The use or disclosure of the debtor information is authorised if it is in accordance with rules of court that comply with regulations under subsection (8).

(8)   Regulations may make provision about the circumstances, if any, in which rules of court may allow any of the following –

    (a)   access to, or the supply of, debtor information;

    (b)   access to, or the supply of copies of, any attachment of earnings order which has been directed to an employer using debtor information.

(9)   It is a defence for a person charged with an offence under subsection (2) to prove that he reasonably believed that the disclosure was lawful.

(10) A person guilty of an offence under subsection (2) is liable –

    (a)   on conviction on indictment, to imprisonment for a term not exceeding two years, to a fine, or to both;

    (b)   on summary conviction, to imprisonment for a term not exceeding twelve months, to a fine not exceeding the statutory maximum, or to both.

## 15C  Regulations

(1)   It is for the Lord Chancellor to make regulations under section 15B.

(2)   But the Lord Chancellor may make regulations under section 15B only with the agreement of the Commissioners.

(3)   Regulations under section 15B are to be made by statutory instrument.

(4)   A statutory instrument containing regulations under section 15B may not be made unless a draft of the instrument has been laid before and approved by a resolution of each House of Parliament.

## 15D  Interpretation

(1)   For the purposes of sections 15A to 15C (and this section) –

    "the Commissioners" means the Commissioners for Her Majesty's Revenue and Customs;

    "information" means information held in any form;

    "the lapsed order" means the attachment of earnings order referred to in section 15A(1);

    "the proper authority" is determined in accordance with subsections (2) to (5).

(2)   If the lapsed order was made by the High Court, the proper authority is the High Court.

(3)   If the lapsed order was made by a county court, the proper authority is a county court.

(4)   If the lapsed order was made by a magistrates' court under this Act, the proper authority is –

    (a)   a magistrates' court, or

    (b)   the designated officer for a magistrates' court.

(5)  If the lapsed order was made by a magistrates' court or a fines officer under Schedule 5 to the Courts Act 2003, the proper authority is –

    (a)  a magistrates' court, or

    (b)  a fines officer.'

(2)  This section applies in relation to any attachment of earnings order, whether made before or after the commencement of this section.

(3)  In relation to an offence committed before the commencement of section 154(1) of the Criminal Justice Act 2003 (c. 44), the reference in section 15B(10)(b) of the Attachment of Earnings Act 1971 (c. 32) to 12 months is to be read as a reference to 6 months.

## Charging orders

### 93  Payment by instalments: making and enforcing charging orders

(1)  Subsections (2), (3) and (4) make amendments to the Charging Orders Act 1979 (c. 53).

(2)  In section 1 (charging orders), after subsection (5) insert –

    '(6)  Subsections (7) and (8) apply where, under a judgment or order of the High Court or a county court, a debtor is required to pay a sum of money by instalments.

    (7)  The fact that there has been no default in payment of the instalments does not prevent a charging order from being made in respect of that sum.

    (8)  But if there has been no default, the court must take that into account when considering the circumstances of the case under subsection (5).'

(3)  In section 3 (provisions supplementing sections 1 and 2), after subsection (4) insert –

    '(4A)  Subsections (4C) to (4E) apply where –

      (a)  a debtor is required to pay a sum of money in instalments under a judgment or order of the High Court or a county court (an "instalments order"), and

      (b)  a charge has been imposed by a charging order in respect of that sum.

    (4B)  In subsections (4C) to (4E) references to the enforcement of a charge are to the making of an order for the enforcement of the charge.

    (4C)  The charge may not be enforced unless there has been default in payment of an instalment under the instalments order.

    (4D)  Rules of court may –

      (a)  provide that, if there has been default in payment of an instalment, the charge may be enforced only in prescribed cases, and

      (b)  limit the amounts for which, and the times at which, the charge may be enforced.

    (4E)  Except so far as otherwise provided by rules of court under subsection (4D) –

      (a)  the charge may be enforced, if there has been default in payment of an instalment, for the whole of the sum of money secured by the charge and the costs then remaining unpaid, or for such part as the court may order, but

      (b)  the charge may not be enforced unless, at the time of enforcement, the whole or part of an instalment which has become due under the instalments order remains unpaid.'

(4)  In section 6(2) (meaning of references to judgment or order of High Court or county court), for 'section 1' substitute 'sections 1 and 3'.
(5)  In section 313(4) of the Insolvency Act 1986 (c. 45) (charge on bankrupt's home: certain provisions of section 3 of Charging Orders Act 1979 to apply), for the words before 'section 3' substitute 'Subsection (1), (2), (4), (5) and (6) of'.
(6)  This section does not apply in a case where a judgment or order of the High Court or a county court under which a debtor is required to pay a sum of money by instalments was made, or applied for, before the coming into force of this section.

## 94  Charging orders: power to set financial thresholds

In the Charging Orders Act 1979 (c. 53), after section 3 there is inserted –

### '3A Power to set financial thresholds

(1)  The Lord Chancellor may by regulations provide that a charge may not be imposed by a charging order for securing the payment of money of an amount below that determined in accordance with the regulations.
(2)  The Lord Chancellor may by regulations provide that a charge imposed by a charging order may not be enforced by way of order for sale to recover money of an amount below that determined in accordance with the regulations.
(3)  Regulations under this section may –

(a)  make different provision for different cases;
(b)  include such transitional provision as the Lord Chancellor thinks fit.

(4)  The power to make regulations under this section is exercisable by statutory instrument.
(5)  The Lord Chancellor may not make the first regulations under subsection (1) or (2) unless (in each case) a draft of the statutory instrument containing the regulations has been laid before, and approved by a resolution of, each House of Parliament.
(6)  A statutory instrument containing any subsequent regulations under those subsections is subject to annulment in pursuance of a resolution of either House of Parliament.'

## Information requests and orders

### 95  Application for information about action to recover judgment debt

(1)  A person who is the creditor in relation to a judgment debt may apply to the High Court or a county court for information about what kind of action it would be appropriate to take in court to recover that particular debt.
(2)  An application under subsection (1) must comply with any provision made in regulations about the making of such applications.

### 96  Action by the court

(1)  This section applies if the creditor in relation to a judgment debt makes an application for information under section 95.
(2)  The relevant court may make one or more of the following in relation to the debtor –

(a)  a departmental information request;
(b)  an information order.

(3)  The relevant court may exercise its powers under subsection (2) only if it is satisfied that to do so will help it to deal with the creditor's application.
(4)  Before exercising its powers under subsection (2), the relevant court must give notice to the debtor that the court intends to make a request or order.

(5) The relevant court may not make a departmental information request to the Commissioners unless regulations are in force that have been made under section 102(4) and (7) and relate to the use or disclosure of debtor information disclosed by the Commissioners.

(6) The relevant court may disclose such information (including information identifying the debtor) as it considers necessary to assist the recipient of a request or order to comply with the request or order.

(7) A disclosure under subsection (6) is not to be taken to breach any restriction on the disclosure of information (however imposed).

(8) Nothing in this section is to be taken to prejudice any power that exists apart from this section to request or order the disclosure of information.

### 97   Departmental information requests

(1) A departmental information request is a request for the disclosure of information held by, or on behalf of, a government department.

(2) The request is to be made to the Minister of the Crown, or other person, who is in charge of the department.

(3) In the case of a request made to the designated Secretary of State, the disclosure of some or all of the following information may be requested –

  (a) the full name of the debtor;
  (b) the address of the debtor;
  (c) the date of birth of the debtor;
  (d) the national insurance number of the debtor;
  (e) prescribed information.

(4) In the case of a request made to the Commissioners, the disclosure of some or all of the following information may be requested –

  (a) whether or not the debtor is employed;
  (b) the name and address of the employer (if the debtor is employed);
  (c) the national insurance number of the debtor;
  (d) prescribed information.

(5) In the case of any other request, the disclosure of prescribed information may be requested.

(6) In this section –

  'designated Secretary of State' means the Secretary of State designated for the purpose of this section by regulations;
  'government department' does not include the following –

  (a) any part of the Scottish Administration;
  (b) a Northern Ireland department;
  (c) the Welsh Assembly Government or any member of staff appointed under section 52 of the Government of Wales Act 2006 (c. 32);

  'prescribed information', in relation to a departmental information request, means information that falls within the category or categories of information (if any) prescribed by regulations in relation to the department to which the request relates.

### 98   Information orders

(1) An information order is an order of the relevant court which –

  (a) specifies a prescribed person ('the information discloser'),
  (b) specifies prescribed information relating to the debtor ('the required information'), and
  (c) orders the information discloser to disclose the required information to the relevant court.

(2) In subsection (1) 'prescribed' means prescribed in regulations.

(3) Regulations under this section may be made by reference to –

    (a) particular persons or particular descriptions of person (or both);

    (b) particular information or particular descriptions of information (or both).

(4) Regulations may, in particular, be made under this section so as to ensure that –

    (a) an information order made against a particular person, or a person of a particular description, may order that person to disclose only particular information, or information of a particular description;

    (b) an information order that orders the disclosure of particular information, or information of a particular description, may only be made against a particular person, or a person of a particular description.

(5) Regulations under this section must not make provision that would allow the relevant court to order –

    (a) the disclosure of information by the debtor, or

    (b) the disclosure of information held by, or on behalf of, a government department.

## 99 Responding to a departmental information request

(1) This section applies if the relevant court makes a departmental information request.

(2) The recipient of the request may disclose to the relevant court any information (whether held by the department or on its behalf) that the recipient considers is necessary to comply with the request.

(3) A disclosure under subsection (2) is not to be taken to breach any restriction on the disclosure of information (however imposed).

(4) Nothing in this section is to be taken to prejudice any power that exists apart from this section to disclose information.

## 100 Information order: required information not held etc.

(1) An information discloser is not to be regarded as having breached an information order because of a failure to disclose some or all of the required information, if that failure is for one of the permitted reasons.

(2) These are the permitted reasons –

    (a) the information provider does not hold the information;

    (b) the information provider is unable to ascertain whether the information is held, because of the way in which the information order identifies the debtor;

    (c) the disclosure of the information would involve the information discloser in unreasonable effort or expense.

(3) It is to be presumed that a failure to disclose required information is for a permitted reason if –

    (a) the information discloser gives the relevant court a certificate that complies with subsection (4), and

    (b) there is no evidence that the failure is not for a permitted reason.

(4) The certificate must state –

    (a) which of the required information is not being disclosed;

    (b) what the permitted reason is, or permitted reasons are, for the failure to disclose that information.

(5) Any reference in this section to the information discloser holding, or not holding, information includes a reference to the information being held, or not being held, on the information discloser's behalf.

**101  Using the information about the debtor**

(1)  This section applies if –

    (a)  the creditor in relation to a judgment debt makes an application for information under section 95, and

    (b)  information ('debtor information') is disclosed to the relevant court in compliance with a request or order made under section 96.

(2)  The relevant court may use the debtor information for the purpose of making another request or order under section 96 in relation to the debtor.

(3)  The relevant court may use the debtor information for the purpose of providing the creditor with information about what kind of action (if any) it would be appropriate to take in court (whether the relevant court or another court) to recover the judgment debt.

(4)  If the creditor takes any action in the relevant court to recover the judgment debt, the relevant court may use the debtor information in carrying out functions in relation to that action.

(5)  If the creditor takes any action in another court to recover the judgment debt –

    (a)  the relevant court may disclose the debtor information to the other court, and

    (b)  the other court may use that information in carrying out functions in relation to that action.

(6)  Debtor information may be used or disclosed under any of subsections (3) to (5) only if –

    (a)  regulations about such use or disclosure of information are in force, and

    (b)  the use or disclosure complies with those regulations.

(7)  In addition, if the debtor information was disclosed by the Commissioners, the information may be used or disclosed under any of subsections (3) to (5) only with the consent of the Commissioners.

(8)  Consent for the purposes of subsection (7) may be given –

    (a)  in relation to particular use or a particular disclosure, or

    (b)  in relation to use, or a disclosure made, in such circumstances as may be specified or described in the consent.

(9)  The use or disclosure of information in accordance with this section is not to be taken to breach any restriction on the use or disclosure of information (however imposed).

(10) Nothing in this section is to be taken to prejudice any power that exists apart from this section to use or disclose information.

**102  Offence of unauthorised use or disclosure**

(1)  This section applies if –

    (a)  an application is made under section 95 in relation to recovery of a judgment debt ('the relevant judgment debt'),

    (b)  a departmental information request or an information order is made in consequence of that application, and

    (c)  information ('debtor information') is disclosed in accordance with the request or order.

(2)  A person to whom the debtor information is disclosed commits an offence if he –

    (a)  uses or discloses the debtor information, and

    (b)  the use or disclosure is not authorised by any of subsections (3) to (6).

(3)  The use or disclosure of the debtor information is authorised if it is in accordance with section 101.

(4)  The use or disclosure of the debtor information is authorised if it is –

    (a)  in accordance with an enactment or order of court, or

(b)  for the purposes of any proceedings before a court,

and it is in accordance with regulations.

(5)  The use or disclosure of the debtor information is authorised if the information has previously been lawfully disclosed to the public.

(6)  The use or disclosure of the debtor information is authorised if it is in accordance with rules of court that comply with regulations under subsection (7).

(7)  Regulations may make provision about the circumstances, if any, in which rules of court may allow access to, or the supply of, information disclosed in accordance with a department information request or an information order.

(8)  It is a defence for a person charged with an offence under subsection (2) to prove that he reasonably believed that the use or disclosure was lawful.

(9)  A person guilty of an offence under subsection (2) is liable –

(a)  on conviction on indictment, to imprisonment for a term not exceeding two years, to a fine or to both;

(b)  on summary conviction, to imprisonment for a term not exceeding twelve months, to a fine not exceeding the statutory maximum, or to both.

## 103  Regulations

(1)  It is for the Lord Chancellor to make information regulations.

(2)  But the Lord Chancellor may make the following regulations only with the agreement of the Commissioners –

(a)  regulations under section 97(4)(d);

(b)  regulations under section 102(4) or (7) so far as the regulations relate to the use or disclosure of debtor information disclosed by the Commissioners.

(3)  Information regulations are to be made by statutory instrument.

(4)  A statutory instrument containing information regulations may not be made unless a draft of the instrument has been laid before and approved by a resolution of each House of Parliament.

(5)  But subsection (4) does not apply in the case of a statutory instrument that contains only –

(a)  regulations under section 95, or

(b)  regulations under section 97 which designate a Secretary of State for the purpose of that section.

(6)  In such a case, the statutory instrument is subject to annulment in pursuance of a resolution of either House of Parliament.

(7)  In this section 'information regulations' means regulations under any of sections 95 to 102.

## 104  Interpretation

(1)  This section applies for the purposes of sections 95 to 103.

(2)  In those provisions –

'Commissioners' means the Commissioners for Her Majesty's Revenue and Customs;

'creditor', in relation to a judgment debt, means –

(a)  the person to whom the debt is payable (whether directly or through an officer of any court or another person);

(b)  where the debt is payable under an administration order (within the meaning of Part 6 of the County Courts Act 1984 (c. 28)), any one of the creditors scheduled to the order;

'debtor', in relation to a judgment debt, means the person by whom the debt is payable;

'departmental information request' has the meaning given by section 97;

'information' means information held in any form;

'information discloser', in relation to an information order, has the meaning given by section 98(1)(a);

'information order' has the meaning given by section 98;

'judgment debt' means either of the following –

    (a)  a sum which is payable under a judgment or order enforceable by the High Court or a county court;

    (b)  a sum which, by virtue of an enactment, is recoverable as if it were payable under a judgment or order of the High Court or of a county court (including a sum which is so recoverable because a court so orders);

'required information', in relation to an information order, has the meaning given by section 98(1)(b);

'relevant court', in relation to an application under section 95, means the court to which the application is made.

(3)  Any reference to information held on behalf of a government department, or on behalf of an information discloser, includes a reference to any information which –

    (a)  is held by a person who provides services to the department or to the information discloser, and

    (b)  is held by that person in connection with the provision of those services.

### 105   Application and transitional provision

(1)  Sections 95 to 104 apply in relation to any judgment debt, whether it became payable, or recoverable, before or after the commencement of those sections.

(2)  In relation to an offence committed before the commencement of section 154(1) of the Criminal Justice Act 2003 (c. 44), the reference in section 102(9)(b) to 12 months is to be read as a reference to 6 months.

## PART 5   DEBT MANAGEMENT AND RELIEF

## CHAPTER 1   ADMINISTRATION ORDERS

### 106   Administration orders

(1)  For Part 6 of the County Courts Act 1984 (c. 28) (administration orders) substitute –

#### 'PART 6   ADMINISTRATION ORDERS

*Administration orders*

#### 112A   Administration orders

An administration order is an order –

    (a)  to which certain debts are scheduled in accordance with section 112C, 112D or 112Y(3) or (4),

    (b)  which imposes the requirement specified in section 112E on the debtor, and

    (c)  which imposes the requirements specified in sections 112F to 112I on certain creditors.

#### 112B   Power to make order

(1)  A county court may make an administration order if the conditions in subsections (2) to (7) are met.

(2)  The order must be made in respect of an individual who is a debtor under two or more qualifying debts.

(3)  That individual ("the debtor") must not be a debtor under any business debts.

(4)  The debtor must not be excluded under any of the following –

    (a)   the AO exclusion;

    (b)   the voluntary arrangement exclusion;

    (c)   the bankruptcy exclusion.

(5)  The debtor must be unable to pay one or more of his qualifying debts.

(6)  The total amount of the debtor's qualifying debts must be less than, or the same as, the prescribed maximum.

(7)  The debtor's surplus income must be more than the prescribed minimum.

(8)  Before making an administration order, the county court must have regard to any representations made –

    (a)   by any person about why the order should not be made, or

    (b)   by a creditor under a debt about why the debt should not be taken into account in calculating the total amount of the debtor's qualifying debts.

*Scheduling debts*

### 112C  Scheduling declared debts

(1)  This section applies to a qualifying debt ("the declared debt") if –

    (a)   an administration order is made, and

    (b)   when the order is made, the debt is taken into account in calculating the total amount of the debtor's qualifying debts for the purposes of section 112B(6).

(2)  If the declared debt is already due at the time the administration order is made, the proper county court must schedule the debt to the order when the order is made.

(3)  If the declared debt becomes due after the administration order is made, the proper county court must schedule the debt to the order if the debtor, or the creditor under the debt, applies to the court for the debt to be scheduled.

(4)  This section is subject to section 112AG(5).

### 112D  Scheduling new debts

(1)  This section applies to a qualifying debt ("the new debt") if the debt –

    (a)   arises after an administration order is made, and

    (b)   becomes due during the currency of the order.

(2)  The proper county court may schedule the new debt to the administration order if these conditions are met –

    (a)   the debtor, or the creditor under the new debt, applies to the court for the debt to be scheduled;

    (b)   the total amount of the debtor's qualifying debts (including the new debt) is less than, or the same as, the prescribed maximum.

*Requirements imposed by order*

### 112E  Repayment requirement

(1)  An administration order must, during the currency of the order, impose a repayment requirement on the debtor.

(2)  A repayment requirement is a requirement for the debtor to repay the scheduled debts.

(3)  The repayment requirement may provide for the debtor to repay a particular scheduled debt in full or to some other extent.

(4)  The repayment requirement may provide for the debtor to repay different scheduled debts to different extents.

(5)  In the case of a new debt scheduled to the order in accordance with section 112D, the repayment requirement may provide that no due repayment in respect of the new debt is to be made until the debtor has made all due repayments in respect of declared debts.

(6)  The repayment requirement must provide that the due repayments are to be made by instalments.

(7)  It is for the proper county court to decide when the instalments are to be made.

(8)  But the proper county court is to determine the amount of the instalments in accordance with repayment regulations.

(9)  Repayment regulations are regulations which make provision for instalments to be determined by reference to the debtor's surplus income.

(10) The repayment requirement may provide that the due repayments are to be made by other means (including by one or more lump sums) in addition to the instalments required in accordance with subsection (6).

(11) The repayment requirement may include provision in addition to any that is required or permitted by this section.

(12) In this section –

"declared debt" has the same meaning as in section 112C (and for this purpose it does not matter whether a declared debt is scheduled to the administration order when it is made, or afterwards);

"due repayments" means repayments which the repayment requirement requires the debtor to make;

"new debt" has the same meaning as in section 112D.

### 112F  Presentation of bankruptcy petition

(1)  An administration order must, during the currency of the order, impose the following requirement.

(2)  The requirement is that no qualifying creditor of the debtor is to present a bankruptcy petition against the debtor in respect of a qualifying debt, unless the creditor has the permission of the proper county court.

(3)  The proper county court may give permission for the purposes of subsection (2) subject to such conditions as it thinks fit.

### 112G  Remedies other than bankruptcy

(1)  An administration order must, during the currency of the order, impose the following requirement.

(2)  The requirement is that no qualifying creditor of the debtor is to pursue any remedy for the recovery of a qualifying debt unless –

(a)  regulations under subsection (3) provide otherwise, or

(b)  the creditor has the permission of the proper county court.

(3)  Regulations may specify classes of debt which are exempted (or exempted for specified purposes) from the restriction imposed by subsection (2).

(4)  The proper county court may give permission for the purposes of subsection (2)(b) subject to such conditions as it thinks fit.

(5)  This section does not have any effect in relation to bankruptcy proceedings.

### 112H  Charging of interest etc

(1)  An administration order must, during the currency of the order, impose the following requirement.

(2)  The requirement is that no creditor under a scheduled debt is to charge any sum by way of interest, fee or other charge in respect of that debt.

**112I  Stopping supplies of gas or electricity**

(1)  An administration order must, during the currency of the order, impose the requirement in subsection (3).

(2)  In relation to that requirement, a domestic utility creditor is any person who –

(a)  provides the debtor with a supply of mains gas or mains electricity for the debtor's own domestic purposes, and

(b)  is a creditor under a qualifying debt that relates to the provision of that supply.

(3)  The requirement is that no domestic utility creditor is to stop the supply of gas or electricity, or the supply of any associated services, except in the cases in subsections (4) to (6).

(4)  The first case is where the reason for stopping a supply relates to the non-payment by the debtor of charges incurred in connection with that supply after the making of the administration order.

(5)  The second case is where the reason for stopping a supply is unconnected with the non-payment by the debtor of any charges incurred in connection with –

(a)  that supply, or

(b)  any other supply of mains gas or mains electricity, or of associated services, that is provided by the domestic utility creditor.

(6)  The third case is where the proper county court gives permission to stop a supply.

(7)  The proper county court may give permission for the purposes of subsection (6) subject to such conditions as it thinks fit.

(8)  A supply of mains gas is a supply of the kind mentioned in section 5(1)(b) of the Gas Act 1986.

(9)  A supply of mains electricity is a supply of the kind mentioned in section 4(1)(c) of the Electricity Act 1989.

*Making an order*

**112J  Application for an order**

(1)  A county court may make an administration order only on the application of the debtor.

(2)  The debtor may make an application for an administration order whether or not a judgment has been obtained against him in respect of any of his debts.

**112K  Duration**

(1)  A county court may, at the time it makes an administration order, specify a day on which the order will cease to have effect.

(2)  The court may not specify a day which falls after the last day of the maximum permitted period.

(3)  If the court specifies a day under this section, the order ceases to have effect on that day.

(4)  If the court does not specify a day under this section, the order ceases to have effect at the end of the maximum permitted period.

(5)  The maximum permitted period is the period of five years beginning with the day on which the order is made.

(6)  This section is subject to –

(a)  section 112S (variation of duration);

(b)  section 112W (effect of revocation).

(7)   This section is also subject to the following (effect of enforcement restriction order or debt relief order on administration order) –

    (a)   section 117I of this Act;
    (b)   section 251F of the Insolvency Act 1986.

*Effects of order*

**112L  Effect on other debt management arrangements**

(1)   This section applies if –

    (a)   an administration order is made, and
    (b)   immediately before the order is made, other debt management arrangements are in force in respect of the debtor.

(2)   The other debt management arrangements cease to be in force when the administration order is made.

(3)   If the proper county court is aware of the other debt management arrangements, the court must give the relevant authority notice that the order has been made.

(4)   In a case where the proper county court is aware of other debt management arrangements at the time it makes the order, it must give the notice as soon as practicable after making the order.

(5)   In a case where the proper county court becomes aware of those arrangements after it makes the order, it must give the notice as soon as practicable after becoming aware of them.

(6)   "Other debt management arrangements" means any of the following –

    (a)   an enforcement restriction order under Part 6A of this Act;
    (b)   a debt relief order under Part 7A of the Insolvency Act 1986;
    (c)   a debt repayment plan arranged in accordance with a debt management scheme that is approved under Chapter 4 of Part 5 of the Tribunals, Courts and Enforcement Act 2007.

(7)   "The relevant authority" means –

    (a)   in relation to an enforcement restriction order: the proper county court (within the meaning of Part 6A);
    (b)   in relation to a debt relief order: the official receiver;
    (c)   in relation to a debt repayment plan: the operator of the debt management scheme in accordance with which the plan is arranged.

(8)   For the purposes of this section a debt relief order is "in force" if the moratorium applicable to the order under section 251H of the Insolvency Act 1986 has not yet ended.

**112M  Duty to provide information**

(1)   This section applies if, and for as long as, an administration order has effect in respect of a debtor.

(2)   The debtor must, at the prescribed times, provide the proper county court with particulars of his –

    (a)   earnings,
    (b)   income,
    (c)   assets, and
    (d)   outgoings.

(3)   The debtor must provide particulars of those matters –

    (a)   as the matters are at the time the particulars are provided, and
    (b)   as the debtor expects the matters to be at such times in the future as are prescribed.

(4) If the debtor intends to dispose of any of his property he must, within the pre-scribed period, provide the proper county court with particulars of the following matters –

    (a)   the property he intends to dispose of;
    (b)   the consideration (if any) he expects will be given for the disposal;
    (c)   such other matters as may be prescribed;
    (d)   such other matters as the court may specify.

(5) But subsection (4) does not apply if the disposal is of –

    (a)   goods that are exempt goods for the purposes of Schedule 12 to the Tribunals, Courts and Enforcement Act 2007,
    (b)   goods that are protected under any other enactment from being taken control of under that Schedule, or
    (c)   prescribed property.

(6) The duty under subsection (4) to provide the proper county court with particulars of a proposed disposal of property applies whether the debtor is the sole owner, or one of several owners, of the property.

(7) In any provision of this section "prescribed" means prescribed in regulations for the purposes of that provision.

### 112N  Offence if information not provided

(1) A person commits an offence if he fails to comply with –

    (a)   section 112M(2) and (3), or
    (b)   section 112M(4).

(2) A person who commits an offence under subsection (1) may be ordered by a judge of the proper county court to pay a fine of not more than £250 or to be imprisoned for not more than 14 days.

(3) Where under subsection (2) a person is ordered to be imprisoned by a judge of the proper county court, the judge may at any time –

    (a)   revoke the order, and
    (b)   if the person is already in custody, order his discharge.

(4) Section 129 of this Act (enforcement of fines) applies to payment of a fine imposed under subsection (2).

(5) For the purposes of section 13 of the Administration of Justice Act 1960 (appeal in cases of contempt of court), subsection (2) is to be treated as an enactment enabling a county court to deal with an offence under subsection (1) as if it were a contempt of court.

(6) A district judge or deputy district judge shall have the same powers under this section as a judge of a county court.

### 112O  Existing county court proceedings to be stayed

(1) This section applies if these conditions are met –

    (a)   an administration order is made;
    (b)   proceedings in a county court (other than bankruptcy proceedings) are pending against the debtor in respect of a qualifying debt;
    (c)   by virtue of a requirement included in the order by virtue of section 112G, the creditor under the qualifying debt is not entitled to continue the proceedings in respect of the debt;
    (d)   the county court receives notice of the administration order.

(2) The county court must stay the proceedings.

(3) The court may allow costs already incurred by the creditor.

(4) If the court allows such costs, it may on application or of its motion add them –

    (a)    to the debt, or

    (b)    if the debt is a scheduled debt, to the amount scheduled to the order in respect of the debt.

(5) But the court may not add the costs under subsection (4)(b) if the court is under a duty under section 112U(6)(b) to revoke the order because the total amount of the debtor's qualifying debts (including the costs) is more than the prescribed maximum.

### 112P   Appropriation of money paid

(1) Money paid into court under an administration order is to be appropriated –

    (a)    first in satisfaction of any relevant court fees, and

    (b)    then in liquidation of debts.

(2) Relevant court fees are any fees under an order made under section 92 of the Courts Act 2003 which are payable by the debtor in respect of the administration order.

### 112Q   Discharge from debts

(1) If the debtor repays a scheduled debt to the extent provided for by the administration order, the proper county court must –

    (a)    order that the debtor is discharged from the debt, and

    (b)    de-schedule the debt.

(2) If the debtor repays all of the scheduled debts to the extent provided for by the administration order, the proper county court must revoke the order.

(3) Subsections (1) and (2) apply to all scheduled debts, including any which, under the administration order, are to be repaid other than to their full extent.

*Variation*

### 112R   Variation

(1) The proper county court may vary an administration order.

(2) The power under this section is exercisable –

    (a)    on the application of the debtor;

    (b)    on the application of a qualifying creditor;

    (c)    of the court's own motion.

### 112S   Variation of duration

(1) The power under section 112R includes power to vary an administration order so as to specify a day, or (if a day has already been specified under section 112K or this subsection) a different day, on which the order will cease to have effect.

(2) But the new termination day must fall on or before the last day of the maximum permitted period.

(3) If the proper county court varies an administration under subsection (1), the order ceases to have effect on the new termination day.

(4) In this section –

    (a)    "new termination day" means the day on which the order will cease to have effect in accordance with the variation under subsection (1);

    (b)    "maximum permitted period" means the period of five years beginning with the day on which the order was originally made.

(5) This section is subject to section 112W (effect of revocation).

## 112T  De-scheduling debts

(1)  The power under section 112R includes power to vary an administration order by de-scheduling a debt.

(2)  But the debt may be de-scheduled only if it appears to the proper county court that it is just and equitable to do so.

*Revocation*

## 112U  Duty to revoke order

(1)  The proper county court must revoke an administration order in either of these cases –

   (a)  where it becomes apparent that, at the time the order was made, the condition in subsection 112B(2) was not met (debtor in fact did not have two or more qualifying debts);

   (b)  where the debtor is no longer a debtor under any qualifying debts.

(2)  The proper county court must revoke an administration order in either of these cases –

   (a)  where it becomes apparent that, at the time the order was made, the condition in subsection 112B(3) was not met (debtor in fact had business debt), and he is still a debtor under the business debt, or any of the business debts, in question;

   (b)  where the debtor subsequently becomes a debtor under a business debt, and he is still a debtor under that debt.

(3)  The proper county court must revoke an administration order where it becomes apparent that, at the time the order was made, the condition in section 112B(4) was not met (debtor in fact excluded under AO, voluntary arrangement or bankruptcy exclusion).

(4)  The proper county court must revoke an administration order where, after the order is made –

   (a)  the debtor becomes excluded under the voluntary arrangement exclusion, or

   (b)  a bankruptcy order is made against the debtor, and is still in force.

(5)  The proper county court must revoke an administration order in either of these cases –

   (a)  where it becomes apparent that, at the time the order was made, the condition in section 112B(5) was not met (debtor in fact able to pay qualifying debts);

   (b)  where the debtor is now able to pay all of his qualifying debts.

(6)  The proper county court must revoke an administration order in either of these cases –

   (a)  where it becomes apparent that, at the time the order was made, the condition in section 112B(6) was not met (debtor's qualifying debts in fact more than prescribed maximum);

   (b)  where the total amount of the debtor's qualifying debts is now more than the prescribed maximum.

(7)  The proper county court must revoke an administration order in either of these cases –

   (a)  where it becomes apparent that, at the time the order was made, the condition in section 112B(7) was not met (debtor's surplus income in fact less than, or the same as, the prescribed minimum);

   (b)  where the debtor's surplus income is now less than, or the same as, the prescribed minimum.

### 112V  Power to revoke order

(1) The proper county court may revoke an administration order in any case where there is no duty under this Part to revoke it.

(2) The power of revocation under this section may, in particular, be exercised in any of the following cases –

   (a) where the debtor has failed to make two payments (whether consecutive or not) required by the order;

   (b) where the debtor has failed to provide the proper county court with the particulars required by –

      (i) section 112M(2) and (3), or

      (ii) section 112M(4).

(3) The power of revocation under this section is exercisable –

   (a) on the application of the debtor;

   (b) on the application of a qualifying creditor;

   (c) of the court's own motion.

### 112W  Effect of revocation

(1) This section applies if, under any duty or power in this Part, the proper county court revokes an administration order.

(2) The order ceases to have effect in accordance with the terms of the revocation.

*Notification of certain events*

### 112X  Notice when order made, varied, revoked etc

(1) If a notifiable event occurs in relation to an administration order, the proper county court must send notice of the event to the creditor under every scheduled debt.

(2) There is a notifiable event in any of the following cases –

   (a) when the administration order is made;

   (b) when a debt is scheduled to the administration order at any time after the making of the order;

   (c) when the administration order is varied;

   (d) when the administration order is revoked;

   (e) when the proper county court is given notice under any of the provisions listed in section 112K(7) (effect of enforcement restriction order or debt relief order on administration order).

*Total amount of qualifying debts not properly calculated*

### 112Y  Failure to take account of all qualifying debts

(1) This section applies if –

   (a) an administration order has been made, but

   (b) it becomes apparent that the total amount of the debtor's qualifying debts was not properly calculated for the purposes of section 112B(6), because of an undeclared debt.

(2) A debt is undeclared if it ought to have been, but was not, taken into account in the calculation for the purposes of section 112B(6).

(3) If these conditions are met –

   (a) the undeclared debt is due (whether it became due before or after the making of the order);

   (b) the total debt is less than, or the same as, the prescribed maximum;

the proper county court must schedule the undeclared debt to the order.

(4) If these conditions are met –

(a)   the undeclared debt is not due;

(b)   the total debt is less than, or the same as, the prescribed maximum;

the proper county court must schedule the undeclared debt to the order when the debt becomes due.

(5) If the total debt is more than the prescribed maximum, the proper county court must revoke the administration order (whether or not the undeclared debt is due).

(6) In this section "total debt" means the total amount of the debtor's qualifying debts (including the undeclared debt).

(7) Subsections (3) and (4) are subject to section 112AG(5).

*Interpretation*

### 112Z  Introduction

Sections 112AA to 112AH apply for the purposes of this Part.

### 112AA  Main definitions

(1) In this Part –

"administration order" has the meaning given by section 112A;

"debtor" has the meaning given by section 112B;

"prescribed maximum" means the amount prescribed in regulations for the purposes of section 112B(6);

"prescribed minimum" means the amount prescribed in regulations for the purposes of section 112B(7);

"qualifying creditor" means a creditor under a qualifying debt.

(2) References to the currency of an administration order are references to the period which –

(a)   begins when the order first has effect, and

(b)   ends when the order ceases to have effect.

(3) In relation to an administration order, references to the proper county court are references to the county court that made the order.

(4) But that is subject to rules of court as to the venue for, and transfer of, proceedings in county courts.

### 112AB  Expressions relating to debts

(1) All debts are qualifying debts, except for the following –

(a)   any debt secured against an asset;

(b)   any debt of a description specified in regulations.

(2) A business debt is any debt (whether or not a qualifying debt) which is incurred by a person in the course of a business.

(3) Only debts that have already arisen are included in references to debts; and accordingly such references do not include any debt that will arise only on the happening of some future contingency.

### 112AC  Inability to pay debts

(1) In a case where an individual is the debtor under a debt that is repayable by a single payment, the debtor is to be regarded as unable to pay the debt only if –

(a)   the debt has become due,

(b)   the debtor has failed to make the single payment, and

(c)   the debtor is unable to make that payment.

(2) In a case where an individual is the debtor under a debt that is repayable by a number of payments, the debtor is to be regarded as unable to pay the debt only if –

    (a) the debt has become due,

    (b) the debtor has failed to make one or more of the payments, and

    (c) the debtor is unable to make all of the missed payments.

**112AD  Calculating the debtor's qualifying debts**

(1) The total amount of a debtor's qualifying debts is to be calculated in accordance with subsections (2) and (3).

(2) All of the debtor's qualifying debts which have arisen before the calculation must be taken into account (whether or not the debts are already due at the time of the calculation).

(3) Regulations must make further provision about how the total amount of a debtor's qualifying debts is to be calculated.

(4) Regulations may make provision about how the amount of any particular qualifying debt is to be calculated.

(5) That includes the calculation of the amount of a debt for these purposes –

    (a) calculating the total amount of the debtor's qualifying debts;

    (b) scheduling the debt to an administration order.

**112AE  Calculating the debtor's surplus income**

(1) The debtor's surplus income is to be calculated in accordance with regulations.

(2) Regulations under this section must, in particular, make the following provision –

    (a) provision about what is surplus income;

    (b) provision about the period by reference to which the debtor's surplus income is to be calculated.

(3) Regulations under this section may, in particular, provide for the debtor's assets to be taken account of when calculating his surplus income.

**112AF  Debts becoming due**

(1) A debt that is repayable by a single payment becomes due when the time for making that payment is reached.

(2) A debt that is repayable by a number of payments becomes due when the time for making the first of the payments is reached.

**112AG  Scheduling and de-scheduling debts**

(1) A debt is scheduled to an administration order if the relevant information is included in a schedule to the order.

(2) A debt is de-scheduled if the relevant information is removed from a schedule in which it was included as mentioned in subsection (1).

(3) In relation to a debt, the relevant information is –

    (a) the amount of the debt, and

    (b) the name of the creditor under the debt.

(4) A scheduled debt is a debt that is scheduled to an administration order.

(5) The proper county court must not schedule a debt to an administration order unless the court has had regard to any representations made by any person about why the debt should not be scheduled.

(6) But subsection (5) does not apply to any representations which are made by the debtor in relation to the scheduling of a debt under section 112Y.

(7) The proper county court must not de-schedule a debt unless the court has had regard to any representations made by any person about why the debt should not be de-scheduled.

(8) But subsection (7) does not apply in relation to the de-scheduling of a debt under section 112Q.

(9) A court must not schedule a debt to an administration order, or de-schedule a debt, except in accordance with the provisions of this Part.

### 112AH  The AO, voluntary arrangement and bankruptcy exclusions

(1) The debtor is excluded under the AO exclusion if –

    (a)   an administration order currently has effect in respect of him, or

    (b)   an administration order has previously had effect in respect of him, and the period of 12 months – beginning with the day when that order ceased to have effect – has yet to finish.

(2) But in a case that falls within subsection (1)(b), the debtor is not excluded under the AO exclusion if the previous administration order –

    (a)   ceased to have effect in accordance with any of the provisions listed in section 112K(7) (effect of enforcement restriction order or debt relief order on administration order), or

    (b)   was revoked in accordance with section 112U(1)(b) (debtor no longer has any qualifying debts).

(3) The debtor is excluded under the voluntary arrangement exclusion if –

    (a)   an interim order under section 252 of the Insolvency Act 1986 has effect in respect of him (interim order where debtor intends to make proposal for voluntary arrangement), or

    (b)   he is bound by a voluntary arrangement approved under Part 8 of the Insolvency Act 1986.

(4) The debtor is excluded under the bankruptcy exclusion if –

    (a)   a petition for a bankruptcy order to be made against him has been presented but not decided, or

    (b)   he is an undischarged bankrupt.

*Regulations*

### 112AI  Regulations under this Part

(1) It is for the Lord Chancellor to make regulations under this Part.

(2) Any power to make regulations under this Part is exercisable by statutory instrument.

(3) A statutory instrument containing regulations under this Part is subject to annulment in pursuance of a resolution of either House of Parliament.'

(2) Schedule 16 makes amendments consequential on the substitution of the new Part 6 in the 1984 Act.

(3) This section does not apply to any case in which an administration order was made, or an application for such an order was made, before the day on which this section comes into force.

## CHAPTER 2  ENFORCEMENT RESTRICTION ORDERS

### 107  Enforcement restriction orders

(1) After Part 6 of the County Courts Act 1984 (c. 28) (administration orders) insert –

'PART 6A   ENFORCEMENT RESTRICTION ORDERS

*Enforcement restriction orders*

### 117A  Enforcement restriction orders

(1) An enforcement restriction order is an order that imposes the requirements specified in sections 117C to 117E on certain creditors.
(2) An enforcement restriction order may also impose a requirement in accordance with section 117F on the debtor.

### 117B  Power to make order

(1) A county court may make an enforcement restriction order if the conditions in subsections (2) to (8) are met.
(2) The order must be made in respect of an individual who is a debtor under two or more qualifying debts.
(3) That individual ("the debtor") must not be a debtor under any business debts.
(4) The debtor must not be excluded under any of the following –

   (a)   the ERO exclusion;
   (b)   the voluntary arrangement exclusion;
   (c)   the bankruptcy exclusion.

(5) The debtor must be unable to pay one or more of his qualifying debts.
(6) The debtor must be suffering from a sudden and unforeseen deterioration in his financial circumstances.
(7) There must be a realistic prospect that the debtor's financial circumstances will improve within the period of six months beginning when the order is made.
(8) It must be fair and equitable to make the order.
(9) Before making an enforcement restriction order, the county court must have regard to any representations made by any person about why the order should not be made.
(10) Subsection (9) is subject to Civil Procedure Rules.

*Requirements imposed by order*

### 117C  Presentation of bankruptcy petition

(1) An enforcement restriction order must, during the currency of the order, impose the following requirement.
(2) The requirement is that no qualifying creditor of the debtor is to present a bankruptcy petition against the debtor in respect of a qualifying debt, unless the creditor has the permission of the proper county court.
(3) The proper county court may give permission for the purposes of subsection (2) subject to such conditions as it thinks fit.

### 117D  Remedies other than bankruptcy

(1) An enforcement restriction order must, during the currency of the order, impose the following requirement.
(2) The requirement is that no qualifying creditor of the debtor is to pursue any remedy for the recovery of a qualifying debt unless –

   (a)   regulations under subsection (3) provide otherwise, or
   (b)   the creditor has the permission of the proper county court.

(3) Regulations may specify classes of debt which are exempted (or exempted for specified purposes) from any requirement imposed by subsection (2).
(4) The proper county court may give permission for the purposes of subsection (2)(b) subject to such conditions as it thinks fit.
(5) This section does not have any effect in relation to bankruptcy proceedings.

**117E  Stopping supplies of gas or electricity**

(1)  An enforcement restriction order must, during the currency of the order, impose the requirement in subsection (3).

(2)  In relation to that requirement, a domestic utility creditor is any person who –

    (a)  provides the debtor with a supply of mains gas or mains electricity for the debtor's own domestic purposes, and

    (b)  is a creditor under a qualifying debt that relates to the provision of that supply.

(3)  The requirement is that no domestic utility creditor is to stop the supply of gas or electricity, or the supply of any associated services, except in the cases in subsections (4) to (6).

(4)  The first case is where the reason for stopping a supply relates to the non-payment by the debtor of charges incurred in connection with that supply after the making of the enforcement restriction order.

(5)  The second case is where the reason for stopping a supply is unconnected with the non-payment by the debtor of any charges incurred in connection with –

    (a)  that supply, or

    (b)  any other supply of mains gas or mains electricity, or of associated services, that is provided by the domestic utility creditor.

(6)  The third case is where the proper county court gives permission to stop a supply.

(7)  The proper county court may give permission for the purposes of subsection (6) subject to such conditions as it thinks fit.

(8)  A supply of mains gas is a supply of the kind mentioned in section 5(1)(b) of the Gas Act 1986.

(9)  A supply of mains electricity is a supply of the kind mentioned in section 4(1)(c) of the Electricity Act 1989.

**117F  Repayment requirement**

(1)  An enforcement restriction order may impose a repayment requirement on the debtor.

(2)  The county court may include the requirement in the order at the time it makes the order.

(3)  The proper county court may, at any time after an enforcement restriction order has been made, vary the order so as to include a repayment requirement.

(4)  The proper county court may, at any time when an enforcement restriction order includes a repayment requirement, vary the order so as to –

    (a)  remove the repayment requirement, or

    (b)  include a different repayment requirement.

(5)  A repayment requirement is a requirement that the debtor make payments, in respect of one or more of his qualifying debts, to the person or persons to whom he owes the debt or debts.

(6)  A county court may include a repayment requirement in an order only if –

    (a)  the debtor has surplus income at the time of the inclusion of the requirement, and

    (b)  the inclusion of the requirement would be fair and equitable.

(7)  The debtor's surplus income is to be calculated in accordance with regulations.

(8)  Regulations under subsection (7) must make the following provision –

    (a)  provision about what is surplus income;

    (b)  provision about the period by reference to which the debtor's surplus income is to be calculated.

(9) Regulations under subsection (7) may, in particular, provide for the debtor's assets to be taken account of for the purpose of calculating his surplus income.
(10) The proper county court may vary an enforcement restriction order under this section –

    (a)   of its own motion;
    (b)   on the application of the debtor;
    (c)   on the application of a qualifying creditor.

*Making an order*

### 117G  Application for order

(1) A county court may make an enforcement restriction order only on the application of the debtor.
(2) The debtor may make an application for an enforcement restriction order whether or not a judgment has been obtained against him in respect of any of his debts.

### 117H  Duration

(1) A county court may, at the time it makes an enforcement restriction order, specify a day on which the order will cease to have effect.
(2) The court may not specify a day which falls after the last day of the maximum permitted period.
(3) If the court specifies a day under this section, the order ceases to have effect on that day.
(4) If the court does not specify a day under this section, the order ceases to have effect at the end of the maximum permitted period.
(5) The maximum permitted period is the period of 12 months beginning with the day on which the order is made.
(6) This section is subject to –

    (a)   section 117N (variation of duration);
    (b)   section 117Q (effect of revocation).

(7) This section is also subject to the following (effect of administration order or debt relief order on enforcement restriction order) –

    (a)   section 112L of this Act;
    (b)   section 251F of the Insolvency Act 1986.

*Effects of order*

### 117I  Effect on other debt management arrangements

(1) This section applies if –

    (a)   an enforcement restriction order is made, and
    (b)   immediately before the order is made, other debt management arrangements are in force in respect of the debtor.

(2) The other debt management arrangements cease to be in force when the enforcement restriction order is made.
(3) If the proper county court is aware of the other debt management arrangements, the court must give the relevant authority notice that the order has been made.
(4) In a case where the proper county court is aware of those arrangements at the time it makes the order, it must give the notice as soon as practicable after making the order.
(5) In a case where the proper county court only becomes aware of those arrangements after it makes the order, it must give the notice as soon as practicable after becoming aware of them.
(6) "Other debt management arrangements" means any of the following –

    (a)    an administration order under Part 6 of this Act;

    (b)    a debt relief order under Part 7A of the Insolvency Act 1986;

    (c)    a debt repayment plan arranged in accordance with a debt management scheme that is approved under Chapter 4 of Part 5 of the Tribunals, Courts and Enforcement Act 2007.

(7)  "The relevant authority" means –

    (a)    in relation to an administration order: the proper county court (within the meaning of Part 6);

    (b)    in relation to a debt relief order: the official receiver;

    (c)    in relation to a debt repayment plan: the operator of the debt management scheme in accordance with which the plan is arranged.

(8)  For the purposes of this section a debt relief order is "in force" if the moratorium applicable to the order under section 251H of the Insolvency Act 1986 has not yet ended.

## 117J  Duty to provide information

(1)  This section applies if, and for as long as, an enforcement restriction order has effect in respect of a debtor.

(2)  The debtor must, at the prescribed times, provide the proper county court with particulars of his –

    (a)    earnings,

    (b)    income,

    (c)    assets, and

    (d)    outgoings.

(3)  The debtor must provide particulars of those matters –

    (a)    as the matters are at the time the particulars are provided, and

    (b)    as the debtor expects the matters to be at such times in the future as may be prescribed.

(4)  If the debtor intends to dispose of any of his property he must, within the prescribed period, provide the proper county court with particulars of the following matters –

    (a)    the property he intends to dispose of;

    (b)    the consideration (if any) he expects will be given for the disposal;

    (c)    such other matters as may be prescribed;

    (d)    such other matters as the court may specify.

(5)  But subsection (4) does not apply if the disposal is of –

    (a)    goods that are exempt goods for the purposes of Schedule 12 to the Tribunals, Courts and Enforcement Act 2007,

    (b)    goods that are protected under any other enactment from being taken control of under that Schedule, or

    (c)    prescribed property.

(6)  The duty under subsection (4) to provide the proper county court with particulars of a proposed disposal of property applies whether the debtor is the sole owner, or one of several owners, of the property.

(7)  In any provision of this section "prescribed" means prescribed in regulations for the purposes of that provision.

## 117K  Offence if information not provided

(1)  A person commits an offence if he fails to comply with –

    (a)    section 117J(2) and (3), or

    (b)    section 117J(4).

(2) A person who commits an offence under subsection (1) may be ordered by a judge of the proper county court to pay a fine of not more than £250 or to be imprisoned for not more than 14 days.

(3) Where under subsection (2) a person is ordered to be imprisoned by a judge of the proper county court, the judge may at any time –

    (a)   revoke the order, and

    (b)   if the person is already in custody, order his discharge.

(4) Section 129 of this Act (enforcement of fines) applies to payment of a fine imposed under subsection (2).

(5) For the purposes of section 13 of the Administration of Justice Act 1960 (appeal in cases of contempt of court), subsection (2) is to be treated as an enactment enabling a county court to deal with an offence under subsection (1) as if it were a contempt of court.

(6) A district judge or deputy district judge shall have the same powers under this section as a judge of a county court.

### 117L Existing county court proceedings to be stayed

(1) This section applies if these conditions are met –

    (a)   an enforcement restriction order is made;

    (b)   proceedings in a county court (other than bankruptcy proceedings) are pending against the debtor in respect of a qualifying debt;

    (c)   by virtue of a requirement included in the order by virtue of section 117D, the creditor under the qualifying debt is not entitled to continue the proceedings in respect of the debt;

    (d)   the county court receives notice of the enforcement restriction order.

(2) The county court must stay the proceedings.

(3) The county court –

    (a)   may allow costs already incurred by the creditor, and

    (b)   if the court allows such costs, may on application or of its own motion add them to the debt owed to the creditor.

### 117M Charges

(1) This section applies during, and after, the currency of an enforcement restriction order.

(2) A qualifying creditor may not make any charge in respect of a protected qualifying debt, unless the charge –

    (a)   is interest, or

    (b)   is not interest but relates to a time before or after the currency of the order.

(3) A charge made in breach of subsection (2) is not recoverable.

(4) In subsection (2) "protected qualifying debt" means any qualifying debt under which the debtor was a debtor at some time during the currency of the enforcement restriction order.

*Variation of duration*

### 117N Variation of duration

(1) The proper county court may vary an enforcement restriction order so as to specify a day, or (if a day has already been specified under section 117H or this section) a different day, on which the order will cease to have effect.

(2) But the new termination day must fall on or before the last day of the maximum permitted period.

(3) If the proper county court varies an enforcement restriction order under subsection (1), the order ceases to have effect on the new termination day.

(4)  The power under this section is exercisable –

    (a)  on the application of the debtor;

    (b)  on the application of a qualifying creditor;

    (c)  of the court's own motion.

(5)  In this section –

    (a)  "new termination day" means the day on which the order will cease to have effect in accordance with the variation under subsection (1);

    (b)  "maximum permitted period" means the period of 12 months beginning with the day on which the order was originally made.

(6)  This section is subject to section 117Q (effect of revocation).

### *Revocation of order*

### 117O  Duty to revoke order

(1)  The proper county court must revoke an enforcement restriction order in either of these cases –

    (a)  where it becomes apparent that, at the time the order was made, the condition in subsection 117B(2) was not met (debtor in fact did not have two or more qualifying debts);

    (b)  where the debtor is no longer a debtor under any qualifying debts.

(2)  The proper county court must revoke an enforcement restriction order in either of these cases –

    (a)  where it becomes apparent that, at the time the order was made, the condition in subsection 117B(3) was not met (debtor in fact had business debt), and he is still a debtor under the business debt, or any of the business debts, in question;

    (b)  where the debtor subsequently becomes a debtor under a business debt, and he is still a debtor under that debt.

(3)  The proper county court must revoke an enforcement restriction order where it becomes apparent that, at the time the order was made, the condition in section 117B(4) was not met (debtor in fact excluded under ERO, voluntary arrangement or bankruptcy exclusion).

(4)  The proper county court must revoke an enforcement restriction order where, after the order is made –

    (a)  the debtor becomes excluded under the voluntary arrangement exclusion, or

    (b)  a bankruptcy order is made against the debtor, and is still in force.

(5)  The proper county court must revoke an enforcement restriction order in either of these cases –

    (a)  where it becomes apparent that, at the time the order was made, the condition in section 117B(5) was not met (debtor in fact able to pay qualifying debts);

    (b)  where the debtor is now able to pay all of his qualifying debts.

(6)  The proper county court must revoke an enforcement restriction order in either of these cases –

    (a)  where it becomes apparent that, at the time the order was made, the condition in section 117B(6) was not met (debtor in fact not suffering from sudden and unforeseen deterioration in financial circumstances);

    (b)  where the debtor is no longer suffering from the deterioration in financial circumstances which was taken into account for the purposes of section 117B(6) (even if he is suffering from some other sudden and unforeseen deterioration in his financial circumstances).

(7)  The proper county court must revoke an enforcement restriction order in either of these cases –

    (a)  where it becomes apparent that, at the time the order was made, the condition in section 117B(7) was not met (in fact no realistic prospect of improvement in debtor's financial circumstances);

    (b)  where there is no longer a realistic prospect that the debtor's financial circumstances will improve during the period within which the order would continue to have effect (if not revoked).

(8)  The proper county court must revoke an enforcement restriction order in either of these cases –

    (a)  where it becomes apparent that, at the time the order was made, the condition in section 117B(8) was not met (not in fact fair and equitable to make order);

    (b)  where it is not fair and equitable for the order to continue to have effect.

### 117P  Power to revoke order

(1)  The proper county court may revoke an enforcement restriction order in any case where there is no duty under this Part to revoke it.

(2)  The power of revocation under this section may, in particular, be exercised in any of the following cases –

    (a)  where the order includes, or has previously included, a repayment requirement, and the debtor has failed to comply with that requirement;

    (b)  where the debtor has failed to provide the proper county court with the particulars required by –

        (i)   section 117J(2) and (3), or

        (ii)  section 117J(4).

(3)  The power of revocation under this section is exercisable –

    (a)  on the application of the debtor;

    (b)  on the application of a qualifying creditor;

    (c)  of the court's own motion.

### 117Q  Effect of revocation

(1)  This section applies if, under any duty or power in this Part, the proper county court revokes an enforcement restriction order.

(2)  The order ceases to have effect in accordance with the terms of the revocation.

*Notification of certain events*

### 117R  Notice when order made, varied, revoked etc.

(1)  If a notifiable event occurs in relation to an enforcement restriction order, the proper county court must give notice of the event to every identified qualifying creditor of the debtor.

(2)  There is a notifiable event in any of the following cases –

    (a)  when the enforcement restriction order is made;

    (b)  when the enforcement restriction order is varied;

    (c)  when the enforcement restriction order is revoked;

    (d)  when the proper county court is given notice under any of the provisions listed in section 117H(7) (effect of administration order or debt relief order on enforcement restriction order).

(3)  A person is an identified qualifying creditor of the debtor if –

(a)   the debtor has notified the proper county court, or another court whilst it was previously the proper county court, that the person is a qualifying creditor, or

(b)   the proper county court is satisfied that the person is a qualifying creditor.

*Interpretation*

### 117S  Introduction

Sections 117T to 117W apply for the purposes of this Part.

### 117T  Main definitions

(1)  In this Part –

"enforcement restriction order" has the meaning given by section 117A;
"debtor" has the meaning given by section 117B;
"qualifying creditor" means a creditor under a qualifying debt.

(2)  References to the currency of an enforcement restriction order are references to the period which –

(a)   begins when the order first has effect, and
(b)   ends when the order ceases to have effect.

(3)  In relation to an enforcement restriction order, references to the proper county court are references to the county court that made the order.

(4)  But that is subject to rules of court as to the venue for, and transfer of, proceedings in county courts.

### 117U  Expressions relating to debts

(1)  All debts are qualifying debts, except for the following –

(a)   any debt secured against an asset;
(b)   any debt of a description specified in regulations.

(2)  A business debt is any debt (whether or not a qualifying debt) which is incurred by a person in the course of a business.

(3)  Only debts that have already arisen are included in references to debts; and accordingly such references do not include any debt that will arise only on the happening of some future contingency.

### 117V  Inability to pay debts

(1)  In a case where an individual is the debtor under a debt that is repayable by a single payment, the debtor is to be regarded as unable to pay the debt only if –

(a)   the time for making the payment has been reached,
(b)   the debtor has failed to make the single payment, and
(c)   the debtor is unable to make that payment.

(2)  In a case where an individual is the debtor under a debt that is repayable by a number of payments, the debtor is to be regarded as unable to pay the debt only if –

(a)   the time for making the first of the payments has been reached,
(b)   the debtor has failed to make one or more of the payments, and
(c)   the debtor is unable to make all of the missed payments.

### 117W  The ERO, voluntary arrangement and bankruptcy exclusions

(1)  The debtor is excluded under the ERO exclusion if –

(a)   an enforcement restriction order currently has effect in respect of him, or
(b)   an enforcement restriction order has previously had effect in respect of

him, and the period of 12 months – beginning with the day when that order ceased to have effect – has yet to finish.

(2) But in a case that falls within subsection (1)(b), the debtor is not excluded under the ERO exclusion if the previous enforcement restriction order –

(a) ceased to have effect in accordance with any of the provisions listed in section 117H(7) (effect of administration order or debt relief order on enforcement restriction order), or

(b) was revoked in accordance with section 117O(1)(b) (debtor no longer has any qualifying debts).

(3) The debtor is excluded under the voluntary arrangement exclusion if –

(a) an interim order under section 252 of the Insolvency Act 1986 has effect in respect of him (interim order where debtor intends to make proposal for voluntary arrangement), or

(b) he is bound by a voluntary arrangement approved under Part 8 of the Insolvency Act 1986.

(4) The debtor is excluded under the bankruptcy exclusion if –

(a) a petition for a bankruptcy order to be made against him has been presented but not decided, or

(b) he is an undischarged bankrupt.

*Regulations*

**117X  Power to make regulations**

(1) It is for the Lord Chancellor to make regulations under this Part.

(2) Any power to make regulations under this Part is exercisable by statutory instrument.

(3) A statutory instrument containing regulations under this Part is subject to annulment in pursuance of a resolution of either House of Parliament.'

(2) In Schedule 6A to the Magistrates' Courts Act 1980 (c. 43) (fines that may be altered under section 143 of the 1980 Act) insert the following entry at the appropriate place in the entries relating to the County Courts Act 1984 (c. 28) –

'Section 117K(1) (enforcement restriction orders:           £250'
failure to provide information)

(3) In section 98 of the Courts Act 2003 (c. 39) (register of judgments and orders etc.), in subsection (1), for paragraph (d) substitute –

'(d) enforcement restriction orders under Part 6A of that Act (power of county courts to make enforcement restriction orders);'.

## CHAPTER 3    DEBT RELIEF ORDERS

**108  Debt relief orders and debt relief restrictions orders etc.**

(1) In the Second Group of Parts of the Insolvency Act 1986 (c. 45) (insolvency of individuals), before Part 8 there is inserted, as Part 7A, the Part set out in Schedule 17.

(2) After Schedule 4 to that Act there is inserted, as Schedules 4ZA and 4ZB, the Schedules set out in Schedules 18 and 19.

(3) Schedule 20 (which makes amendments consequential on provisions contained in Schedule 17) has effect.

## CHAPTER 4    DEBT MANAGEMENT SCHEMES

### *Introductory*

**109  Debt management schemes**

(1)  A debt management scheme is a scheme that meets the conditions in this section.

(2)  The scheme must be open to some or all non-business debtors.

(3)  A scheme is open to a non-business debtor if it allows him to make a request to the scheme operator for a debt repayment plan to be arranged for him.

(4)  The scheme must provide that, if such a request is made –

    (a)  a decision must be made about whether a debt repayment plan is to be arranged for the non-business debtor, and

    (b)  such a plan must be arranged (if that is the decision made).

(5)  The scheme must be operated by a body of persons (whether a body corporate or not).

**110  Debt repayment plans**

(1)  A debt repayment plan is a plan that meets the conditions in this section.

(2)  The plan must specify all of the debtor's qualifying debts.

(3)  The plan must require the debtor to make payments in respect of each of the specified debts.

(4)  It does not matter if –

    (a)  the plan requires payments of different amounts to be made in respect of a specified debt at different times;

    (b)  the payments that the plan requires to be made in respect of a specified debt would, if all made, repay the debt only in part.

### *Approval of schemes*

**111  Approval by supervising authority**

(1)  The supervising authority may approve one or more debt management schemes.

(2)  Regulations may make provision about any or all of the following –

    (a)  conditions that must be met before the supervising authority may approve a debt management scheme;

    (b)  considerations that the supervising authority must, or must not, take into account in deciding whether to approve a debt management scheme.

(3)  Regulations under this section may, in particular, make provision about conditions or considerations that relate to any matter listed in Schedule 21.

(4)  The supervising authority may approve a debt management scheme whether a body is –

    (a)  operating the scheme at the time of the approval, or

    (b)  proposing to operate the scheme from a time in the future.

**112  Applications for approval**

(1)  Regulations may specify a procedure for making an application for approval of a debt management scheme.

(2)  Regulations under this section may, in particular, specify a procedure that requires any or all of the following –

    (a)  an application to be made in a particular form;

    (b)  information to be supplied in support of an application;

    (c)  a fee to be paid in respect of an application.

### 113  Terms of approval

(1)  The approval of a debt management scheme has effect subject to any relevant terms.
(2)  Relevant terms are –

  (a)  the terms (if any) specified in regulations that relate to the approval, and
  (b)  the terms (if any) that the supervising authority includes in the approval.

(3)  Relevant terms may, in particular, deal with all or any of the following –

  (a)  the start of the approval;
  (b)  the expiry of the approval;
  (c)  the termination of the approval, including termination because of the breach of some other term.

(4)  Relevant terms may, in particular, impose requirements on the scheme operator.
(5)  Relevant terms may, in particular, relate to any matter listed in Schedule 21.
(6)  Regulations may make provision about terms that the supervising authority must, or must not, include in an approval.

## Effect of plans etc.

### 114  Discharge from specified debts

(1)  This section applies if –

  (a)  a debt repayment plan is arranged for a non-business debtor in accordance with an approved scheme, and
  (b)  the plan comes into effect.

(2)  The debtor is discharged from the debts that are specified in the plan.
(3)  The discharge from a particular specified debt takes effect at the time when all the required payments have been made.
(4)  The required payments are the payments in respect of the debt that are required by the provision included in the plan in accordance with section 110(3).

### 115  Presentation of bankruptcy petition

(1)  This section applies during the currency of a debt repayment plan arranged in accordance with an approved scheme.
(2)  No qualifying creditor of the debtor is to present a bankruptcy petition against the debtor in respect of a qualifying debt, unless –

  (a)  regulations provide otherwise, or
  (b)  the creditor has the permission of a county court.

(3)  A county court may give permission for the purposes of subsection (2)(b) subject to such conditions as it thinks fit.
(4)  The reference to the currency of a debt repayment plan is a reference to the period which –

  (a)  begins when the plan first has effect, and
  (b)  ends when the plan ceases to have effect.

### 116  Remedies other than bankruptcy

(1)  This section applies in relation to a non-business debtor during a period of protection.
(2)  No qualifying creditor of the debtor is to pursue any remedy for the recovery of a qualifying debt, unless –

  (a)  regulations provide otherwise, or
  (b)  the creditor has the permission of a county court.

(3)  A county court may give permission for the purposes of subsection (2)(b) subject to such conditions as it thinks fit.

(4)  This section does not have any effect in relation to bankruptcy proceedings.

## 117  Charging of interest etc.

(1)  This section applies in relation to a non-business debtor during a period of protection.

(2)  No qualifying creditor is to charge any sum by way of interest, fee or other charge in respect of a qualifying debt, unless –

(a)  regulations provide otherwise, or

(b)  the creditor has the permission of a county court.

(3)  A county court may give permission for the purposes of subsection (2)(b) subject to such conditions as it thinks fit.

## 118  Stopping supplies of gas or electricity

(1)  This section applies in relation to a non-business debtor during a period of protection.

(2)  In relation to the debtor, a domestic utility creditor is any person who –

(a)  provides the debtor with a supply of mains gas or mains electricity for the debtor's own domestic purposes, and

(b)  is a creditor under a qualifying debt that relates to the provision of that supply.

(3)  No domestic utility creditor is to stop the supply of gas or electricity, or the supply of any associated services, except in the cases in subsections (4) to (7).

(4)  The first case is where the reason for stopping a supply relates to the non-payment by the debtor of charges incurred in connection with that supply after the start of the period of protection.

(5)  The second case is where the reason for stopping a supply is unconnected with the non-payment by the debtor of any charges incurred in connection with –

(a)  that supply, or

(b)  any other supply of mains gas or mains electricity, or of associated services, that is provided by the domestic utility creditor.

(6)  The third case is where regulations allow the supply to be stopped.

(7)  The fourth case is where a county court gives permission to stop a supply.

(8)  A county court may give permission for the purposes of subsection (7) subject to such conditions as it thinks fit.

(9)  A supply of mains gas is a supply of the kind mentioned in section 5(1)(b) of the Gas Act 1986 (c. 44).

(10) A supply of mains electricity is a supply of the kind mentioned in section 4(1)(c) of the Electricity Act 1989 (c. 29).

## 119  Existing county court proceedings to be stayed

(1)  This section applies if these conditions are met –

(a)  a debt repayment plan is arranged for a non-business debtor in accordance with an approved scheme;

(b)  proceedings in a county court (other than bankruptcy proceedings) are pending against the debtor in respect of a qualifying debt;

(c)  by virtue of section 116, the creditor under the qualifying debt is not entitled to continue the proceedings in respect of the debt;

(d)  the county court receives notice of the debt repayment plan.

(2)  The county court must stay the proceedings.

(3)  The court may allow costs already incurred by the creditor.

(4)  Subsection (5) applies if –

(a)  the court allows such costs, and

(b)  the qualifying debt is a specified debt.

(5)  The operator of the approved scheme may, if requested to do so by –

    (a)  the non-business debtor, or

    (b)  the creditor under the qualifying debt,

    add the costs to the amount specified in the plan in respect of the debt.

(6)  But the operator may not add the costs under subsection (5) if, under the terms of the approved scheme, the operator is under a duty to terminate the plan.

## 120  Registration of plans

(1)  Regulations may make provision about the registration of either or both of the following –

    (a)  any request made to the operator of an approved scheme for a debt repayment plan to be arranged in accordance with the scheme;

    (b)  any debt repayment plan arranged for a non-business debtor in accordance with an approved scheme.

(2)  In subsection (1) 'registration' means registration in the register maintained under section 98 of the Courts Act 2003 (c. 39) (the register of judgments and orders etc).

(3)  Regulations under this section may amend section 98 of the 2003 Act.

## 121  Other debt management arrangements in force

(1)  This section applies if –

    (a)  a debt repayment plan is arranged for a debtor in accordance with an approved scheme, and

    (b)  immediately before the plan is arranged, other debt management arrangements are in force in respect of the debtor.

(2)  The plan is not to come into effect unless the other debt management arrangements cease to be in force.

(3)  Any provision (whether in the plan or elsewhere) about when the plan is to come into effect is subject to subsection (2).

(4)  If the operator of the approved scheme is aware of the other debt management arrangements, the operator must give the relevant authority notice that the plan has been arranged.

(5)  In a case where the operator is aware of other debt management arrangements at the time the plan is arranged, it must give the notice as soon as practicable after the plan is arranged.

(6)  In a case where the operator becomes aware of those arrangements after the plan is arranged, it must give the notice as soon as practicable after becoming aware of them.

(7)  'Other debt management arrangements' means any of the following –

    (a)  an administration order under Part 6 of the County Courts Act 1984 (c. 28);

    (b)  an enforcement restriction order under Part 6A of the County Courts Act 1984;

    (c)  a debt relief order under Part 7A of the Insolvency Act 1986 (c. 45).

(8)  'The relevant authority' means –

    (a)  in relation to an administration order: the proper county court (within the meaning of Part 6 of the County Courts Act 1984);

    (b)  in relation to an enforcement restriction order: the proper county court (within the meaning of Part 6A of the County Courts Act 1984);

    (c)  in relation to a debt relief order: the official receiver.

(9)  For the purposes of this section a debt relief order is 'in force' if the moratorium applicable to the order under section 251H of the Insolvency Act 1986 has not yet ended.

## *Appeals*

### 122 Right of appeal

(1) This section applies if a debt repayment plan is arranged for a debtor in accordance with an approved scheme.

(2) An affected creditor may appeal to a county court against any of the following –

    (a) the fact that the plan has been arranged;

    (b) the fact that a debt owed to the affected creditor has been specified in the plan;

    (c) the terms of the plan (including any provision included in the plan in accordance with section 110(3)).

(3) Subsection (2)(c) does not allow an affected creditor to appeal against the fact that a debt owed to any other creditor has been specified in the plan.

(4) In this section 'affected creditor' means the creditor under any debt which is specified in the plan.

### 123 Dealing with appeals

(1) This section applies if an appeal is made to a county court under section 122.

(2) The county court may determine the appeal in any way that it thinks fit.

(3) The county court may make such orders as may be necessary to give effect to the determination of the appeal.

(4) The county court may, in particular, order the scheme operator to do any of the following –

    (a) to reconsider the decision to arrange the plan;

    (b) to reconsider any decision about the terms of the plan;

    (c) to modify the debt repayment plan;

    (d) to revoke the debt repayment plan.

(5) The county court may make such interim provision as it thinks fit in relation to the period before the appeal is determined.

(6) The county court is the county court to which the appeal is made.

## *Approved schemes: charging*

### 124 Charges by operator of approved scheme

(1) The operator of an approved scheme may recover its costs by charging debtors or affected creditors (or both).

(2) In this section –

'costs' means the costs which the operator incurs, taking one year with another, in connection with the approved scheme, so far as those costs are reasonable;

'debtors' means –

    (a) debtors who make requests for debt repayment plans to be arranged in accordance with the approved scheme, and

    (b) debtors for whom debt repayment plans are arranged in accordance with the approved scheme.

## *Termination of approval*

### 125 Procedure for termination

(1) Regulations may specify a procedure for terminating the approval of a debt management scheme.

(2) Regulations under this section may, in particular, specify a procedure that requires any or all of the following –

(a)  notice of, or the reasons for, an intended termination to be given (whether to the supervising authority, the scheme operator, the Lord Chancellor or any other person);

(b)  conditions to be met before a termination takes effect;

(c)  a particular period of time to elapse before a termination takes effect.

### 126  Terminating an approval

The approval of a debt management scheme may be terminated only if the termination is in accordance with all of the following (so far as they are relevant) –

(a)  any terms to which the approval is subject by virtue of section 113;

(b)  any provision made in regulations under section 125;

(c)  any other provision made in other regulations under this Chapter.

### 127  Alternatives to termination

(1)  Regulations may make provision to allow the supervising authority to deal with a termination case other than by terminating the approval.

(2)  A termination case is a case in which the supervising authority would be entitled to terminate the approval of a debt management scheme.

(3)  Regulations under this section may, in particular, make provision to allow the supervising authority to transfer the operation of the scheme –

(a)  to itself, or

(b)  to any other body.

## Effects of end of approval

### 128  Effects of end of approval

(1)  Regulations may make provision about the effects if the approval of a debt management scheme comes to an end.

(2)  Regulations under this section may, in particular, make provision about the treatment of debt repayment plans arranged for non-business debtors before the scheme came to an end.

(3)  That includes provision to treat a plan –

(a)  as though the approval had not come to an end, or

(b)  as though the plan had been made in accordance with a different approved scheme.

(4)  Regulations under this section may, in particular, make provision about cases where, at the time the scheme comes to an end, the scheme operator is in breach of a relevant obligation.

(5)  That includes provision to ensure that the operator is not released from the relevant obligation by virtue of the termination.

(6)  In subsections (4) and (5) 'relevant obligation' means any obligation (including a requirement or condition) however arising, that relates to –

(a)  the scheme in question (including its operation),

(b)  the approval of that scheme, or

(c)  the termination of that approval.

## The supervising authority

### 129  The supervising authority

(1)  The supervising authority is –

(a)  the Lord Chancellor, or

(b)  any person that the Lord Chancellor has authorised to approve debt management schemes under section 111.

(2)  Subsections (3) and (4) apply in any case where an authorisation under subsection (1)(b) starts or ends.

(3)  The start or end of the authorisation does not affect the validity of an approval that is in force at the relevant time.

(4)  The new supervising authority may exercise all of its functions in relation to an approval that is in force at the relevant time as though it had given the approval itself.

(5)  In this section –

'approval' means an approval of a debt management scheme given under section 111;
'relevant time' means the time when an authorisation starts or ends.

## Various

### 130  Regulations

(1)  It is for the Lord Chancellor to make regulations.

(2)  The power to make regulations is exercisable by statutory instrument.

(3)  A statutory instrument containing regulations is subject to annulment in pursuance of a resolution of either House of Parliament.

(4)  But subsection (3) does not apply in the case of a statutory instrument that contains either or both of the following –

(a)  the first regulations under a particular section of this Chapter;

(b)  any regulations under section 118(6);

(c)  any regulations under section 120 that amend section 98 of the Courts Act 2003 (c. 39);

(d)  any regulations that amend section 122 or 123.

(5)  In such a case the statutory instrument may not be made unless a draft of the instrument has been laid before, and approved by a resolution of, each House of Parliament.

(6)  Regulations may make different provision in relation to different cases.

(7)  Regulations may make any or all of the following provision if the Lord Chancellor thinks it is necessary or expedient –

(a)  supplementary, incidental or consequential provision;

(b)  transitory, transitional or saving provision.

(8)  Provision under subsection (7) may, in particular, amend section 122 or 123 (including by making provision for further grounds of appeal).

(9)  In this section (except in subsection (4)(a) to (c)) 'regulations' means regulations under any provision of this Chapter.

### 131  Main definitions

(1)  In this Chapter –

'affected creditor' has the meaning given by section 122;
'approved scheme' means a debt management scheme that is approved under section 111;
'debt management scheme' has the meaning given by section 109;
'debt repayment plan' has the meaning given by section 110;
'non-business debtor' means any individual who –

(a)  is a debtor under one or more qualifying debts, but

(b)  is not a debtor under any business debts;

'period of protection' has the meaning given by section 133;
'qualifying creditor' means a creditor under a qualifying debt;

'scheme operator' means the body that operates a debt management scheme;
'specified debt' means a debt specified in a debt repayment plan;
'supervising authority' has the meaning given by section 129.

(2)   Any reference to a county court is subject to rules of court as to the venue for, and transfer of, proceedings in county courts.

## 132  Expressions relating to debts

(1)   All debts are qualifying debts, except the following –

    (a)   any debt secured against an asset;

    (b)   in relation to a debt repayment plan which has been requested or arranged, any debt which could not, by virtue of the terms of the debt management scheme, be specified in the plan.

(2)   A business debt is any debt (whether or not a qualifying debt) which is incurred by a person in the course of a business.

## 133  Periods of protection

(1)   A 'period of protection', in relation to a non-business debtor, is a period which begins and ends as specified in this section.

(2)   The period begins if, and when, the debtor makes a request to the operator of an approved scheme for a debt repayment plan to be arranged in accordance with the scheme.

(3)   The period ends as follows –

    (a)   if a debt repayment plan is not arranged in consequence of the request: when the decision is made not to arrange the plan;

    (b)   if a debt repayment plan is arranged in consequence of the request: when that plan ceases to have effect.

(4)   But if other debt management arrangements are in force in relation to debtor immediately before he makes the request, the period does not begin unless, and until, a debt repayment plan –

    (a)   is arranged in consequence of the request, and

    (b)   comes into effect in accordance with section 121(2).

(5)   In this section the reference to other debt management arrangements which are in force has the same meaning as such references in section 121.

*****

# PART 7   MISCELLANEOUS

## Compulsory purchase

### 139  Enforcement by enforcement officers

(1)   In section 3 of the Lands Clauses Consolidation Act 1845 (c. 18) (interpretations in this and the special Act), at the end insert –

'Where any matter in relation to any lands is required to be done by an enforcement officer, the expression 'the enforcement officer' means the officer or officers identified for that purpose in paragraph 3A of Schedule 7 to the Courts Act 2003.'

(2)   In section 91 of that Act (proceedings in case of refusal to deliver possession of lands) –

(a) after 'the sheriff' in the first place insert 'or the enforcement officer';

(b) for 'the sheriff' in the second place substitute 'the person to whom it is issued';

(c) for 'the sheriff' in the third place substitute 'the person executing the warrant';

(d) after the existing words, which (as amended) become subsection (1), insert –

'(2) If, by virtue of paragraph 3A of Schedule 7 to the Courts Act 2003, the warrant is issued to two or more persons collectively, the duty in subsection (1) to deliver possession of lands shall apply to the person to whom the warrant is allocated in accordance with the approved arrangements mentioned in that Schedule.'

(3) Subsections (1) and (2) extend only to England and Wales.

(4) Section 13 of the Compulsory Purchase Act 1965 (c. 56) (refusal to give possession to acquiring authority) is amended as follows.

(5) In subsection (1), for the words from 'the sheriff' to the end substitute

' –

(a) the sheriff, or

(b) the enforcement officer,

to deliver possession of it to the person appointed in the warrant to receive it.'

(6) In subsection (2), for 'the sheriff' substitute 'the person to whom it is issued'.

(7) After subsection (2) insert –

'(2A) If, by virtue of paragraph 3A of Schedule 7 to the Courts Act 2003, the warrant is issued to two or more persons collectively, the duty in subsection (2) of this section shall apply to the person to whom the warrant is allocated in accordance with the approved arrangements mentioned in that Schedule.'

(8) In subsection (3), for 'the sheriff' substitute 'the person executing the warrant'.

(9) In subsection (6), after 'In this section' insert

' –

"the enforcement officer", in relation to a warrant to deliver possession of land under this section, means the officer or officers identified for that purpose in paragraph 3A of Schedule 7 to the Courts Act 2003, and'.

(10) Schedule 22 makes consequential amendments.

## 140 Supplementary

(1) Schedule 7 to the Courts Act 2003 (c. 39) (High Court writs of execution) is amended as follows.

(2) After paragraph 3 insert –

*'Issue of certain warrants to enforcement officers*

3A(1) Sub-paragraph (2) applies for the purpose of identifying the enforcement officer to whom a warrant may be issued under –

(a) section 91(1) of the Lands Clauses Consolidation Act 1845 (proceedings in case of refusal to deliver possession of lands), or

(b) section 13(1) of the Compulsory Purchase Act 1965 (refusal to give possession to acquiring authority).

(2) The enforcement officer, in relation to such a warrant, is –

(a) the enforcement officer assigned to a relevant district or, if two or more enforcement officers are assigned to that district, those officers collectively, or

(b) a named enforcement officer who, whether or not assigned to a relevant district, has undertaken to execute the warrant.

    (3)  In sub-paragraph (2), "a relevant district", in relation to a warrant, means –

        (a)   the district where the land in respect of which the warrant was issued is situated, or

        (b)   if that land (being land in one ownership) is not situated wholly in one district, a district where any part of that land is situated.'

(3)  Paragraph 4 is amended as set out in subsections (4) to (7).

(4)  In sub-paragraph (1), at the end insert 'and warrants issued to one or more enforcement officers under an enactment mentioned in paragraph 3A(1)(a) or (b)'.

(5)  After sub-paragraph (2) insert –

    '(2A)  The relevant officer has, in relation to the warrant, the duties, powers, rights, privileges and liabilities that a sheriff of a county would have had at common law if –

        (a)   the warrant had been issued to him, and

        (b)   the district in which it is to be executed had been within his county.'

(6)  For sub-paragraph (3) substitute –

    '(3)   "The relevant officer" means –

        (a)   in relation to a writ –

            (i)     if the writ is directed to a single enforcement officer under paragraph 3(1)(a) or (c), that officer;

            (ii)    if the writ is directed to two or more enforcement officers collectively under paragraph 3(1)(b), the officer to whom, in accordance with approved arrangements, the execution of the writ is allocated,

        (b)   in relation to a warrant –

            (i)     if the warrant is issued to a single enforcement officer in accordance with paragraph 3A(2)(a) or (b), that officer;

            (ii)    if the warrant is issued to two or more enforcement officers collectively in accordance with paragraph 3A(2)(a), the officer to whom, in accordance with approved arrangements, the execution of the warrant is allocated.'

(7)  For sub-paragraph (4) substitute –

    '(4)  Sub-paragraphs (2) and (2A) apply to a person acting under the authority of the relevant officer as they apply to the relevant officer.'

(8)  In paragraph 5, after 'writ' insert 'or warrant'.

(9)  In paragraph 12(2)(d)(ii), after 'officers' insert ', or warrants issued to enforcement officers under an enactment mentioned in paragraph 3A(1)(a) or (b),'.

(10) Accordingly –

    (a)   in section 99 of that Act (High Court writs of execution), in subsection (1) at the end insert 'and about warrants issued in connection with the compulsory acquisition of land';

    (b)   in Schedule 7 to that Act –

        (i)    for the heading 'High Court Writs of Execution' substitute 'Enforcement of Certain Writs and Warrants';

        (ii)   in the heading immediately preceding paragraph 1, for 'of execution' substitute 'and warrants'.

\*\*\*\*\*

## PART 8   GENERAL

\*\*\*\*\*

### 146  Repeals

Schedule 23 contains repeals.

### 147  Extent

(1) Parts 1, 2 and 6 and this Part extend to England and Wales, Scotland and Northern Ireland.
(2) The other provisions of this Act extend only to England and Wales.
(3) Subsections (1) and (2) are subject to subsections (4) and (5).
(4) Unless provided otherwise, amendments, repeals and revocations in this Act extend to any part of the United Kingdom to which the provisions amended, repealed or revoked extend.
(5) The following extend also to the Isle of Man –

  (a)  section 143(1) and (2),
  (b)  the repeal by this Act of any provision specified in Part 6 of Schedule 23 that extends to the Isle of Man,
  (c)  sections 145 and 148(5) to (7) so far as relating to –

    (i)   section 143(1) and (2), and
    (ii)  the provisions of this Act by which the repeals mentioned in paragraph (b) are effected, and

  (d)  this section and section 149.

### 148  Commencement

(1) Section 60 comes into force at the end of the period of two months beginning with the day on which this Act is passed.
(2) The provisions of Chapter 3 of Part 5 come into force in accordance with provision made by the Lord Chancellor or the Secretary of State by order.
(3) The provisions of Part 6 come into force, except as provided by subsection (4), in accordance with provision made by the Secretary of State by order.
(4) The provisions of Part 6 come into force, in so far as they extend to Scotland, in accordance with provision made by the Scottish Ministers by order.
(5) The remaining provisions of this Act, except sections 53, 55, 56, 57, 145, 147, 149, this section and Schedule 11, come into force in accordance with provision made by the Lord Chancellor by order.
(6) An order under this section may make different provision for different purposes.
(7) The power to make an order under this section is exercisable by statutory instrument.

### 149  Short title

This Act may be cited as the Tribunals, Courts and Enforcement Act 2007.

\*\*\*\*\*

## SCHEDULE 12   TAKING CONTROL OF GOODS

Section 62(1)

### PART 1   INTRODUCTORY

### *The procedure*

1   (1)   Using the procedure in this Schedule to recover a sum means taking control of goods and selling them to recover that sum in accordance with this Schedule and regulations under it.

    (2)   In this Schedule a power to use the procedure to recover a particular sum is called an 'enforcement power'.

    (3)   The following apply in relation to an enforcement power.

    (4)   'Debt' means the sum recoverable.

    (5)   'Debtor' means the person liable to pay the debt or, if two or more persons are jointly or jointly and severally liable, any one or more of them.

    (6)   'Creditor' means the person for whom the debt is recoverable.

### *Enforcement agents*

2   (1)   In this Schedule 'enforcement agent' means an individual authorised by section 63(2) to act as an enforcement agent.

    (2)   Only an enforcement agent may take control of goods and sell them under an enforcement power.

    (3)   An enforcement agent, if he is not the person on whom an enforcement power is conferred, may act under the power only if authorised by that person.

    (4)   In relation to goods taken control of by an enforcement agent under an enforcement power, references to the enforcement agent are references to any person for the time being acting as an enforcement agent under the power.

### *General interpretation*

3   (1)   In this Schedule –

    'amount outstanding' is defined in paragraph 50(3);

    'control' (except in paragraph 5(4)(a)) means control under an enforcement power;

    'controlled goods' means goods taken control of that –

        (a)   have not been sold or abandoned,

        (b)   if they have been removed, have not been returned to the debtor (unless subject to a controlled goods agreement), and

        (c)   if they are goods of another person, have not been returned to that person;

    'controlled goods agreement' has the meaning given by paragraph 13(4);

    'co-owner' in relation to goods of the debtor means a person other than the debtor who has an interest in the goods, but only if the enforcement agent –

        (a)   knows that the person has an interest in the particular goods, or

        (b)   would know, if he made reasonable enquiries;

    'the court', unless otherwise stated, and subject to rules of court, means –

        (a)   the High Court, in relation to an enforcement power under a writ of the High Court;

    (b)   a county court, in relation to an enforcement power under a warrant issued by a county court;

    (c)   in any other case, a magistrates' court;

'disposal' and related expressions, in relation to securities, are to be read in accordance with paragraph 48(2);

'exempt goods' means goods that regulations exempt by description or circumstances or both

'goods' means property of any description, other than land;

'interest' means a beneficial interest;

'money' means money in sterling or another currency;

'premises' means any place, and in particular includes –

    (a)   a vehicle, vessel, aircraft or hovercraft;

    (b)   a tent or movable structure;

'securities' includes bills of exchange, promissory notes, bonds, specialties and securities for money.

(2)   In this Schedule –

    (a)   references to goods of the debtor or another person are references to goods in which the debtor or that person has an interest, but

    (b)   references to goods of the debtor do not include references to trust property in which either the debtor or a co-owner has an interest not vested in possession.

## PART 2    THE PROCEDURE

### Binding property in the debtor's goods

4    (1)   For the purposes of any enforcement power, the property in all goods of the debtor, except goods that are exempt goods for the purposes of this Schedule or are protected under any other enactment, becomes bound in accordance with this paragraph.

    (2)   Where the power is conferred by a writ issued from the High Court the writ binds the property in the goods from the time when it is received by the person who is under a duty to endorse it.

    (3)   Where the power is conferred by a warrant to which section 99 of the County Courts Act 1984 (c. 28) or section 125ZA of the Magistrates' Courts Act 1980 (c. 43) applies, the warrant binds the property in the goods from the time when it is received by the person who is under a duty to endorse it under that section.

    (4)   Where sub-paragraphs (2) and (3) do not apply but notice is given to the debtor under paragraph 7(1), the notice binds the property in the goods from the time when the notice is given.

### Effect of property in goods being bound

5    (1)   An assignment or transfer of any interest of the debtor's in goods while the property in them is bound for the purposes of an enforcement power –

    (a)   is subject to that power, and

    (b)   does not affect the operation of this Schedule in relation to the goods, except as provided by paragraph 61 (application to assignee or transferee).

    (2)   Sub-paragraph (1) does not prejudice the title to any of the debtor's goods that a person acquires –

    (a)   in good faith,

(b)   for valuable consideration, and
(c)   without notice.

(3)   For the purposes of sub-paragraph (2)(a), a thing is to be treated as done in good faith if it is in fact done honestly (whether it is done negligently or not).

(4)   In sub-paragraph (2)(c) 'notice' means –

(a)   where the property in the goods is bound by a writ or warrant, notice that the writ or warrant, or any other writ or warrant by virtue of which the goods of the debtor might be seized or otherwise taken control of, had been received by the person who was under a duty to endorse it and that goods remained bound under it;

(b)   where the property in the goods is bound by notice under paragraph 7(1), notice that that notice had been given and that goods remained bound under it.

(5)   In sub-paragraph (4)(a) 'endorse' in relation to a warrant to which section 99 of the County Courts Act 1984 (c. 28) or section 125ZA of the Magistrates' Courts Act 1980 (c. 43) applies, means endorse under that section.

## Time when property ceases to be bound

6    (1)   For the purposes of any enforcement power the property in goods of the debtor ceases to be bound in accordance with this paragraph.

(2)   The property in any goods ceases to be bound –

(a)   when the goods are sold;
(b)   in the case of money used to pay any of the amount outstanding, when it is used.

(3)   The property in all goods ceases to be bound when any of these happens –

(a)   the amount outstanding is paid, out of the proceeds of sale or otherwise;
(b)   the instrument under which the power is exercisable ceases to have effect;
(c)   the power ceases to be exercisable for any other reason.

## Notice of enforcement

7    (1)   An enforcement agent may not take control of goods unless the debtor has been given notice.

(2)   Regulations must state –

(a)   the minimum period of notice;
(b)   the form of the notice;
(c)   what it must contain;
(d)   how it must be given;
(e)   who must give it.

(3)   The enforcement agent must keep a record of the time when the notice is given.

(4)   If regulations authorise it, the court may order in prescribed circumstances that the notice given may be less than the minimum period.

(5)   The order may be subject to conditions.

## Time limit for taking control

8    (1)   An enforcement agent may not take control of goods after the prescribed period.

(2)   The period may be prescribed by reference to the date of notice of enforcement or of any writ or warrant conferring the enforcement power or any other date.

(3) Regulations may provide for the period to be extended or further extended by the court in accordance with the regulations.

## Goods which may be taken

9    An enforcement agent may take control of goods only if they are –

(a)   on premises that he has power to enter under this Schedule, or
(b)   on a highway.

10   An enforcement agent may take control of goods only if they are goods of the debtor.

11  (1) Subject to paragraphs 9 and 10 and to any other enactment under which goods are protected, an enforcement agent –

(a)   may take control of goods anywhere in England and Wales;
(b)   may take control of any goods that are not exempt.

(2) Regulations may authorise him to take control of exempt goods in prescribed circumstances, if he provides the debtor with replacements in accordance with the regulations.

## Value of goods taken

12  (1) Unless sub-paragraph (2) applies, an enforcement agent may not take control of goods whose aggregate value is more than –

(a)   the amount outstanding, and
(b)   an amount in respect of future costs, calculated in accordance with regulations.

(2) An enforcement agent may take control of goods of higher value on premises or on a highway, only to the extent necessary, if there are not enough goods of a lower value within a reasonable distance –

(a)   on a highway, or
(b)   on premises that he has power to enter under this Schedule, either under paragraph 14 or under an existing warrant.

(3) For the purposes of this paragraph goods are above a given value only if it is or ought to be clear to the enforcement agent that they are.

(4) Sub-paragraph (1) does not affect the power to keep control of goods if they rise in value once they have been taken.

## Ways of taking control

13  (1) To take control of goods an enforcement agent must do one of the following –

(a)   secure the goods on the premises on which he finds them;
(b)   if he finds them on a highway, secure them on a highway, where he finds them or within a reasonable distance;
(c)   remove them and secure them elsewhere;
(d)   enter into a controlled goods agreement with the debtor.

(2) Any liability of an enforcement agent (including criminal liability) arising out of his securing goods on a highway under this paragraph is excluded to the extent that he acted with reasonable care.

(3) Regulations may make further provision about taking control in any of the ways listed in sub-paragraph (1), including provision –

(a)   determining the time when control is taken;

(b)  prohibiting use of any of those ways for goods by description or circumstances or both.

(4)  A controlled goods agreement is an agreement under which the debtor –

(a)  is permitted to retain custody of the goods,

(b)  acknowledges that the enforcement agent is taking control of them, and

(c)  agrees not to remove or dispose of them, nor to permit anyone else to, before the debt is paid.

## Entry without warrant

14  (1)  An enforcement agent may enter relevant premises to search for and take control of goods.

(2)  Where there are different relevant premises this paragraph authorises entry to each of them.

(3)  This paragraph authorises repeated entry to the same premises, subject to any restriction in regulations.

(4)  If the enforcement agent is acting under section 72(1) (CRAR), the only relevant premises are the demised premises.

(5)  If he is acting under section 121A of the Social Security Administration Act 1992 (c. 5), premises are relevant if they are the place, or one of the places, where the debtor carries on a trade or business.

(6)  Otherwise premises are relevant if the enforcement agent reasonably believes that they are the place, or one of the places, where the debtor –

(a)  usually lives, or

(b)  carries on a trade or business.

## Entry under warrant

15  (1)  If an enforcement agent applies to the court it may issue a warrant authorising him to enter specified premises to search for and take control of goods.

(2)  Before issuing the warrant the court must be satisfied that all these conditions are met –

(a)  an enforcement power has become exercisable;

(b)  there is reason to believe that there are goods on the premises that the enforcement power will be exercisable to take control of if the warrant is issued;

(c)  it is reasonable in all the circumstances to issue the warrant.

(3)  The warrant authorises repeated entry to the same premises, subject to any restriction in regulations.

## Re-entry

16  (1)  This paragraph applies where goods on any premises have been taken control of and have not been removed by the enforcement agent.

(2)  The enforcement agent may enter the premises to inspect the goods or to remove them for storage or sale.

(3)  This paragraph authorises repeated entry to the same premises.

## General powers to use reasonable force

17    Where paragraph 18 or 19 applies, an enforcement agent may if necessary use reasonable force to enter premises or to do anything for which the entry is authorised.

18    This paragraph applies if these conditions are met –

(a)    the enforcement agent has power to enter the premises under paragraph 14 or 16 or under a warrant under paragraph 15;

(b)    he is acting under an enforcement power conferred by a warrant of control under section 76(1) of the Magistrates' Courts Act 1980 (c. 43) for the recovery of a sum adjudged to be paid by a conviction;

(c)    he is entitled to execute the warrant by virtue of section 125A (civilian enforcement officers) or 125B (approved enforcement agencies) of that Act.

19    (1)    This paragraph applies if these conditions are met –

(a)    the enforcement agent has power to enter the premises under paragraph 16;

(b)    he reasonably believes that the debtor carries on a trade or business on the premises;

(c)    he is acting under an enforcement power within sub-paragraph (2).

(2)    The enforcement powers are those under any of the following –

(a)    a writ or warrant of control issued for the purpose of recovering a sum payable under a High Court or county court judgment;

(b)    section 61(1) of the Taxes Management Act 1970 (c. 9);

(c)    section 121A(1) of the Social Security Administration Act 1992 (c. 5);

(d)    section 51(A1) of the Finance Act 1997 (c. 16);

(e)    paragraph 1A of Schedule 12 to the Finance Act 2003 (c. 14).

## Application for power to use reasonable force

20    (1)    This paragraph applies if an enforcement agent has power to enter premises under paragraph 14 or 16 or under a warrant under paragraph 15.

(2)    If the enforcement agent applies to the court it may issue a warrant which authorises him to use, if necessary, reasonable force to enter the premises or to do anything for which entry is authorised.

21    (1)    This paragraph applies if an enforcement agent is applying for power to enter premises under a warrant under paragraph 15.

(2)    If the enforcement agent applies to the court it may include in the warrant provision authorising him to use, if necessary, reasonable force to enter the premises or to do anything for which entry is authorised.

22    (1)    The court may not issue a warrant under paragraph 20 or include provision under paragraph 21 unless it is satisfied that prescribed conditions are met.

(2)    A warrant under paragraph 20 or provision included under paragraph 21 may require any constable to assist the enforcement agent to execute the warrant.

## Other provisions about powers of entry

23    Paragraphs 24 to 30 apply where an enforcement agent has power to enter premises under paragraph 14 or 16 or under a warrant under paragraph 15.

24    (1)    The power to enter and any power to use force are subject to any restriction imposed by or under regulations.

(2)    A power to use force does not include power to use force against persons, except to the extent that regulations provide that it does.

25    (1)    The enforcement agent may enter and remain on the premises only within prescribed times of day.

(2) Regulations may give the court power in prescribed circumstances to authorise him to enter or remain on the premises at other times.

(3) The authorisation –

    (a)   may be by order or in a warrant under paragraph 15;

    (b)   may be subject to conditions.

26  (1)  The enforcement agent must on request show the debtor and any person who appears to him to be in charge of the premises evidence of –

    (a)   his identity, and

    (b)   his authority to enter the premises.

    (2)  The request may be made before the enforcement agent enters the premises or while he is there.

27  (1)  The enforcement agent may take other people onto the premises.

    (2)  They may assist him in exercising any power, including a power to use force.

    (3)  They must not remain on the premises without the enforcement agent.

    (4)  The enforcement agent may take any equipment onto the premises.

    (5)  He may leave equipment on the premises if he leaves controlled goods there.

28  (1)  After entering the premises the enforcement agent must provide a notice for the debtor giving information about what the enforcement agent is doing.

    (2)  Regulations must state –

    (a)   the form of the notice;

    (b)   what information it must give.

    (3)  Regulations may prescribe circumstances in which a notice need not be provided after re-entry to premises.

    (4)  If the debtor is on the premises when the enforcement agent is there, the enforcement agent must give him the notice then.

    (5)  If the debtor is not there, the enforcement agent must leave the notice in a conspicuous place on the premises.

    (6)  If the enforcement agent knows that there is someone else there or that there are other occupiers, a notice he leaves under sub-paragraph (5) must be in a sealed envelope addressed to the debtor.

29      If the premises are occupied by any person apart from the debtor, the enforcement agent must leave at the premises a list of any goods he takes away.

30      The enforcement agent must leave the premises as effectively secured as he finds them.

## *Goods on a highway*

31  (1)  If the enforcement agent applies to the court it may issue a warrant which authorises him to use, if necessary, reasonable force to take control of goods on a highway.

    (2)  The court may not issue a warrant unless it is satisfied that prescribed conditions are met.

    (3)  The warrant may require any constable to assist the enforcement agent to execute it.

    (4)  The power to use force is subject to any restriction imposed by or under regulations.

    (5)  The power to use force does not include power to use force against persons, except to the extent that regulations provide that it does.

32  (1)  The enforcement agent may not exercise any power under this Schedule on a highway except within prescribed times of day.

    (2)  Regulations may give the court power in prescribed circumstances to authorise him to exercise a power at other times.

(3)  The authorisation may be subject to conditions.

33  (1)  If the enforcement agent takes control of goods on a highway or enters a vehicle on a highway with the intention of taking control of goods, he must provide a notice for the debtor giving information about what he is doing.

(2)  Regulations must state –

   (a)   the form of the notice;

   (b)   what information it must give.

(3)  If the debtor is present when the enforcement agent is there, the enforcement agent must give him the notice then.

(4)  Otherwise the enforcement agent must deliver the notice to any relevant premises (as defined by paragraph 14) in a sealed envelope addressed to the debtor.

## Inventory

34  (1)  If an enforcement agent takes control of goods he must provide the debtor with an inventory of them as soon as reasonably practicable.

(2)  But if there are co-owners of any of the goods, the enforcement agent must instead provide the debtor as soon as reasonably practicable with separate inventories of goods owned by the debtor and each co-owner and an inventory of the goods without a co-owner.

(3)  The enforcement agent must as soon as reasonably practicable provide the co-owner of any of the goods with –

   (a)   the inventory of those goods, and

   (b)   a copy of the notice under paragraph 28.

(4)  Regulations must state –

   (a)   the form of an inventory, and

   (b)   what it must contain.

## Care of goods removed

35  (1)  An enforcement agent must take reasonable care of controlled goods that he removes from the premises or highway where he finds them.

(2)  He must comply with any provision of regulations about their care while they remain controlled goods.

## Valuation

36  (1)  Before the end of the minimum period, the enforcement agent must –

   (a)   make or obtain a valuation of the controlled goods in accordance with regulations;

   (b)   give the debtor, and separately any co-owner, an opportunity to obtain an independent valuation of the goods.

(2)  In this paragraph 'minimum period' means the period specified by regulations under –

   (a)   paragraph 49, in the case of securities;

   (b)   paragraph 39, in any other case.

## Best price

37  (1)  An enforcement agent must sell or dispose of controlled goods for the best price that can reasonably be obtained in accordance with this Schedule.

    (2)  That does not apply to money that can be used for paying any of the outstanding amount, unless the best price is more than its value if used in that way.

## Sale

38       Paragraphs 39 to 42 apply to the sale of controlled goods, except where –

         (a)   the controlled goods are securities, or

         (b)   the sale is by exchange of one currency for another.

39  (1)  The sale must not be before the end of the minimum period except with the agreement of the debtor and any co-owner.

    (2)  Regulations must specify the minimum period.

40  (1)  Before the sale, the enforcement agent must give notice of the date, time and place of the sale to the debtor and any co-owner.

    (2)  Regulations must state –

         (a)   the minimum period of notice;

         (b)   the form of the notice;

         (c)   what it must contain (besides the date, time and place of sale);

         (d)   how it must be given.

    (3)  The enforcement agent may replace a notice with a new notice, subject to any restriction in regulations.

    (4)  Any notice must be given within the permitted period.

    (5)  Unless extended the permitted period is 12 months beginning with the day on which the enforcement agent takes control of the goods.

    (6)  Any extension must be by agreement in writing between the creditor and debtor before the end of the period.

    (7)  They may extend the period more than once.

41  (1)  The sale must be by public auction unless the court orders otherwise.

    (2)  The court may make an order only on an application by the enforcement agent.

    (3)  Regulations may make provision about the types of sale the court may order.

    (4)  In an application for an order under sub-paragraph (2) the enforcement agent must state whether he has reason to believe that an enforcement power has become exercisable by another creditor against the debtor or a co-owner.

    (5)  If the enforcement agent states that he does, the court may not consider the application until notice of it has been given to the other creditor in accordance with regulations (or until the court is satisfied that an enforcement power is not exercisable by the other creditor against the debtor or a co-owner).

42       Regulations may make further provision about the sale of controlled goods, including in particular –

         (a)   requirements for advertising;

         (b)   provision about the conduct of a sale.

## Place of sale

43  (1)  Regulations may make provision about the place of sale of controlled goods.

    (2)  They may prescribe circumstances in which the sale may be held on premises where goods were found by the enforcement agent.

    (3)  Except where the regulations provide otherwise, the sale may not be held on those premises without the consent of the occupier.

    (4)  Paragraphs 44 to 46 apply if the sale may be held on those premises.

44  (1)  The enforcement agent and any person permitted by him –

    (a)  may enter the premises to conduct or attend the sale;

    (b)  may bring equipment onto the premises for the purposes of the sale.

  (2)  This paragraph authorises repeated entry to the premises.

  (3)  If necessary the enforcement agent may use reasonable force to enable the sale to be conducted and any person to enter under this paragraph.

45  (1)  The enforcement agent must on request show the debtor and any person who appears to him to be in charge of the premises evidence of –

    (a)  his identity, and

    (b)  his authority to enter and hold the sale on the premises.

  (2)  The request may be made before the enforcement agent enters the premises or while he is there.

46  The enforcement agent must leave the premises as effectively secured as he finds them.

## Holding and disposal of securities

47  Paragraphs 48 and 49 apply to securities as controlled goods.

48  (1)  Regulations may make provision about how securities are to be held and disposed of.

  (2)  In this Schedule, references to disposal include, in relation to securities, realising the sums secured or made payable by them, suing for the recovery of those sums or assigning the right to sue for their recovery.

  (3)  Regulations may in particular make provision for purposes corresponding to those for which provision is made in this Schedule in relation to the disposal of other controlled goods.

  (4)  The power to make regulations under this paragraph is subject to paragraph 49.

49  (1)  The creditor may sue in the name of the debtor, or in the name of any person in whose name the debtor might have sued, for the recovery of any sum secured or made payable by securities, when the time of payment arrives.

  (2)  Before any proceedings under sub-paragraph (1) are commenced or the securities are otherwise disposed of, the enforcement agent must give notice of the disposal to the debtor and any co-owner.

  (3)  Regulations must state –

    (a)  the minimum period of notice;

    (b)  the form of the notice;

    (c)  what it must contain;

    (d)  how it must be given.

  (4)  The enforcement agent may replace a notice with a new notice, subject to any restriction in regulations.

  (5)  Any notice must be given within the permitted period.

  (6)  Unless extended the permitted period is 12 months beginning with the time of payment.

  (7)  Any extension must be by agreement in writing between the creditor and debtor before the end of the period.

  (8)  They may extend the period more than once.

## Application of proceeds

50  (1)  Proceeds from the exercise of an enforcement power must be used to pay the amount outstanding.

  (2)  Proceeds are any of these –

(a)  proceeds of sale or disposal of controlled goods;

(b)  money taken in exercise of the power, if paragraph 37(1) does not apply to it.

(3)  The amount outstanding is the sum of these –

(a)  the amount of the debt which remains unpaid (or an amount that the creditor agrees to accept in full satisfaction of the debt);

(b)  any amounts recoverable out of proceeds in accordance with regulations under paragraph 62 (costs).

(4)  If the proceeds are less than the amount outstanding, which amounts in sub-paragraph (3)(a) and (b) must be paid, and how much of any amount, is to be determined in accordance with regulations.

(5)  If the proceeds are more than the amount outstanding, the surplus must be paid to the debtor.

(6)  If there is a co-owner of any of the goods, the enforcement agent must –

(a)  first pay the co-owner a share of the proceeds of those goods proportionate to his interest;

(b)  then deal with the rest of the proceeds under sub-paragraphs (1) to (5).

(7)  Regulations may make provision for resolving disputes about what share is due under sub-paragraph (6)(a).

## Passing of title

51  (1)  A purchaser of controlled goods acquires good title, with two exceptions.

(2)  The exceptions apply only if the goods are not the debtor's at the time of sale.

(3)  The first exception is where the purchaser, the creditor, the enforcement agent or a related party has notice that the goods are not the debtor's.

(4)  The second exception is where a lawful claimant has already made an application to the court claiming an interest in the goods.

(5)  A lawful claimant in relation to goods is a person who has an interest in them at the time of sale, other than an interest that was assigned or transferred to him while the property in the goods was bound for the purposes of the enforcement power.

(6)  A related party is any person who acts in exercise of an enforcement power, other than the creditor or enforcement agent.

(7)  'The court' has the same meaning as in paragraph 60.

## Abandonment of goods other than securities

52      Paragraphs 53 and 54 apply to controlled goods other than –

(a)  securities;

(b)  money to which paragraph 37(1) does not apply.

53  (1)  Controlled goods are abandoned if the enforcement agent does not give the debtor or any co-owner notice under paragraph 40 (notice of sale) within the permitted period.

(2)  Controlled goods are abandoned if they are unsold after a sale of which notice has been given in accordance with that paragraph.

(3)  Regulations may prescribe other circumstances in which controlled goods are abandoned.

54  (1)  If controlled goods are abandoned then, in relation to the enforcement power concerned, the following apply –

(a)  the enforcement power ceases to be exercisable;

(b)    as soon as reasonably practicable the enforcement agent must make the goods available for collection by the debtor, if he removed them from where he found them.

(2)    Regulations may make further provision about arrangements under sub-paragraph (1)(b), including in particular provision about the disposal of goods uncollected after a prescribed period.

(3)    Where the enforcement power was under a writ or warrant, sub-paragraph (1) does not affect any power to issue another writ or warrant.

## Abandonment of securities

55    Paragraphs 56 and 57 apply to securities as controlled goods.

56    (1)    Securities are abandoned if the enforcement agent does not give the debtor or any co-owner notice under paragraph 49 (notice of disposal) within the permitted period.

(2)    Securities are abandoned if they are not disposed of in accordance with a notice of disposal under that paragraph.

(3)    Regulations may prescribe other circumstances in which securities are abandoned.

57    (1)    If securities are abandoned then, in relation to the enforcement power concerned, the following apply –

(a)    the enforcement power ceases to be exercisable;

(b)    as soon as reasonably practicable the enforcement agent must make the securities available for collection by the debtor, if he removed them from where he found them.

(2)    Where the enforcement power was under a writ or warrant, sub-paragraph (1) does not affect any power to issue another writ or warrant.

## Payment of amount outstanding

58    (1)    This paragraph applies where the debtor pays the amount outstanding in full –

(a)    after the enforcement agent has taken control of goods, and

(b)    before they are sold or abandoned.

(2)    If the enforcement agent has removed the goods he must as soon as reasonably practicable make them available for collection by the debtor.

(3)    No further step may be taken under the enforcement power concerned.

(4)    For the purposes of this paragraph the amount outstanding is reduced by the value of any controlled goods consisting of money required to be used to pay that amount, and sub-paragraph (2) does not apply to that money.

59    (1)    This paragraph applies if a further step is taken despite paragraph 58(3).

(2)    The enforcement agent is not liable unless he had notice, when the step was taken, that the amount outstanding had been paid in full.

(3)    Sub-paragraph (2) applies to a related party as to the enforcement agent.

(4)    If the step taken is sale of any of the goods the purchaser acquires good title unless, at the time of sale, he or the enforcement agent had notice that the amount outstanding had been paid in full.

(5)    A person has notice that the amount outstanding has been paid in full if he would have found it out if he had made reasonable enquiries.

(6)    Sub-paragraphs (2) to (4) do not affect any right of the debtor or a co-owner to a remedy against any person other than the enforcement agent or a related party.

(7)    In this paragraph, 'related party' has the meaning given by paragraph 65(4).

## Third party claiming goods

60  (1)  This paragraph applies where a person makes an application to the court claiming that goods taken control of are his and not the debtor's.

(2)  After receiving notice of the application the enforcement agent must not sell the goods, or dispose of them (in the case of securities), unless directed by the court under this paragraph.

(3)  The court may direct the enforcement agent to sell or dispose of the goods if the applicant fails to make, or to continue to make, the required payments into court.

(4)  The required payments are –

(a)  payment on making the application (subject to sub-paragraph (5)) of an amount equal to the value of the goods, or to a proportion of it directed by the court;

(b)  payment, at prescribed times (on making the application or later), of any amounts prescribed in respect of the enforcement agent's costs of retaining the goods.

(5)  If the applicant makes a payment under sub-paragraph (4)(a) but the enforcement agent disputes the value of the goods, any underpayment is to be –

(a)  determined by reference to an independent valuation carried out in accordance with regulations, and

(b)  paid at the prescribed time.

(6)  If sub-paragraph (3) does not apply the court may still direct the enforcement agent to sell or dispose of the goods before the court determines the applicant's claim, if it considers it appropriate.

(7)  If the court makes a direction under sub-paragraph (3) or (6) –

(a)  paragraphs 38 to 49, and regulations under them, apply subject to any modification directed by the court;

(b)  the enforcement agent must pay the proceeds of sale or disposal into court.

(8)  In this paragraph 'the court', subject to rules of court, means –

(a)  the High Court, in relation to an enforcement power under a writ of the High Court;

(b)  a county court, in relation to an enforcement power under a warrant issued by a county court;

(c)  in any other case, the High Court or a county court.

## Application to assignee or transferee

61  (1)  This Schedule applies as follows where an interest of the debtor's in goods is assigned or transferred while the property in the goods is bound for the purposes of an enforcement power, and the enforcement agent –

(a)  knows that the assignee or transferee has an interest in the particular goods, or

(b)  would know, if he made reasonable enquiries.

(2)  These apply as if the assignee or transferee were a co-owner of the goods with the debtor –

(a)  paragraph 34 (inventory);

(b)  paragraph 36 (valuation);

(c)  paragraphs 39 to 41 (sale);

(d)  paragraph 59(6) (remedies after payment of amount outstanding).

(3)  If the interest of the assignee or transferee was acquired in good faith, for valuable consideration and without notice, paragraph 50(6) applies as if 'co-owner' included the assignee or transferee.

(4) If the interest of the assignee or transferee was not acquired in good faith, for valuable consideration and without notice, the enforcement agent must pay any surplus under paragraph 50(5) to the assignee or transferee and to the debtor (if he retains an interest).

(5) If the surplus is payable to two or more persons it must be paid in shares proportionate to their interests.

(6) Paragraph 5(3) and (4) ('good faith' and 'notice') apply for the purposes of this paragraph.

## Costs

62 (1) Regulations may make provision for the recovery by any person from the debtor of amounts in respect of costs of enforcement-related services.

(2) The regulations may provide for recovery to be out of proceeds or otherwise.

(3) The amount recoverable under the regulations in any case is to be determined by or under the regulations.

(4) The regulations may in particular provide for the amount, if disputed, to be assessed in accordance with rules of court.

(5) 'Enforcement-related services' means anything done under or in connection with an enforcement power, or in connection with obtaining an enforcement power, or any services used for the purposes of a provision of this Schedule or regulations under it.

## Limitation of liability for sale or payment of proceeds

63 (1) Any liability of an enforcement agent or related party to a lawful claimant for the sale of controlled goods is excluded except in two cases.

(2) The first exception is where at the time of the sale the enforcement agent had notice that the goods were not the debtor's, or not his alone.

(3) The second exception is where before sale the lawful claimant had made an application to the court claiming an interest in the goods.

(4) A lawful claimant in relation to goods is a person who has an interest in them at the time of sale, other than an interest that was assigned or transferred to him while the property in the goods was bound for the purposes of the enforcement power.

64 (1) Any liability of an enforcement agent or related party to a lawful claimant for paying over proceeds is excluded except in two cases.

(2) The first exception is where at the time of the payment he had notice that the goods were not the debtor's, or not his alone.

(3) The second exception is where before that time the lawful claimant had made an application to the court claiming an interest in the goods.

(4) A lawful claimant in relation to goods is a person who has an interest in them at the time of sale.

65 (1) Paragraphs 63 and 64 –

(a) do not affect the liability of a person other than the enforcement agent or a related party;

(b) do not apply to the creditor if he is the enforcement agent.

(2) The following apply for the purposes of those paragraphs.

(3) The enforcement agent or a related party has notice of something if he would have found it out if he had made reasonable enquiries.

(4) A related party is any person who acts in exercise of an enforcement power, other than the creditor or enforcement agent.

(5) 'The court' has the same meaning as in paragraph 60.

## Remedies available to the debtor

66 (1) This paragraph applies where an enforcement agent –

    (a) breaches a provision of this Schedule, or

    (b) acts under an enforcement power under a writ, warrant, liability order or other instrument that is defective.

  (2) The breach or defect does not make the enforcement agent, or a person he is acting for, a trespasser.

  (3) But the debtor may bring proceedings under this paragraph.

  (4) Subject to rules of court, the proceedings may be brought –

    (a) in the High Court, in relation to an enforcement power under a writ of the High Court;

    (b) in a county court, in relation to an enforcement power under a warrant issued by a county court;

    (c) in any other case, in the High Court or a county court.

  (5) In the proceedings the court may –

    (a) order goods to be returned to the debtor;

    (b) order the enforcement agent or a related party to pay damages in respect of loss suffered by the debtor as a result of the breach or of anything done under the defective instrument.

  (6) A related party is either of the following (if different from the enforcement agent) –

    (a) the person on whom the enforcement power is conferred,

    (b) the creditor.

  (7) Sub-paragraph (5) is without prejudice to any other powers of the court.

  (8) Sub-paragraph (5)(b) does not apply where the enforcement agent acted in the reasonable belief –

    (a) that he was not breaching a provision of this Schedule, or

    (b) (as the case may be) that the instrument was not defective.

  (9) This paragraph is subject to paragraph 59 in the case of a breach of paragraph 58(3).

## Remedies available to the creditor

67 If a debtor wrongfully interferes with controlled goods and the creditor suffers loss as a result, the creditor may bring a claim against the debtor in respect of the loss.

## Offences

68 (1) A person is guilty of an offence if he intentionally obstructs a person lawfully acting as an enforcement agent.

  (2) A person is guilty of an offence if he intentionally interferes with controlled goods without lawful excuse.

  (3) A person guilty of an offence under this paragraph is liable on summary conviction to –

    (a) imprisonment for a term not exceeding 51 weeks, or

    (b) a fine not exceeding level 4 on the standard scale, or

    (c) both.

(4)   In relation to an offence committed before the commencement of section 281(5) of the Criminal Justice Act 2003 (c. 44), the reference in sub-paragraph (3)(a) to 51 weeks is to be read as a reference to 6 months.

## Relation to insolvency provisions

69      This Schedule is subject to sections 183, 184 and 346 of the Insolvency Act 1986 (c. 45).

## SCHEDULE 13   TAKING CONTROL OF GOODS: AMENDMENTS

Section 62(3)

### Inclosure Act 1773 (c. 81)

1       The Inclosure Act 1773 is amended as follows.
2       (1)   Section 4 (expenses how to be defrayed) is amended as follows.
        (2)   For 'levied by distress and sale of the goods and chattels of' substitute 'recovered, by using the procedure in Schedule 12 to the Tribunals, Courts and Enforcement Act 2007 (taking control of goods), from'.
        (3)   Omit the words from 'rendering' to the end.
3       (1)   Section 16 (assessments to be levied for the improving of wastes where there are stinted commons) is amended as follows.
        (2)   For 'levied by distress and sale of the goods and chattels of' substitute 'recovered, by using the procedure in Schedule 12 to the Tribunals, Courts and Enforcement Act 2007 (taking control of goods), from'.
        (3)   Omit the words from 'rendering' to the end.

### Oaths Act 1775 (c. 39)

4       In the Oaths Act 1775 (justices to administer oaths for levying penalties etc.) at the end insert –

        'In this Act references to making a distress include references to using the procedure in Schedule 12 to the Tribunals, Courts and Enforcement Act 2007 (taking control of goods) to recover a sum.'

### Sale of Farming Stock Act 1816 (c. 50)

5       The Sale of Farming Stock Act 1816 ceases to have effect.

### Judgments Act 1838 (c. 110)

6       In the Judgments Act 1838 omit section 12 (sheriff may seize money, banknotes, etc.).

### Lands Clauses Consolidation Act 1845 (c. 18)

7       (1)   In section 91 of the Lands Clauses Consolidation Act 1845 (proceedings in case of refusal to deliver possession of lands) for 'levied by distress' substitute

'recovered by using the procedure in Schedule 12 to the Tribunals, Courts and Enforcement Act 2007 (taking control of goods),'.

(2)   This paragraph extends only to England and Wales.

## Inclosure Act 1845 (c. 118)

8      The Inclosure Act 1845 is amended as follows.

9      In section 151 (recovery of share of expenses) for 'levied by distress' substitute 'recovered by using the procedure in Schedule 12 to the Tribunals, Courts and Enforcement Act 2007 (taking control of goods).'

10     In section 159 (recovery of penalties and forfeitures) for the words from 'to levy' to the end substitute 'to recover such penalties and forfeitures by using the procedure in Schedule 12 to the Tribunals, Courts and Enforcement Act 2007 (taking control of goods).'

## Railways Clauses Act 1863 (c. 92)

11     The Railways Clauses Act 1863 is amended as follows.

12     In section 33 (recovery of money by distress) at the end insert –

'In this section as it applies in England and Wales –

(a)   for "levied by distress" substitute "recovered using the procedure in Schedule 12 to the Tribunals, Courts and Enforcement Act 2007 (taking control of goods)";

(b)   for "warrant of distress" substitute "warrant of control".'

13     In section 34 (several names in one warrant) at the end insert –

'In this section as it applies in England and Wales for "warrant of distress" substitute "warrant of control".'

## Summary Jurisdiction (Process) Act 1881 (c. 24)

14     The Summary Jurisdiction (Process) Act 1881 is amended as follows.

15     In section 5 (provision as to execution of process) after 'warrant of distress' in the first place insert 'or warrant of control'.

16     In section 8 (definitions) after 'warrant of distress,' insert 'any warrant of control,'.

## Bills of Sale Act (1878) Amendment Act 1882 (c. 43)

17     The Bills of Sale Act (1878) Amendment Act 1882 is amended as follows.

18     In section 7 (bill of sale with power to seize except in certain events to be void), in paragraph (2) after 'distrained' insert ', or taken control of using the power in Schedule 12 to the Tribunals, Courts and Enforcement Act 2007,'.

19     In section 14 (bill of sale not to protect chattels against poor and parochial rates), after 'warrant' insert, 'or subject to a warrant of control,'.

## Sheriffs Act 1887 (c. 55)

20     In section 20 of the Sheriffs Act 1887 (fees and poundage), after subsection (2) insert –

'(2A)    Subsection (2) does not apply to the execution of process under a power to use the procedure in Schedule 12 to the Tribunals, Courts and Enforcement Act 2007 (taking control of goods).'

## Deeds of Arrangement Act 1914 (c. 47)

21        In section 17 of the Deeds of Arrangement Act 1914 (preferential payment to creditor an offence), after 'by distress' insert 'or by using the procedure in Schedule 12 to the Tribunals, Courts and Enforcement Act 2007 (taking control of goods),'.

## Maintenance Orders (Facilities for Enforcement) Act 1920 (c. 33)

22    (1)    Section 6 of the Maintenance Orders (Facilities for Enforcement) Act 1920 (mode of enforcing orders) is amended as follows.
      (2)    In subsection (3), after 'distress' insert, 'control'.
      (3)    After subsection (3) insert –

            '(4)    For the purposes of its execution under subsection (3) in England and Wales, a warrant of distress has effect as a warrant of control.
            (5)    For the purposes of its execution under subsection (3) elsewhere than in England and Wales, a warrant of control has effect as a warrant of distress.'

## Agricultural Credits Act 1928 (c. 43)

23        In section 8 of the Agricultural Credits Act 1928 (supplemental provisions about agricultural charges), in subsection (7) after 'distress for' insert, 'or the exercise of a power to use the procedure in Schedule 12 to the Tribunals, Courts and Enforcement Act 2007 (taking control of goods) to recover,'.

## Reserve and Auxiliary Forces (Protection of Civil Interests) Act 1951 (c. 65)

24        In section 2 of the Reserve and Auxiliary Forces (Protection of Civil Interests) Act 1951 (general restrictions on execution and other remedies), in subsection (2)(a) after 'the levying of distress;' insert –

            'using the procedure in Schedule 12 to the Tribunals, Courts and Enforcement Act 2007 (taking control of goods);'.

## Agriculture (Miscellaneous Provisions) Act 1954 (c. 39)

25        In section 5 of the Agriculture (Miscellaneous Provisions) Act 1954 (power of Agricultural Land Tribunal to award costs), in subsection (3) for 'by execution issued from the county court' substitute 'under section 85 of the County Courts Act 1984'.

## Criminal Justice Act 1961 (c. 39)

26        In section 39 of the Criminal Justice Act 1961 (interpretation) after subsection (1) insert –

'(1ZA)   In the definition of "default" in subsection (1) the reference to want of sufficient distress to satisfy a fine or other sum includes a reference to circumstances where –

(a)   there is power to use the procedure in Schedule 12 to the Tribunals, Courts and Enforcement Act 2007 to recover the fine or other sum from a person, but

(b)   it appears, after an attempt has been made to exercise the power, that the person's goods are insufficient to pay the amount outstanding (as defined by paragraph 50(3) of that Schedule).'

## Compulsory Purchase Act 1965 (c. 56)

27      The Compulsory Purchase Act 1965 is amended as follows.

28  (1)  Section 13 (refusal to give possession to acquiring authority) is amended as follows.

    (2)  In subsection (4) for 'levied by distress' substitute 'recovered by using the procedure in Schedule 12 to the Tribunals, Courts and Enforcement Act 2007 (taking control of goods)'.

    (3)  Omit subsection (5).

29      Omit section 29 (irregularities in proceedings under the Act).

## Criminal Justice Act 1967 (c. 80)

30      In section 104 of the Criminal Justice Act 1967 (general provisions as to interpretation) after subsection (1) insert –

'(1A)   In the definition of "sentence of imprisonment" in subsection (1) the reference to want of sufficient distress to satisfy a sum includes a reference to circumstances where –

(a)   there is power to use the procedure in Schedule 12 to the Tribunals, Courts and Enforcement Act 2007 to recover the sum from a person, but

(b)   it appears, after an attempt has been made to exercise the power, that the person's goods are insufficient to pay the amount outstanding (as defined by paragraph 50(3) of that Schedule).'

## Sea Fisheries Act 1968 (c. 77)

31      In section 12 of the Sea Fisheries Act 1968 (recovery of fines imposed on master etc. or crew), in subsection (3) –

(a)   for 'warrants of distress)' substitute 'warrants), as they apply to warrants of the kinds mentioned there,';

(b)   omit the words from 'as they apply' to the end.

## Taxes Management Act 1970 (c. 9)

32      The Taxes Management Act 1970 is amended as follows.

33  (1)  Section 61 (distraint by collectors) is amended as follows.

    (2)  In subsection (1), after 'the collector may' insert

         ' –

(a)   in England and Wales, use the procedure in Schedule 12 to the Tribunals, Courts and Enforcement Act 2007 (taking control of goods) to recover that sum;

(b)   in Northern Ireland,'.

(3)   After subsection (1) insert –

'(1A)   Subsections (2) to (6) apply to distraint under subsection (1)(b).'

34        In section 62 (priority of claim for tax) at the end insert –

'(4)      This section does not extend to England and Wales.'

## Administration of Justice Act 1970 (c. 31)

35        In section 41 of the Administration of Justice Act 1970 (recovery of costs and compensation awarded by magistrates etc.) in subsection (3) for 'writ of fieri facias' substitute 'writ of control'.

## Attachment of Earnings Act 1971 (c. 32)

36        In section 3 of the Attachment of Earnings Act 1971 (application for order and conditions of court's power to make it), in subsection (4)(b), for 'distress' substitute 'taking control of goods'.

## Criminal Justice Act 1972 (c. 71)

37        In section 66 of the Criminal Justice Act 1972 (interpretation etc.), in subsection (2) omit the words from '"sentence of imprisonment"' to the end.

## Rehabilitation of Offenders Act 1974 (c. 53)

38        In section 1 of the Rehabilitation of Offenders Act 1974 (rehabilitated persons and spent convictions) after subsection (3) insert –

'(3A)   In subsection (3)(a), the reference to want of sufficient distress to satisfy a fine or other sum includes a reference to circumstances where –

(a)   there is power to use the procedure in Schedule 12 to the Tribunals, Courts and Enforcement Act 2007 to recover the fine or other sum from a person, but

(b)   it appears, after an attempt has been made to exercise the power, that the person's goods are insufficient to pay the amount outstanding (as defined by paragraph 50(3) of that Schedule).'

## Patents Act 1977 (c. 37)

39        The Patents Act 1977 is amended as follows.
40        In section 41 (amount of compensation of employees), in subsection (9) for 'by execution issued from the county court' substitute 'under section 85 of the County Courts Act 1984'.
41        In section 61 (proceedings for infringement of patent), in subsection (7)(a) for 'by execution issued from the county court' substitute 'under section 85 of the County Courts Act 1984'.

42        In section 93 (enforcement of orders for costs), in paragraph (a) for 'by execu-
          tion issued from the county court' substitute 'under section 85 of the County
          Courts Act 1984'.
43        In section 107 (costs and expenses in proceedings before the comptroller), in
          subsection (2) for 'by execution issued from the county court' substitute 'under
          section 85 of the County Courts Act 1984'.

## Customs and Excise Management Act 1979 (c. 2)

44        In section 149 of the Customs and Excise Management Act 1979 (non-payment
          of penalties etc: maximum terms of imprisonment) after subsection (1) insert –

          '(1A)   In subsection (1)(b) as it applies to a magistrates' court in England
                  or Wales the reference to default of sufficient distress to satisfy the
                  amount of the penalty is a reference to want of sufficient goods to
                  satisfy the amount, within the meaning given by section 79(4) of
                  the Magistrates' Courts Act 1980.'

## Magistrates' Courts Act 1980 (c. 43)

45        The Magistrates' Courts Act 1980 is amended as follows.
46   (1)  Section 76 (enforcement of sums adjudged to be paid) is amended as follows.
     (2)  In subsection (1) for 'issue a warrant of distress for the purpose of levying the
          sum' substitute 'issue a warrant of control for the purpose of recovering the
          sum'.
     (3)  In subsection (2)(a) –

          (a)   for 'warrant of distress' substitute 'warrant of control';
          (b)   for 'satisfy the sum with the costs and charges of levying the sum' substi-
                tute 'pay the amount outstanding, as defined by paragraph 50(3) of
                Schedule 12 to the Tribunals, Courts and Enforcement Act 2007'.

     (4)  In subsection (2)(b) for 'warrant of distress' substitute 'warrant of control'.
47        In section 77 (postponement of issue of warrant), in subsection (1) for 'warrant
          of distress' substitute 'warrant of control'.
48   (1)  Section 79 (release from custody and reduction of detention on payment) is
          amended as follows.
     (2)  In subsection (1) –

          (a)   for 'distress' in the first place substitute 'goods';
          (b)   for 'and distress' substitute ', or (as the case may be) on the payment of the
                amount outstanding,'.

     (3)  In subsection (2) –

          (a)   for 'distress' in the first place substitute 'goods';
          (b)   for the words from 'to so much of the said sum' to the end substitute

                ' –

                (a)   to the amount outstanding at the time the period of detention was
                      imposed, if the procedure in Schedule 12 to the Tribunals, Courts and
                      Enforcement Act 2007 (taking control of goods) had been used for
                      recovering the sum;
                (b)   otherwise, to so much of the sum as was due at that time.'

     (4)  After subsection (3) insert –

          '(4)   In this Act, references to want of sufficient goods to satisfy a sum of
                 money are references to circumstances where –

    (a)   a warrant of control has been issued for the sum to be recovered from a person, but

    (b)   it appears on the return to the warrant that the person's money and goods are insufficient to pay the amount outstanding.

  (5)  In this section, "the amount outstanding" has the meaning given by paragraph 50(3) of Schedule 12 to the Tribunals, Courts and Enforcement Act 2007.'

49    In section 80 (application of money found on defaulter to satisfy sum adjudged), in subsection (2) for 'distress' substitute 'goods'.

50    In section 81 (enforcement of fines imposed on young offenders) in subsections (1) and (3) for 'distress' substitute 'goods'.

51    (1)  Section 82 (restriction on power to impose imprisonment for default) is amended as follows.

  (2)  In subsection (3), for 'distress' substitute 'goods'.

  (3)  In subsection (4A)(a), for 'warrant of distress' substitute 'warrant of control'.

52    In section 87 (enforcement of payment of fines by High Court and county court) in subsection (1) for 'writ of fieri facias' substitute 'writ of control'.

53    (1)  Section 87A (fines imposed on companies) is amended as follows.

  (2)  In subsection (1)(b), for 'warrant of distress' substitute 'warrant of control'.

  (3)  For subsection (1)(c) substitute –

    '(c)   it appears on the return to the warrant that the company's money and goods are insufficient to pay the amount outstanding,'.

  (4)  At the end insert –

    '(3)   In this section, "the amount outstanding" has the meaning given by paragraph 50(3) of Schedule 12 to the Tribunals, Courts and Enforcement Act 2007.'

54    In section 88 (supervision pending payment) in subsections (4) and (6) for 'distress' substitute 'goods'.

55    In section 96 (civil debt: complaint for non-payment), in subsection (1) for 'distress' substitute 'goods'.

56    In section 120 (forfeiture of recognizance), in subsection (4) for 'warrant of distress' substitute 'warrant of control'.

57    (1)  In section 125 (warrants) subsection (2) is amended as follows.

  (2)  For 'warrant of distress', in the first place, substitute 'warrant of control'.

  (3)  Omit the words from 'This subsection' to the end.

58    (1)  Section 125A (civilian enforcement officers) is amended as follows.

  (2)  In subsection (3), for 'distress' substitute 'control'.

  (3)  In subsection (3A), for 'distress' substitute 'control'.

  (4)  In subsection (4), for 'against whom distress is levied' substitute ', in the case of a warrant of control, against whom the warrant is issued'.

59    In section 125B (execution by approved enforcement agency), in subsection (4) for 'against whom distress is levied' substitute ', in the case of a warrant of control, against whom the warrant is issued'.

60    In section 125CA (power to make disclosure order), in subsection (2) for 'distress' substitute 'control'.

61    (1)  Section 125D (execution by person not in possession of warrant) is amended as follows.

  (2)  Omit subsection (3)(c).

  (3)  In subsection (4), for 'against whom distress is levied' substitute ', in the case of a warrant of control, against whom the warrant is issued'.

62    In section 133 (consecutive terms of imprisonment) in subsections (4) and (5) for 'distress' substitute 'goods'.

63    (1)  Section 150 (interpretation) is amended as follows.

(2)  In subsection (1) in the definitions of 'impose imprisonment' and 'sentence', for 'distress' substitute 'goods'.

(3)  After subsection (3) insert –

'(3A)   References in this Act to want of sufficient goods to satisfy a fine or other sum of money have the meaning given by section 79(4).'

64      Omit section 151.

65      In Schedule 4A (powers of authorised officers executing warrants), omit paragraph 3.


## Supreme Court Act 1981 (c. 54)

66  (1)  Section 43ZA of the Supreme Court Act 1981 (power of High Court to vary committal in default) is amended as follows.

(2)  In subsection (1) for 'distress' in both places substitute 'goods'.

(3)  After subsection (2) insert –

'(3)   In subsection (1) references to want of sufficient goods to satisfy a sum are references to circumstances where –

(a)   there is power to use the procedure in Schedule 12 to the Tribunals, Courts and Enforcement Act 2007 to recover the sum from a person, but

(b)   it appears, after an attempt has been made to exercise the power, that the person's goods are insufficient to pay the amount outstanding (as defined by paragraph 50(3) of that Schedule).'


## British Fishing Boats Act 1983 (c. 8)

67      In section 5 of the British Fishing Boats Act 1983 (recovery of fines), in subsection (3) –

(a)   for 'warrants of distress)' substitute 'warrants), as they apply to warrants of the kinds mentioned there,';

(b)   omit the words from 'as they apply' to the end.


## County Courts Act 1984 (c. 28)

68      The County Courts Act 1984 is amended as follows.

69  (1)  Section 85 (execution of judgments or orders for payment of money) is amended as follows.

(2)  In subsection (1), for the words from 'by execution' to the end substitute 'under a warrant under subsection (2).'

(3)  In subsection (2) –

(a)   for 'warrant of execution in the nature of a writ of fieri facias' substitute 'warrant of control';

(b)   for the words from 'levy' to the end substitute 'use the procedure in Schedule 12 to the Tribunals, Courts and Enforcement Act 2007 (taking control of goods) to recover the money payable under the judgment or order.'

(4)  After that subsection insert –

'(2A)   The person to whom a warrant under subsection (2) must be directed is to be determined in accordance with arrangements made by a person authorised by or on behalf of the Lord Chancellor.'

(5)   Omit subsection (3).

70   (1)   Section 86 (execution of orders for payment by instalments) is amended as follows.

(2)   In subsection (1) for 'execution on the order' substitute 'a warrant of control to recover any of that sum'.

(3)   In subsection (2) –

(a)   for 'execution is to issue' substitute 'a warrant of control is to be issued';

(b)   for 'execution may issue' substitute 'a warrant of control may be issued'.

(4)   In subsection (3) –

(a)   for 'execution or successive executions may issue' substitute 'a warrant or successive warrants of control may be issued';

(b)   for the words from 'no execution' to 'it issues' substitute 'no warrant of control may be issued unless when it is issued'.

71   (1)   Section 87 (execution to be superseded on payment) is amended as follows.

(2)   In subsection (1) –

(a)   for 'warrant of execution' substitute 'warrant of control';

(b)   for 'levied' substitute 'recovered'.

(3)   Omit subsection (2).

(4)   For the heading 'Execution to be superseded on payment' substitute 'Indorsement of amount on warrant'.

72      Omit sections 89 to 91.

73      In section 92 (penalty for rescuing goods seized), after subsection (2) insert –

'(3)   This section does not apply in the case of goods seized under Schedule 12 to the Tribunals, Courts and Enforcement Act 2007.'

74      Omit sections 93 to 100.

75      In section 101 (interpleader by district judge), after subsection (3) insert –

'(4)   This section does not apply in the case of goods seized under Schedule 12 to the Tribunals, Courts and Enforcement Act 2007.'

76      Omit sections 102 and 103.

77      In section 104 (information as to writs and warrants of execution) in subsection (2) for 'A bailiff of a county court' substitute 'The person to whom a warrant issued by a county court is directed'.

78      Omit section 123.

79   (1)   Section 124 (liability of bailiff for neglect to levy execution) is amended as follows.

(2)   In subsection (1) –

(a)   for the words from 'a bailiff' to 'the execution' substitute 'a county court issues a warrant of execution, control, possession or delivery and the person to whom it is directed loses the opportunity of executing it';

(b)   for 'judge of that court' substitute 'district judge'.

(3)   In subsection (2) –

(a)   for 'the bailiff' substitute 'that person';

(b)   for 'execution' substitute 'warrant was'.

80   In section 125 (irregularity in executing warrants) in subsection (1) after 'but' insert ', except in the case of a warrant of control (to which Schedule 12 to the Tribunals, Courts and Enforcement Act 2007 applies),'.

81   (1)   Section 126 (actions against bailiffs acting under warrants) is amended as follows.

(2)   In subsection (3) omit the words from 'but' to the end.

(3)   In subsection (4) –

    (a)   after 'section' insert '"bailiff" in relation to a warrant means the person to whom the warrant is directed, and';

    (b)   omit 'bailiff';

    (c)   for 'a bailiff' substitute 'that person'.

(4)  After subsection (4) insert –

    '(5)   This section does not apply to an action for anything done under a power to use the procedure in Schedule 12 to the Tribunals, Courts and Enforcement Act 2007.'

82   In section 147 (interpretation) in subsection (1) omit the definition of 'bailiff'.

## Finance Act 1984 (c. 43)

83      In the Finance Act 1984 omit section 16 (unpaid car tax and VAT: distress).

## Gas Act 1986 (c. 44)

84      In paragraph 29 of Schedule 2B to the Gas Act 1986 (gas meters and fittings not to be subject to distress) in sub-paragraph (1)(a) after 'liable' insert 'to be taken control of under Schedule 12 to the Tribunals, Courts and Enforcement Act 2007, or'.

## Insolvency Act 1986 (c. 45)

85      In section 436 of the Insolvency Act 1986 (expressions used generally) insert in the appropriate place –

   '"distress" includes use of the procedure in Schedule 12 to the Tribunals, Courts and Enforcement Act 2007, and references to levying distress, seizing goods and related expressions shall be construed accordingly;'.

## Dartford-Thurrock Crossing Act 1988 (c. 20)

86  (1)  Section 15 of the Dartford-Thurrock Crossing Act 1988 (termination: supplementary provisions) is amended as follows.

   (2)  In subsection (2) –

    (a)   after 'distress' in the first place insert 'or any power to use the procedure in Schedule 12 to the Tribunals, Courts and Enforcement Act 2007 (taking control of goods)';

    (b)   after 'levied' insert 'or that power was exercised'.

   (3)  In subsection (3) after 'levied' insert 'or the power there mentioned was exercisable'.

## Local Government Finance Act 1988 (c. 41)

87      The Local Government Finance Act 1988 is amended as follows.

88      After section 62 insert –

   **'62A   Recovery by taking control of goods**

   Where a liability order has been made against a person under regulations under Schedule 9, the billing authority may use the procedure in Schedule 12 to the Tribunals, Courts and Enforcement Act 2007 (taking control of goods) to recover the amount in respect of which the order was made, to the extent that it remains unpaid.'

89 (1) Schedule 9 (non-domestic rating: administration) is amended as follows.
   (2) In paragraph 1 for 'recovery' substitute 'the recovery, otherwise than under Schedule 12 to the Tribunals, Courts and Enforcement Act 2007 (taking control of goods),'.
   (3) In paragraph 3 –
     (a) omit sub-paragraph (2)(b);
     (b) in sub-paragraph (4)(b), after 'method' in the second place insert 'provided for in section 62A above or'.

## Electricity Act 1989 (c. 29)

90 In paragraph 11 of Schedule 6 to the Electricity Act 1989 (electrical plant etc not to be liable to be taken in execution), in sub-paragraph (2)(b) after 'liable' insert 'to be taken control of under Schedule 12 to the Tribunals, Courts and Enforcement Act 2007, or'.

## Companies Act 1989 (c. 40)

91 In section 180 of the Companies Act 1989 (proceedings against market property by unsecured creditors) in subsection (1) after 'levied,' insert 'and no power to use the procedure in Schedule 12 to the Tribunals, Courts and Enforcement Act 2007 (taking control of goods) may be exercised,'.

## New Roads and Street Works Act 1991 (c. 22)

92 (1) Paragraph 3 of Schedule 1 to the New Roads and Street Works Act 1991 (recovery of property taken in distress etc.) is amended as follows.
   (2) In sub-paragraph (1) –
     (a) after 'distress' in the first place insert 'or under any power to use the procedure in Schedule 12 to the Tribunals, Courts and Enforcement Act 2007 (taking control of goods)';
     (b) after 'levied' insert 'or that power was exercised'.
   (3) In sub-paragraph (2) –
     (a) For 'This' substitute 'Sub-paragraph (1)';
     (b) after 'levied' insert 'or the power mentioned there was exercisable'.

## Child Support Act 1991 (c. 48)

93 The Child Support Act 1991 is amended as follows.
94 (1) Section 35 (enforcement of liability orders by distress) is amended as follows.
   (2) In the heading for 'distress' substitute 'taking control of goods'.
   (3) In subsection (1) for the words from 'levy' to the end substitute 'use the procedure in Schedule 12 to the Tribunals, Courts and Enforcement Act 2007 (taking control of goods) to recover the amount in respect of which the order was made, to the extent that it remains unpaid.'
   (4) Omit subsections (2) to (8).
95 In section 39A (commitment to prison and disqualification from driving), in subsection (1)(a), for 'levy an amount by distress under this Act' substitute 'recover an amount by virtue of section 35(1)'.

96          In section 40 (commitment to prison) for subsection (4)(a)(i) substitute –

'(i)    the amount outstanding, as defined by paragraph 50(3) of Schedule 12 to the Tribunals, Courts and Enforcement Act 2007 (taking control of goods); and'.

97          In section 40B (disqualification from driving: further provision) for subsection (3)(a) substitute –

'(a)    the amount outstanding, as defined by paragraph 50(3) of Schedule 12 to the Tribunals, Courts and Enforcement Act 2007 (taking control of goods); and'.

## Water Industry Act 1991 (c. 56)

98          In section 179 of the Water Industry Act 1991 (vesting of works in undertaker), in subsection (4)(b) after 'liable' insert 'to be taken control of under Schedule 12 to the Tribunals, Courts and Enforcement Act 2007, or'.

## Water Resources Act 1991 (c. 57)

99          In Schedule 15 to the Water Resources Act 1991 (supplemental provisions with respect to drainage charges), in paragraph 12(2)(b) for 'warrant of distress' substitute 'warrant of control'.

## Land Drainage Act 1991 (c. 59)

100         In section 54 of the Land Drainage Act 1991 (powers for enforcing payment of drainage rates), in subsection (2)(b) for 'warrant of distress' substitute 'warrant of control'.

## Social Security Administration Act 1992 (c. 5)

101         The Social Security Administration Act 1992 is amended as follows.
102         In section 71 (overpayments: general), in subsection (10)(a) for 'by execution issued from the county court' substitute 'under section 85 of the County Courts Act 1984'.
103         In section 75 (overpayments of housing benefit), in subsection (7)(a) for 'by execution issued from the county court' substitute 'under section 85 of the County Courts Act 1984'.
104 (1)     Section 121A (recovery of contributions etc in England and Wales) is amended as follows.
    (2)     In subsection (1) –

(a)    in paragraph (b) after 'relates' insert '("the sums due")';
(b)    for the words from 'distrain' to the end substitute 'use the procedure in Schedule 12 to the Tribunals, Courts and Enforcement Act 2007 (taking control of goods) to recover the sums due'.

    (3)     Omit subsections (2) to (8) and (10).

## Local Government Finance Act 1992 (c. 14)

105         The Local Government Finance Act 1992 is amended as follows.

106      In section 14 (administration, penalties and enforcement), after subsection (3) insert –

'(4)   Where a liability order has been made against a person under regulations under Schedule 4, the billing authority concerned may use the procedure in Schedule 12 to the Tribunals, Courts and Enforcement Act 2007 (taking control of goods) to recover the amount in respect of which the order was made, to the extent that it remains unpaid.'

107  (1)   Schedule 4 (enforcement: England and Wales) is amended as follows.

(2)   In paragraph 1(1) and (2) after 'recovery' insert ', otherwise than under Schedule 12 to the Tribunals, Courts and Enforcement Act 2007 (taking control of goods),'.

(3)   In paragraph 5 (attachment of earnings etc) –

(a)   in sub-paragraph (1A)(a) for '; and' substitute '(unless paragraph (b) applies);';

(b)   in sub-paragraph (1A)(b) for sub-paragraph (i) and the words before it substitute –

'(b)   where a person authorised to act under the power conferred by section 14(4) (power to use the procedure in Schedule 12 to the Tribunals, Courts and Enforcement Act 2007) has reported to the authority concerned that he was unable (for whatever reason) to find sufficient goods of the debtor to pay the amount outstanding –

(i)   the amount outstanding at the time when the attachment of earnings order is made, and';

(c)   at the end insert –

'(9)   In this paragraph "the amount outstanding" has the meaning given by paragraph 50(3) of Schedule 12 to the Tribunals, Courts and Enforcement Act 2007.'

(4)   Omit paragraph 7 (distress).

(5)   In paragraph 8 (commitment to prison) –

(a)   in sub-paragraph (1)(a) –

(i)   omit the words from 'an authority' to 'paragraph 7 above';

(ii)   for the words from 'the person' to 'levy the amount' substitute 'there are insufficient goods to satisfy an amount under section 14(4)';

(b)   after sub-paragraph (1) insert –

'(1A)   In sub-paragraph (1) the reference to insufficient goods to satisfy an amount under section 14(4) is a reference to circumstances where a person authorised to act under the power conferred by section 14(4) (power to use the procedure in Schedule 12 to the Tribunals, Courts and Enforcement Act 2007) has reported to the authority concerned that he was unable (for whatever reason) to find sufficient goods of the debtor to pay the amount outstanding.';

(c)   for sub-paragraph (2)(a) substitute –

'(a)   the amount outstanding at the time when the warrant of commitment is issued; and';

(d)   at the end insert –

'(4)   In this paragraph "the amount outstanding" has the meaning given by paragraph 50(3) of Schedule 12 to the Tribunals, Courts and Enforcement Act 2007.'

(6) In paragraph 12 (relationship between remedies) in sub-paragraph (1) –

    (a)  omit paragraph (c);

    (b)  in paragraph (d), for 'distress' substitute 'the power conferred by section 14(4)';

    (c)  in paragraph (e), for 'distress' substitute 'exercise of the power conferred by section 14(4)';

    (d)  in paragraph (f), for 'distress' substitute 'exercise of the power conferred by section 14(4)'.

(7) Omit paragraph 19 (3).

## Trade Union and Labour Relations (Consolidation) Act 1992 (c. 52)

108    Schedule A1 to the Trade Union and Labour Relations (Consolidation) Act 1992 (collective bargaining: recognition) is amended as follows.

109 (1)  Paragraph 19E is amended as follows.

(2)  In sub-paragraph (5) for 'by execution issued from that court' substitute 'under section 85 of the County Courts Act 1984'.

(3)  In sub-paragraph (6) for the words from the beginning to 'carried out' substitute 'Where a warrant of control is issued under section 85 of the 1984 Act to recover an amount in accordance with sub-paragraph (5), the power conferred by the warrant is exercisable'.

110 (1)  Paragraph 28 is amended as follows.

(2)  In sub-paragraph (6) for 'by execution issued from that court' substitute 'under section 85 of the County Courts Act 1984'.

(3)  In sub-paragraph (6A) for the words from the beginning to 'carried out' substitute 'Where a warrant of control is issued under section 85 of the 1984 Act to recover an amount in accordance with sub-paragraph (6), the power conferred by the warrant is exercisable'.

111 (1)  Paragraph 120 is amended as follows.

(2)  In sub-paragraph (6) for 'by execution issued from that court' substitute 'under section 85 of the County Courts Act 1984'.

(3)  In sub-paragraph (6A) for the words from the beginning to 'carried out' substitute 'Where a warrant of control is issued under section 85 of the 1984 Act to recover an amount in accordance with sub-paragraph (6), the power conferred by the warrant is exercisable'.

## Railways Act 1993 (c. 43)

112    In section 27 of the Railways Act 1993 (transfer of franchise assets and shares), in subsection (6) after 'levied' insert 'and no power to use the procedure in Schedule 12 to the Tribunals, Courts and Enforcement Act 2007 may be exercised'.

## Finance Act 1994 (c. 9)

113 (1)  The Finance Act 1994 is amended as follows.

114    After section 10 insert –

    '10A   Breaches of controlled goods agreements

(1) This section applies where an enforcement agent acting under the power conferred by section 51(A1) of the Finance Act 1997 (power to use the procedure in Schedule 12 to the Tribunals, Courts and Enforcement Act 2007) has entered into a controlled goods agreement with the person against whom the power is exercisable ("the person in default").

(2) In this section, "controlled goods agreement" has the meaning given by paragraph 13(4) of that Schedule.

(3) Subject to subsection (4) below, if the person in default removes or disposes of goods (or permits their removal or disposal) in breach of the controlled goods agreement, he is liable to a penalty equal to half of the unpaid duty or other amount recoverable under section 51(A1) of the Finance Act 1997.

(4) The person in default shall not be liable to a penalty under subsection (3) above if he satisfies the Commissioners or, on appeal, an appeal tribunal that there is a reasonable excuse for the breach in question.

(5) This section extends only to England and Wales.'

115    In section 11 (breaches of walking possession agreements), for subsection (5) substitute –

'(5)   This section extends only to Northern Ireland.'

116 (1) Schedule 7 (insurance premium tax) is amended as follows.

(2) After paragraph 18 insert –

'18A(1)   This paragraph applies where an enforcement agent acting under the power conferred by section 51(A1) of the Finance Act 1997 (power to use the procedure in Schedule 12 to the Tribunals, Courts and Enforcement Act 2007) has entered into a controlled goods agreement with the person against whom the power is exercisable ("the person in default").

(2) In this paragraph, "controlled goods agreement" has the meaning given by paragraph 13(4) of that Schedule.

(3) Subject to sub-paragraph (4) below, if the person in default removes or disposes of goods (or permits their removal or disposal) in breach of the controlled goods agreement, he is liable to a penalty equal to half of the tax or other amount recoverable under section 51(A1) of the Finance Act 1997.

(4) The person in default shall not be liable to a penalty under sub-paragraph (3) above if he satisfies the Commissioners or, on appeal, an appeal tribunal, that there is a reasonable excuse for the breach in question.

(5) This paragraph extends only to England and Wales.'

(3) In paragraph 19, for sub-paragraph (5) substitute –

'(5)   This paragraph extends only to Northern Ireland.'

## Value Added Tax Act 1994 (c. 23)

117    The Value Added Tax Act 1994 is amended as follows.

118    In section 48 (VAT representatives), in subsection (7A) after 'enforcement' insert 'by taking control of goods or, in Northern Ireland,'.

119    After section 67 (failure to notify and unauthorised invoices) insert –

'67A   Breach of controlled goods agreement

(1) This section applies where an enforcement agent acting under the power conferred by section 51(A1) of the Finance Act 1997 (power to

use the procedure in Schedule 12 to the Tribunals, Courts and Enforcement Act 2007) has entered into a controlled goods agreement with the person against whom the power is exercisable ("the person in default").

(2)    In this section, "controlled goods agreement" has the meaning given by paragraph 13(4) of that Schedule.

(3)    Subject to subsection (4) below, if the person in default removes or disposes of goods (or permits their removal or disposal) in breach of the controlled goods agreement, he is liable to a penalty equal to half of the VAT or other amount recoverable under section 51(A1) of the Finance Act 1997.

(4)    The person in default shall not be liable to a penalty under subsection (3) above if he satisfies the Commissioners or, on appeal, a tribunal that there is a reasonable excuse for the breach in question.

(5)    This section extends only to England and Wales.'

120    In section 68 (breach of walking possession agreements) for subsection (5) substitute –

'(5)    This section extends only to Northern Ireland.'

## Pensions Act 1995 (c. 26)

121    In section 10 of the Pensions Act 1995 (civil penalties), in subsection (8A)(a) for 'by execution issued from the county court' substitute 'under section 85 of the County Courts Act 1984'.

## Finance Act 1996 (c. 8)

122    Schedule 5 to the Finance Act 1996 (landfill tax) is amended as follows.

123    After paragraph 23 insert –

'Controlled Goods Agreements

23A(1)    This paragraph applies where an enforcement agent acting under the power conferred by section 51(A1) of the Finance Act 1997 (power to use the procedure in Schedule 12 to the Tribunals, Courts and Enforcement Act 2007) has entered into a controlled goods agreement with the person against whom the power is exercisable ("the person in default").

(2)    In this paragraph, "controlled goods agreement" has the meaning given by paragraph 13(4) of that Schedule.

(3)    If the person in default removes or disposes of goods (or permits their removal or disposal) in breach of the controlled goods agreement, he is liable to a penalty equal to half of the tax or other amount recoverable under section 51(A1) of the Finance Act 1997.

(4)    The person in default shall not be liable to a penalty under sub-paragraph (3) above if he satisfies the Commissioners or, on appeal, an appeal tribunal, that there is a reasonable excuse for the breach in question.

(5)    This paragraph extends only to England and Wales.'

124    In paragraph 24, for sub-paragraph (4) substitute –

'(4)    This paragraph extends only to Northern Ireland.'

## Employment Tribunals Act 1996 (c. 17)

125    In section 15 of the Employment Tribunals Act 1996 (enforcement), in subsection (1) for 'by execution issued from the county court' substitute 'under section 85 of the County Courts Act 1984'.

## Finance Act 1997 (c. 16)

126 (1)    Section 51 of the Finance Act 1997 (enforcement by distress) is amended as follows.

(2)    Before subsection (1) insert –

'(A1)    The Commissioners may, in England and Wales, use the procedure in Schedule 12 to the Tribunals, Courts and Enforcement Act 2007 (taking control of goods) to recover any of these that a person refuses or neglects to pay –

(a)    any amount of relevant tax due from him;

(b)    any amount recoverable as if it were relevant tax due from him.'

(3)    In subsection (1) after 'by regulations' insert 'not having effect in England and Wales or Scotland'.

(4)    Omit subsection (7).

## Social Security (Recovery of Benefits) Act 1997 (c. 27)

127    In section 7 of the Social Security (Recovery of Benefits) Act 1997 (recovery of payments due under section 6), in subsection (4) for 'by execution issued from the county court' substitute 'under section 85 of the County Courts Act 1984'.

## National Minimum Wage Act 1998 (c. 39)

128    In section 21 of the National Minimum Wage Act 1998 (financial penalty for non-compliance), in subsection (5)(a) for 'by execution issued from the county court' substitute 'under section 85 of the County Courts Act 1984'.

## Road Traffic (NHS Charges) Act 1999 (c. 3)

129    In section 5 of the Road Traffic (NHS Charges) Act 1999 (recovery of NHS charges), in subsection (4) (so far as it continues to have effect) for 'by execution issued from the county court' substitute 'under section 85 of the County Courts Act 1984'.

## Greater London Authority Act 1999 (c. 29)

130    In section 216 of the Greater London Authority Act 1999 (protection of key system assets), in subsection (4) after 'levied' insert 'and no power to use the procedure in Schedule 12 to the Tribunals, Courts and Enforcement Act 2007 (taking control of goods) may be exercised'.

## *Powers of Criminal Courts (Sentencing) Act 2000 (c. 6)*

131   The Powers of Criminal Courts (Sentencing) Act 2000 is amended as follows.

132 (1)   Section 78 (limit on magistrates' courts' power to impose imprisonment etc.) is (until its repeal by the Criminal Justice Act 2003 (c. 44) comes into force) amended as follows.

(2)   In subsection (4) for 'distress' substitute 'goods'.

(3)   After subsection (4) insert –

'(4A)   In subsection (4) the reference to want of sufficient goods to satisfy a fine is a reference to circumstances where –

(a)   there is power to use the procedure in Schedule 12 to the Tribunals, Courts and Enforcement Act 2007 to recover the fine from a person, but

(b)   it appears, after an attempt has been made to exercise the power, that the person's goods are insufficient to pay the amount outstanding (as defined by paragraph 50(3) of that Schedule).'

133 (1)   Section 163 (general definition) is amended as follows.

(2)   The existing words become subsection (1).

(3)   After that subsection insert –

'(2)   In the definition of "sentence of imprisonment" in subsection (1) the reference to want of sufficient distress to satisfy a sum includes a reference to circumstances where –

(a)   there is power to use the procedure in Schedule 12 to the Tribunals, Courts and Enforcement Act 2007 to recover the sum from a person, but

(b)   it appears, after an attempt has been made to exercise the power, that the person's goods are insufficient to pay the amount outstanding (as defined by paragraph 50(3) of that Schedule).'

## *Financial Services and Markets Act 2000 (c. 8)*

134   In Schedule 17 to the Financial Services and Markets Act 2000 (the ombudsman scheme), in paragraph 16(a) for 'by execution issued from the county court' substitute 'under section 85 of the County Courts Act 1984'.

## *Finance Act 2000 (c. 17)*

135   Schedule 6 to the Finance Act 2000 (climate change levy) is amended as follows.

136   After paragraph 89 insert –

'*Controlled goods agreements*

89A(1)   This paragraph applies where an enforcement agent acting under the power conferred by section 51(A1) of the Finance Act 1997 (power to use the procedure in Schedule 12 to the Tribunals, Courts and Enforcement Act 2007) has entered into a controlled goods agreement with the person against whom the power is exercisable ("the person in default").

(2)   In this paragraph, "controlled goods agreement" has the meaning given by paragraph 13(4) of that Schedule.

(3)   Subject to sub-paragraph (4), if the person in default removes or disposes of goods (or permits their removal or disposal) in breach

of the controlled goods agreement, he is liable to a penalty equal to half of the levy or other amount recoverable under section 51(A1) of the Finance Act 1997.

(4)    The person in default shall not be liable to a penalty under sub-paragraph (3) above if he satisfies the Commissioners or, on appeal, an appeal tribunal, that there is a reasonable excuse for the breach in question.

(5)    This paragraph extends only to England and Wales.'

137    In paragraph 90 for sub-paragraph (5) substitute –

'(5)   This paragraph extends only to Northern Ireland.'

## Postal Services Act 2000 (c. 26)

138    In section 104 of the Postal Services Act 2000 (inviolability of mails), in subsection (2) after paragraph (b) insert –

'(ba)   in England and Wales, being taken control of under Schedule 12 to the Tribunals, Courts and Enforcement Act 2007,'.

## Finance Act 2001 (c. 9)

139    Schedule 5 to the Finance Act 2001 (aggregates levy: recovery and interest) is amended as follows.

140    After paragraph 14 insert –

'Controlled goods agreements

14A(1)  This paragraph applies where an enforcement agent acting under the power conferred, by virtue of paragraph 14 above, by section 51(A1) of the Finance Act 1997 (power to use the procedure in Schedule 12 to the Tribunals, Courts and Enforcement Act 2007) has entered into a controlled goods agreement with the person against whom the power is exercisable ("the person in default").

(2)    In this paragraph, "controlled goods agreement" has the meaning given by paragraph 13(4) of that Schedule.

(3)    Subject to sub-paragraph (4), if the person in default removes or disposes of goods (or permits their removal or disposal) in breach of the controlled goods agreement, he is liable to a penalty equal to half of the levy or other amount recoverable under section 51(A1) of the Finance Act 1997.

(4)    The person in default shall not be liable to a penalty under sub-paragraph (3) above if he satisfies the Commissioners or, on appeal, an appeal tribunal, that there is a reasonable excuse for the breach in question.

(5)    This paragraph extends only to England and Wales.'

141    In paragraph 15 for sub-paragraph (5) substitute –

'(5)   This paragraph extends only to Northern Ireland.'

## Proceeds of Crime Act 2002 (c. 29)

142    The Proceeds of Crime Act 2002 is amended as follows.

143    In section 58 (restraint orders: restrictions), in subsection (2) after 'levied' insert ', and no power to use the procedure in Schedule 12 to the Tribunals, Courts and Enforcement Act 2007 (taking control of goods) may be exercised,'.

144    In section 59 (enforcement receivers: restrictions), in subsection (2) after 'levied' insert ', and no power to use the procedure in Schedule 12 to the Tribunals, Courts and Enforcement Act 2007 (taking control of goods) may be exercised,'.

145    In section 60 (Director's receivers: restrictions), in subsection (2) after 'levied' insert ', and no power to use the procedure in Schedule 12 to the Tribunals, Courts and Enforcement Act 2007 (taking control of goods) may be exercised,'.

146    In section 253 (interim receiving orders: restriction on proceedings and remedies) in subsection (1)(b) after 'levied' insert ', and no power to use the procedure in Schedule 12 to the Tribunals, Courts and Enforcement Act 2007 (taking control of goods) may be exercised,'.

## Finance Act 2003 (c. 14)

147 (1)  Schedule 12 to the Finance Act 2003 (stamp duty land tax: collection and recovery of tax) is amended as follows.

(2)  After paragraph 1 insert –

'Recovery of tax by taking control of goods

1A    In England and Wales, if a person neglects or refuses to pay the sum charged, the collector may use the procedure in Schedule 12 to the Tribunals, Courts and Enforcement Act 2007 (taking control of goods) to recover the sum.'

(3)  In paragraph 2(1) omit 'England and Wales or'.

## Courts Act 2003 (c. 39)

148    The Courts Act 2003 is amended as follows.

149    In Part 9 of Schedule 5 (operation of collection orders after increase imposed), in paragraph 38(1)(a), for 'warrant of distress' substitute 'warrant of control'.

150    In Schedule 6 (discharge of fines by unpaid work), in paragraph 2(1)(a)(i), for 'warrant of distress' substitute 'warrant of control'.

151 (1)  Schedule 7 (High Court writs of execution) is amended as follows.

(2)  In paragraph 4, after sub-paragraph (1) insert –

'(1A)    But it is subject to Schedule 12 to the Tribunals, Courts and Enforcement Act 2007 in the case of a writ conferring power to use the procedure in that Schedule.'

(3)  For paragraph 6 substitute –

'6(1)    Paragraph 7 applies to any writ of execution against goods which is issued from the High Court.

(2)    Paragraphs 8 to 11 –

(a)    do not apply to any writ that confers power to use the procedure in Schedule 12 to the Tribunals, Courts and Enforcement Act 2007, but

(b)    apply to any other writ of execution against goods which is issued from the High Court.'

(4)  Omit paragraph 8(5).

## Health and Social Care (Community Health and Standards) Act 2003 (c. 43)

152    In section 155 of the Health and Social Care (Community Health and Standards) Act 2003 (recovery of NHS charges), in subsection (7) for 'by execution issued

from the county court' substitute 'under section 85 of the County Courts Act 1984'.

## *Criminal Justice Act 2003 (c. 44)*

153    The Criminal Justice Act 2003 is amended as follows.

154 (1)  Section 154 (general limit on magistrates' power to impose imprisonment) is amended as follows.

   (2)  In subsections (4) and (6) for 'distress' substitute 'goods'.

   (3)  After subsection (7) insert –

'(8)  In this section references to want of sufficient goods to satisfy a fine or other sum of money have the meaning given by section 79(4) of the Magistrates' Courts Act 1980.'

155    In section 305 (interpretation of Part 12) after subsection (1) insert –

'(1A)  In the definition of "sentence of imprisonment" in subsection (1) the reference to want of sufficient distress to satisfy a sum includes a reference to circumstances where –

(a)  there is power to use the procedure in Schedule 12 to the Tribunals, Courts and Enforcement Act 2007 to recover the sum from a person, but

(b)  it appears, after an attempt has been made to exercise the power, that the person's goods are insufficient to pay the amount outstanding (as defined by paragraph 50(3) of that Schedule).'

## *Traffic Management Act 2004 (c. 18)*

156    In the Traffic Management Act 2004 omit –

(a)  section 82(3)(a);

(b)  section 83.

## *Income Tax Act 2007 (c. 3)*

157    In section 955(4) of the Income Tax Act 2007 (proceedings before set-off claim is made) after 'attachment' insert 'or under Schedule 12 to the Tribunals, Courts and Enforcement Act 2007 (taking control of goods)'.

## SCHEDULE 14   RENT ARREARS RECOVERY: AMENDMENTS

Section 86

### *Distress for Rent Act 1689 (c. 5)*

1    The Distress for Rent Act 1689 ceases to have effect.

### *Landlord and Tenant Act 1709 (c. 18)*

2    In the Landlord and Tenant Act 1709 omit the following –

(a)  section 1;

(b)  sections 6 to 8.

## Landlord and Tenant Act 1730 (c. 28)

3          In the Landlord and Tenant Act 1730 omit section 5.

## Distress for Rent Act 1737 (c. 19)

4          In the Distress for Rent Act 1737 the following cease to have effect –
           (a)    sections 1 to 10;
           (b)    sections 16 and 17;
           (c)    section 19.

## Deserted Tenements Act 1817 (c. 52)

5          The Deserted Tenements Act 1817 ceases to have effect.

## Fines and Recoveries Act 1833 (c. 74)

6     (1)   In section 67 of the Fines and Recoveries Act 1833 (assignees to recover rent of
           the lands of a bankrupt), for the words from 'or may distrain' to 'recovering of
           rent in arrear;' substitute 'or, so far as the power under section 72(1) of the
           Tribunals, Courts and Enforcement Act 2007 (commercial rent arrears recovery)
           is exercisable to recover any of those rents and profits, may exercise that power,
           as if they were the landlord, on behalf of the creditors;'.
      (2)   This paragraph does not extend to Northern Ireland.

## Metropolitan Police Courts Act 1840 (c. 84)

7          The Metropolitan Police Courts Act 1840 ceases to have effect.

## Execution Act 1844 (c. 96)

8          The Execution Act 1844 ceases to have effect.

## Lands Clauses Consolidation Act 1845 (c. 18)

9     (1)   In section 11 of the Lands Clauses Consolidation Act 1845 (payment of rents to
           be charged on tolls) omit the words from 'or it shall be lawful' to the end.
      (2)   This paragraph extends only to England and Wales.

## Inclosure Act 1845 (c. 118)

10         In section 112 of the Inclosure Act 1845 (recovery of rents of allotment) for 'by
           distress' substitute 'under section 72(1) of the Tribunals, Courts and
           Enforcement Act 2007 (commercial rent arrears recovery)'.

## Markets and Fairs Clauses Act 1847 (c. 14)

11    (1)   Section 38 of the Markets and Fairs Clauses Act 1847 (recovery of stallage, rents
           or tolls) is amended as follows.

(2) The existing words become subsection (1).

(3) After 'England' insert '(subject to subsection (2))'.

(4) After subsection (1) insert –

'(2) Subsection (1) does not apply to the levying of rent in respect of premises in England and Wales to the extent that the power under section 72(1) of the Tribunals, Courts and Enforcement Act 2007 (commercial rent arrears recovery) is exercisable to recover such rent.

(3) Where that power is exercisable to recover such rent, either the undertakers or their lessee, if not the landlord for the purposes of section 72(1) of that Act, may exercise that power as if they or he were the landlord.'

(5) This paragraph extends only to England and Wales.

## Sequestration Act 1849 (c. 67)

12 (1) Section 1 of the Sequestration Act 1849 (sequestrator enabled to sue etc. in his own name) is amended as follows.

(2) For 'levy any distress' substitute 'exercise the power under section 72(1) of the Tribunals, Courts and Enforcement Act 2007 (commercial rent arrears recovery)'.

(3) Omit the words 'levy' and 'distress' in the second place where each occurs.

(4) Omit 'levied'.

## Landlord and Tenant Act 1851 (c. 25)

13 (1) The Landlord and Tenant Act 1851 ceases to have effect.

(2) This paragraph extends only to England and Wales.

## Common Law Procedure Act 1852 (c. 76)

14    The Common Law Procedure Act 1852 is amended as follows.

15    In section 210 (proceedings in ejectment by landlord for non-payment of rent), for 'and that no sufficient distress was to be found on the demised premises, countervailing the arrears then due' substitute 'and that either of the conditions in section 210A was met in relation to the arrears'.

16    After that section insert –

'210A    Conditions relating to commercial rent arrears recovery

(1) The first condition is that the power under section 72(1) of the Tribunals, Courts and Enforcement Act 2007 (commercial rent arrears recovery) was not exercisable to recover the arrears.

(2) The second condition is that there were not sufficient goods on the premises to recover the arrears by that power.'

## Improvement of Land Act 1864 (c. 114)

17 (1) In section 64 of the Improvement of Land Act 1864 (interest on arrears of rentcharges), for the words from 'a sufficient distress' to 'charges of such distress' substitute 'goods that would be sufficient to pay the amount outstanding under Schedule 12 to the Tribunals, Courts and Enforcement Act 2007 (taking control of goods)'.

(2) This paragraph extends only to England and Wales.

## *Railway Rolling Stock Protection Act 1872 (c. 50)*

18  (1)  The Railway Rolling Stock Protection Act 1872 ceases to have effect.
    (2)  This paragraph extends only to England and Wales.

## *Law of Distress Amendment Act 1888 (c. 21)*

19      The Law of Distress Amendment Act 1888 ceases to have effect.

## *Law of Distress Amendment Act 1908 (c. 53)*

20      The Law of Distress Amendment Act 1908 ceases to have effect.

## *Law of Property Act 1925 (c. 20)*

21      The Law of Property Act 1925 is amended as follows.
22      In section 109 (powers etc. of receiver appointed by mortgagee), in subsection (3), for ', distress' substitute 'or under section 72(1) of the Tribunals, Courts and Enforcement Act 2007 (commercial rent arrears recovery)'.
23      Section 121(2) ceases to have effect.
24      In section 150 (surrender of a lease, without prejudice to underleases with a view to the grant of a new lease), in subsection (5), for 'by distress or' substitute 'under section 72(1) of the Tribunals, Courts and Enforcement Act 2007 (commercial rent arrears recovery) or by'.
25      In section 162 (restrictions on the perpetuity rule) in subsection (1) omit paragraph (a).
26      In section 189 (indemnities against rents) omit subsection (1).
27  (1)  Section 190 (equitable apportionment of rents and remedies for non-payment or breach of covenant) is amended as follows.
    (2)  Omit subsection (2).
    (3)  For subsections (4) and (5) substitute –

        '(4)  Subsection (5) applies where –

            (a)  any default is made in payment of the whole or part of a rent by the person ("the defaulter") who, by reason of a charge or apportionment within subsection (3), is liable to pay it, and

            (b)  the lessee for the time being of any other land comprised in the lease, in whom, as respects that land, the residue of the term or interest created by the lease is vested, ("the paying lessee") pays or is required to pay the whole or part of the rent which ought to have been paid by the defaulter.

        (5)  Section 72(1) of the Tribunals, Courts and Enforcement Act 2007 (commercial rent arrears recovery) applies, subject to the other provisions of Chapter 2 of Part 3 of that Act, to the recovery by the paying lessee from the defaulter of the rent paid by the paying lessee which ought to have been paid by the defaulter, as if the paying lessee were the landlord, and the defaulter his tenant, under the lease.'

    (4)  In subsection (7) omit 'owner or'.

## Administration of Estates Act 1925 (c. 23)

28  (1)  Section 26 of the Administration of Estates Act 1925 (rights of action by and against personal representative) is amended as follows.
    (2)  Omit subsection (3).
    (3)  For subsection (4) substitute –

        '(4)  To recover rent due or accruing to the deceased, a personal representative may exercise any power under section 72(1) (commercial rent arrears recovery) or 81 (right to rent from sub-tenant) of the Tribunals, Courts and Enforcement Act 2007 that would have been exercisable by the deceased if he had still been living.'

## Leasehold Reform Act 1967 (c. 88)

29  In section 15 of the Leasehold Reform Act 1967 (terms of tenancy to be granted on extension), in subsection (3) for 'distress, re-entry or otherwise' substitute 're-entry or otherwise (subject to section 85 of the Tribunals, Courts and Enforcement Act 2007)'.

## Agriculture Act 1970 (c. 40)

30  In section 85 of the Agriculture Act 1970 (exemption for certain sales), in paragraph (d) after 'warrant of distress' insert 'or warrant of control'.

## Rent (Agriculture) Act 1976 (c. 80)

31  Section 8 of the Rent (Agriculture) Act 1976 ceases to have effect.

## Rent Act 1977 (c. 42)

32  The Rent Act 1977 is amended as follows
33  In section 141(5) (county court jurisdiction) (until its repeal by the Courts and Legal Services Act 1990 (c. 41) comes into force) for 'sections 147 and' substitute 'section'.
34  Section 147 ceases to have effect.

## Limitation Act 1980 (c. 58)

35  The Limitation Act 1980 is amended as follows
36  In section 19 (time limit for actions to recover rent) for 'or distress made' substitute 'and the power conferred by section 72(1) of the Tribunals, Courts and Enforcement Act 2007 shall not be exercisable'.
37  In section 38 (interpretation) omit 'rentcharges and' and 'rent or'.

## County Courts Act 1984 (c. 28)

38  The County Courts Act 1984 is amended as follows.
39  Section 116 ceases to have effect.
40  In section 139, for subsection (1)(c) substitute –

'(c)    the power under section 72(1) of the Tribunals, Courts and Enforcement Act 2007 (commercial rent arrears recovery) is exercisable to recover the arrears; and

(d)    there are not sufficient goods on the premises to recover the arrears by that power,'.

## Agricultural Holdings Act 1986 (c. 5)

41      The Agricultural Holdings Act 1986 is amended as follows.

42      Omit sections 16 to 19.

43      In section 24 (restriction of landlord's remedies for breach of contract of tenancy) omit ', by distress or otherwise,'.

## Insolvency Act 1986 (c. 45)

44   (1)  Section 347 of the Insolvency Act 1986 (distress etc.) is amended as follows.

(2)  In subsection (1) for the words from the beginning to 'available' substitute 'CRAR (the power of commercial rent arrears recovery under section 72(1) of the Tribunals, Courts and Enforcement Act 2007) is exercisable where the tenant is an undischarged bankrupt'.

(3)  In subsection (2) –

(a)    for the words from the beginning to 'goods and effects of' substitute 'Where CRAR has been exercised to recover rent from';

(b)    for 'that distress' substitute 'CRAR';

(c)    for 'the distress was levied' substitute 'goods were taken control of under CRAR'.

(4)  In subsection (5) for the words from the beginning to 'upon' substitute 'CRAR is not exercisable at any time after the discharge of a bankrupt against'.

(5)  Omit subsections (6) and (7).

(6)  Omit subsection (11).

## Housing Act 1988 (c. 50)

45      Omit section 19 of the Housing Act 1988.

## Water Industry Act 1991 (c. 56)

46      In section 179 of the Water Industry Act 1991 (vesting of works in undertaker) in subsection (4)(b) omit 'or to the landlord's remedy for rent'.

## Leasehold Reform, Housing and Urban Development Act 1993 (c. 28)

47      In section 57 of the Leasehold Reform Act 1967 (terms on which new lease is to be granted), in subsection (2)(b)(ii) for 'distress, re-entry or otherwise' substitute 're-entry or otherwise (subject to section 85 of the Tribunals, Courts and Enforcement Act 2007)'.

## Constitutional Reform Act 2005 (c. 4)

48      In Schedule 7 to the Constitutional Reform Act 2005 (protected functions of the Lord Chancellor), in paragraph 4, omit the entry for the Law of Distress Amendment Act 1888.

## SCHEDULE 15   ATTACHMENT OF EARNINGS ORDERS: DEDUCTIONS AT FIXED RATES                Section 91

## PART 1   MAIN AMENDMENTS

### Introduction

1       This Schedule amends the Attachment of Earnings Act 1971 (c. 32).

### Amendment of section 6: Effect and contents of order

2      (1)  For section 6(1)(a) (instruction to employer to make deductions from debtor's earnings) substitute –

'(a)   to make periodical deductions from the debtor's earnings, as specified in the order; and'.

(2)  After section 6(1) insert –

'(1A)   If a county court makes an attachment of earnings order to secure payment of a judgment debt, the order must specify that periodical deductions are to be made in accordance with the fixed deductions scheme.

(1B)   If a court (whether a county court or another court) makes any other attachment of earnings order, the order must specify that periodical deductions are to be made in accordance with Part 1 of Schedule 3.'

(3)  In section 6(5) (order to specify normal deduction and protected earnings rates), for 'the order' substitute 'a Schedule 3 deductions order'.

### Insertion of new section 6A

3       After section 6 insert –

'6A   The fixed deductions scheme

(1)   In this Act "fixed deductions scheme" means any scheme that the Lord Chancellor makes which specifies the rates and frequencies at which deductions are to be made under attachment of earnings orders so as to secure the repayment of judgment debts.

(2)   The Lord Chancellor is to make the fixed deductions scheme by regulations.

(3)   The power to make regulations under subsection (2) is exercisable by statutory instrument.

(4)   The Lord Chancellor may not make a statutory instrument containing the first regulations under subsection (2) unless a draft of the instrument has been laid before, and approved by resolution of, each House of Parliament.

(5)    A statutory instrument containing any subsequent regulations under subsection (2) is subject to annulment in pursuance of a resolution of either House of Parliament.'

## Amendment of section 9: Variation, lapse and discharge of orders

4        After section 9(1) (power of court to vary order) insert –

'(1A)    Subsection (1) is subject to Schedule 3A (which deals with the variation of certain attachment of earnings orders by changing the basis of deductions).'

## Insertion of new section 9A

5        After section 9 insert –

'9A    Suspension of fixed deductions orders

(1)    A county court must make an order suspending a fixed deductions order if the court is satisfied of either or both of the following –

(a)    that the fixed deductions order requires periodical deductions to be made at a rate which is not appropriate;

(b)    that the fixed deductions order requires periodical deductions to be made at times which are not appropriate.

(2)    The county court is to make the suspension order on the following terms –

(a)    if the condition in subsection (1)(a) is met: on terms specifying the rate at which the debtor must make repayments (whether higher or lower than the rate at which the order requires the deductions to be made);

(b)    if the condition in subsection (1)(b) is met: on terms specifying the times at which the debtor must make repayments;

(c)    if either or both conditions are met: on any additional terms that the court thinks appropriate.

(3)    If the employer is given notice of the suspension order, the employer must cease to make the deductions required by the fixed deductions order; but the employer is under no liability for non-compliance before seven days have elapsed since service of the notice.

(4)    A county court –

(a)    must revoke the suspension order if any of the terms of the suspension order are broken;

(b)    may revoke the suspension order in any other circumstances if the court thinks that it is appropriate to do so.

(5)    Rules of court may make provision as to the circumstances in which a county court may of its own motion –

(a)    make a suspension order; or

(b)    revoke a suspension order.

(6)    The suspension of a fixed deductions order under this section does not prevent the order from being treated as remaining in force subject to the provisions of this section.

(7)    This section is without prejudice to any other powers of a court to suspend attachment of earnings orders or to revoke the suspension of such orders.

(8)    In this section, in relation to a fixed deductions order, "repayments" means repayments of the judgment debt to which the order relates.'

## Amendment of section 25: General interpretation

6       In section 25(1) (meaning of particular words and phrases) insert the following
        entries at the appropriate place –

        ' "fixed deductions order" means an attachment of earnings order under
            which periodical deductions are to be made in accordance with the
            fixed deductions scheme;';
        ' "fixed deductions scheme" has the meaning given by section 6A(1);';
        ' "Schedule 3 deductions order" means an attachment of earnings order
            under which periodical deductions are to be made in accordance with
            Part 1 of Schedule 3;';
        ' "suspension order" means an order under section 9A suspending a fixed
            deductions order;'.

## Insertion of new Schedule 3A

7       After Schedule 3 insert –

### 'SCHEDULE 3A    CHANGING THE BASIS OF DEDUCTIONS

### PART 1    CHANGING TO THE FIXED DEDUCTIONS SCHEME

*Introduction*

1       This Part of this Schedule deals with the variation of a certain kind of
        attachment of earnings order – referred to as a Schedule 3 judgment
        debt order – by changing the basis of deductions.
2       A Schedule 3 judgment debt order is a Schedule 3 deductions order
        made by a county court to secure payment of a judgment debt.
3       References to variation of a Schedule 3 judgment debt order by
        changing the basis of deductions are references to the variation of the
        order so that it specifies that periodical deductions are to be made in
        accordance with the fixed deductions scheme.

*Variation at discretion of court*

4(1)    A county court may vary a Schedule 3 judgment debt order by
        changing the basis of deductions.
(2)     The county court may make the variation –
        (a)    in consequence of an application made to the court, or
        (b)    of its own motion.
(3)     The variation takes effect on the date that it is made.

*Variation by court upon redirection*

5(1)    A county court must vary a Schedule 3 judgment debt order by
        changing the basis of deductions if –
        (a)    the order lapses, and
        (b)    the county court directs the order to a person in accordance
               with section 9(4).

(2)    The variation must be made at the same time as the county court directs the order in accordance with section 9(4).

(3)    The variation takes effect on the date that it is made.

*Automatic variation on changeover date*

6(1)    On the changeover date, all Schedule 3 judgment debt orders are to be treated as if a county court had varied them by changing the basis of deductions.

(2)    The variation takes effect on the changeover date.

(3)    The changeover date is the date which the Lord Chancellor specifies for the purposes of this paragraph.

(4)    The Lord Chancellor is to specify the changeover date in an order made by statutory instrument.

(5)    A statutory instrument containing an order under sub-paragraph (4) is subject to annulment in pursuance of a resolution of either House of Parliament.

*Notice of variation still required*

7    Section 9(2) (service by court of notice of variation) applies to the variation of an order under this Part of this Schedule (including variation in accordance with paragraph 6) as it applies to any other variation of an attachment of earnings order.

## PART 2    CHANGING FROM THE FIXED DEDUCTIONS SCHEME

*Introduction*

8    This Part of this Schedule deals with the variation of fixed deductions orders by changing the basis of deductions.

9    References to variation of a fixed deductions order by changing the basis of deductions are references to the variation of the order so that it specifies that periodical deductions are to be made in accordance with Part 1 of Schedule 3.

*General prohibition on changing from the fixed deductions basis*

10    A court may not vary a fixed deductions order by changing the basis of deductions unless the variation is in accordance with this Part of this Schedule.

*Fixed deductions order directed to secure payments under an administration order*

11(1)    A county court must vary a fixed deductions order by changing the basis of deductions if, under section 5, the county court directs the order to take effect as an order to secure payments required by an administration order.

(2)    The variation must be made at the same time as the county court gives that direction under section 5.

(3)    The variation takes effect on the date that it is made.

(4)    Section 9(2) (service by court of notice of variation) applies to the variation of an order under this paragraph as it applies to any other variation of an attachment of earnings order.'

## PART 2   CONSEQUENTIAL AMENDMENTS

### *Amendment of section 5: Securing payments under administration order*

8      In section 5(3) (power of county court to direct existing attachment of earnings order to secure administration order), for the words in brackets substitute '(with the variation required by paragraph 11 of Schedule 3A and such other variations, if any, as the court thinks appropriate)'.

### *Amendment of section 14: Power of court to obtain information*

9      In section 14(1) (power of court to order debtor and employer to provide specified information), for 'an attachment of earnings order' substitute 'a Schedule 3 deductions order'.

10     After section 14(1) insert –

> '(1A)   Where in any proceedings a county court has power to make a fixed deductions order, the court may order the debtor to give to the court, within a specified period, a statement signed by him of –
>
> > (a)   the name and address of any person by whom earnings are paid to him; and
> >
> > (b)   specified particulars for enabling the debtor to be identified by any employer of his.'

11     In section 14(2) (powers of court after attachment of earnings order has been made), for the words from 'Where' to 'in force –' substitute 'At any time when a Schedule 3 deductions order is in force, the court or the fines officer, as the case may be, may –'.

12     After section 14(2) insert –

> '(2A)   At any time when a fixed deductions order is in force, the court may –
>
> > (a)   make such an order as is described in subsection (1A) above; and
> >
> > (b)   order the debtor to attend before it on a day and at a time specified in the order to give the information described in subsection (1A) above.'

13     In section 14(4) (rules of court about notice of application for attachment or earnings order), for the words from 'give' to 'the application.' substitute ', within such period and in such manner as may be prescribed, give the court a statement in accordance with subsection (4A) or (4B).'

14     After section 14(4) insert –

> '(4A) In a case where the attachment of earnings order would, if made, be a Schedule 3 deductions order, the debtor must give a statement in writing of –
>
> > (a)   the matters specified in subsection (1)(a) above, and
> >
> > (b)   any other prescribed matters which are, or may be, relevant under section 6 of this Act to the determination of the normal deduction rate and the protected earnings rate to be specified in any attachment of earnings order made on the application.
>
> (4B)   In a case where the attachment of earnings order would, if made, be a fixed deductions order, the debtor must give a statement in writing of the matters specified in subsection (1A) above.'

15　　In section 14(5) (certain statements in proceedings for making or varying etc attachment of earnings orders deemed to be evidence of facts stated), after 'subsection (1)(a) or (b)' insert 'or (1A)'.

## Amendment of section 15: Obligation of debtor and employer to notify changes

16　(1)　Section 15(1) is amended as follows.

　　(2)　In paragraph (b) (obligation to notify of court of earnings under new employment) at the beginning insert 'if the order is a Schedule 3 deductions order,'.

　　(3)　In paragraph (c) (obligation of employer to notify court of debtor's new employment and earnings) for 'and include' insert 'and, if the order is a Schedule 3 deductions order, include'.

## Amendment of section 17: Consolidated attachment orders

17　(1)　Section 17(3) (rules of court made in connection with consolidated attachment orders) is amended as follows.

　　(2)　In paragraph (b) (rules relating to powers of court to which order etc transferred), after 'vary' insert ', suspend'.

　　(3)　In paragraph (e) (rules modifying or excluding statutory provisions), after 'provisions of this Act' insert ', the fixed deductions scheme'.

18　　After section 17(3) insert –

　　　　'(4)　Section 6(1A) applies to a consolidated attachment order which a county court makes to secure the payment of two or more judgment debts even if, immediately before the order is made, one or more of those debts is secured by a Schedule 3 deductions order.'

## Amendment of section 23: Enforcement provisions

19　　Section 23 is amended as follows.

20　　In subsection (1) (failure of debtor to attend hearing) –

　　(a)　for the words from 'notice of an application' to 'such an order' substitute 'relevant notice,';

　　(b)　for 'for any hearing of the application' substitute 'in the notice for any hearing,'.

21　　After subsection (1) insert –

　　　　'(1ZA)　In subsection (1) "relevant notice" means any of the following –

　　　　　(a)　notice of an application to a county court to make, vary or suspend an attachment of earnings order;

　　　　　(b)　notice that a county court is, of its own motion, to consider making, varying or suspending an attachment of earnings order.'

22　　In subsection (2)(c) and (f) (offences related to attachment of earnings orders) –

　　(a)　after 'section 14(1)' insert 'or (1A)'.

　　(b)　after 'attachment of earnings order' insert 'or suspension order'.

## SCHEDULE 16    ADMINISTRATION ORDERS: CONSEQUENTIAL AMENDMENTS     Section 106

### *Attachment of Earnings Act 1971 (c. 32)*

1    (1)   Section 4 of the Attachment of Earnings Act 1971 (extension of power to make administration order) is amended as follows.

     (2)   For subsections (2) and (2A) substitute –

           '(2)   The court may make an administration order in respect of the debtor's estate if, after receipt of the list referred to in subsection (1)(b) above, the court is satisfied that the conditions in sections 112B(2) to (7) of the County Courts Act 1984 (conditions to power to make administration orders) are met in relation to the debtor.'

     (3)   In subsection (4) for 'section 112' substitute 'section 112J'.

### *Magistrates' Courts Act 1980 (c. 43)*

2    (1)   Schedule 6A to the Magistrates' Courts Act 1980 (fines that may be altered under section 143 of the 1980 Act) is amended as follows.

     (2)   Insert the following entry at the appropriate place in the entries relating to the County Courts Act 1984 (c. 28) –

           'Section 112N(1) (administration orders:          £250'
           failure to provide information)

### *Insolvency Act 1986 (c. 45)*

3    (1)   Section 429 of the Insolvency Act 1986 (disabilities on revocation of administration order against an individual) is amended as follows.

     (2)   For subsections (1) and (2) substitute –

           '(1)   This section applies if a county court revokes an administration order made in respect of an individual ("the debtor") on one of the relevant grounds.

           (2)    The court may, at the time it revokes the administration order, make an order directing that this section and section 12 of the Company Directors Disqualification Act 1986 shall apply to the debtor for such period, not exceeding one year, as may be specified in the order.

           (2A)   Each of the following is a relevant ground –

                  (a)   the debtor had failed to make two payments (whether consecutive or not) required by the order;

                  (b)   at the time the order was made –

                        (i)    the total amount of the debtor's qualifying debts was more than the prescribed maximum for the purposes of Part 6 of the 1984 Act, but

                        (ii)   because of information provided, or not provided, by the debtor, that amount was thought to be less than, or the same as, the prescribed maximum.'

     (3)   In subsection (3) for 'a person' in the first place substitute 'an individual'.

     (4)   In subsection (4) for 'a person' substitute 'an individual'.

     (5)   In subsection (5) for 'person' substitute 'individual'.

4    (1)   Section 440 (extent: Scotland) is amended as follows.

(2)  In subsection (2)(a) (provisions in the third Group of Parts that do not extend to Scotland) for 'section 429(1) and (2)' substitute 'section 429(1) to (2A)'.

## Company Directors Disqualification Act 1986 (c. 46)

5    (1)  Section 12 of the Company Directors Disqualification Act 1986 (failure to pay under county court administration order) is amended as follows.
     (2)  For the title of the section substitute 'Disabilities on revocation of administration order'.
     (3)  Omit subsection (1).
     (4)  In subsection (2), for the words from 'that section' to '429(2)(b)' substitute 'section 429 of the Insolvency Act applies by virtue of an order under subsection (2) of that section'.

## Courts and Legal Services Act 1990 (c. 41)

6          Omit section 13 of the Courts and Legal Services Act 1990.

## Charities Act 1993 (c. 10)

7    (1)  Section 72 of the Charities Act 1993 (persons disqualified for being trustees of a charity) is amended as follows.
     (2)  In subsection (1)(f), for the words from 'section 429(2)(b)' to the end substitute 'section 429(2) of the Insolvency Act 1986 (disabilities on revocation of county court administration order).'

## Pensions Act 1995 (c. 26)

8    (1)  Section 29 of the Pensions Act 1995 (persons disqualified for being trustees of a trust scheme) is amended as follows.
     (2)  In subsection (1)(f), for the words from 'section 429(2)(b)' to the end substitute 'section 429(2) of the Insolvency Act 1986 (disabilities on revocation of county court administration order).'

## Police Act 1996 (c. 16)

9    (1)  The Police Act 1996 is amended as follows.
     (2)  In paragraph 11 of Schedule 2 (disqualification for being appointed as or being member of a police authority), in sub-paragraph (1)(c), for 'section 429(2)(b)' to the end substitute 'section 429(2) of the Insolvency Act 1986 (disabilities on revocation of county court administration order); or'.
     (3)  In paragraph 7 of Schedule 2A (disqualification for being appointed as or being member of the Metropolitan Police Authority), in sub-paragraph (1)(c), for the words from 'section 429(2)(b)' to the end substitute 'section 429(2) of the Insolvency Act 1986 (disabilities on revocation of county court administration order); or'.

## Housing Act 1996 (c. 52)

10   (1)  Paragraph 4 of Schedule 1 to the Housing Act 1996 (power to remove director, trustee etc. of registered social landlord) is amended as follows.

(2) In sub-paragraph (2)(c), for the words from 'section 429(2)(b)' to the end substitute 'section 429(2) of the Insolvency Act 1986 (disabilities on revocation of county court administration order);'.

## Police Act 1997 (c. 50)

11 (1) The Police Act 1997 is amended as follows.

(2) In section 91 (the Commissioners), in subsection (7)(b), for 'section 429(2)(b) of the Insolvency Act 1986 (failure to pay under county court administration order)' substitute 'section 429(2) of the Insolvency Act 1986 (disabilities on revocation of county court administration order)'.

(3) In paragraph 3 of Schedule 2 (disqualification for being appointed as or being member of a Service Authority), in sub-paragraph (1)(c), for the words from 'section 429(2)(b)' to the end substitute 'section 429(2) of the Insolvency Act 1986 (disabilities on revocation of county court administration order); or'.

## Criminal Justice and Police Act 2001 (c. 16)

12 (1) Paragraph 3 of Schedule 3 to the Criminal Justice and Police Act 2001 (persons disqualified for being appointed as or being member of the Central Police Training and Development Authority) is amended as follows.

(2) In sub-paragraph (1)(b), for the words from 'section 429(2)(b)' to the end substitute 'section 429(2) of the Insolvency Act 1986 (disabilities on revocation of county court administration order); or'.

## Police Reform Act 2002 (c. 30)

13 (1) Schedule 2 to the Police Reform Act 2002 (the Independent Police Complaints Commission) is amended as follows.

(2) In paragraph 1(5) (grounds for removal of chairman), in paragraph (e)(ii), for the words from 'section 429(2)(b)' to the end substitute 'section 429(2) of the Insolvency Act 1986 (disabilities on revocation of county court administration order);'.

(3) In paragraph 2(6) (grounds for removal of ordinary members), in paragraph (e)(ii), for the words from 'section 429(2)(b)' to the end substitute 'section 429(2) of the Insolvency Act 1986 (disabilities on revocation of county court administration order);'.

## Railways and Transport Safety Act 2003 (c. 20)

14 (1) Paragraph 7 of Schedule 4 to the Railways and Transport Safety Act 2003, (eligibility for appointment as member of British Transport Police Authority) is amended as follows.

(2) In sub-paragraph (3)(c), for 'section 429(2)(b)' substitute 'section 429(2)'.

## Courts Act 2003 (c. 39)

15 (1) Section 98 of the Courts Act 2003 (register of judgments and orders) is amended as follows.

(2) In subsection (1)(b) (administration orders) for 'section 112' substitute 'Part 6'.

## SCHEDULE 17   PART 7A OF THE INSOLVENCY
## ACT 1986

### 'PART 7A   DEBT RELIEF ORDERS

*Preliminary*

**251A   Debt relief orders**

(1) An individual who is unable to pay his debts may apply for an order under this Part ("a debt relief order") to be made in respect of his qualifying debts.

(2) In this Part "qualifying debt" means (subject to subsection (3)) a debt which –

  (a) is for a liquidated sum payable either immediately or at some certain future time; and

  (b) is not an excluded debt.

(3) A debt is not a qualifying debt to the extent that it is secured.

(4) In this Part "excluded debt" means a debt of any description prescribed for the purposes of this subsection.

*Applications for a debt relief order*

**251B   Making of application**

(1) An application for a debt relief order must be made to the official receiver through an approved intermediary.

(2) The application must include –

  (a) a list of the debts to which the debtor is subject at the date of the application, specifying the amount of each debt (including any interest, penalty or other sum that has become payable in relation to that debt on or before that date) and the creditor to whom it is owed;

  (b) details of any security held in respect of any of those debts; and

  (c) such other information about the debtor's affairs (including his creditors, debts and liabilities and his income and assets) as may be prescribed.

(3) The rules may make further provision as to –

  (a) the form of an application for a debt relief order;

  (b) the manner in which an application is to be made; and

  (c) information and documents to be supplied in support of an application.

(4) For the purposes of this Part an application is not to be regarded as having been made until –

  (a) the application has been submitted to the official receiver; and

  (b) any fee required in connection with the application by an order under section 415 has been paid to such person as the order may specify.

**251C   Duty of official receiver to consider and determine application**

(1) This section applies where an application for a debt relief order is made.

(2)    The official receiver may stay consideration of the application until he has received answers to any queries raised with the debtor in relation to anything connected with the application.

(3)    The official receiver must determine the application by –

(a)    deciding whether to refuse the application;

(b)    if he does not refuse it, by making a debt relief order in relation to the specified debts he is satisfied were qualifying debts of the debtor at the application date;

but he may only refuse the application if he is authorised or required to do so by any of the following provisions of this section.

(4)    The official receiver may refuse the application if he considers that –

(a)    the application does not meet all the requirements imposed by or under section 251B;

(b)    any queries raised with the debtor have not been answered to the satisfaction of the official receiver within such time as he may specify when they are raised;

(c)    the debtor has made any false representation or omission in making the application or on supplying any information or documents in support of it.

(5)    The official receiver must refuse the application if he is not satisfied that –

(a)    the debtor is an individual who is unable to pay his debts;

(b)    at least one of the specified debts was a qualifying debt of the debtor at the application date;

(c)    each of the conditions set out in Part 1 of Schedule 4ZA is met.

(6)    The official receiver may refuse the application if he is not satisfied that each condition specified in Part 2 of Schedule 4ZA is met.

(7)    If the official receiver refuses an application he must give reasons for his refusal to the debtor in the prescribed manner.

(8)    In this section "specified debt" means a debt specified in the application.

**251D    Presumptions applicable to the determination of an application**

(1)    The following presumptions are to apply to the determination of an application for a debt relief order.

(2)    The official receiver must presume that the debtor is an individual who is unable to pay his debts at the determination date if –

(a)    that appears to the official receiver to be the case at the application date from the information supplied in the application and he has no reason to believe that the information supplied is incomplete or inaccurate; and

(b)    he has no reason to believe that, by virtue of a change in the debtor's financial circumstances since the application date, the debtor may be able to pay his debts.

(3)    The official receiver must presume that a specified debt (of the amount specified in the application and owed to the creditor so specified) is a qualifying debt at the application date if –

(a)    that appears to him to be the case from the information supplied in the application; and

(b)    he has no reason to believe that the information supplied is incomplete or inaccurate.

(4)   The official receiver must presume that the condition specified in paragraph 1 of Schedule 4ZA is met if –

    (a)   that appears to him to be the case from the information supplied in the application;

    (b)   any prescribed verification checks relating to the condition have been made; and

    (c)   he has no reason to believe that the information supplied is incomplete or inaccurate.

(5)   The official receiver must presume that any other condition specified in Part 1 or 2 of Schedule 4ZA is met if –

    (a)   that appears to him to have been the case as at the application date from the information supplied in the application and he has no reason to believe that the information supplied is incomplete or inaccurate;

    (b)   any prescribed verification checks relating to the condition have been made; and

    (c)   he has no reason to believe that, by virtue of a change in circumstances since the application date, the condition may no longer be met.

(6)   References in this section to information supplied in the application include information supplied to the official receiver in support of the application.

(7)   In this section "specified debt" means a debt specified in the application.

*Making and effect of debt relief order*

**251E   Making of debt relief orders**

(1)   This section applies where the official receiver makes a debt relief order on determining an application under section 251C.

(2)   The order must be made in the prescribed form.

(3)   The order must include a list of the debts which the official receiver is satisfied were qualifying debts of the debtor at the application date, specifying the amount of the debt at that time and the creditor to whom it was then owed.

(4)   The official receiver must –

    (a)   give a copy of the order to the debtor; and

    (b)   make an entry for the order in the register containing the prescribed information about the order or the debtor.

(5)   The rules may make provision as to other steps to be taken by the official receiver or the debtor on the making of the order.

(6)   Those steps may include in particular notifying each creditor to whom a qualifying debt specified in the order is owed of –

    (a)   the making of the order and its effect,

    (b)   the grounds on which a creditor may object under section 251K, and

    (c)   any other prescribed information.

(7)   In this Part the date on which an entry relating to the making of a debt relief order is first made in the register is referred to as "the effective date".

**251F Effect of debt relief order on other debt management arrangements**

(1) This section applies if –

    (a) a debt relief order is made, and

    (b) immediately before the order is made, other debt management arrangements are in force in respect of the debtor.

(2) The other debt management arrangements cease to be in force when the debt relief order is made.

(3) In this section "other debt management arrangements" means –

    (a) an administration order under Part 6 of the County Courts Act 1984;

    (b) an enforcement restriction order under Part 6A of that Act;

    (c) a debt repayment plan arranged in accordance with a debt management scheme that is approved under Chapter 4 of Part 5 of the Tribunals, Courts and Enforcement Act 2007.

**251G Moratorium from qualifying debts**

(1) A moratorium commences on the effective date for a debt relief order in relation to each qualifying debt specified in the order ("a specified qualifying debt").

(2) During the moratorium, the creditor to whom a specified qualifying debt is owed –

    (a) has no remedy in respect of the debt, and

    (b) may not –

        (i) commence a creditor's petition in respect of the debt, or

        (ii) otherwise commence any action or other legal proceedings against the debtor for the debt,

    except with the permission of the court and on such terms as the court may impose.

(3) If on the effective date a creditor to whom a specified qualifying debt is owed has any such petition, action or other proceeding as mentioned in subsection (2)(b) pending in any court, the court may –

    (a) stay the proceedings on the petition, action or other proceedings (as the case may be), or

    (b) allow them to continue on such terms as the court thinks fit.

(4) In subsection (2)(a) and (b) references to the debt include a reference to any interest, penalty or other sum that becomes payable in relation to that debt after the application date.

(5) Nothing in this section affects the right of a secured creditor of the debtor to enforce his security.

**251H The moratorium period**

(1) The moratorium relating to the qualifying debts specified in a debt relief order continues for the period of one year beginning with the effective date for the order, unless –

    (a) the moratorium terminates early; or

    (b) the moratorium period is extended by the official receiver under this section or by the court under section 251M.

(2) The official receiver may only extend the moratorium period for the purpose of –

(a) carrying out or completing an investigation under section 251K;

(b) taking any action he considers necessary (whether as a result of an investigation or otherwise) in relation to the order; or

(c) in a case where he has decided to revoke the order, providing the debtor with the opportunity to make arrangements for making payments towards his debts.

(3) The official receiver may not extend the moratorium period for the purpose mentioned in subsection (2)(a) without the permission of the court.

(4) The official receiver may not extend the moratorium period beyond the end of the period of three months beginning after the end of the initial period of one year mentioned in subsection (1).

(5) The moratorium period may be extended more than once, but any extension (whether by the official receiver or by the court) must be made before the moratorium would otherwise end.

(6) References in this Part to a moratorium terminating early are to its terminating before the end of what would otherwise be the moratorium period, whether on the revocation of the order or by virtue of any other enactment.

**251I  Discharge from qualifying debts**

(1) Subject as follows, at the end of the moratorium applicable to a debt relief order the debtor is discharged from all the qualifying debts specified in the order (including all interest, penalties and other sums which may have become payable in relation to those debts since the application date).

(2) Subsection (1) does not apply if the moratorium terminates early.

(3) Subsection (1) does not apply in relation to any qualifying debt which the debtor incurred in respect of any fraud or fraudulent breach of trust to which the debtor was a party.

(4) The discharge of the debtor under subsection (1) does not release any other person from –

(a) any liability (whether as partner or co-trustee of the debtor or otherwise) from which the debtor is released by the discharge; or

(b) any liability as surety for the debtor or as a person in the nature of such a surety.

(5) If the order is revoked by the court under section 251M after the end of the moratorium period, the qualifying debts specified in the order shall (so far as practicable) be treated as though subsection (1) had never applied to them.

*Duties of debtor*

**251J  Providing assistance to official receiver etc**

(1) The duties in this section apply to a debtor at any time after the making of an application by him for a debt relief order.

(2) The debtor must –

(a) give to the official receiver such information as to his affairs,

(b) attend on the official receiver at such times, and

(c) do all such other things,

as the official receiver may reasonably require for the purpose of carrying out his functions in relation to the application or, as the case may be, the debt relief order made as a result of the application.

(3)    The debtor must notify the official receiver as soon as reasonably practicable if he becomes aware of –

(a)    any error in, or omission from, the information supplied to the official receiver in, or in support of, the application;

(b)    any change in his circumstances between the application date and the determination date that would affect (or would have affected) the determination of the application.

(4)    The duties under subsections (2) and (3) apply after (as well as before) the determination of the application, for as long as the official receiver is able to exercise functions of the kind mentioned in subsection (2).

(5)    If a debt relief order is made as a result of the application, the debtor must notify the official receiver as soon as reasonably practicable if –

(a)    there is an increase in his income during the moratorium period applicable to the order;

(b)    he acquires any property or any property is devolved upon him during that period;

(c)    he becomes aware of any error in or omission from any information supplied by him to the official receiver after the determination date.

(6)    A notification under subsection (3) or (5) must give the prescribed particulars (if any) of the matter being notified.

*Objections, investigations and revocation*

**251K    Objections and investigations**

(1)    Any person specified in a debt relief order as a creditor to whom a specified qualifying debt is owed may object to –

(a)    the making of the order;

(b)    the inclusion of the debt in the list of the debtor's qualifying debts; or

(c)    the details of the debt specified in the order.

(2)    An objection under subsection (1) must be –

(a)    made during the moratorium period relating to the order and within the prescribed period for objections;

(b)    made to the official receiver in the prescribed manner;

(c)    based on a prescribed ground;

(d)    supported by any information and documents as may be prescribed;

and the prescribed period mentioned in paragraph (a) must not be less than 28 days after the creditor in question has been notified of the making of the order.

(3)    The official receiver must consider every objection made to him under this section.

(4)    The official receiver may –

(a)    as part of his consideration of an objection, or

(b)    on his own initiative,

carry out an investigation of any matter that appears to the official receiver to be relevant to the making of any decision mentioned in subsection (5) in relation to a debt relief order or the debtor.

(5)    The decisions to which an investigation may be directed are –

(a)    whether the order should be revoked or amended under section 251L;

(b)    whether an application should be made to the court under section 251M; or

(c)    whether any other steps should be taken in relation to the debtor.

(6)    The power to carry out an investigation under this section is exercisable after (as well as during) the moratorium relating to the order.

(7)    The official receiver may require any person to give him such information and assistance as he may reasonably require in connection with an investigation under this section.

(8)    Subject to anything prescribed in the rules as to the procedure to be followed in carrying out an investigation under this section, an investigation may be carried out by the official receiver in such manner as he thinks fit.

**251L    Power of official receiver to revoke or amend a debt relief order**

(1)    The official receiver may revoke or amend a debt relief order during the applicable moratorium period in the circumstances provided for by this section.

(2)    The official receiver may revoke the order on the ground that –

(a)    any information supplied to him by the debtor –

(i)    in, or in support of, the application, or

(ii)    after the determination date,

was incomplete, incorrect or otherwise misleading;

(b)    the debtor has failed to comply with a duty under section 251J;

(c)    a bankruptcy order has been made in relation to the debtor; or

(d)    the debtor has made a proposal under Part 8 (or has notified the official receiver of his intention to do so).

(3)    The official receiver may revoke the order on the ground that he should not have been satisfied –

(a)    that the debts specified in the order were qualifying debts of the debtor as at the application date;

(b)    that the conditions specified in Part 1 of Schedule 4ZA were met;

(c)    that the conditions specified in Part 2 of that Schedule were met or that any failure to meet such a condition did not prevent his making the order.

(4)    The official receiver may revoke the order on the ground that either or both of the conditions in paragraphs 7 and 8 of Schedule 4ZA (monthly surplus income and property) are not met at any time after the order was made.

For this purpose those paragraphs are to be read as if references to the determination date were references to the time in question.

(5)    Where the official receiver decides to revoke the order, he may revoke it either –

(a)    with immediate effect, or

(b)    with effect from such date (not more than three months after the date of the decision) as he may specify.

(6)    In considering when the revocation should take effect the official receiver must consider (in the light of the grounds on which the decision to revoke was made and all the other circumstances of the case)

whether the debtor ought to be given the opportunity to make arrangements for making payments towards his debts.

(7) If the order has been revoked with effect from a specified date the official receiver may, if he thinks it appropriate to do so at any time before that date, revoke the order with immediate effect.

(8) The official receiver may amend a debt relief order for the purpose of correcting an error in or omission from anything specified in the order.

(9) But subsection (8) does not permit the official receiver to add any debts that were not specified in the application for the debt relief order to the list of qualifying debts.

(10) The rules may make further provision as to the procedure to be followed by the official receiver in the exercise of his powers under this section.

*Role of the court*

### 251M   Powers of court in relation to debt relief orders

(1) Any person may make an application to the court if he is dissatisfied by any act, omission or decision of the official receiver in connection with a debt relief order or an application for such an order.

(2) The official receiver may make an application to the court for directions or an order in relation to any matter arising in connection with a debt relief order or an application for such an order.

(3) The matters referred to in subsection (2) include, among other things, matters relating to the debtor's compliance with any duty arising under section 251J.

(4) An application under this section may, subject to anything in the rules, be made at any time.

(5) The court may extend the moratorium period applicable to a debt relief order for the purposes of determining an application under this section.

(6) On an application under this section the court may dismiss the application or do one or more of the following –

   (a) quash the whole or part of any act or decision of the official receiver;

   (b) give the official receiver directions (including a direction that he reconsider any matter in relation to which his act or decision has been quashed under paragraph (a));

   (c) make an order for the enforcement of any obligation on the debtor arising by virtue of a duty under section 251J;

   (d) extend the moratorium period applicable to the debt relief order;

   (e) make an order revoking or amending the debt relief order;

   (f) make an order under section 251N; or

   (g) make such other order as the court thinks fit.

(7) An order under subsection (6)(e) for the revocation of a debt relief order –

   (a) may be made during the moratorium period applicable to the debt relief order or at any time after that period has ended;

   (b) may be made on the court's own motion if the court has made a bankruptcy order in relation to the debtor during that period;

   (c) may provide for the revocation of the order to take effect on such terms and at such a time as the court may specify.

(8)   An order under subsection (6)(e) for the amendment of a debt relief order may not add any debts that were not specified in the application for the debt relief order to the list of qualifying debts.

### 251N   Inquiry into debtor's dealings and property

(1)   An order under this section may be made by the court on the application of the official receiver.

(2)   An order under this section is an order summoning any of the following persons to appear before the court –

(a)   the debtor;

(b)   the debtor's spouse or former spouse or the debtor's civil partner or former civil partner;

(c)   any person appearing to the court to be able to give information or assistance concerning the debtor or his dealings, affairs and property.

(3)   The court may require a person falling within subsection (2)(c) –

(a)   to provide a written account of his dealings with the debtor; or

(b)   to produce any documents in his possession or under his control relating to the debtor or to the debtor's dealings, affairs or property.

(4)   Subsection (5) applies where a person fails without reasonable excuse to appear before the court when he is summoned to do so by an order under this section.

(5)   The court may cause a warrant to be issued to a constable or prescribed officer of the court –

(a)   for the arrest of that person, and

(b)   for the seizure of any records or other documents in that person's possession.

(6)   The court may authorise a person arrested under such a warrant to be kept in custody, and anything seized under such a warrant to be held, in accordance with the rules, until that person is brought before the court under the warrant or until such other time as the court may order.

*Offences*

### 251O   False representations and omissions

(1)   A person who makes an application for a debt relief order is guilty of an offence if he knowingly or recklessly makes any false representation or omission in making the application or providing any information or documents to the official receiver in support of the application.

(2)   A person who makes an application for a debt relief order is guilty of an offence if –

(a)   he intentionally fails to comply with a duty under section 251J(3) in connection with the application; or

(b)   he knowingly or recklessly makes any false representation or omission in providing any information to the official receiver in connection with such a duty or otherwise in connection with the application.

(3)   It is immaterial for the purposes of an offence under subsection (1) or (2) whether or not a debt relief order is made as a result of the application.

(4) A person in respect of whom a debt relief order is made is guilty of an offence if –

    (a) he intentionally fails to comply with a duty under section 251J(5) in connection with the order; or

    (b) he knowingly or recklessly makes any false representation or omission in providing information to the official receiver in connection with such a duty or otherwise in connection with the performance by the official receiver of functions in relation to the order.

(5) It is immaterial for the purposes of an offence under subsection (4) –

    (a) whether the offence is committed during or after the moratorium period; and

    (b) whether or not the order is revoked after the conduct constituting the offence takes place.

### 251P   Concealment or falsification of documents

(1) A person in respect of whom a debt relief order is made is guilty of an offence if, during the moratorium period in relation to that order –

    (a) he does not provide, at the request of the official receiver, all his books, papers and other records of which he has possession or control and which relate to his affairs;

    (b) he prevents the production to the official receiver of any books, papers or other records relating to his affairs;

    (c) he conceals, destroys, mutilates or falsifies, or causes or permits the concealment, destruction, mutilation or falsification of, any books, papers or other records relating his affairs;

    (d) he makes, or causes or permits the making of, any false entries in any book, document or record relating to his affairs; or

    (e) he disposes of, or alters or makes any omission in, or causes or permits the disposal, altering or making of any omission in, any book, document or record relating to his affairs.

(2) A person in respect of whom a debt relief order is made is guilty of an offence if –

    (a) he did anything falling within paragraphs (c) to (e) of subsection (1) during the period of 12 months ending with the application date; or

    (b) he did anything falling within paragraphs (b) to (e) of subsection (1) after that date but before the effective date.

(3) A person is not guilty of an offence under this section if he proves that, in respect of the conduct constituting the offence, he had no intent to defraud or to conceal the state of his affairs.

(4) In its application to a trading record subsection (2)(a) has effect as if the reference to 12 months were a reference to two years.

(5) In subsection (4) "trading record" means a book, document or record which shows or explains the transactions or financial position of a person's business, including –

    (a) a periodic record of cash paid and received,

    (b) a statement of periodic stock-taking, and

    (c) except in the case of goods sold by way of retail trade, a record of goods sold and purchased which identifies the buyer and seller or enables them to be identified.

(6)   It is immaterial for the purposes of an offence under this section whether or not the debt relief order in question is revoked after the conduct constituting the offence takes place (but no offence is committed under this section by virtue of conduct occurring after the order is revoked).

### 251Q   Fraudulent disposal of property

(1)   A person in respect of whom a debt relief order is made is guilty of an offence if he made or caused to be made any gift or transfer of his property during the period between –

(a)   the start of the period of two years ending with the application date; and

(b)   the end of the moratorium period.

(2)   The reference in subsection (1) to making a transfer of any property includes causing or conniving at the levying of any execution against that property.

(3)   A person is not guilty of an offence under this section if he proves that, in respect of the conduct constituting the offence, he had no intent to defraud or to conceal the state of his affairs.

(4)   For the purposes of subsection (3) a person is to be taken to have proved that he had no such intent if –

(a)   sufficient evidence is adduced to raise an issue as to whether he had such intent; and

(b)   the contrary is not proved beyond reasonable doubt.

(5)   It is immaterial for the purposes of this section whether or not the debt relief order in question is revoked after the conduct constituting an offence takes place (but no offence is committed by virtue of conduct occurring after the order is revoked).

### 251R   Fraudulent dealing with property obtained on credit

(1)   A person in respect of whom a debt relief order is made is guilty of an offence if during the relevant period he disposed of any property which he had obtained on credit and, at the time he disposed of it, had not paid for it.

(2)   Any other person is guilty of an offence if during the relevant period he acquired or received property from a person in respect of whom a debt relief order was made (the "debtor") knowing or believing –

(a)   that the debtor owed money in respect of the property, and

(b)   that the debtor did not intend, or was unlikely to be able, to pay the money he so owed.

(3)   In subsections (1) and (2) 'relevant period' means the period between –

(a)   the start of the period of two years ending with the application date; and

(b)   the determination date.

(4)   A person is not guilty of an offence under subsection (1) or (2) if the disposal, acquisition or receipt of the property was in the ordinary course of a business carried on by the debtor at the time of the disposal, acquisition or receipt.

(5)   In determining for the purposes of subsection (4) whether any property is disposed of, acquired or received in the ordinary course of a

business carried on by the debtor, regard may be had, in particular, to the price paid for the property.

(6) A person is not guilty of an offence under subsection (1) if he proves that, in respect of the conduct constituting the offence, he had no intent to defraud or to conceal the state of his affairs.

(7) In this section references to disposing of property include pawning or pledging it; and references to acquiring or receiving property shall be read accordingly.

(8) It is immaterial for the purposes of this section whether or not the debt relief order in question is revoked after the conduct constituting an offence takes place (but no offence is committed by virtue of conduct occurring after the order is revoked).

### 251S    Obtaining credit or engaging in business

(1) A person in respect of whom a debt relief order is made is guilty of an offence if, during the relevant period –

    (a) he obtains credit (either alone or jointly with any other person) without giving the person from whom he obtains the credit the relevant information about his status; or

    (b) he engages directly or indirectly in any business under a name other than that in which the order was made without disclosing to all persons with whom he enters into any business transaction the name in which the order was made.

(2) For the purposes of subsection (1)(a) the relevant information about a person's status is the information that –

    (a) a moratorium is in force in relation to the debt relief order,

    (b) a debt relief restrictions order is in force in respect of him, or

    (c) both a moratorium and a debt relief restrictions order is in force,

as the case may be.

(3) In subsection (1) "relevant period" means –

    (a) the moratorium period relating to the debt relief order, or

    (b) the period for which a debt relief restrictions order is in force in respect of the person in respect of whom the debt relief order is made,

as the case may be.

(4) Subsection (1)(a) does not apply if the amount of the credit is less than the prescribed amount (if any).

(5) The reference in subsection (1)(a) to a person obtaining credit includes the following cases –

    (a) where goods are bailed to him under a hire-purchase agreement, or agreed to be sold to him under a conditional sale agreement;

    (b) where he is paid in advance (in money or otherwise) for the supply of goods or services.

### 251T    Offences: supplementary

(1) Proceedings for an offence under this Part may only be instituted by the Secretary of State or by or with the consent of the Director of Public Prosecutions.

(2) It is not a defence in proceedings for an offence under this Part that anything relied on, in whole or in part, as constituting the offence was done outside England and Wales.

(3)  A person guilty of an offence under this Part is liable to imprisonment or a fine, or both (but see section 430).

*Supplementary*

**251U    Approved intermediaries**

(1)  In this Part "approved intermediary" means an individual for the time being approved by a competent authority to act as an intermediary between a person wishing to make an application for a debt relief order and the official receiver.

(2)  In this section "competent authority" means a person or body for the time being designated by the Secretary of State for the purposes of granting approvals under this section.

(3)  Designation as a competent authority may be limited so as to permit the authority only to approve persons of a particular description.

(4)  The Secretary of State may by regulations make provision as to –

    (a)  the procedure for designating persons or bodies as competent authorities;

    (b)  descriptions of individuals who are ineligible to be approved under this section;

    (c)  the procedure for granting approvals under this section;

    (d)  the withdrawal of designations or approvals under this section;

and provision made under paragraph (a) or (c) may include provision requiring the payment of fees.

(5)  The rules may make provision about the activities to be carried out by an approved intermediary in connection with an application for a debt relief order, which may in particular include –

    (a)  assisting the debtor in making the application;

    (b)  checking that the application has been properly completed;

    (c)  sending the application to the official receiver.

(6)  The rules may also make provision about other activities to be carried out by approved intermediaries.

(7)  An approved intermediary may not charge a debtor any fee in connection with an application for a debt relief order.

(8)  An approved intermediary is not liable to any person in damages for anything done or omitted to be done when acting (or purporting to act) as an approved intermediary in connection with a particular application by a debtor for a debt relief order.

(9)  Subsection (8) does not apply if the act or omission was in bad faith.

(10)  Regulations under subsection (4) shall be made by statutory instrument subject to annulment in pursuance of a resolution of either House of Parliament.

**251V    Debt relief restrictions orders and undertakings**

Schedule 4ZB (which makes provision about debt relief restrictions orders and debt relief restrictions undertakings) has effect.

**251W    Register of debt relief orders etc**

The Secretary of State must maintain a register of matters relating to –

    (a)  debt relief orders;

    (b)  debt relief restrictions orders; and

    (c)  debt relief restrictions undertakings.

**251X   Interpretation**

(1)   In this Part –

"the application date", in relation to a debt relief order or an application for a debt relief order, means the date on which the application for the order is made to the official receiver;

"approved intermediary" has the meaning given in section 251U(1);

"debt relief order" means an order made by the official receiver under this Part;

"debtor" means –

(a)   in relation to an application for a debt relief order, the applicant; and

(b)   in relation to a debt relief order, the person in relation to whom the order is made;

"debt relief restrictions order" and "debt relief restrictions undertaking" means an order made, or an undertaking accepted, under Schedule 4ZB;

"the determination date", in relation to a debt relief order or an application for a debt relief order, means the date on which the application for the order is determined by the official receiver;

"the effective date" has the meaning given in section 251E(7);

"excluded debt" is to be construed in accordance with section 251A;

"moratorium" and "moratorium period" are to be construed in accordance with sections 251G and 251H;

"qualifying debt", in relation to a debtor, has the meaning given in section 251A(2);

"the register" means the register maintained under section 251W;

"specified qualifying debt" has the meaning given in section 251G(1).

(2)   In this Part references to a creditor specified in a debt relief order as the person to whom a qualifying debt is owed by the debtor include a reference to any person to whom the right to claim the whole or any part of the debt has passed, by assignment or operation of law, after the date of the application for the order.'

SCHEDULE 18   **SCHEDULE 4ZA TO THE**
**INSOLVENCY ACT 1986**                    Section 108(2)

## 'SCHEDULE 4ZA   CONDITIONS FOR MAKING A DEBT RELIEF ORDER

## PART 1   CONDITIONS WHICH MUST BE MET

*Connection with England and Wales*

1     (1)   The debtor –

(a)   is domiciled in England and Wales on the application date; or

(b)   at any time during the period of three years ending with that date –

(i)   was ordinarily resident, or had a place of residence, in England and Wales; or

            (ii)    carried on business in England and Wales.
    (2)    The reference in sub-paragraph (1)(b)(ii) to the debtor carrying
            on business includes –
            (a)    the carrying on of business by a firm or partnership of
                   which he is a member;
            (b)    the carrying on of business by an agent or manager for
                   him or for such a firm or partnership.

*Debtor's previous insolvency history*

2            The debtor is not, on the determination date –
             (a)    an undischarged bankrupt;
             (b)    subject to an interim order or voluntary
                    arrangement under Part 8; or
             (c)    subject to a bankruptcy restrictions order or a debt
                    relief restrictions order.

3            A debtor's petition for the debtor's bankruptcy under Part 9 –
             (a)    has not been presented by the debtor before the
                    determination date;
             (b)    has been so presented, but proceedings on the peti-
                    tion have been finally disposed of before that date;
                    or
             (c)    has been so presented and proceedings in relation
                    to the petition remain before the court at that date,
                    but the court has referred the debtor under section
                    274A(2) for the purposes of making an application
                    for a debt relief order.

4            A creditor's petition for the debtor's bankruptcy under Part 9 –
             (a)    has not been presented against the debtor at any
                    time before the determination date;
             (b)    has been so presented, but proceedings on the peti-
                    tion have been finally disposed of before that date;
                    or
             (c)    has been so presented and proceedings in relation
                    to the petition remain before the court at that date,
                    but the person who presented the petition has con-
                    sented to the making of an application for a debt
                    relief order.

5            A debt relief order has not been made in relation to the debtor
             in the period of six years ending with the determination date.

*Limit on debtor's overall indebtedness*

6    (1)    The total amount of the debtor's debts on the determination
            date, other than unliquidated debts and excluded debts, does
            not exceed the prescribed amount.
     (2)    For this purpose an unliquidated debt is a debt that is not for a
            liquidated sum payable to a creditor either immediately or at
            some future certain time.

*Limit on debtor's monthly surplus income*

7    (1)    The debtor's monthly surplus income (if any) on the determina-
            tion date does not exceed the prescribed amount.

(2)   For this purpose "monthly surplus income" is the amount by which a person's monthly income exceeds the amount necessary for the reasonable domestic needs of himself and his family.

(3)   The rules may –

(a)   make provision as to how the debtor's monthly surplus income is to be determined;

(b)   provide that particular descriptions of income are to be excluded for the purposes of this paragraph.

*Limit on value of debtor's property*

8   (1)   The total value of the debtor's property on the determination date does not exceed the prescribed amount.

(2)   The rules may –

(a)   make provision as to how the value of a person's property is to be determined;

(b)   provide that particular descriptions of property are to be excluded for the purposes of this paragraph.

## PART 2   OTHER CONDITIONS

9   (1)   The debtor has not entered into a transaction with any person at an undervalue during the period between –

(a)   the start of the period of two years ending with the application date; and

(b)   the determination date.

(2)   For this purpose a debtor enters into a transaction with a person at an undervalue if –

(a)   he makes a gift to that person or he otherwise enters into a transaction with that person on terms that provide for him to receive no consideration;

(b)   he enters into a transaction with that person in consideration of marriage or the formation of a civil partnership; or

(c)   he enters into a transaction with that person for a consideration the value of which, in money or money's worth, is significantly less than the value, in money or money's worth, of the consideration provided by the individual.

10   (1)   The debtor has not given a preference to any person during the period between –

(a)   the start of the period of two years ending with the application date; and

(b)   the determination date.

(2)   For this purpose a debtor gives a preference to a person if –

(a)   that person is one of the debtor's creditors to whom a qualifying debt is owed or is a surety or guarantor for any such debt, and

(b)   the debtor does anything or suffers anything to be done which (in either case) has the effect of putting that person into a position which, in the event that a debt relief order is made in relation to the debtor, will be better than the position he would have been in if that thing had not been done.'

## SCHEDULE 19   SCHEDULE 4ZB TO THE INSOLVENCY ACT 1986

Section 108(2)

### 'SCHEDULE 4ZB   DEBT RELIEF RESTRICTIONS ORDERS AND UNDERTAKINGS

*Debt relief restrictions order*

1    (1)    A debt relief restrictions order may be made by the court in relation to a person in respect of whom a debt relief order has been made.

(2)    An order may be made only on the application of –

(a)    the Secretary of State, or

(b)    the official receiver acting on a direction of the Secretary of State.

*Grounds for making order*

2    (1)    The court shall grant an application for a debt relief restrictions order if it thinks it appropriate to do so having regard to the conduct of the debtor (whether before or after the making of the debt relief order).

(2)    The court shall, in particular, take into account any of the following kinds of behaviour on the part of the debtor –

(a)    failing to keep records which account for a loss of property by the debtor, or by a business carried on by him, where the loss occurred in the period beginning two years before the application date for the debt relief order and ending with the date of the application for the debt relief restrictions order;

(b)    failing to produce records of that kind on demand by the official receiver;

(c)    entering into a transaction at an undervalue in the period beginning two years before the application date for the debt relief order and ending with the date of the determination of that application;

(d)    giving a preference in the period beginning two years before the application date for the debt relief order and ending with the date of the determination of that application;

(e)    making an excessive pension contribution;

(f)    a failure to supply goods or services that were wholly or partly paid for;

(g)    trading at a time, before the date of the determination of the application for the debt relief order, when the debtor knew or ought to have known that he was himself to be unable to pay his debts;

(h) incurring, before the date of the determination of the application for the debt relief order, a debt which the debtor had no reasonable expectation of being able to pay;

(i) failing to account satisfactorily to the court or the official receiver for a loss of property or for an insufficiency of property to meet his debts;

(j) carrying on any gambling, rash and hazardous speculation or unreasonable extravagance which may have materially contributed to or increased the extent of his inability to pay his debts before the application date for the debt relief order or which took place between that date and the date of the determination of the application for the debt relief order;

(k) neglect of business affairs of a kind which may have materially contributed to or increased the extent of his inability to pay his debts;

(l) fraud or fraudulent breach of trust;

(m) failing to co-operate with the official receiver.

(3) The court shall also, in particular, consider whether the debtor was an undischarged bankrupt at some time during the period of six years ending with the date of the application for the debt relief order.

(4) For the purposes of sub-paragraph (2) –

"excessive pension contribution" shall be construed in accordance with section 342A;

"preference" shall be construed in accordance with paragraph 10(2) of Schedule 4ZA;

"undervalue" shall be construed in accordance with paragraph 9(2) of that Schedule.

*Timing of application for order*

3      An application for a debt relief restrictions order in respect of a debtor may be made –

(a) at any time during the moratorium period relating to the debt relief order in question, or

(b) after the end of that period, but only with the permission of the court.

*Duration of order*

4   (1) A debt relief restrictions order –

(a) comes into force when it is made, and

(b) ceases to have effect at the end of a date specified in the order.

(2) The date specified in a debt relief restrictions order under sub-paragraph (1)(b) must not be –

(a) before the end of the period of two years beginning with the date on which the order is made, or

(b) after the end of the period of 15 years beginning with that date.

*Interim debt relief restrictions order*

5    (1)    This paragraph applies at any time between –

        (a)    the institution of an application for a debt relief restrictions order, and

        (b)    the determination of the application.

    (2)    The court may make an interim debt relief restrictions order if the court thinks that –

        (a)    there are prima facie grounds to suggest that the application for the debt relief restrictions order will be successful, and

        (b)    it is in the public interest to make an interim debt relief restrictions order.

    (3)    An interim debt relief restrictions order may only be made on the application of –

        (a)    the Secretary of State, or

        (b)    the official receiver acting on a direction of the Secretary of State.

    (4)    An interim debt relief restrictions order –

        (a)    has the same effect as a debt relief restrictions order, and

        (b)    comes into force when it is made.

    (5)    An interim debt relief restrictions order ceases to have effect –

        (a)    on the determination of the application for the debt relief restrictions order,

        (b)    on the acceptance of a debt relief restrictions undertaking made by the debtor, or

        (c)    if the court discharges the interim debt relief restrictions order on the application of the person who applied for it or of the debtor.

6    (1)    This paragraph applies to a case in which both an interim debt relief restrictions order and a debt relief restrictions order are made.

    (2)    Paragraph 4(2) has effect in relation to the debt relief restrictions order as if a reference to the date of that order were a reference to the date of the interim debt relief restrictions order.

*Debt relief restrictions undertaking*

7    (1)    A debtor may offer a debt relief restrictions undertaking to the Secretary of State.

    (2)    In determining whether to accept a debt relief restrictions undertaking the Secretary of State shall have regard to the matters specified in paragraph 2(2) and (3).

8        A reference in an enactment to a person in respect of whom a debt relief restrictions order has effect (or who is 'the subject of' a debt relief restrictions order) includes a reference to a person in respect of whom a debt relief restrictions undertaking has effect.

9    (1)    A debt relief restrictions undertaking –

        (a)    comes into force on being accepted by the Secretary of State, and

        (b)    ceases to have effect at the end of a date specified in the undertaking.

(2)   The date specified under sub-paragraph (1)(b) must not be –

   (a)   before the end of the period of two years beginning with the date on which the undertaking is accepted, or

   (b)   after the end of the period of 15 years beginning with that date.

(3)   On an application by the debtor the court may –

   (a)   annul a debt relief restrictions undertaking;

   (b)   provide for a debt relief restrictions undertaking to cease to have effect before the date specified under sub-paragraph (1)(b).

*Effect of revocation of debt relief order*

10       Unless the court directs otherwise, the revocation at any time of a debt relief order does not –

   (a)   affect the validity of any debt relief restrictions order, interim debt relief restrictions order or debt relief restrictions undertaking which is in force in respect of the debtor;

   (b)   prevent the determination of any application for a debt relief restrictions order, or an interim debt relief restrictions order, in relation to the debtor that was instituted before that time;

   (c)   prevent the acceptance of a debt relief restrictions undertaking that was offered before that time; or

   (d)   prevent the institution of an application for a debt relief restrictions order or interim debt relief restrictions order in respect of the debtor, or the offer or acceptance of a debt relief restrictions undertaking by the debtor, after that time.'

## SCHEDULE 20   DEBT RELIEF ORDERS: CONSEQUENTIAL AMENDMENTS

Section 108(3)

## PART 1   AMENDMENTS TO THE INSOLVENCY ACT 1986

1       The Insolvency Act 1986 (c. 45) is amended as follows.

2   (1)   In section 31 (disqualification of bankrupt) in subsection (1) –

   (a)   at the end of paragraph (a) (before 'or') insert –

   '(aa)   a moratorium period under a debt relief order applies in relation to him,';

   (b)   in paragraph (b) after 'order' insert 'or a debt relief restrictions order'.

(2)   In the heading to that section after '**bankrupt**' insert '**or person in respect of whom a debt relief order is made**'.

3      After section 274 insert –

**'274A   Debtor who meets conditions for a debt relief order**

(1) This section applies where, on the hearing of a debtor's petition –

   (a)   it appears to the court that a debt relief order would be made in relation to the debtor if, instead of presenting the petition, he had made an application under Part 7A; and

(b)    the court does not appoint an insolvency practitioner under section 273.

(2) If the court thinks it would be in the debtor's interests to apply for a debt relief order instead of proceeding on the petition, the court may refer the debtor to an approved intermediary (within the meaning of Part 7A) for the purposes of making an application for a debt relief order.

(3) Where a reference is made under subsection (2) the court shall stay proceedings on the petition on such terms and conditions as it thinks fit; but if following the reference a debt relief order is made in relation to the debtor the court shall dismiss the petition.'

4       In section 384(2) (meaning of prescribed amount) –

(a)    at the beginning of the list of provisions insert 'section 251S(4);';
(b)    in the list omit 'and' after 'section 361(2);' and
(c)    at the end of the list insert 'paragraphs 6 to 8 of Schedule 4ZA,'.

5   (1)  Section 385(1) (definitions) is amended as follows.
   (2)  In the definition of 'the debtor', before paragraph (a) insert –

'(za)   in relation to a debt relief order or an application for such an order, has the same meaning as in Part 7A,'.

   (3)  After the definition of 'debtor's petition' insert –

'"debt relief order" means an order made by the official receiver under Part 7A;'.

6   (1)  Section 390 (persons not qualified to act as insolvency practitioners) is amended as follows.
   (2)  In subsection (4) after paragraph (a) insert –

'(aa)   a moratorium period under a debt relief order applies in relation of him,'.

   (3)  In subsection (5) after 'order' insert 'or a debt relief restrictions order'.

7   (1)  Section 399 (appointment etc of official receivers) is amended as follows.
   (2)  In subsection (1) for 'or individual voluntary arrangement' (in both places) substitute ', individual voluntary arrangement, debt relief order or application for such an order'.
   (3)  In subsection (4) for 'or individual voluntary arrangement' substitute ', individual voluntary arrangement, debt relief order or application for such an order'.

8       In section 412(1) (individual insolvency rules) for 'Parts VIII to XI' substitute 'Parts 7A to 11'.

9   (1)  Section 415 (fees orders) is amended as follows.
   (2)  In subsection (1) before paragraph (a) insert –

'(za)   the costs of persons acting as approved intermediaries under Part 7A,'.

   (3)  In that subsection in paragraph (a) for 'Parts VIII to XI' substitute 'Parts 7A to 11'.

10      In section 415A (fees orders: general), before subsection (1) insert –

'(A1)   The Secretary of State –

(a)    may by order require a person or body to pay a fee in connection with the grant or maintenance of a designation of that person or body as a competent authority under section 251U, and
(b)    may refuse to grant, or may withdraw, any such designation where a fee is not paid.'

11      In section 418(1) (monetary limits) –

(a)    at the beginning of the list of provisions insert –

'section 251S(4) (maximum amount of credit which a person in respect of whom a debt relief order is made may obtain without disclosure of his status);';

(b)    at the end of the list of provisions insert –

'paragraphs 6 to 8 of Schedule 4ZA (maximum amount of a person's debts, monthly surplus income and property for purposes of obtaining a debt relief order);'.

12   (1)   Section 426A (disqualification from Parliament) is amended as follows.

(2)   In subsection (1) after 'bankruptcy restrictions order' insert 'or a debt relief restrictions order'.

(3)   In subsection (5) after 'interim order' insert ', or a debt relief restrictions order or an interim debt relief restrictions order,'.

(4)   In subsection (6) after 'bankruptcy restrictions undertaking' insert 'or a debt relief restrictions undertaking'.

13   (1)   Section 426B (devolution) is amended as follows.

(2)   In subsection (1) after 'Wales,' insert 'or makes a debt relief restrictions order or interim debt relief restrictions order in respect of such a member,'.

(3)   In subsection (2) after 'bankruptcy restrictions undertaking' insert 'or a debt relief restrictions undertaking'.

14   (1)   Schedule 9 is amended as follows.

(2)   In paragraph 1 for 'Parts VIII to XI' substitute 'Parts 7A to 11'.

(3)   In paragraph 5 for 'Parts VIII to XI' substitute 'Parts 7A to 11'.

(4)   In paragraph 6 for 'Parts VIII to XI' substitute 'Parts 7A to 11'.

(5)   After paragraph 7 insert –

*Debt relief orders*

7A    Provision as to the manner in which the official receiver is to carry out his functions under Part 7A.

7B    Provision as to the manner in which any requirement that may be imposed by the official receiver on a person under Part 7A is to take effect.

7C    Provision modifying the application of Part 7A in relation to an individual who has died at a time when a moratorium period under a debt relief order applies in relation to him.

*Debt relief restrictions orders and undertakings*

7D    Provision about debt relief restrictions orders, interim orders and undertakings, including provision about evidence.

*Register of debt relief orders and debt relief restrictions orders etc*

7E    Provision about the register required to be maintained by section 251W and the information to be contained in it, including provision –

(a)   enabling the amalgamation of the register with another register;

(b)   enabling inspection of the register by the public.'

15   (1)   The Table in Schedule 10 (punishment of offences) is amended as follows.

(2)   In the entry relating to section 31, in the column describing the general nature of the offence, after 'bankrupt' insert 'or person in respect of whom a debt relief order is made'.

(3)   Insert the following entries after the entry relating to section 235(5) –

| '251O(1) | False representations or omissions in making an application for a debt relief order. | 1. On indictment 2. Summary | 7 years or a fine, or both. 12 months or the statutory maximum, or both. |
|---|---|---|---|
| 251O(2)(a) | Failing to comply with duty in connection with an application for a debt relief order. | 1. On indictment 2. Summary | 2 years or a fine, or both. 12 months or the statutory maximum, or both. |

| 251O(2)(b) | False representations or omissions in connection with duty in relation to an application for a debt relief order. | 1. On indictment<br>2. Summary | 7 years or a fine, or both.<br>12 months or the statutory maximum, or both. |
|---|---|---|---|
| 251O(4)(a) | Failing to comply with duty in connection with a debt relief order. | 1. On indictment<br>2. Summary | 2 years or a fine, or both.<br>12 months or the statutory maximum, or both. |
| 251O(4)(b) | False representations or omissions in connection with a duty in relation to a debt relief order. | 1. On indictment<br>2. Summary | 7 years or a fine, or both.<br>12 months or the statutory maximum, or both. |
| 251P(1) | Failing to deliver books, records and papers to official receiver, concealing or destroying them or making false entries in them by person in respect of whom a debt relief order is made. | 1. On indictment<br>2. Summary | 7 years or a fine, or both.<br>12 months or the statutory maximum, or both. |
| 251P(2) | Person in respect of whom debt relief order is made doing anything falling within paragraphs (c) to (e) of section 251P(1) during the period of 12 months ending with the application date or doing anything falling within paragraphs (b) to (e) of section 251P(1) after that date but before the effective date. | 1. On indictment<br>2. Summary | 7 years or a fine, or both<br>12 months or the statutory maximum, or both. |
| 251Q(1) | Fraudulent disposal of property by person in respect of whom a debt relief order is made. | 1. On indictment<br>2. Summary | 2 years or a fine, or both.<br>12 months or the statutory maximum, or both. |
| 251R(1) | Disposal of property that is not paid for by person in respect of whom a debt relief order is made. | 1. On indictment<br>2. Summary | 7 years or a fine, or both.<br>12 months or the statutory maximum, or both. |
| 251R(2) | Obtaining property in respect of which money is owed by a person in respect of whom a debt relief order is made. | 1. On indictment<br>2. Summary | 7 years or a fine, or both.<br>12 months or the statutory maximum, or both. |
| 251S(1) | Person in respect of whom a debt relief order is made obtaining credit or engaging in business without disclosing his status or name. | 1. On indictment<br>2. Summary | 2 years or a fine, or both.<br>12 months or the statutory maximum, or both.' |

(4)  In the application of those entries in relation to offences committed before the commencement of section 154(1) of the Criminal Justice Act 2003 (c. 44) (limit on magistrates' court powers to impose imprisonment), the references in the fourth column to '12 months' are to be read as references to '6 months'.

## PART 2   AMENDMENTS TO OTHER LEGISLATION

16   (1)   Section 11(1) of the Company Directors Disqualification Act 1986 (c. 46) (undischarged bankrupts) (as substituted in relation to England and Wales by the Enterprise Act 2002 (c. 40)) is amended as follows.

(2)   At the end of paragraph (a) (before 'or') insert –

'(aa)   a moratorium period under a debt relief order applies in relation to him,'.

(3)   In paragraph (b) after 'bankruptcy restrictions order' insert 'or a debt relief restrictions order'.

17   In section 183(2) of the Employment Rights Act 1996 (c. 18) (insolvency of an employer who is individual), in paragraph (a) before sub-paragraph (i) insert –

'(ai)   a moratorium period under a debt relief order applies in relation to him,'.

## SCHEDULE 21   REGULATIONS UNDER SECTIONS 111 AND 113

Sections 111 and 113

1   The first column of this table lists the matters referred to in sections 111(3) and 113(5).

2   A matter listed in the first column includes the aspects set out in the appropriate part of the second column.

| Matter about which particular provision may be made: | Including these aspects: |
| --- | --- |
| 1. The scheme operator. | (a) The constitution of the scheme operator. <br> (b) The governance of the scheme operator. <br> (c) The size of the scheme operator's undertaking. <br> (d) The financial standing of the scheme operator. <br> (e) Whether or not a scheme operator is a profit-making organisation. |
| 2. The terms of a debt management scheme. | (a) The non-business debtors to whom the scheme is open. <br> (b) The kinds of debts which may be specified in a plan arranged in accordance with the scheme. |
| 3. The operation of a debt management scheme. | (a) How decisions are made about whether debt repayment plans are to be arranged. <br> (b) How debt repayment plans are arranged. <br> (c) How decisions are made about the terms of debt repayment plans, including decisions about– <br>    (i)   what payments will be required in relation to the specified debts; <br>    (ii)   the amounts, times and recipients of payments; <br>    (iii)   the duration of the plan. <br> (d) The format of debt repayment plans. <br> (e) When debt repayment plans begin to have effect. <br> (f) How changes are to be made to debt repayment plans (including the specification of debts after a plan has been arranged). <br> (g) How decisions are made about whether debt repayment plans are to be terminated. <br> (h) How debt repayment plans are terminated. |

| Matter about which particular provision may be made: | Including these aspects: |
|---|---|
| 4. Changes that affect the scheme operator. | |
| 5. Changes to –<br>(i) the terms of a debt management scheme;<br>(ii) the operation of a debt management scheme. | (a) Whether changes may be made.<br>(b) How changes are made. |
| 6. The transfer of the operation of a debt | (a) Whether the operation of the scheme management scheme to another body. may be transferred.<br>(b) How the operation of the scheme is transferred. |

## SCHEDULE 22    COMPULSORY PURCHASE: CONSEQUENTIAL AMENDMENTS          Section 139

### Local Government (Miscellaneous Provisions) Act 1976 (c. 57)

1    In Part 2 of Schedule 1 to the Local Government (Miscellaneous Provisions) Act 1976 (compulsory purchase of rights: adaptation of 1965 Act), in paragraph 9 for 'sheriff's warrant' substitute 'enforcement officer's or sheriff's warrant'.

### Local Government, Planning and Land Act 1980 (c. 65)

2    In Part 4 of Schedule 28 to the Local Government, Planning and Land Act 1980 (acquisition of rights), in paragraph 23(4) for 'sheriff's warrant' substitute 'enforcement officer's or sheriff's warrant'.

### Highways Act 1980 (c. 66)

3    In Part 2 of Schedule 19 to the Highways Act 1980 (compulsory acquisition of rights: adaptation of 1965 Act), in paragraph 9 for 'sheriff's warrant' substitute 'enforcement officer's or sheriff's warrant'.

### Gas Act 1986 (c. 44)

4    In Part 2 of Schedule 3 to the Gas Act 1986 (compulsory acquisition of land and rights: procedure etc), in paragraph 10 for 'sheriff's warrant' substitute 'enforcement officer's or sheriff's warrant'.

### Channel Tunnel Act 1987 (c. 53)

5    In Part 3 of Schedule 5 to the Channel Tunnel Act 1987 (supplementary provisions as to acquisition of land), in paragraph 8(d) for 'sheriff's warrant' substitute 'enforcement officer's or sheriff's warrant'.

### Housing Act 1988 (c. 50)

6    In Part 3 of Schedule 10 to the Housing Act 1988 (acquisition of rights), in paragraph 23(2), for 'sheriff's warrant' substitute 'enforcement officer's or sheriff's warrant'.

## Electricity Act 1989 (c. 29)

7        In Part 2 of Schedule 3 to the Electricity Act 1989 (compulsory acquisition of land and rights: procedure etc), in paragraph 11 for 'sheriff's warrant' substitute 'enforcement officer's or sheriff's warrant'.

## Leasehold Reform, Housing and Urban Development Act 1993 (c. 28)

8        In Part 3 of Schedule 20 to the Leasehold Reform, Housing and Urban Development Act 1993 (acquisition of rights), in paragraph 23(2) for 'sheriff's warrant' substitute 'enforcement officer's or sheriff's warrant'.

## Channel Tunnel Rail Link Act 1996 (c. 61)

9        In Part 3 of Schedule 4 to the Channel Tunnel Rail Link Act 1996 (supplementary provisions as to acquisition of land), in paragraph 9(5), for 'sheriff's warrant' there is substituted 'enforcement officer's or sheriff's warrant'.

## Regional Development Agencies Act 1998 (c. 45)

10       In Part 2 of Schedule 5 to the Regional Development Agencies Act 1998 (acquisition of rights), in paragraph 5(2), for 'sheriff's warrant' there is substituted 'enforcement officer's or sheriff's warrant'.

## Postal Services Act 2000 (c. 26)

11       In Part 2 of Schedule 5 to the Postal Services Act 2000 (acquisition of land and rights: procedure etc), in paragraph 10, for 'sheriff's warrant' there is substituted 'enforcement officer's or sheriff's warrant'.

## SCHEDULE 23   REPEALS

*****

## PART 3   ENFORCEMENT BY TAKING CONTROL OF GOODS

| Reference | Extent of repeal |
| --- | --- |
| Inclosure Act 1773 (c. 81) | In section 4, the words from 'rendering' to the end.<br>In section 16, the words from 'rendering' to the end. |
| Sale of Farming Stock Act 1816 (c. 50) | The whole Act. |
| Judgments Act 1838 (c. 110) | Section 12. |
| Compulsory Purchase Act 1965 (c. 56) | Section 13(5).<br>Section 29. |
| Sea Fisheries Act 1968 (c. 77) | In section 12(3), the words from 'as they apply' to the end. |
| Criminal Justice Act 1972 (c. 71) | In section 66(2), the words from '"sentence of imprisonment"' to the end. |

| Reference | Extent of repeal |
|---|---|
| Magistrates' Courts Act 1980 (c. 43) | In section 125(2), the words from 'This subsection' to the end.<br>Section 125D(3)(c).<br>Section 151.<br>In Schedule 4A, paragraph 3. |
| British Fishing Boats Act 1983 (c. 8) | In section 5(3), the words from 'as they apply' to the end. |
| County Courts Act 1984 (c. 28) | Section 85(3).<br>Section 87(2).<br>Sections 89 to 91.<br>Sections 93 to 100.<br>Sections 102 and 103.<br>Section 123.<br>In section 126 –<br>(a)  in subsection (3) the words from 'but' to the end;<br>(b)  in subsection (4) 'bailiff'.<br>In section 147(1) the definition of 'bailiff'. |
| Finance Act 1984 (c. 43) | Section 16. |
| Local Government Finance Act 1988 (c. 41) | In Schedule 9, paragraph 3(2)(b). |
| Child Support Act 1991 (c. 48) | Section 35(2) to (8). |
| Social Security Administration Act 1992 (c. 5) | Section 121A(2) to (8) and (10). |
| Local Government Finance Act 1992 (c. 14) | In Schedule 4 –<br>(a)  paragraph 7;<br>(b)  in paragraph 8(1)(a) the words from 'an authority' to 'paragraph 7 above';<br>(c)  paragraph 12(1)(c);<br>(d)  paragraph 19(3). |
| Finance Act 1997 (c. 16) | Section 51(7). |
| Courts Act 2003 (c. 39) | In Schedule 7, paragraph 8(5). |
| Traffic Management Act 2004 (c. 18) | Section 82(3)(a).<br>Section 83. |

## PART 4    RENT ARREARS RECOVERY

| Reference | Extent of repeal |
|---|---|
| Distress for Rent Act 1689 (c. 5) | The whole Act. |
| Landlord and Tenant Act 1709 (c. 18) | Section 1.<br>Sections 6 to 8. |
| Landlord and Tenant Act 1730 (c. 28) | Section 5. |
| Distress for Rent Act 1737 (c. 19) | Sections 1 to 10.<br>Sections 16 and 17.<br>Section 19. |
| Deserted Tenements Act 1817 (c. 52) | The whole Act. |
| Metropolitan Police Courts Act 1840 (c. 84) | The whole Act. |

| Reference | Extent of repeal |
|---|---|
| Execution Act 1844 (c. 96) | The whole Act. |
| Lands Clauses Consolidation Act 1845 (c. 18) | In section 11 the words from 'or it shall be lawful' to the end. |
| Sequestration Act 1849 (c. 67) | In section 1 the words 'levy' and 'distress' in the second place where each occurs, and 'levied'. |
| Landlord and Tenant Act 1851 (c. 25) | The whole Act. |
| Railway Rolling Stock Protection Act 1872 (c. 50) | The whole Act. |
| Law of Distress Amendment Act 1888 (c. 21) | The whole Act. |
| Law of Distress Amendment Act 1908 (c. 53) | The whole Act. |
| Law of Property Act 1925 (c. 20) | Section 121(2). Section 162(1)(a). Section 189(1). In section 190 – (a) subsection (2); (b) in subsection (7), 'owner or'. |
| Administration of Estates Act 1925 (c. 23) | Section 26(3). |
| Rent (Agriculture) Act 1976 (c. 80) | Section 8. |
| Rent Act 1977 (c. 42) | Section 147. |
| Limitation Act 1980 (c. 58) | In section 38, 'rentcharges and' and 'rent or'. |
| County Courts Act 1984 (c. 28) | Section 116. |
| Agricultural Holdings Act 1986 (c. 5) | Sections 16 to 19. In section 24, ', by distress or otherwise,'. |
| Insolvency Act 1986 (c. 45) | Section 347(6), (7) and (11). |
| Housing Act 1988 (c. 50) | Section 19. |
| Water Industry Act 1991 (c. 56) | In section 179(4)(b), 'or to the landlord's remedy for rent'. |
| Constitutional Reform Act 2005 (c. 4) | In Schedule 7, in the table in paragraph 4, the entry for the Law of Distress Amendment Act 1888. |

## PART 5   ADMINISTRATION ORDERS

| Reference | Extent of repeal |
|---|---|
| Company Directors Disqualification Act 1986 (c. 46) | Section 12(1). |
| Courts and Legal Services Act 1990 (c. 41) | Section 13. |

## PART 6   APPEAL TRIBUNAL UNDER SECTION 28 OF THE REGISTERED DESIGNS ACT 1949: ABOLITION

| *Reference* | *Extent of repeal* |
| --- | --- |
| Registered Designs Act 1949 (c. 88) | Section 28.<br>In section 37(3), the words 'or on the Appeal Tribunal' and the words from 'and the Statutory Instruments Act 1946 shall apply' to the end.<br><br>In section 44(1), the definition of 'Appeal Tribunal'. |
| Administration of Justice Act 1969 (c. 58) | Section 24.<br>In Schedule 1, the entry in respect of the Registered Designs Act 1949. |
| Administration of Justice Act 1970 (c. 31) | Section 10. |
| Patents Act 1977 (c. 37) | In Schedule 5, paragraph 5. |
| Copyright, Designs and Patents Act 1988 (c. 48) | Section 249(2).<br>In Schedule 3, paragraph 17. |
| Constitutional Reform Act 2005 (c. 4) | In Schedule 4, paragraphs 37 and 66. |

# INDEX